The Struggle for Soviet Jewry in American Politics

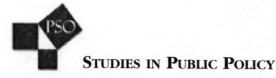

STUDIES IN PUBLIC POLICY

Series Editor: Paul J. Rich, Policy Studies Organization

Lexington Books and the Policy Studies Organization's **Studies in Public Policy** series brings together the very best in new and original scholarship, spanning the range of global policy questions. Its multi-disciplinary texts combine penetrating analysis of policy formulation at the macro level with innovative and practical solutions for policy implementation. The books provide the political and social scientist with the latest academic research and the policy maker with effective tools to tackle the most pressing issues faced by government today. Not least, the books are invaluable resources for teaching public policy. For ideas about curriculum use, visit www.ipsonet.org.

The Struggle for Soviet Jewry in American Politics

Israel versus the American Jewish Establishment

Fred A. Lazin

LEXINGTON BOOKS
Lanham • Boulder • New York • Toronto • Oxford

LEXINGTON BOOKS

A division of Rowman & Littlefield Publishers, Inc.
A wholly owned subsidiary of The Rowman & Littlefield Publishing Group, Inc.
4501 Forbes Boulevard, Suite 200
Lanham, Maryland 20706

PO Box 317
Oxford
OX2 9RU, UK

British Library Cataloguing in Publication Information Available

Library of Congress Cataloging-in-Publication Data

Lazin, Frederick A., 1943–
  The struggle for Soviet Jewry in American politics : Israel versus the American
Jewish establishment / Fred A. Lazin.
    p. cm. — (Studies in public policy)
  Includes bibliographic references and index.
  1. Jews—Soviet Union—Migrations. 2. Jews—Migrations—Government
policy—Soviet Union. 3. Soviet Union—Emigration and immigration—Government
policy—History—20th century. 4. Israel—Emigration and immigration—Government
policy—History—20th century. 5. United States—Emigration and immigration—
Government policy—History—20th century. 6. Jews—United States—Politics and
government—20th century. 7. Israel and the diaspora. I. Title. II. Series.
  DS135.R92L39 2005   325'.247'095694048—dc22

ISBN 0-7391-0842-5 (cloth: alk. paper)
ISBN 0-7391-1343-7 (paper)

Printed in the United States of America

∞™ The paper used in this publication meets the minimum requirements of
American National Standard for Information Sciences—Permanence of Paper
for Printed Library Materials, ANSI/NISO Z39.48-1992.

Dedicated to Guenter Lewy,
teacher, scholar, and friend

Contents

Foreword

This major work by Professor Fred Lazin, uncommonly interesting and sure to become an indispensable reference, is based on a vast array of documents and sources about one of the great and somewhat underreported movements of people in the later part of the twentieth century: the immigration of Jews from the Soviet Union to Israel and the United States. Importantly, it is also about American politics, Jewish pressure groups, friction between Israel and Jews in the Diaspora, and (inevitably) the continuing crisis in the Middle East. Professor Lazin is unusually successful in treating both parties with fairness, which is not an easy task. All concerned will probably criticize him for his unflattering objectivity.

The volume may not inspire optimism about the future of the Middle East because it highlights the difficulty of resolving a situation in Israel in which leaders must deal not only with Palestinians but also with an amazing variety of American Jewish lobbies. Even now, with the death of Yasser Arafat and new hope for the peace process, negotiators will still have to contend with a wide range of interests that must be satisfied. It is rather like a tennis match with a dozen players on each side of the court.

This is hardly the only wisdom to be gained from the following pages. Since many Arab leaders are convinced of hidden conspiracies, surely this involved story of the American and Israeli disputes and debates should provide convincing evidence that policy in democratic states is made in an arena where parties vie in embarrassingly open contention and public disagreement.

While Professor Lazin explores the impediment that Americans and Israelis posed to Soviet Jewish immigration, his study is a clear narrative of how policy is forged on the ground and how politics play out in a democratic society. His book is thus a doubly welcome addition to the Policy Studies Organization's series with Lexington Books.

It is a well-crafted work that can and should be read on several levels—certainly as a much-needed resource on immigration, surely as a study of power and pressure in American and Israeli politics, but also as a prime example of just how policy wars in democratic cultures are never tidy, pristine, or for the meek. Lazin leaves it up to the reader to decide who emerges as principled and high-minded, though we may instead conclude that practicality rather than nobility is the virtue that prevails.

Paul J. Rich
Series Editor

Acknowledgments

I wish to express my appreciation to several persons who have influenced my interest in American and ethnic politics, immigration, and Soviet Jewry. I would also like to thank several persons whose cooperation made this research effort doable.

At the University of Massachusetts at Amherst I studied American politics and history in courses taught by Luther Allen, Mario DePillis, Sheldon Goldman, Glen Gordon, David Mayhew and Louis Ruchames. I continued these scholarly pursuits at the University of Chicago with David Greenstone, E. W. Kelley, Ted Lowi, and Grant McConnell.

As a graduate student at the University of Chicago I wrote an MA thesis about Jews in American politics under the guidance of Hans J. Morgenthau. I focused on the response of District 6 B'nai B'rith to Hitler's anti-Jewish policies and German Jewish refugees during the 1930s. The guidance of Jeremy Azreal and Joseph Cropsey helped me broaden the focus of the thesis to deal with the American Jewish response to Hitler. Rabbis Max Ticktin and Danny Leifer arranged for me to present my first academic talk on the subject at Hillel at the University of Chicago.

Many individuals were most cooperative and helpful in my research efforts for this book. Among them were Carl Glick (HIAS), Ralph Goldman and Sherry Melzer Hyman (JDC), Don Irvine and Steve Solender (United Jewish Communities) and Howard Weisband (Jewish Agency for Israel). Also helpful were the staff at the Dorot Jewish Division of the New York Public Library.

Several colleagues provided encouragement, insight and guidance. These include Sam Aroni and Joel Aberbach at UCLA; Henry Feingold at Baruch College; Lee Sigelman at GWU; Alon Gal and Benjamin Pinkus of Ben Gurion University; Robert Selzer and Ken Sherrill at Hunter College; Ira Sharkansky at Hebrew University; and Mark Holzer at Rutgers University. A special debt is owed to Aristide Zolberg of the New School University for his interest, support, and encouragement.

I am indebted to the members of the Hurst Family—Alan and Linda, Steve and Sonny, David and Melissa—for their continued support of my incumbency of the Lynn and Lloyd Hurst Family Chair in Local Government. Their backing facilitated my pursuit of this research project.

I would like to thank Ayelet Haimpur-Zuckerman, Etty Hadad and Lital Grundland, my research assistants at Ben Gurion University, who helped with library work and checked sources.

Finally, I would like to express a special thanks to my wife Rachel who encouraged me from the start to pursue and finish this project. Her preference for summer teaching at GWU led to my first interview for the project. Had we not gone to Washington I doubt that I would have started this research.

1

Introduction

On May 8, 1989, Mr. Simcha Dinitz, the Chairman of the Jewish Agency Executive wrote Israeli Prime Minster Yitzhak Shamir that the Soviet government would allow American authorities to issue visas in Moscow to Russian Jews wanting to immigrate to the United States. Until this time Soviet authorities had denied most Soviet Jews the option of applying for American visas in Moscow; those wanting to immigrate to the United States left on visas for Israel via Vienna. In Vienna, Jewish and non-Jewish American aid organizations provided care and maintenance, transferred them to Rome and assisted them to apply for entry into the United States as refugees. In his response to Simcha Dinitz on May 17, 1989, Prime Minister Yitzhak Shamir's chief of staff, Mr. Yossi Ben-Aharon, confirmed that the Israeli government supported the proposed new visa arrangements in Moscow.[1]

Ostensibly this response contradicted the Israeli government's official position at the time that all Soviet Jewish émigrés should settle in Israel. For decades, Israeli prime ministers had criticized "dropouts," Soviet Jews who emigrated on Israeli visas but chose to resettle in other countries, and had urged several American Jewish organizations to desist from helping them reach the United States.[2] Recently, Prime Minister Yitzhak Shamir had urged the American government to deny refugee status to Soviet Jews. Ben-Aharon's letter, however, suggests that Israel may have been a party to an agreement involving the governments of the United States and Soviet Union and American Jewish leaders which provided for a limit on the number of Soviet Jewish refugees allowed to enter the United States, the issuance of American visas in Moscow, and "direct flights" to Israel.[3]

Following General Secretary Mikhail Gorbachev's decisions in 1987–1988 to allow free emigration of Soviet Jews, it became evident that over 90 percent

1

preferred to resettle in the United States. Few desired to go to Israel. The negotiated understanding in Washington, D.C. permitted the annual entry as refugees of 40,000 Soviet Jews who had immediate family in the United States. Once a backlog of Soviet Jewish refugee applicants was cleared in Rome then the United States would cease to issue refugee visas to Soviet Jews outside of the Soviet Union. These restrictions ended the "dropout" phenomenon. For most Soviet Jews unable to obtain entry to the United States, the choice became one of either staying in the Soviet Union or immigrating to Israel. By the end of 1992 almost 400,000 had chosen to settle in Israel (see appendix).

This book deals with the conflict between 1967 and 1989 involving Israeli political leaders and several American Jewish organizations over the issue of where Soviet Jews émigrés should resettle. Initially the Israeli government and most American Jewish leaders viewed the Russian Jewish émigré issue as one of *Aliyah*—immigration to Israel.[4] This consensus fell apart in the late 1970s when the majority of Soviet Jewish émigrés preferred to come to the United States. The American Jewish community responded sympathetically; they pressured their government to admit Soviet Jews as refugees and provide resettlement assistance. They organized resettlement in Jewish communities throughout the United States and assisted with housing, jobs, and health care.

In response the Israeli government demanded that the American Jewish organizations desist from aiding Russian Jews to immigrate to the United States. It argued that Israel needed the maximum number of Soviet Jews. It portrayed the potential immigration as essential for Israel's continued existence emphasizing that past absorption of many uneducated and unskilled immigrants from Arab lands gave Israel the right to receive the highly educated and skilled Jews of the Soviet Union. Officially, the Israeli government argued that those leaving on Israeli visas had an obligation to come to Israel. Moreover, they suggested that the deception of not coming to Israel might lead the Soviets to close the gates entirely. Finally, it argued that those émigrés coming to Israel had a better chance of remaining Jews than those who went to the United States and other Western countries.

This situation created a dilemma for American Jewish leaders. Many empathized with Israel's need for a maximum number of Soviet Jews, especially those that were well educated and skilled. Yet, many remembered that during the Holocaust the American government had refused entry to Jews fleeing Hitler's Germany. Would the American Jewish community now block the entry of Soviet Jews fleeing persecution in a Communist dictatorship? Moreover, the absence of an American option might cause many to remain in the Soviet Union. What if their lives would be physically threatened in the future? Some cited the Jewish tradition of rescuing prisoners (*Piduyon Shvuim*). Others defended assisting Soviet Jews by espousing the principle of "freedom of choice"; émigrés should be allowed to decide where they wanted to settle. Who were the Israeli's or the American Jewish community to deny Soviet Jews freedom to choose where to live? Defenders of "freedom of choice" also argued that if American Jewish organizations ceased aiding "dropouts" that other non-Jewish and anti-Zionist groups would assist their entry into the United States and be reimbursed by the United States government.[5] Finally, a minority of Jewish leaders and organizational professionals favored a maximum number coming to the United States. One federation official justified this position on grounds that since the closing of the gates of the United States to refugees in 1924 the American Jewish community had yet to be replenished.

The issue became very complex as the positions of the American Jewish community and Israeli leaders often changed. Whereas Prime Ministers Golda Meir, Yitzhak Rabin and Yitzhak Shamir pushed a hard line on "dropouts," Menachem Begin often placed family needs and preferences before immigration to Israel. He refused to request that the American government (or any other government) deny entry to Soviet Jews as refugees. As prime minister he asked American Jews not to aid dropouts in Vienna but urged them to welcome and assist Russian Jewish émigrés who managed to reach their communities. Importantly, Israeli governments tolerated differences with the American Jewish establishment in matters of Soviet Jewry.[6] Despite threats and anger on the subject Israeli governments consistently sought good relations with the American Jewish community. This may suggest that during the 1970s and 1980s that the Soviet Jewry issue had a lower priority for Israeli political leaders than their concern for good relations with American Jewry (and the United States government).

The American Jewish establishment also oscillated on the subject. While in November 1976 the American Jewish establishment defended the principle of "freedom of choice" against Israeli pressure to force Soviet Jews to come to Israel, early in 1979, several major Jewish federations expressed reservations about resettling Soviet Jewish émigrés in their communities. They were either disillusioned with the lack of idealism of those that came and/or concerned about the costs of resettlement (Simon 1997:77,78). In the late 1980s, following Gorbachev's coming to power and a major change in Soviet policy toward Jewish emigration most mainstream American Jewish leaders abandoned their commitment to freedom of choice. They supported "direct flights" to Israel (via Bucharest) and later agreed to an American government proposed quota on Soviet Jewish refugees allowed to enter the United States. They preferred that most Soviet Jews go to Israel where they were wanted and needed and stood a better chance of remaining Jews.

SIGNIFICANCE

This book deals with the broader issue of ethnicity and American politics. It focuses on the changing role of Jews in American politics during the past half century. The analysis of the response of American Jewish leaders to the plight of Soviet Jewry from the late 1960s to 1989 provides important information about the political behavior, influence and style of a well-established minority group in the United States. American Jewry came of age during the Soviet Jewry movement (Friedman 1999:1,2). Since the 1960s American Jews "have come to wield considerable influence in American economic, cultural, intellectual and political life." By the 1980s and 1990s they played "a major role in electoral politics and public policy . . . [and] wield[ed] considerable influence in the nation's public life" (Ginsberg 1993:139,1,2).[7] According to Biale (1986:177–178), "Today this community has access to the highest corridors of power and possesses considerable ability to influence, if not always decisively, the government of the United States in favor of Jewish interests."

Importantly, the group's acceptance, security, wealth and political power were recent. In the 1930s American Jews were seen by many and often by themselves as outsiders and strangers. Many Jews believed that one had to give up being Jewish to succeed and "make it" in America (Silberman 1985:62–85). They lacked political influence and felt insecure as American-Jews. They believed that American Jews, as a minority, should not lobby publicly for a specific Jewish issue (Lazin 1979). Their response to the plight of German Jews in the 1930s and the Holocaust is revealing (Lazin 1979 and Ne'eman Arad 2000): Most major American Jewish leaders urged caution in approaching their government on behalf of German Jews; they feared that public agitation for rescue could lead to anti-Semitism (Novick 1999:40). For example, in the 1930s key members of the most powerful American Jewish organization, the American Jewish Committee, who worked closely with President Roosevelt, refused to raise with him the issue of the persecution of Jews in Germany.[8] Lookstein (1988:113,114) argues that the "established leadership of the Jewish community . . . chose not to [pressure Roosevelt]— being frightened, dazzled by the president's charm or simply indifferent to the slaughter."[9] According to Ginsberg (1993:3), "The Jewish community lacked sufficient influence to induce the United States government to take any action that might have impeded the slaughter of European Jewry."

The depression, anti-immigration sentiment, the existence of widespread anti-Semitism in the United States and a sense of insecurity as Americans influenced the response of American Jewish leaders. "Anti-Jewish hostility was so widespread and so respectable, that even a President who was sympathetic toward Jews had to weigh the formidable risks of helping them" (Goldberg 1996:116–117).[10]

Americans changed their attitude toward American Jews shortly after World War II; "hating Jews was no longer a respectable political stance" (Goldberg 1996:117; Novick 1999:40,41). Many factors contributed to this change including sympathy for the victims of the Holocaust, revulsion against the evils of prejudice and good will of the 1950s. The birth of Israel eroded the old stereotype of Jew as weakling. Also, at the end of the Second World War, American Jewish organizations launched a campaign to end prejudice and discrimination in America. They formed coalitions with Afro-Americans, labor and liberal churches (Goldberg 119–120).[11] Silberman (1985:109) suggests that the election of John F. Kennedy as President in 1960 transformed the United States from an "essentially Protestant to a religiously pluralistic society."

According to Biale (1986:184) the Six Day War in 1967 became the focus of American Jewish power and enhanced it. The War influenced the self-perception of American Jews and the way other Americans perceived them (Goldberg 1996:134). The victory marked the end "of one era and the beginning of another in the life of the American Jewish community, the moment, it is often said, when American Jews gained pride in being Jewish" (Silberman 1985:137).[12] It was a time in which "American Jews had tried to persuade themselves as well as Gentiles, that they were just like everybody else, only more so, and a period in which they acknowledged, even celebrated their distinctiveness (Silberman 1985:223)."

By the 1970s America had changed and so had the standing and influence of its Jewish community. Biale (1986:186) suggests that the failure of the melting pot led to Jews redefining themselves "in ethnic terms."[13] Silberman (1985:9–22) describes an American society that opened to Jews and other ethnic and religious groups in ways unexpected a generation ago. American Jews now felt much more at home and secure as Jews in America. They now had more freedoms and equal opportunities; "equality is a fact, not just an aspiration" (Silberman 1985:23,110–112). They were wealthy, well educated, assertive, influential, and powerful.

There had also been a leadership change which had begun in the 1930s. By the 1960s and 1970s the children and grandchildren of Eastern European Jews had replaced the American Jewish leaders of German origin. (Golden 1992:72–73).[14] They asserted themselves as Jews on the American political agenda (Biale 1986:179).

In the 1970s the struggle for Soviet Jewry became a national Jewish crusade (Goldberg 1996:144; Sarna and Golden 2000:88). Many American Jewish leaders pressured openly to put the issue of Soviet Jewry on the American public agenda. They sought support in Congress and the Administration and even battled publicly against the President of the United States over the Jackson-Vanik Amendment. They did not hesitate to support the Israeli request for United States government aid to resettle Soviet Jews. They pressured their government to declare Soviet Jews refugees in order to give them special standing and privileges and to fund their resettlement in the United States. This, Orbach (1979:124,125) argues, "reflected a growing Jewish self-confidence—it was no longer considered disloyal to express Jewish interests." Nevertheless, they exercised restraint and caution. In the late 1980s, when it looked like a million or more wanted to come live in the *Goldene Medina* (golden land), they agreed to limit the number of Soviet Jewish refugees allowed to enter the United States.

Clearly, the focus on the changing role of Jews in American politics contributes to a better understanding of the process of Americanization of groups considered at one time outsiders, strangers and politically ineffective. Understanding the way American Jews participate as organized interest groups in American politics since the 1970s should provide an interesting marker for other groups who have more recently entered American society. How do children and grandchildren of immigrants behave politically on issues relating to their perceived ethnic group interests? How does their perception of themselves as Americans and as Jews influence the political behavior of leaders of organized American Jewry in the American political system from the 1970s to the present? Hopefully, the study will add to the growing body of literature about immigration politics begun by Rogers Brubaker, Gary Freeman (1989) (1995), and Aristide Zolberg (1995, 1998). The findings should provide a potential paradigm for understanding what may happen to second and third generation children of newer immigrants who today are considered outsiders and newcomers.

The book also provides a fascinating and important case study of "sponsored" immigrant politics—the political involvement of a foreign country with its "former citizens" in the United States. David Biale (1986:197) notes that in redefining themselves "in ethnic terms according to national origins." American Jews substituted Israel for "nation of origin."

A central focus here is the role that the Israeli government played in influencing the response and policies of American Jewish leaders and their government toward Soviet Jewry. This study, therefore, can be used for comparison with older ethnic communities as well as the post-1965 communities and their former homelands (Portes and Rumbau 1996:109). The findings are especially relevant for understanding the politics of transnational migrants in contemporary American society which has become an important issue for American politics today with the political awareness and activism of growing numbers of Mexican, Asian and other ethnic groups. To what extent does this study of American Jews presage a forthcoming role for Mexican or Asian groups in American politics?

David Biale (1986:186) notes that Israel's "political and diplomatic representatives serve as agents for organizing American Jewish political activity on its behalf." An important issue here is the degree to which the Israeli government orchestrated the activities and efforts of the Soviet Jewry advocacy movement in the United States. Another issue is the role Israeli officials played in influencing United States refugee and resettlement policies. It will be shown here how the Israelis shaped American public opinion essential to pressure action by the American government on behalf of Soviet Jewry. At first the Israelis encouraged and even manipulated the involvement of American Jews and their organizations to act on behalf of Soviet Jewry. They tapped Holocaust guilt and deference to Israel to foster the American Soviet Jewry movement (see Spiegel 2001:257).

In his study of the relationship between American Jews and Israel, Steven Rosenthal writes that "By 1975, American Jews' identification with Israel and their loyalty to the Jewish state had become so strong that such emotions appeared unremarkable and routine. American Jews had embraced Israel as the culmination of Jewish history, as the highest expression of Jewish virtue, and as an indispensable component of modern Jewish identity. They saw their roles as providing automatic financial and political support for whatever goals or policies the Jewish state chose to pursue. Critics of Israel were simply read out of the organized Jewish community."[15]

He goes on to argue that by the "1970s and 1980s the vast majority of American Jews meekly and uncritically supported the policies of the Begin government despite widespread and vigorous dissent within Israel itself. Even when American Jews disagreed with Israel they almost invariably shunned public criticism on grounds that revealing disunity would give comfort to Israel's enemies (23)."

The study here, however, reveals that on the Soviet Jewry issue the American Jewish establishment disagreed with the Israelis as early as the mid-1970s. They took public positions contrary to that of the Israeli government. Therefore, it will be argued here that throughout much of the period American Jewish leaders pursued their own interests as organizations representing Jews living in the United States. It supports Rosenthal's thesis that "despite emotional support of Israel, American Jews' priorities remained overwhelmingly American."[16]

Ironically the participation of American Jews in the Soviet Jewry movement helped direct them away from concern with Israel to focus on Jews elsewhere and eventually their own communities. They came to see their "Jewish interests" as differing from those of the Israelis. Many American Jewish leaders put "freedom of choice" before "Israel's national interest." This contributed to an awareness of a new Jewish identity (more inward than Israeli oriented) among American Jewry. When the Soviet Jewry movement had achieved success by 1990, the centrality of Israel has given way in the American Jewish community to local and internal concerns.[17] As Israeli journalist Nahum Barnea wrote in January 1977: The Soviet Jewry issue is the "start of a challenge to Israel's preeminence in American Jewish communal affairs."[18]

Finally the focus on the Soviet Jewry advocacy movement and in particular its interaction with the State Department, White House and Congress supplements other analyses of understanding Soviet policy on Jewish emigration. For example, the details of American Jewish efforts to influence their government to pressure Mikhail Gorbachev are presented here. They are based on archival materials not reviewed by previous authors dealing with Soviet emigration policy. While Salitan's (1992:34,154) analysis of Soviet domestic factors in explaining emigration policy is very important, the pressures of American Jews on their government may also have influenced Soviet emigration policy. While she downplays the importance of Soviet-American relations she does not discount them. She may have underestimated them.

THE CONTENTS OF THE BOOK

The book is divided into three sections. Part I traces the role of the Israeli government in making American Jews and Americans in general aware of the plight of Soviet Jewry. For most Americans, Jews and non-Jews, there was no Soviet Jewry problem until the mid- or late 1960s.

In 1952, the highest level of the Israeli government approved the establishment of a special department in the Office of the Prime Minister to "rescue" Soviet Jewry. It later became known as the Liaison Bureau. It established contact with Jews within the Soviet Union, fostered Jewish identity and encouraged interest in emigration to Israel (Levanon 1999:71).[19] A second branch, named *Bar*, focused on stimulating interest in Soviet Jewry among Jews and non-Jews in the West in order to influence Western governments to pressure the USSR to let its Jews immigrate to Israel.

The book focuses on efforts by Liaison Bureau personnel in the United States to initiate, nurture and create the Soviet Jewry issue and bring it to the attention of the American Jewish community, public opinion at large, and to political decision makers in Washington, D.C. One Liaison Bureau person served as an Israeli Consul in New York City with responsibility for contact with American Jewish organizations. A second served in the Washington Embassy with responsibility for dealing with Congress and the Administration. The Liaison Bureau also employed Israeli journalists on assignment in the United States and at least one American Jewish intellectual. Considerable attention is given to the "Israeli role" in establishing the National Conference of Soviet Jewry (NCSJ) (1971) and its predecessor the American Jewish Conference on Soviet Jewry (AJCSJ). Both served as the American Jewish establishment's umbrella organization for the advocacy of the Soviet Jewry movement in the United States. Once established as American Jewish organizations, Liaison Bureau personnel continued to participate actively in them. At the same time, however, these organizations became independent entities. An important issue here is the degree of Israeli influence and direction of these organizations.

Also examined is the role of other establishment Jewish organizations in the Soviet Jewry movement in the United States. These include the Hebrew

Immigrant Aid Society (HIAS), the American Joint Distribution Committee (JDC) and the Council of Jewish Federations and Welfare Funds (CJF). HIAS helped Soviet émigrés get visas to Western countries and coordinated their resettlement in the United States with the New York Association for New Americans (NYANA) and the federations (Sanders 1988:181–193,589–591 and http://www.hias.org/splash.html, August 23, 2004). HIAS would be a major actor in setting American Jewish policy toward Soviet Jews in the early and mid-1970s. JDC provided care and maintenance for Russian émigrés in Europe (Goldberg 1996:106 and http://www.jdc.org, August 23, 2004).[20] It also funded many of the Liaison bureau activities in the Soviet Union including the packages program. Its lay leadership and professionals played a major role in the American Soviet Jewry movement. CJF represented almost 200 federations (Goldberg 1996:52,105). In the mid-1970s its General Assembly became a sounding board for advocacy policies on behalf of Soviet Jews.[21] Its influence and power within the American Jewish Community expanded throughout the period. In the mid-1970s it would restrict or block various Israeli initiatives on Soviet Jewry and by the late 1980s it set "Soviet Jewish policy" for the American Jewish establishment.[22] It also played a major role in the resettlement of Soviet Jews in the United States. While most of its lay leaders and staff were "pro-Israeli" CJF often acted independently of Israeli government interests.

Lesser attention is given to the National Jewish Community Relations Councils (NJCRAC), the Conference of Presidents of Major American Jewish Organizations (Presidents Conference), the American Jewish Committee (AJC) and the American Jewish Congress.[23]

The book does not record in detail the policies and activities of two other important American Soviet Jewry advocacy organizations—the non-mainstream Union of Councils and the Student Struggle for Soviet Jewry (SSSJ).[24] Their neglect here is not intended to minimize their role in the Soviet Jewry movement. Credit is given to them throughout the manuscript. The emphasis on the establishment organizations reflects their central role in influencing American Jewry, American public opinion and the American government; without their efforts much less would have been achieved. It also reflects archival sources used by the author.[25]

The study reviews the efforts in the mid-1970s of several American Jewish organizations to secure visas and entry for Soviet Jewish émigrés and funds for their resettlement in the United States.[26] This section ends with a discussion of the Jackson-Vanik Amendment, which denied the Soviet Union '*Most Favored Nation*' (*MFN*) status in dealings with the United States. Despite Goldberg's (1996) assertion that the Israeli government stayed out of the conflict, the Israelis and the Liaison Bureau played a major role in getting support for the amendment. More important, the organized American Jewish community publicly opposed the President of the United States and the

Secretary of State on the issue—a far cry from the Jewish timidity and restraint of the 1930s.

Part II of the book examines the "dropout" phenomenon and the freedom of choice debate from the early 1970s through 1982 when the Soviet Union temporarily closed its gates to Soviet Jewish emigration. The issue brought Israel, its Liaison Bureau and the Jewish Agency into conflict with the American Jewish establishment.[27] At the core of the disagreement was the issue whether the American Jewish community should aid dropouts and facilitate their immigration and resettlement in the United States and other Western countries. With an increasing number of émigrés choosing not to come to Israel, Israelis feared that they would loose those Jews for whom they had worked for decades to free. Ironically, to achieve the exit of Soviet Jews, the Israelis had mobilized American Jews, who increasingly supported and funded the resettlement of Soviet Jews in the United States. Without the "American" resettlement option many more might have chosen to come to Israel. These activities provide important insights into the efforts of the Israeli and American Governments as well as American Jewish organizations to influence the final destination of Soviet Jewish émigrés.

Due to the absence of direct flights most Soviet Jews leaving on visas for Israel traveled to Vienna and were then flown to Israel. Initially, Israel controlled the émigrés in Austria and may (or may not) have denied them other destination options.[28] This changed in late summer 1973 when, following a Palestinian terrorist incident, the Austrian government assumed authority for Soviet émigrés in transit. While they allowed the Jewish Agency to meet and receive almost all persons leaving the Soviet Union on Israeli visas, Austrian authorities insured each émigré the freedom to decide his or her final destination. Accordingly, the Jewish Agency transferred Jewish émigrés not going to Israel to the American Joint Distribution Committee (JDC) and the Hebrew Immigrant Aid Society (HIAS), both sponsored and funded by the American Jewish community. Other organizations, including Caritas, Tolstoy Foundation, International Rescue Committee and later Rav Tov (associated with the Brooklyn-based Satmer Rebbe) also offered assistance to individual émigrés who did not want to continue on to Israel. HIAS transported "dropouts" to Rome where it helped them obtain visas to the United States and other countries.

Once the dropout rate reached 50 percent in the mid-1970s the Israeli authorities pressured HIAS and JDC to stop aiding those not wanting to come to Israel. Israeli efforts convinced leaders of several national Jewish organizations to support its position. Others, however, including HIAS and key federation lay leaders and professionals resisted Israeli pressure and supported "freedom of choice" for Soviet Jews. By 1978 the Israelis had backed down and accepted defeat on this issue. Three years later in 1981, with Soviet Jewish emigration in sharp decline, Mr. Aryeh Dulzin, head of the Jewish Agency

Executive, acted unilaterally to pressure JDC and HIAS to stop aiding Soviet Jewish "dropouts" in Vienna. For a short period of time they acquiesced. Many of these activities came to a halt in 1982 when the Soviet Union significantly limited the number of Jews allowed to emigrate. The gates would close for several years.

The final section of the book deals with the American Soviet Jewry advocacy movement during the Gorbachev era.[29] It is divided into two parts. The first analyzes the strategy of the American Jewish establishment to make free emigration by Soviet Jews a pre-condition of détente. This created at least three dilemmas for American Jewish leaders. First, they were uncertain as to whether it would be wise to link Soviet Jewish emigration with disarmament. They were uneasy about requesting that their government go slow on nuclear disarmament until the Soviets allowed more Jews to emigrate. Second, they had to decide whether to press the Soviet Union for free emigration for Soviet Jews or for all of its citizens? In other words, if the Soviet Union allows all Jews to leave should the struggle for free emigration end (Appelbaum 1986:632ff)? Third, a changed, more liberal and open Soviet Union might offer an option of Jews remaining in the Soviet Union with cultural and religious freedom (Salitan 1992:67). Should this option be supported?

A second part of this section deals with the response by American Jewry, Israel, Congress and the Administration to the expected mass Soviet Jewish emigration following Gorbachev's decision to allow free emigration of Soviet Jews. By 1987 it became clear that the Soviet Union would open its gates and a million or more Jews might leave. More than 90 percent wanted to go to the United States; few preferred Israel. This embarrassed and incensed the Israeli government. In practical terms, Israel would receive few if any Soviet Jews. Therefore, Israel wanted to block the entry of Soviet Jews into the United States. At the same time, neither the United States Government nor the American Jewish establishment favored accepting so many Jewish refugees. Several issues developed. First, the USA had a limited number of annual places and funding for refugees. Jewish leaders did not want to alienate other immigrant aid groups by giving undue preference for Soviet Jewish refugees. Second, some American Jewish leaders as well as American government officials questioned the refugee status of Soviet Jews especially in light of the new liberal policies of Gorbachev. Third, the expenses involved in resettlement weighed heavily on the United States government and the American Jewish community. Fourth, many Jewish federations and community felt that they had reached their capacity to absorb and resettle Soviet Jews. In light of all of the above more and more American Jewish leaders came to see Israel as the preferred destination for Soviet Jews. American Jewish support for the Lautenberg Amendment which granted all Jews, Pentecostal Christians and members of the Ukrainian Catholic and Ukrainian Autocephalous Orthodox Church in the Soviet Union refugee status based on

group membership hid the real opposition of the American Jewish establishment to open gates for Soviet Jews to immigrate to the United States.

Part II traces the important negotiations involving the American Jewish
leadership led by Max Fisher, the White House, State Department, Immigration and Nationalization Service (INS) and Congress that resulted in a compromise whereby the United States restricted annual immigration of Soviet
Jews to 40,000 persons with close relatives (family reunification) in the
United States.[30] The negotiations were part of a consultation process established by the Refugee Act of 1980 whereby the President consulted with
members of Congress to set the number of refugee entries for the coming
Fiscal Year (FY). The compromise required the cooperation of the Soviet
government. Members of the negotiating teams also consulted with the Israeli government. In a situation of either waiting years for an American visa
(as the quota for the first two years filled immediately) or going at once to Israel, hundreds of thousands of Jews decided to leave for Israel. Gitelman
(1999:86) refers to this as panic migration (1989–1994) when 750,000 Jews,
including growing number of non-Jews attached to Jewish family members
"fled what they saw as a collapsing economy, state and social order."

METHODOLOGY

In the late 1980s the author had access to extensive archival material in the
Jewish Agency dealing with Israel's absorption of Soviet and Ethiopian immigrants. The files contained considerable information about Jewish Agency
efforts to influence the final destination of Soviet Jewish émigrés. Some of
these materials dealt with the issue of "dropouts" in Vienna, "freedom of
choice" and the conflict as to whether Soviet Jews should go either to Israel
or the United States. Among the documents were the letters between Simcha
Dinitz and Yossi Ben-Aharon, which at the time confused the author: How
could Prime Minister Yitzhak Shamir support the American policy of granting Soviet Jews refugee visas in Moscow?

While teaching at George Washington University in Washington, D.C., during the summer of 1995 the author interviewed several officials in Jewish organizations, Congressional staffs and Executive Agencies about the Soviet
Jewry movement and Soviet Jewish immigration to the United States in the
late 1980s. They provided considerable but incomplete information about
negotiations involving Max Fisher and a dual exit policy (Israel and the
United States [Western countries] from the USSR and a quota on Soviet immigrants to the USA. In the fall of 1996 in New York City, during a six month
stay at the Center for Global Change and Governance at Rutgers University
in Newark, he continued interviews with leaders in Jewish organizations and
gained access to the archives of the American Joint Distribution Committee.

At that time, Mr. Steve Solender, then Executive Vice President of the UJA-Federation of New York City, claimed that the issues of the preferred destination for Soviet Jews—Israel or the United States in the 1980s—had first surfaced during the early 1970s. This led the author to broaden the research to the issue of "Freedom of Choice" in the early 1970s. The author pursued this subject during a two and half year stay in New York City beginning in the fall of 1998. He read archival materials at the JDC, HIAS and the United Jewish Communities (formerly the CJF, UIA, and UJA). At JDC the author had access to files relating to the career of former Executive Vice President Mr. Ralph Goldman who had dealt actively with Soviet Jewish issues until the mid-1980s. Despite promises, HIAS did not grant the author free access to its files. Fortunately, many important HIAS documents were found in the archives of JDC and the CJF. At the offices of the United Jewish Communities, the author had complete access to available files.[31]

Another valuable source of information on the Soviet Jewry movement in the United States was the Dorot Archives at the New York Public Library. It contains an Oral History of the Soviet Jewry movement conducted originally by the American Jewish Committee. The collection contains personal accounts of many of the key Israeli Liaison Bureau personnel, and American Jewish leaders active in the Soviet Jewry advocacy movement. The oral histories read are cited in the bibliography.

The author supplemented the archival materials with extensive open-ended interviews with activists in American Jewish Organizations and officials in the Jewish Agency, and the United States and Israeli governments (see appendix). The interviews were conducted from 1994 to the present. Extensive uses of secondary sources including newspaper accounts, memoirs, relevant scholarly articles, books and the World Wide Web have been used.

NOTES

1. Both letters are in the archives of the Jewish Agency for Israel in Jerusalem, Israel.
2. The Hebrew word for dropouts is *Noshrim*.
3. Initially, those Soviet Jews going to Israel were to fly from Eastern European cities.
4. Gitelman (1999:85,89) contends that within the Soviet Union it was always an *Aliyah* movement, even when the overwhelming majority wanted to go to the United States in the 1980s. Those wanting America did not set up a separate movement nor did they make immigration to the United States or elsewhere a public goal. Where to go was private while they publicly fought to establish the right to leave the country.
5. By the 1970s the United States government reimbursed these organizations the cost of transportation, care and maintenance in Europe, and initial resettlement in the United States for Soviet Jewish refugees.
6. The term "American Jewish establishment" refers to the leaders of mainstream national American Jewish organizations including the American Jewish Committee,

American Jewish Congress, Council of Jewish Federations (CJF), local Jewish Federations, National Jewish Community Relations Advisory Councils (NJCRAC), B'nai
B'rith, Anti-Defamation League, Presidents Conference of Major American Jewish organizations and others.

7. Ginsberg (1993:23) refers to more than \$3b per annum in aid to Israel and a
decline of anti-Semitism as indicators of Jewish influence. Also see Greenberg and
Wald 2001:188.

8. Later, during World War II, actions by Henry Mogenthau, President Roosevelt's
Jewish Secretary of the Treasury, would prove to be an exception (Silberman 1985:104).

9. Riemer (1996:6) writes that "Jewish organizations were reluctant to agitate for the
admission of Jewish refugees." Based on Wyman, Riemer (1996:9) asserts that while the
United States could not have prevented the Holocaust, it could have saved several hundred thousand Jews had Roosevelt acted. Wyman argues (1984) that among other
heads of government FDR was the least indifferent to the Jewish catastrophe.

10. Goldberg (115–116) referring to Wyman (1984) writes that American public
opinion was hostile to rescuing European Jews: "Opposition to helping Jews was not
merely widespread, it was intense." Hyman Bookbinder, in 1985, referred to "the
non-existence of the kind of Jewish political power we now exercise in this country.
If . . . we had in place institutions and techniques and professionals that could get 70
Senators or 350 Congressmen in matter of days or hours joining together to demand
action . . . or . . . the alliances we have today with other ethnic religious groups we
might have saved more Jews."

11. The American Jewish Committee, for example, launched a legal assault on
American anti-Semitism based on a plan of Alexander Pekelis titled "Full Equality in
a Free Society."

12. Goldberg argues that this transformation started with the waiting period before
the war when many American Jews feared that Israel may be destroyed. "Amid their
exhilaration, Jewish leaders and activists were left with an overwhelming feeling of
vulnerability and isolation." In Silberman's (1984:177,201,205) view this caused them
to become more interested in the Holocaust and led to a discovery of Jewish partic-
ularism (1985:177,201,205). They believed that the world might have let Israel be de-
stroyed, thus the world is a hostile place. Goldberg (1996:137–145) argues that American left and developing world perception of Israel as a military and imperial power
along with the Ocean Hill Brownsville New York City school decentralization controversy "conspired to reinforce bitterness of siege and erase the joy of victory." "Dri-
ven by fear of anti-Semitism, by guilt over past Jewish timidity, and by suspicion of
Gentiles, liberalism, and coalition politics, the new particularists simply took over the
machinery of American Jewish politics." For Goldberg (1996:149) the new leadership
is made up of Orthodox Jews, secular Zionists and Neo-Conservatives. Bookbinder
(1985) attributes Jewish power after 1967 to the many leaders and professionals and
the large number of national, regional and local organizations networks. "It is the
sum-total of thousands of organized Jewish branches and units and lodges in hundreds of American communities."

13. Biale also notes that in the 1930s there was considerably less legitimacy for
ethnic politics. Michael Novick (1999:34) cites a revival of ethnic identity in the 1960s.

14. Silberman (1985:223) also distinguishes between the older generation born before and during World War II and the younger generation who "Never having known

their parents' fear, young Jews do not need the vicarious sense of potency their parents derive from Israeli's military accomplishments."

15. Ginsberg (2001:23) writes "Beginning in late 1950s after Israel's victory over Egypt in the Suez War, and heightened after Israel's spectacular victory over all Arab nations in the 1967 Israeli-Arab War, Israel became the central focus of American Jewish life." In Novick's (1999:148–149) words, the aftermath of the Six Day War "effected a permanent reorientation in the agenda of organized American Jewry. Israel moved to the top of that agenda—in fund raising, in lobbying and in electoral politics."

16. Raffel (2002:121) notes that the American Jewish community was never a rubber stamp "for decisions made in Jerusalem."

17. In 1990, Charlotte Jacobson, former president of Hadassah and World Zionist Organization (American section) official commented that during the last two years the American Jewish community was moving away from Israel. Contributing factors had been the issue of "who is a Jew?" and the realization by American Jewish leaders that they had more power over activities here than in Israel.

18. Reported by Malka Rabinowitz in the *Jerusalem Post*. See Rosenthal 2001: 170–177; Ginsberg 2001:23. Novick (1999:168) argues that by 1984 the Holocaust replaced Israel as the primary concern of many American Jews. Both Rosenthal and Greenberg and Wald (2001:195) emphasize the decline of support for Israeli policy among American Jews due to Israeli policy in the occupied territories.

19. Its code name in Hebrew was *Nativ*. It assigned three Russian speaking families to the Israeli Embassy in Moscow and worked out of Israeli embassies in Bucharest and Prague. It established clandestine contacts with Jews, distributed materials and helped some persons escape from behind the Iron Curtain.

20. In 1935 JDC and the American Zionists established the Allied Jewish Appeal which became the United Jewish Appeal (UJA) for Overseas Relief in 1939 (Goldberg 1996:107; Silberman 1985:186).

21. Biale (1986:187–188) notes that the General Assembly is "considered by those involved in Jewish politics as the yearly national congress of American Jews." In 1976 CJF established a Washington Action Office which helped get refugee admission numbers and lobbied for immigration and resettlement legislation and funding (Carp 2002:208).

22. See Elazar 2002:7. In the late 1990s the CJF, UJA and United Israel Appeal merged to form the United Jewish Communities (UJC) (http://www.ujc.org, August 23, 2004).

23. The National Community Relations Advisory Council (NCRAC) was established in 1944 by the General Assembly of the CJF (Goldberg 1996:105 & Chernin 1999:17; http://www.jewishpublicaffairs.org/publications/JPP_94-95_appendix.html, August 23, 2004). In 1969 it became the National Jewish Community Relations Advisory Council or NJCRAC (Goldberg (1996:123–125). In 1998 it became the Jewish Council for Public Affairs. It is an umbrella organization which coordinates the policies of 13 national organizations, including major defense and synagogue groups, with 120 local Jewish community relations councils (Chanes 2001:109;Chernin 1999:17 & Goldberg 1996:127).

The Conference of Presidents of Major American Jewish Organizations, established in 1955 by Nahum Goldmann to bring together leaders of major American Jewish

organizations to coordinate their position on issues relating to Israel (http://www.
conferenceofpresidents.org/fence.html, August 23, 2004). It was viewed by many as
an Israeli front (Orbach 1979:72 and Goldberg 1996:xviii). Nahum Goldmann set it up
working with Philip Klutznick of B'nai B'rith and Israel's Ambassador to the USA
Abba Eban. Yehuda Hellman, a colleague of Goldman's from Israel became executive director and served until his death in 1986 (Raffel 2002:114).

The American Jewish Committee was established in 1906 by German American
Jews to deal with the plight of Russian Jews following the pogroms of 1905 and to
fight anti-Semitism at home (Goldberg 1996:101; Sanders 1988:235; Windmueller
2002:16,40–41 and http://www.ajc.org/, August 23, 2004). During the 1970s and
1980s it remained an elite organization, very active on the issue of Soviet Jewry. It
generally cooperated with the Liaison Bureau representatives. It played a pivotal role
in establishing the American Jewish Conference on Soviet Jewry and the NCSJ.

The American Jewish Congress was initially set up in December 1918 to seek national rights for Eastern European Jews at the Paris Peace Conference of April 1919
(Sanders 1988:349; Goldberg 1996:102,103 and http://www.ajcongress.org, August
23, 2004). Rabbi Stephen S. Wise revived the organization in 1922. It became a "personal platform for his private blend of Jewish nationalism and militant liberalism."
During this period Soviet Jewry became a major concern of Congress. It also cooperated with the Liaison Bureau.

24. Formed in 1970, the Union of Councils was an umbrella organization of 22 local Soviet Jewry committees (in 1978) in various American cities and communities
(Ruby 1999:204; Naftalin 1999:229 and http://www.fsumonitor.com/, August 23,
2004). In 1985 it moved its headquarters to D.C. In 1988 it claimed 100,000 members
and overseas affiliations in the United Kingdom, Australia, Canada, France, Israel and
the Soviet Union. In 1988, 3 major Refusenik groups affiliated with the Union of
Councils and held annual meetings in Leningrad and Moscow in 1989 (Naftalin
1999:233). It defined itself as nonestablishment; most committees did not receive
funding from the local federations and the Councils usually did not coordinate its efforts with the Israelis (Ruby 1999:200–203). They perceived of themselves as being
the "American voice" of Refuseniks. Freedman (1989b:95) credits them with challenging Israeli leadership on Soviet Jewry issue by calling for a more active policy.
The Student Struggle for Soviet Jewry (SSSJ) was a student group in New York City of
college age (and older) activists. Although non-establishment and very activist it accepted funding from federations and often coordinated its activities with the Liaison
Bureau. At times it remained outspoken and critical (Halevi 2004).

25. Sarna and Golden 2000:88ff cite the neglect of these organizations by the
American Jewish Yearbook.

26. Previously, they lobbied to have Congress fund Israel's absorption of Soviet Jews.

27. Established in 1929 the Jewish Agency represented world Jewry and the World
Zionist Organization (WZO) in efforts to establish a Jewish State (Stock 1988:7ff). In
formal agreements in 1952 (Law of Status of the WZO and the Jewish Agency for the
Land of Israel) and Covenant in 1954, the Israeli government delegated to it primary
responsibility for the initial care of new immigrants. Although partially controlled by
the government's coalition parties the Agency can be independent in policy making.
It receives its funds from the UJA in the United States and the *Keren Hayesod* elsewhere (Katz et al. 1987).

28. Salitan (1992:32–45) argues that pre-1974 Soviet policies encouraged Zionists to leave. Most of them wanted to immigrate to Israel. In contrast, after 1973 most of the émigrés were non-Zionists who left for economic reasons. They preferred to go West.

29. Leonid Brezhnev died on November 24, 1982 and was succeeded by Yuri Andropov as Secretary of the Communist Party. His successor Konstantin Chernenko served from February 9, 1984 until March 1985. Mikhail Sergeyevich Gorbachev succeeded him on March 11, 1985 (Shultz 1993:124,471,526).

30. At the time, Mr. Carmi Schwartz, Executive Vice President of the CJF sought out Max Fisher, a private citizen, to approach the State Department about the growing number of Soviet Jewish émigrés in Ladispoli, Italy, many of whom were denied refugee status by the INS in Rome (Golden 1992:469).

31. CJF archives are located at the United Jewish Communities (UJC) in New York City.

2

Putting the Soviet Jewry Issue on the Public Agenda in the United States: From Indifference to the Jackson-Vanik Amendment

This chapter documents the efforts of the Liaison Bureau of the Israeli government and several American Jewish organizations to convince American public opinion that there existed a Soviet Jewish issue worthy of governmental concern. In the early 1960s few persons in the United States, Jew or Gentile, perceived of a Soviet Jewry problem. Initial efforts focused on "educating" the American Jewish community about Soviet Jewry. Subsequent activities targeted the American public, Congress and the Administration to take up the issue of human rights for Soviet Jews. When it became apparent that Soviet Jews could not enjoy equal rights guaranteed in the Soviet constitution, the goal shifted to a demand for family reunification in their national homeland—Israel. Later, this was broadened to the right of emigration and cultural and religious rights for those that remained.[1]

A central issue in this chapter is the degree to which the Israeli Liaison Bureau initiated and directed the Soviet Jewry advocacy movement in the United States. According to Howard Morley Sachar (1992:906) the government of Israel "conceived, launched and executed the campaign to establish a relationship with the vast mother lode of European Jewry" in the United States. Others support the claim. Malcolm Hoenlein (1989:23), for example, argues, "recognition has to be given to the role that the Israelis played . . . without them, no Soviet Jewry Movement here!"[2] "Without the Israelis," asserts Rabbi Israel Miller (1990:14) "none of this would have happened." A mark of their success may be that at the height of the Soviet Jewry movement in the late 1980s, some American Jews criticized Israel for its silence and inactivity.

Elazar (1999:iii) may have overstated the case when he observed that "the American Jewish community had moved beyond Israel and evolved into the prime force in the Soviet Jewry movement." Clearly, once organized, the establishment's Soviet Jewry advocacy movement became very independent and took on a life of its own. Nevertheless, the Israeli Liaison Bureau remained very much involved. Formally, its personnel participated in executive committee meetings of the National Conference on Soviet Jewry (NCSJ) and the Greater New York Conference on Soviet Jewry (GNYCSJ). They also participated actively, for example, in planning the 1987 Washington, D.C. rally before the Reagan-Gorbachev summit (Interview with David Harris, August 13, 2003). And, as late as 1987 the head of the Conference of Presidents consulted with Nehemia Levanon of the Liaison Bureau before taking critical policy decisions (Abram 1989). In contrast, many federations and even the CJF often opposed the Liaison Bureau on specific issues relating to Soviet Jewish advocacy in the United States.

JEWS IN THE SOVIET UNION

During the late-nineteenth century over five million Jews lived as a persecuted minority in Czarist Russia. Since 1804 most were confined to the Pale of Settlement "an area of some 386,000 square miles from the Baltic to the Black Seas, located in western and southwestern Russia and the Ukraine" (Edelman 1983:215 and Salitan 1992:21). Czar Alexander II instituted reforms in the 1850s which ended the cantonist system for Jewish boys in the army, allowed greater freedom of residence in certain cities, and permitted entry to the civil service and limited access to universities and professions (Sanders 1888:8–10 and Buwalda (1997:7).

Following the assassination of Alexander II in 1881, the resulting pogroms, expulsions from villages and cities, and increased restrictions on employment led to a mass exodus of Jews from Russia and Eastern Europe (Edelman 1983:216). By 1914 over two million Russian Jews emigrated and settled in the United States (Sanders 1988: xii, 85–91,222; Buwalda 1997:10; Silberman 1985:49). Others went to Western Europe and Canada and a small minority participated in the Zionist enterprise in Ottoman Palestine (Sanders 1988:115–128).

At the height of this exodus of Russian Jews the Zionists criticized the large resettlement in the United States. Max Nordau told Alexander Harkavy of HIAS that "America saves the man, not the Jew." Israeli Zangwill stated "America is the euthanasia of the Jew and Judaism" (Sanders 1988:246,247). These criticisms would repeat themselves seventy years later in the conflict over where Soviet Jewish émigrés should be resettled—Israel or the United States.

For those Jews that remained, the potential for change and/or coping came in the form of several alternatives (Mendelsohn 1993). Some joined the anti-Czarist socialist underground which hoped to replace Czarist Russia with a workers state in which Jewish identity may or may not continue to exist, depending on one's ideological bent. Jews became active among the Bolsheviks and Mensheviks. Another avenue was the Bund, the Jewish Worker's Federation of Russia and Poland, founded in Vilna in 1897, a socialist party that favored a Jewish political entity based on Yiddish culture in the new socialist/Communist regime to be set up after the revolution (Sanders 1988:194). It claimed over 30,000 members in 1917. Much larger was the Zionist movement with over 300,000 members. The Zionists favored emigration and the establishment of a Jewish State in the ancient Jewish homeland of the Land of Israel. Others chose to assimilate into Russian culture. Perhaps a plurality either sought refugee in their religion or remained indifferent to the regime and continued to live in isolation and poverty.

Many of the estimated 3 million Jews of Russia welcomed the revolutions of 1917. While Jews were 3 to 4 percent of the population in 1917 they made up 20 percent of the revolutionary movement (Salitan 1992:12). Lenin included the Jews in a Declaration of Rights of Nationalities in November 1917 (Sanders 1988:299–303). In 1918 the Party established a Jewish Section (*Evsektsya*). The Civil War, however, brought much suffering and death to over 60,000 Jews (Buwalda 1997:11 and Sanders 1988:358).[3] Once the fighting ended, Jewish cultural life in the Soviet Union enjoyed a brief period of prosperity.[4] Many Jews served in high positions in the Communist Party and in the new government. Jews made up 5 percent of the party membership in 1922.

Lenin favored assimilating Jews in Soviet society. The Bund opposed this policy (Shapiro 1978:77). Since Jews lacked a national territory of their own within the Soviet Union, Salitan (1992:14) argues that they lost the chance of preserving separate cultural rights. Soon, the regime closed down and suppressed Jewish religious and cultural institutions.[5] The Stalin purges in the 1930s ended the lives of thousands of Jewish party members and exiled and then systematically killed Jewish cultural, political and religious cadres and leaders (Salitan 1992:18).

In 1932 the Soviet Union established a system of internal passports in which Jews were marked *Yevrei* (Buwalda 1997:15). This decision helped preserve Jewish identity without substance or content (Chernin 1999:22). For example, while 80 percent of the Jews in the 1949 census listed Yiddish as their native tongue, there were no schools or instruction in Yiddish (Lawrence 1970:107).[6]

With the Soviet invasion of Poland in 1939 and annexation of the Baltic States the Jewish population of the Soviet Union grew to 5.2 million. Before and during the German invasion in 1941 more than 300,000 Polish and Baltic Jews either fled or were deported further east into the Soviet Union.[7] During the Second World War the invading German forces killed between 2.5 and 3.3 million Jews in the Soviet Union. According to Pinkus (1992:375) the

Holocaust and Soviet anti-Semitism during World War II reawakened Jewish identity among many Soviet Jews.

In 1948 the Soviet Union recognized Israel and both countries established diplomatic relations.[8] Many in Israel saw the Red Army as the primary victor over Hitler's armies and the liberator of the concentration camps. Several left-wing kibbutzim hung the red flag and Stalin's picture in their dining halls. Mapam and other leftist and Marxist political groups in Israel favored an Israeli alliance with the Soviet Bloc. Initially some in the USSR believed that Israel might serve as its anti-British foothold in the region. This was dispelled by 1951 (Buwalda 1997:18).

Golda Meir served as Israel's first minister to the Soviet Union. Her visit to a Moscow synagogue during *Rosh Hashanah* (Jewish New Year) on October 16, 1948, caused a near riot. An estimated ten thousand Soviet Jews flocked to the streets around the synagogue to greet her (Lawrence 1970:152). When she returned to the Synagogue ten days later a similar response infuriated Soviet authorities (Orbach 1979:13). A wild, almost ecstatic outburst by Jews demonstrating a common bond with the Jewish State contradicted a widely held assumption that the Jews of the Soviet Union, after a generation or more of Communist indoctrination and persecution, had assimilated. The response to Golda Meir indicated that the condition of Soviet Jewish identity remained an open question. Meir Rosenne (1989:25) observed, "this was a traumatic experience of the Russians . . . they never thought that Jews remained so much attached to Israel despite of all those years of war and separation." Clearly, in 1948 the State of Israel "engendered a new pride, a new spirit in Soviet Jewry" (Orbach 1979:12).

Following a hiatus during World War II when the Soviet Union used Soviet Jews to improve ties and solidarity with the United States, Stalin's regime continued its policies of suppressing Jewish culture and identity.[9] Soviet authorities executed Yiddish cultural figures in 1948 and closed Jewish cultural and religious institutions. In August 1953 the Soviet regime executed another 23 Yiddish poets and journalists. In the 1953 "doctor's plot" Stalin accused Jewish doctors of trying to kill him.[10] Stalin's death on March 5, 1953, sidelined any plans for increased persecution of Jews.[11] Levanon (1999:72) refers to a loosening up of suppression of Jewish culture following Stalin's death. Nevertheless, for the next 35 years the regime would suppress Jewish life, culture, religion and almost any form of Jewish social or political organization.

In the early 1970s there were over 2 million Jews in the Soviet Union.[12] They lived throughout the USSR without their own territorial base (Heitman 1989:121,122). Many Soviet Jews, identified by nationality in their passports, faced various forms of discrimination. Although openly violent anti-Semitism disappeared by the 1970s a "deep seated anti-Jewish bias remained" (Shapiro 1978:79).

Nevertheless, Soviet Jews achieved a high degree of professional and economic success. By 1970 Jews had a "higher education level than both the Russian and local majority population in the five republics with high Jewish populations" (Simon 1997:53). Salitan (1992:17) traces the social mobility of Jews back to 1925 when many went to cities and entered higher education and professional fields including education, medicine, economics, natural sciences, engineering and arts. Many of these educated Jews benefited from the "personal and material rewards offered to intellectually productive citizens. Professors, scientists, creative individuals and professionals received proportionately better compensation than in many Western societies" (Simon 1997:53,54).

They became a new generation of Jews largely "alienated from its ethnic and religious roots" (Simon 1997). Many if not most followed a path toward assimilation into Soviet society and culture. This was especially true of the Ashkenazi (European or Western) Jews of the Soviet heartland. "The irony of Soviet anti-Jewish policy is that it makes the assimilation of Jews, which continues to be the stated policy of the regime, impossible" (Shapiro 1978:98). Salitan (1992:19) concurs when she argues that the neglect of Jewish aspects of the Holocaust and increased anti-Semitism "left Soviet Jews acutely aware of their Jewish identity and their position as outsiders."

A minority of Jews (*Zapadniki*) from the western republics annexed to the Soviet Union in 1939–1940 retained a greater degree of Jewish identity. Many spoke Yiddish (Heitman 1989:122–126).

Non-Ashkenazi Jews were the majority in Georgia and the Asian or Muslim republics of the USSR. Here the regime interfered less with religion and Jewish religious life was more common and open. Many of these Jews were craftsmen and white collar workers.

Despite Stalin's policies and a ban on emigration many Israeli leaders including David Ben-Gurion viewed Soviet Jews as the best hope of a future large scale European Jewish immigration to Israel. The Zionist movement and Israel's founders very much wanted to maximize the number of European Jewish immigrants who shared a common cultural bond with Israel's European Jewish establishment. They had disdain for many of the culturally different, less educated and skilled and poorer Jews from Arab countries (Sepharadim or Oriental Jews). For Ben-Gurion and his generation the Jewish State was to have been the homeland of masses of Jews from Eastern Europe.[13]

THE LIAISON BUREAU

In the early 1950s the Israeli government initiated a long-term effort to bring the Jews of the Soviet Union to Israel. It established an organization which later became known as the *Liaison Bureau* (*Lishkat Hakesher*). While initially part of the Foreign Office it became responsible to the Prime Minister (Buwalda 1997:35).[14] Its guiding force became Shaul Avigur who had been very active in the illegal immigration movement (*Aliyah Bet*) in the 1940s that brought hundreds of thousands of Jewish survivors from Eastern Europe to displaced persons camps in Western Europe and then to Palestine. Peter Novick (1999:78,79) suggests that the Israeli emissaries discouraged Jews in DP camps from immigrating to countries other than Israel.

Since conditions in the Soviet Union of the early 1950s did not permit emigration, the Liaison Bureau worked to foster Jewish identity and culture and contact with Israel and the Jewish world until such time as immigration would be possible.[15] Few expected to see results in their lifetime.[16] Nevertheless, many in Israel were encouraged when the Soviets began to let out some elderly Jews for the purpose of family reunion in 1954. Although few in number, they provided an incentive to work for more (Dominitz 1996:115).

Concerned about its own relations with the Soviet Union, Israel often neglected the Soviet Jewry issue.[17] For example, it chose not to publicize information about the arrests and executions of Soviet Jews from 1948 to 1952 (Pinkus 1992:384–385). Israel's use of radio broadcasts also reflected this caution. Israel began beaming Russian language broadcasts to the Soviet Union in 1957 and until 1961 limited them to Friday evening and Saturday. In the 1960s they increased them to four times a week. Not until 1969 did Israel use Kol Israel intensively for the Soviet Jewry movement (Pinkus 1992:392–393).[18]

Nehemia Levanon headed the first Liaison mission of two or three Russian speaking couples to work in the Israeli Embassy in Moscow in 1953.[19] In 1955 the Soviets expelled him and two others on charges of spying. Until the 1967 break in Israeli-Soviet diplomatic relations, the Liaison Bureau sent its embassy personnel over the length and breadth of the Soviet Union.[20] In 1957 it organized a large Israeli delegation to participate in the world youth festival in Moscow (Levanon 1999:75; Pinkus 1992:376). Later, it sent Israeli entertainers on concert tours in the Soviet Union until 1967.[21]

The Liaison Bureau also organized and coordinated the sending of packages of clothing to Jews in the Soviet Union. Financed and operated by the American Joint Distribution Committee (JDC), these packages legally reached Soviet Jewish citizens who sold their contents. After 1968, a single package could cover the cost of exit fees and support a family for as long as six months (Decter 1990:22). Most packages got through (Gold 1990:19).[22] This helped many Soviet Jews, especially those who had lost jobs after applying to immigrate to Israel, survive economically. It also made them realize that World Jewry and Israel had not forgotten them. Throughout the period studied here, JDC, funded by the American United Jewish Appeal (UJA), financed many of the Liaison Bureau operations and activities for Soviet Jewry.

The Liaison Bureau also used many clandestine avenues to bring in educational materials—printed matter, books, and pamphlets. Over the years they solicited the cooperation of Western business people, politicians and others who were often not checked by Soviet authorities. The Liaison Bureau also took advantage of the semi-annual Moscow Book Fair to bring in books and materials for Soviet Jews.[23]

In 1958 the Soviet Union allowed the repatriation (emigration) of thousands of persons and their families who arrived in the Soviet Union from Poland between 1939 and 1941. Upon return to Poland most left for Israel (Dominitz 1996:117; Sanders 1988:594).[24] Gitelman (1972:8) argued that Israeli policy played down this Soviet and East European immigration because they feared it would embarrass the Soviets among Arab nations.

During the Khrushchev era from 1956 to 1963 some saw potential change for Soviet Jews especially after his denunciation of Stalin at the 20th Party Congress in 1956. During his tenure, however, many synagogues were closed (as part of an anti-religious campaign) and 55 percent of the 250 persons executed for economic crimes were Jews.[25] At this time Jews were also excluded from security positions, upper level army ranks and the foreign service.

The rapid industrialization and modernization of the Soviet Union in the 1960s created more competition for access and entry into higher education, jobs and careers among Soviet nationalities. A new influx into urban areas of non-Russian ethnic groups led to affirmative action (quotas) for various ethnic nationalities which reduced the access of Jews to higher education and professional jobs. This in turn eroded the security of many Soviet Jews as they and especially their children now had fewer opportunities in academia and professions.[26] Successful professionals now feared for the future of their children. The effect of these policies, in Salitan's view (1992:22–24) was to make assimilated Jews feel as outsiders; it impeded their integration into Soviet society. This may explain why many well established assimilated Jews chose to leave when emigration became a viable option (Salitan 1972:25).

The need for United States grain might have led Khrushchev to ease up on the cultural plight of Soviet Jews (Freedman 1989b:67). The regime allowed the publication of the Yiddish periodical *Sovietische Heimland* and in 1963 it permitted the baking of Matzoth. Overall, Soviet policy toward Israel was guided more by its ties with the Arabs then by issues of Soviet Jewry (Freedman 1989b:68).

The Liaison Bureau organized a second branch, code named Bar, in 1955 to place the issue of Soviet Jewry on the public agenda in several Western countries (Levanon 1999:73).[27] It hoped that an aware Western public would influence their governments to pressure the Soviet Union on the status of its Jewish citizens. The Liaison Bureau *(Bar)* emphasized that Jews, unlike other peoples and groups were systematically being denied their collective and individual rights guaranteed by the Soviet Constitution. It tried to separate the Soviet Jewry issue from the Cold War by not being anti-Soviet. In doing so it hoped to win over leftists and persons friendly to the Soviet cause (Levanon 1999:74). This would alienate some liberals who favored supporting the cause of anti-Communist dissidents in the Soviet Union (Schroeter 1974:392).

Liaison Bureau emissaries attached to Israeli consulates and embassies recruited local Jewish and non-Jewish individuals and groups into the Soviet Jewry advocacy effort. They organized several conferences and enlisted the support of intellectuals and public and political figures (Orbach 1979:97).[28] They sometimes clashed with the more conservative Jewish establishment organizations in European countries.[29] Levanon (1989) says that Jewish leaders "were so hesitant to challenge the Soviets and it was difficult at times to persuade them to act."

In efforts to establish Soviet Jewry advocacy in the West Israel kept a low public profile. While this led to criticism by some Jewish leaders and Israelis that Israel neglected the Soviet Jewry issue, it insured that a successful Soviet Jewry advocacy movement would not jeopardize Israel's own diplomatic standing with the powerful Soviet Union.

LIAISON BUREAU ACTIVITIES IN THE UNITED STATES

Liaison Bureau personnel believed that American Jewry was the key to reaching the powerful American government which "had leverage on the Soviets" (Frankel 1989:19). "Without the involvement of the Jews of America, the Soviet Jewry movement was doomed to failure, regardless of how much Israel did and Israel did a great deal" (Gold 1990:51).[30]

From the early 1960s the Liaison Bureau sent emissaries to several cities in the United States.[31] An agent, serving as a consul in New York City, coordinated contacts with the American Jewish organizations. He/she reported to the Liaison Bureau and the Prime Minister rather than to the Foreign Office.[32] It also sent a senior person to work in an official diplomatic role in the Israeli Embassy in Washington. Nehemiah Levanon served there from July 1965 through 1970.[33] They worked with members of the media, academics, people in the arts, elected officials and the American Jewish Community.

Uri Raanan was an early Liaison Bureau emissary who worked as a correspondent in New York for the Israeli newspaper *Haaretz* (Levanon 1999:75).[34] He worked with American journalists including several at the *New York Times*, and he cultivated Jewish intellectuals and others in New York City and elsewhere. He supplied information, for example to Moshe Decter, the editor of the *New Leader* who published a September 15, 1959, double issue on Soviet Jews.[35]

In 1960 Binyamin Eliav recruited Moshe Decter to work for the Liaison Bureau in the United States alongside Raanan and others that would follow.[36] Moshe Decter established an organization called the Jewish Minorities Research Bureau, which occupied a carriage house on the grounds of the American Jewish Congress in New York City.[37] Importantly, Decter did not acknowledge ties to the Liaison Bureau; most probably the activists in his organization were unaware of his Israeli connection.

One of the first activities of the Research Bureau was to draft a letter to Khrushchev on behalf of Soviet Jews asking for an end to discrimination, the same cultural rights enjoyed by other minorities in the Soviet Union, and family reunification outside the Soviet Union. Eleanor Roosevelt, Supreme Court Justice William O. Douglas, Thurgood Marshall of the National Association of the Advancement of Colored Peoples and the Protestant theologian Reinhold Niebuhr signed the letter.[38] News of the letter made the front page of the *New York Times*. The Research Bureau held a "Conference on the Status of Soviet Jews" at the Carnegie Foundation in New York City on October 21, 1963. Sponsors and/or participants included Saul Bellow, Martin Luther King, Senator Herbert Lehman, Arthur Miller, Bishop James Pike, Walter Reuther, Norman Thomas, and Robert Penn Warren (Goodman 1965:313).[39] Orbach (1979:20) argued that the conference demonstrated general, non-Jewish concern for Soviet Jewry. On many of its publications, the Research Bureau became the "Conference on the Status of Soviet Jews" located in New York City a "private group of eminent intellectuals, academicians, scientists and artists, labor and civil rights leaders . . . founded in 1963 by . . . Norman Thomas, Walter Reuther, William O. Douglas, Martin Luther King, Jr. and Arthur Miller." The Bureau urged these people to speak out and to influence others on the plight of Soviet Jews. Their involvement proved newsworthy.

When Meir Rosenne took charge of Liaison work in New York City he, together with Yehuda Hellman of the Presidents Conference, mobilized American Jewish organizations and public opinion on behalf of Soviet Jewry.[40] They organized a protest march in New York City in 1963. Rosenne also brought to the attention of Morris Abram, the head of the American delegation at the United Nation Commission on Human Rights, the anti-Semitic publication of the Ukrainian Communist Party, the Tophim Kichko book, *Judaism without Embellishment*. The resulting publicity led the Soviets to withdraw the publication.[41] The consuls often turned to American Jewish organizations and wealthy American Jews for financial assistance. They met few refusals. For example, Yoram Dinstein (1989:17) received considerable support (financial and other) from Mr. Simon Segal of the American Jewish Committee staff.[42] Meir Rosenne recalls the active support of the reform movement and the Synagogue Council of America.[43]

In general the Liaison Bureau did not cultivate ties with the grassroots movement for Soviet Jewry. Levanon (1995:198–200) believed that the key to success in America lay with the establishment organizations that had the crucial political and social power. He realized that pressure from the grassroots groups, however, could move establishment to act quicker.[44] While some of the consuls worked with grassroots groups, others had conflicts with them.[45]

Other activities of the Liaison Bureau involved coordinating visits to the United States of recent émigrés from the Soviet Union including Prisoners of Zion and Refuseniks. Speaking tours were set up for Liaison Bureau Operatives including Lova Eliav, former secretary of the Israeli Embassy in Moscow, who met with Arthur Schlessinger in President Kennedy's office.

AMERICAN JEWISH CONFERENCE ON SOVIET JEWRY (AJCSJ)

Meir Rosenne approached several American Jewish leaders, mostly in New York, some of them with strong Zionist affiliations, to establish an umbrella organization for the sole purpose of stimulating interest in the cause of Soviet Jewry. This was not an easy task at the time. According to Goodman, (1965:312) except for the American Jewish Committee, American Jewish Congress, B'nai B'rith and National Community Relations Advisory Council "Jewish opinion had previously remained unconvinced of the special nature of anti-Jewish discrimination in the USSR." Some American Jewish leaders charged that the problem was artificially created by Israel in an effort to increase immigration of Soviet Jews (Pinkus 1992:392). Rosenne (1989:20) found support for a single Soviet Jewry advocacy organization among the American Jewish Committee, Union of American Hebrew Congregations (reform), Synagogue Council of America and Rabbi Abraham Heschel.[46] Some Zionist groups, the World Jewish Conference and the Presidents' Conference initially opposed it on grounds that it might harm the Jews of the Soviet Union (Chernin 1999:33).[47] Other national Jewish organizations objected to a new national organization. For example, Abraham Foxman of ADL explained that it would be difficult for some defense organizations to give up their autonomy in the area of Soviet Jewry. Yoram Dinstein worked out a modus vivendi with Yehuda Hellman whereby the new organization would involve the Presidents' Conference in approaching the White House and/or Secretary of State.[48]

Following a meeting of national Jewish leaders in New York City in December 1963 a founding conference was held in Washington, D.C., on April 5 and 6, 1964 with over 600 Jewish leaders representing 25 organizations in attendance (Goodman 1965:315).[49] Morris Abram chaired and Supreme Court Justice Arthur Goldberg and Senators Jacob Javits and Abraham Ribicoff addressed the group. The gathering voted to become the American Jewish Conference on Soviet Jewry. Leading roles were played by the American Jewish Committee, B'nai B'rith, Conference of Presidents and ADL.[50] Participants agreed to continue as an ad hoc organization.[51] "Its formation marked a turning point. The leaders of mass organizations of Jews in America were now on record as considering the situation of Soviet Jews sufficiently serious, and their own responsibility to intervene on behalf of those Jews sufficiently clear, to commit the prestige of their organizations to a new body designed to do that and nothing else" (Appelbaum 1986:617).

Thereafter, the American Jewish Conference on Soviet Jewry tried to lead and coordinate the advocacy movement on behalf of Soviet Jews in the United States. It became representative of the established and organized American Jewish Community. Its leaders consulted with Nehemiah Levanon and followed the Liaison Bureau policy of not being anti-Soviet. It sought to avoid Cold War rhetoric and called for mobilization of world public opinion into a moral force to save Soviet Jews from spiritual annihilation. Absent was the Union of Councils. They favored expanding the struggle for Soviet Jewry into general human rights issues which the Liaison Bureau opposed. The Councils also took an anti-Soviet line (Gur-Gurevitz 1996:7).[52] The American Jewish Conference sought to expose "to the world the deprivations, denials and oppressions to which the Jews of Russia are subjected" and "to place this issue on the agenda of the world's major problems, and to keep it there, until it's properly solved."[53] It sought to raise the consciousness of American Jews and non-Jews, influence the American government to pressure the Soviet Union, bring the issue before the United Nations and reach out to Soviet Jews. It focused on public activity and protest (Chernin 1999:34). Its 18 point manifesto issued at the Philadelphia leadership conference in 1966 called for an end to anti-Semitism, support for Jewish cultural activities and for family reunification for those separated by war.[54]

Its structure was that of an umbrella organization governed by a board made up of representatives of constituent organizations. This limited the independence of the new organization which may have been the intent of many of the founding organizations (Orbach 1979:26 and Chernin 1999:38). The 25 constituent groups included the several defense and community relations groups and the various religious and temple movements. It had no permanent lay chair or staff and no budget. Constituent agencies provided $50 each for mailing and other office expenses. The chair would serve for six months or one year and then be replaced by someone from another national Jewish organization (Interviews with Jerry Goodman, January 10, 2001, and Ted Comet, March 4, 1999).[55] Constituent organizations lent a staff person to serve as coordinator for six months to one year. Jerry Goodman of the American Jewish Committee served as first coordinator. Ted Comet of American Zionist Youth Commission followed him.[56] By the late 1960s the Conference became closely associated with the National Jewish Community Relations Advisory Council (NJCRAC) which coordinated and housed its operations.[57]

The American Jewish Conference on Soviet Jewry tried to educate America Jews about the plight of Soviet Jewry. It set up a speakers' bureau, printed information booklets, distributed a manual, organized summer camp programs and reproduced articles and tapes.[58] By 1966, it coordinated demonstrations across the country via NJCRAC's local Community Relations Councils (Orbach 1979:33,39–40 and Chernin 1999:41).[59]

It often used Jewish holidays as a basis of protest, despite some reservations from Orthodox Jews. For example, it organized Soviet Jewry activities during high holidays in September 1966. The following December more than 50,000 persons attended Freedom Lights Chanukah programs for Soviet Jewry in 37 cities (Goodman 1969:113,114). Tens of thousands of persons participated in demonstrations at Simchat Torah in at least 35 cities in 1968. Over 100 demonstrations were held on Simchat Torah in 1970 (Orbach 1979:47). During Pesach it sponsored *Geula* (redemption) marches to the United Nations with 15,000 persons marching in 1966 and it distributed hundreds of thousands of its "Matzoth of Hope" each year.[60] American Jewish pressure (Orbach 1979:33) prompted Congressional resolutions and petitions signed by a majority of both Houses and the House Foreign Affairs Committee held hearings on Soviet Jewry on May 11, 1965 (Chernin 1999:45–50). The Conference also encouraged Jewish organizations to visit the Soviet Union.[61]

INCIDENTS OF CHANGE

Several incidents influenced the course of events for Jews in the Soviet Union as well as the Soviet Jewry advocacy movement in the United States. First, on December 3, 1966 in Paris, Soviet Premier Alexei Kosygin stated in answer to a question at a press conference that "If there are some families divided by the war who want to meet their relatives outside the USSR or even to leave the USSR, we shall do all in our power to help them. The way is open to them and will remain open to them and there is no problem" (Salitan 1992:28; Chernin 1999:54). *Izvestia*'s reprinting of this interview spurred hundreds of Soviet Jewish families to apply to emigrate (Freedman 1989b: 68).[62] Soviet authorities interpreted Kosygin's words to mean family reunification in their homeland, that is, Israel. There may have been many other Soviet citizens and minorities in the Soviet Union who wanted to rejoin family members outside the USSR. In emphasizing repatriation to their "homeland" it set the Jews off from almost every other Soviet minority (except for the Germans). Only they had a "homeland" outside of the USSR.[63] Beginning in January 1967, Soviet authorities allowed 100–200 Soviet Jews per month to emigrate. In a short period of time what started as a Jewish movement in the USSR became a Zionist movement saying "let us go back to the homeland";

they demanded a right to immigrate to "their national Jewish homeland" (Chernin p.56).[64] The emigration figures after 1969 convinced many people, including the skeptics, that there were possibilities for Jews to leave the USSR (see appendix).[65]

A Soviet Jew wishing to join relatives in Israel needed a *vyzov* (invitation from family members addressed to a Soviet citizen extending an invitation to join them in Israel) which he/she brought to the Soviet Office (or Department) of Visas and Registrations (*OVIR*). This had to be a notarized invitation from close relatives, translated into Russian with a stamp from the Israeli government confirming that it was willing to receive the person/persons.[66] Initially the Soviet Union did not demand first degree relatives. The Liaison Bureau set up a cottage industry sending tens and later hundreds of thousands of invitations.[67] Boris Shumilin, Deputy Minister of Internal Affairs of the Soviet Union, admitted that the Soviets realized that many of the Israeli invitations were from "non-existent relatives" (*NYT*, February 3, 1976). At OVIR the applicant filed a request for an exit visa. Applicants had to submit character references from their place of work and from fellow workers, poor relatives had to submit affidavits that did not object to him/her leaving, and no exit was allowed to anyone with military or state secrets (Buwalda 1997: 49–55).[68] After filling out documents one returned them to OVIR and then waited months or years for permission to leave. Recipients of exit visas to Israel would lose their Soviet citizenship.[69]

Recipients of exit visas then applied at the Israeli Embassy for a visa for Israel. Many people received *vysov*'s and did not apply for exit visas. The visas were sometimes valid for a week or month. The Embassy of the Netherlands handled Israeli visas following the cessation of Soviet-Israel diplomatic relations after the 1967 War. Believing that the Israelis wanted all Jews to leave, the Dutch issued Israeli visas to those persons indicating that they intended to go to the United States and not Israel. Buwalda writes "the Israeli government, however much it regretted that misuse (of its visas), apparently always decided in the end that it had an obligation to help all Jews in need" (Buwalda 1997:60,61).[70] This would remain Israeli policy until fall 1989.

The second event was the June 1967 Six Day War which sparked a sense of ethnic national identity among many Soviet Jews who had long sought to assimilate into Soviet society.[71] Bayer (1973:210) wrote: "What began with surface signs of Jewish identity developed into a widespread movement, especially among young people, to leave for Israel." Shapiro argues that Jewish dissidents exhibited resistance to "ethnic and cultural assimilation" (1978:99). Their motto became "Let my people go." They ceased being "passive objects of the state policy of Jewish religious and cultural annihilation. . . . Revived the phenomenon of overt opposition to Soviet practices" (Shapiro 1970:466). Buwalda (1997:xv) writes that following the war "the Jews themselves then began to stir and to demand their right to leave."

Importantly, Jewish dissidents emerging in 1967 chose to act separately from other dissidents.[72] They did not want to change Soviet society or to revitalize Jewish culture. Rather they wanted to go to Israel.[73] Later, a much larger Jewish emigration movement would be non-Zionist and have a different motivation.

Gitelman (1999:86) explains the emergence of Jewish consciousness and a turn to the Zionist agenda due to psychological dissonance of being forced to become Russian culturally while being forced to remain Jewish legally and socially; the influence of million or so *Zapadniki* who entered the USSR in 1939–40 from annexed areas of eastern Poland, the Baltic States, Bessarabia, and Bukovina who had been very Jewish; and the anti-Semitism that told them they were second-class citizens. The increased anti-Zionist policies and propaganda of the Soviet regime after June 1967 inadvertently encouraged many to see emigration as the only solution.[74] In Freedman's (1989b:68–71) view the events of 1967 should be understood together with Prague 1968 which made many Soviet Jews realize that the regime would not change and that leaving for Israel was the only real option.

In 1969 a group of 18 Georgian Jewish families wrote an open letter to Israeli Prime Minister Golda Meir and the head of the United Nation's Human Rights Commission requesting to immigrate to Israel. Significantly, Golda Meir read the letter on the radio (Levanon 1999:80; Orbach 1979:45 and Gitelman 1999:86).[75] This marked a change to a more public approach on Soviet Jewry for the Israeli government. Gitelman (1972:9) argues that from this point on the Israeli government more publicly demanded that the Soviets allow the emigration of their Jewish citizens to Israel.[76]

Yoram Dinstein credits Golda Meir for the change and claims that the petition was an excuse for her to take a more activist position. Pinkus disagrees and argues (1992:382) that her "Moscow experience [with Soviet Jews] did not directly influence Israel's policy and did not even lead to a revision of the usual conception of the matter."[77] Others note that around this time Nehemia Levanon replaced Shaul Avigur as head of the Liaison Bureau. Whereas Avigur always favored secrecy and no publicity (Buwalda 1997:35–37) Levanon may have been less cautious.[78] The change may also reflect the Liaison Bureau being influenced by the willingness of Soviet Jews themselves to put their lives and their families at risk (Orbach 1979:112–115).[79] Pinkus (1992) argues that the arrival of Zionist activists in Israel from the Soviet Union during 1969–1971 reinforced demands for public action.

The upsurge in Jewish identity and identification with Israel among Soviet Jews also influenced an American Jewish community to become more aware of their "brethren" in the USSR. Post-1967 actions by Soviet Jews inspired American Jews to help them.[80] At the same time the Six Day War energized American Jews: "It gave Jews in general a little more iron in their backbone, a little more pride, a little more willingness to take a chance" (Decter 1990:20 and David Geller 1990).[81]

Also important for the development of the Soviet Jewry movement in the United States was Elie Wiesel's book *Jews of Silence*.[82] Markowitz (1995:404,405) has written: "In the 1960s Elie Wiesel . . . shook the Western Jewish world by alerting it to the tragic situation of Soviet Jewry. . . . Wiesel's compelling portrait of 'the Jews of Silence' . . . became the definitive statement of Soviet Jews and their plight. . . . It ignited and intensified movements to free Soviet Jewry, to stop the ethnocide—or cultural denudation— of this people." The Liaison Bureau played a role in generating the book.[83] In the Soviet Union, the Liaison Bureau arranged for Wiesel to meet Jewish activists. In his book, Wiesel wrote of the Soviet Jews he met who had rediscovered their identity, traditions, people, and homeland. For him the Jews of silence were the Jews of America (and the West) who did not protest on behalf of their brethren behind the iron curtain. The book stimulated tremendous interest among American Jews to take up the cause of Soviet Jewry.

Also of interest is Wiesel's association with the Holocaust and the observation by some that the American Jewish response to Soviet Jewry was motivated by guilt over the failure to rescue European Jews during the Holocaust. Appelbaum (1986:619) claims that, early on, activists in the Soviet Jewry advocacy movement emphasized the theme of a potential Holocaust in the Soviet Union.[84] As early as 1965 Rabbi Joachim Prinz, chairman of the Conference of Presidents and a refugee Rabbi from Hitler's Germany, told Congress that the Soviets, like the Nazis, want "to bring to close the long Jewish religious and cultural expression" (Lawrence 1970:10). Max Fisher notes that "the emotion energizing the community as a combustible fusion of sorrow and guilt over the failure to rescue millions of Jews from Nazi brutality. 'Never again' was the shibboleth of the Jewish Defense League, and though most of American Jewry scorned the JDL's militant tactics, this intense emotional commitment to deterring any semblance of a Holocaust was common in the community" (Golden 1992:279).[85]

Yoram Dinstein (1989:28) argues that the Liaison Bureau erred in emphasizing "never again" because the situation of Jews in the Soviet Union never resembled that of Jews in Hitler's Germany. Levanon (1989:67–68) denies the charge. He says that he never equated the situation of Jews in the Soviet Union with Jews in Nazi Germany. In 1990 he held that there is no physical threat in the present but the future could be different.[86]

Ted Comet (1989:30) argues that Wiesel represented "transference of the inability to save Jews during the Holocaust—but here we have a Jewish group that we might save."[87] Rabbi James Rudin (1990:15) at the December 1987 Soviet Jewry demonstration in Washington, D.C., recalled that "the [Holocaust] guilt was there, and there was a sense of 'God damn it, we're going to do in '87 for the Soviet Jews what we could have done and should have done or might have done earlier.'

Gitelman (1999:92) argues that several Western governments also called for action on Soviet Jews out of guilt about their inaction during the Holocaust. The existence of Israel as a place of refuge allowed these countries the luxury of demanding free emigration from the Soviet Union without having to give free entry into their own countries.

Finally, the Leningrad plane hijacking by nine Soviet Jews in 1970 and the resulting trials of thirty-four persons and death sentences for two of the hijackers in December 1971 proved to be pivotal events both for Soviet Jews and the Soviet Jewry advocacy movement in the United States.[88] The courage and daring of Soviet Jews energized American Jewry on their behalf (Bayer 1973:211,212).[89] Abe Foxman (1989) explained that prior to the Leningrad incidents and trials American Jews feared that their actions might lead to repercussions; now they could see that Soviet Jews were willing to go to jail and even risk their lives (Freedman 1989b:72,73). The trials and sentencing led to widespread protests in the USA. Notables including I.B. Singer, Bayard Rustin, Arthur Miller and Hans J. Morgenthau held a press conference in protest (Chernin 1999:58).[90] The death sentences led the Presidents' Conference and the American Jewish Conference on Soviet Jewry (partially through Nehemiah Levanon's initiative) to hold a Washington assembly on December 30, 1970 with 500 Jewish leaders from 65 cities (Orbach 1979:53,54 and Bayer 1973:268,269). They met with Congressmen and foreign diplomats. The leaders, Herschel Schachter of the American Jewish Conference on Soviet Jewry, Max Fisher (CJF) and William Wexler (Presidents' Conference) met first with Secretary of State William Rogers and then with President Richard Nixon. They found President Nixon receptive but unwilling to issue a statement to commute the sentences. He explained how he would react if the Soviets would ask him to commute a sentence against Angela Davis. He suggested that a call from him would be a death sentence. Max Fisher later related that President Nixon argued that a super power like the Soviet Union would not allow the United States to dictate on internal matters (Golden 1992:257). President Nixon asked the Jewish leaders to trust him. Six hours later the sentences were commuted (Golden 1992:257).[91] According to Levanon (1995:354), at the time, protests by European leftists resulted in Spanish President Francisco Franco commuting the death sentences of two Basque terrorists which may have influenced Soviet President Podgorny to commute the death sentences of the Jewish hijackers.

The Soviets also decided to allow many of the leaders and troublemakers among Soviet Jewish activists to emigrate while making it more difficult for others to leave. By late 1971 about 3,000 persons per month were leaving (Buwalda 1997:31,32).

THE FIRST BRUSSELS CONFERENCE

The events of Leningrad in turn facilitated the decision by the Liaison Bureau to convene an international conference in Brussels in 1971. For several years Levanon wanted to establish an international body to coordinate and mobilize the world effort on behalf of Soviet Jewry. Opposition came from the World Jewish Congress, B'nai B'rith, and the World Zionist Organization who opposed another international Jewish body in any form (Levanon 1999:80). When the situation of Soviet Jews deteriorated in 1969 and 1970 the idea for an international conference in Brussels gathered support. Israeli Prime Minister Golda Meir supported the idea. Later on the World Zionist Organization, the World Jewish Congress and B'nai B'rith endorsed Levanon's idea for the Brussels international conference. The American Conference for Soviet Jewry and NJCRAC both supported and helped organize the conference.[92]

The two-day Conference opened on February 23, 1971, with over 600 delegates from 38 countries (Orbach 1979:60).[93] The Liaison Bureau played a major if not controlling role in organizing and running the conference.[94] David Ben Gurion served as chairperson and spoke.[95] Arthur Goldberg gave a key note address. In a speech Nobel Laureate Rene Cassin of France called on the Soviets to allow free emigration for Soviet Jews for the purpose of family reunification recognized in the Soviet Constitution. He also wanted minority rights be granted to Soviet Jews (JDC document on Brussels, February 23–25, 1971, and press release, February 19, 1971, JDC files).

The delegates endorsed resolutions for the "right of Jews who so desire to return to their historical homeland in Israel. . . to enable Jews in the USSR to exercise fully their right to live in accord with Jewish cultural and religious heritage and freely to raise their children in their heritage" (Bayer 1973:22).[96] Lewis Weinstein of NJCRAC found himself alone in wanting to amend the resolution to include the right to emigrate anywhere (Chernin 1999:60,61). The Israelis had argued that the Soviets could more easily deal ideologically with emigration to homeland then with a general plea for open gates. By the time of Brussels II in February 1976 the Liaison Bureau had to accept a resolution on the right of all to leave along with the right to repatriation to the homeland (Geller 1976).[97]

The Brussels conference agreed to have leaders of Soviet Jewry advocacy groups in different countries meet twice yearly in the future in the context of a World Presidium for Soviet Jewry (Buwalda 1979:40). Levanon (1999:81) argues that he arranged this and maneuvered leaders of the different countries to agree. This gave the Liaison Bureau formal contact and influence with activists in every country.[98]

THE NATIONAL CONFERENCE FOR SOVIET JEWRY (NCSJ)

By this time, for many American Jews the Soviet Jewry issue had become the number two issue to security of Israel and number one among some liberal and leftist Jews (Schachter 1974). The Liaison Bureau now pressured American Jewish leaders for a new American organization with its own staff and independent budget for Soviet Jewish advocacy in the United States.[99] They also wanted it independent and separate from NJCRAC which in recent years had housed and staffed the American Jewish Conference on Soviet Jewry.[100]

Opposing the idea of a new single purpose organization were the Conference of Presidents and the National Jewish Community Relations Advisory Committee (NJCRAC). Each preferred to take over the activities and function of the National Conference. The Liaison Bureau ruled out the Presidents' Conference as it was too closely associated with the Israeli government.[101] The leaders of NJCRAC were confident that their organization could direct and implement Soviet Jewry advocacy as part of its regular agenda. The Liaison Bureau operatives, however, had several objections. Organizationally, NJCRAC was an umbrella organization of 11 national constituent organizations. In addition, some national Jewish organizations did not belong. Second, NJCRAC had traditionally supported "freedom of choice" (Bayer 1989). Third, the Israelis distrusted its strong executive director, Isaiah Minkoff, a former Bundist "who loved Israel." Yehoshua Pratt of the Liaison Bureau believed that Minkoff favored reestablishment of Yiddish culture in the USSR and did not care whether Soviet Jews chose to go to Israel or the USA. Finally, whereas Minkoff was cautious the Israelis wanted more activism (Pratt 1989).

In early 1971 Mr. Stanley H. Lowell chaired a committee appointed by the Presidents' Conference and the American Jewish Conference on Soviet Jewry to consider restructuring the American Jewish Conference. It concluded that the Soviet Jewry issue had overwhelmed NJCRAC and interfered with its other tasks.[102] It recommended transferring coordination of national activities to a new independent national umbrella organization with its own full time staff and independent budget.[103] CJF and its federations would become the major source of funding. The new organization would conduct basic planning and strategy for the Soviet Jewry advocacy movement in the United States and coordinate the activities of constituent agencies. It would supplement and not supplant existing programs and resources. There would be a plenum consisting of one representative and one alternate from constituent organizations. There would also be 10 delegates and 10 alternates from the federations and welfare funds.[104] The agreement stipulated that the contacts (written and otherwise) with federal officials as the sponsoring of national and international conferences would be done jointly with the Conference of Presidents.[105]

In June 1971 the NCSJ became an umbrella organization representing and coordinating Soviet Jewry advocacy for most national (and some local) Jewish organizations. Among the 38 constituent members were the American Jewish Committee and the American Jewish Congress, B'nai B'rith, Anti-Defamation League, Student Struggle for Soviet Jewry, Hadassah and the Reform, and Conservative and Orthodox synagogue movements. In addition, there were over 200 local federations, community relations councils and local Soviet Jewry Committees affiliated with it ("What is NCSJ" n.d. [CJF files].[106] Nehemiah Levanon emphasized that the influence and power of NCSJ rested with its constituent organizations and their local chapters that had contact with Congressmen and Senators. He learned (1990:36) that if you want to influence Congress they "must feel that back in their constituencies this is an issue that the Jews are really interested in."

Jerry Goodman became the Executive Director and served until June 1988. Richard Maass of the American Jewish Committee served as the first chairperson for a three year term.[107] CJF and other constituent agencies provided much of the funding in the early years.[108] Goodman claims funding was a serious problem at the start.[109] Its headquarters were in New York City. Initially it used offices of its constituent members for activities in Washington, D.C.

In Shinbaum's (1999:174) words: "our single purpose was to support Soviet Jews in their effort to be reunited with their relatives and the Jewish people in Israel, their historic homeland." Its overall purposes were to educate the public that there is a problem, to mobilize the American Jewish Community, and to keep Congress and the Administration aware of the issue.[110] Yet, an early undated document in the CJF files "What is NCSJ?" indicates that its founding mission was "to help all Soviet Jews who wish to emigrate. . . to leave the Soviet Union for Israel and elsewhere. . . and to help Jews live in the Soviet Union as Jews with all the rights and privileges and freedoms accorded all other groups in the USSR." This suggests less Israeli domination and influence and more input from the CJF and other American groups.

Importantly, NJCRAC received a pivotal role in the new organization. While NCSJ would set national policy, NJCRAC would handle and coordinate implementation on the local level via its community relations councils.[111] This would cause conflict over the years. Goodman and his staff claimed they were denied contact and activity at the local level. They could call for a demonstration but depended on NJCRAC and other grassroots organizations to mobilize the troops (Orbach 1979:7). This conflict would continue for sixteen years until resolved by CJF (See Chapter 7).

Potential conflicts also existed with the Conference of Presidents and other existing national defense agencies (Orbach 1979). For example, several national organizations initially opposed the NCSJ desire to open a Washington Bureau. They assumed that their Washington offices would service the NCSJ. When this proved impractical, the NCSJ again suggested opening a Washington office. Yehuda Hellman of the Conference of Presidents objected while the American Jewish Committee, American Jewish Congress and Anti-Defamation League agreed. Hellman withdrew his objections when NCSJ agreed that the Conference of Presidents would be involved when approaching the President or Secretary of State (Shinbaum 1999:175).[112]

Importantly, representatives of the Liaison Bureau of New York (and Washington) participated in the meetings and executive committee sessions of the NCSJ.[113] They were consulted at every stage. According to Yehoshua Pratt (1989:12), while the Liaison Bureau had to consult with the NJCRAC on decisions in the American Jewish Conference on Soviet Jewry, it could unilaterally decide matters in the NCSJ. The Liaison Bureau provided information and coordinated their activities with efforts on behalf of Soviet Jewry in Israel and around the world. It also provided funding for the "information work" done by the NCSJ after Moshe Decter left in 1978.[114] Nehemiah Levanon cultivated a personal relationship with each of the chairpersons of the NCSJ.

Importantly, at the time, most activists believed that the Israelis had the best information about the situation of Soviet Jewry. Unlike most American Jews, Nehemiah Levanon and many of his associates had lived and worked in the USSR; they knew the situation first hand. They told American Jews what had to be done. Arthur Hertzberg (2002:361) claims that when he was President of the American Jewish Congress in 1963 that Levanon explained to him what position on Soviet Jewry his organization had to take. After the 1967 War it became even easier for Israelis to tell American Jews what to do.[115] This position would change over the years due to the 1967 break in Israeli-Soviet diplomatic relations in 1967 which closed the USSR to most Israelis, the near defeat of Israel in the 1973 Yom Kippur War, the growing direct ties between American and Soviet Jews and the experience and involvement of American Jews in the movement. Yoram Dinstein notes that by the 1970s and 1980s many activists in the American Soviet Jewry movement had been to the USSR and met with Russian Jews and Refuseniks and retained close contacts with them. Some American Jews believed that they knew the situation better than some of the Liaison people who either had been to the USSR years ago or not at all. This included Yehuda Lapidot who replaced Nehemiah Levanon as head of the Liaison Bureau in 1980. He was a professor of biochemistry and had little knowledge of life in the Soviet Union. In time the Liaison Bureau learned that it could not dictate to American Jewry.

On September 15, 1971, the UJA-Federation of New York City established the Greater New York Conference on Soviet Jewry (GNYCSJ) with Malcolm Hoenlein as executive director. Here too, the Liaison Bureau played a major role in the initiative.[116] It shared an office suite with the NCSJ. It became more activist and grassroot oriented than the NCSJ. Malcolm Hoenlein and his successors (Margy-Ruth Davis and Zeesy Schnur) were dynamic, creative and successful. They worked very closely with the Liaison Bureau.[117] Nehemiah Levanon (1989) says "I was a kind of tutor to them. I helped them to learn . . . and offered my advice on targets and methods in the ongoing political struggle for the redemption of Soviet Jewry." They built up the organization to involve 85 constituent organizations, with extensive grassroots support throughout the five city boroughs and Bergen County, New Jersey. It established a Black Coalition for Soviet Jewry, a Medical Coalition for Soviet Jewry and other groups. One of its first activities involved joining the Student Struggle for Soviet Jewry Freedom Lights program at Madison Square Garden in December 1971.[118] In 1972 it began the first solidarity march (*Solidarity Sunday)* to Dag Hammarskjold Plaza at the UN. The first marches drew fewer people than similar demonstrations in Philadelphia. Later they would attract 100,000 and more and become national events.[119] Nehemiah Levanon (1999:79,80) argued that the solidarity marches gave the organization clout in New York City, Washington D.C., and with the Soviets. By the late 1980s the operating budget reached almost $1m. Most of its funding came from the UJA-Federation of New York (Hoenlein 1999:66).[120]

Being in New York City, the center of organized Jewry in the United States, probably contributed to the aspirations of professional and lay leaders to move beyond being just a local organization. The success of its solidarity day parade also enhanced its national status and recognition. In the late 1980s it was renamed Coalition for Soviet Jewry.[121] It often clashed with the NCSJ.

UNION OF COUNCILS

Also on the scene in the United States were grassroots advocacy organizations on behalf of Soviet Jewry. Sarna and Golden (2000:88ff) charge that the *American Jewish Year Book* neglected the "army of housewives" who maintained direct contact with Refuseniks." Some preceded the American Jewish Conference on Soviet Jewry and were independent of Israeli initiative (Friedman 1999:4). For example, in October 1963, Dr. Herbert S. Caron, Dr. Louis Rosenblum and others founded the Cleveland Committee on Soviet Anti-Semitism (CCSA). The Cleveland group involved several reform Rabbis, MDs, labor and revisionist Zionists. Dr. Louis Rosenblum sought to pressure established Jewish organizations in order to bring public pressure on the United States government to act on behalf of Soviet Jewry (Orbach 1979:20).[122] Similar groups in several other cities organized on behalf of Soviet Jewry.

These groups called for active public protests and maximum direct contact with Soviet Jewry. They publicly criticized Jewish leaders and American elected officials and their appointees for their inaction and indifference.

Bayer (1973:213) credits them with developing person to person ties with Soviet Jews by mail and telephone. Later NSCJ would adopt these strategies. The councils prided themselves in serving the true interests of the Refuseniks rather than the Jewish establishment and the government of Israel. Mark Talisman (Interview, October 2, 2002) argues that they had good intelligence on Soviet Jews which became very important when the Israelis "were out." David Harris (1989:55) believes that they humanized the movement. He also thought they were more aggressive than establishment organizations. While they had contacts on the Hill, he argues, the NCSJ was the more powerful force (Interview, August 8, 2002) Later they would favor freedom of choice (Goodman 1969:115 and Baum 1989). Others claimed they were simplistic (Decter 1990). Minimally, they exerted pressure on the establishment organizations to act on behalf of Soviet Jews (Orbach 1979:1; Windmueller 1999:171).

Around 1978 the Cleveland group set up the umbrella organization, the Union of Councils for Soviet Jewry (UCSJ), which quickly grew from 6 to 22 organizations (Orbach 1979:47 and Friedman 1999:4).[123] They would claim to be non-establishment. Phil Baum saw them as not being responsible to the "fat cats" (23). Yoram Dinstein (1989:10), the Liaison Bureau person at the consulate in New York City, clashed openly with them. He told his supervisors "We have . . . to declare war on them." His successor, Yehoshua Pratt stopped fighting them. In sharp contrast Nehemia Levanon supported them. According to Levanon (1999:77–80) the grass roots wanted him to work with them and not with the establishment. In his view the establishment had the troops and masses and was recognized by the White House and Congress: ". . . in the long run what counts is the establishment." He argues (1999) that the establishment and not splinter groups organized Solidarity Days in New York City and they were decisive in D.C. He would use the grass roots to whip the establishment to action. At times he believed that grassroot support for some "shady characters" in the USSR to be irresponsible and unruly and that they sometimes printed untruths.[124]

In the 1970s NCSJ presidents Eugene Gold and Stanley Lowell tried unsuccessfully to bring the Councils into the NCSJ.[125] By the 1980s, however, they too were part of the Conference of President and they would be recognized in the CJF's reorganization of the NCSJ in the late 1980s. They actively participated in the establishment sponsored December 1987 demonstration in Washington, D.C.

Two other groups which played important roles in Soviet Jewry advocacy in the United States should be mentioned. One is the Student Struggle for Soviet Jewry established in 1964 by Jacob Birenbaum and Glen Richter (Halevi 2004).[126] Located in New York City and operating out of Birnbaum's apartment, they took a very strong stand reflecting the activism of the civil rights and anti-war activists of the 1960s.[127] SSSJ was often in the forefront of

demonstrations and activities against Soviet consuls and artistic performances. In the early 1970s they would often act when the adult Jewish establishment would not. Bayer (1973:211) believes that they were the mainstay
in the eastern United States "in sustaining interest in Soviet Jewry" until
around 1970. The SSSJ had good relations with the Israeli government.
Richter admits to quiet help from the Israeli Consulate, especially from Meir
Rosenne. But he claims that the SSSJ fought the Jewish establishment which
followed the lead of the Israeli government. Since the Israelis did not act, he
asserted, then the Jewish establishment did not feel guilty about not acting.
The SSSJ kept their activist and youthful image despite their joining (*"reluctantly"*) the NCSJ in 1972 and the age of its leaders and many of the members (Foxman 1989).[128]

While often identified with the Union of Councils the SSSJ drew much of
its following from the Orthodox community while the Councils were mostly
non-Orthodox Jews. The Councils were also less committed to civil disobe-
dience (Goodman 1969:114 and Ruby 1999:208). Moreover, while SSSJ favored emigration for Soviet Jews to Israel the Union of Councils supported
freedom of choice (Appelbaum 1986:618).

The second group or person is the late Rabbi Meir Kahane and his Jewish
Defense League. He criticized the lethargy of the Jewish establishment in
dealing with Soviet Jewry (Friedman 1999:4). His organization often took
over demonstrations and marches.[129] His sometime violent and even criminal activities proved more newsworthy than some passive demonstrations of
the NCSJ. Some credit him and his organization for bringing the issue of Soviet Jewry to a much wider audience and keeping it in the public eye (Orbach 1979:vii,viii). JDL protests at the time of the Leningrad trials caused a
crisis in Soviet-American relations which led the American Jewish establishment to condemn them (Orbach 1979:7). Kahane and the JDL's contribution
to the Soviet Jewry movement may never be known. He was a fanatic willing to sacrifice human life for the cause. His actions probably frightened the
Jewish establishment from acting.[130]

ACTIVITIES OF THE SOVIET JEWRY ADVOCACY MOVEMENT

The following presents a small sample of the activities of the NCSJ and other
groups in the United States on behalf of the Jews of the Soviet Union. It does
not document the extent and depth of their activities.

First, the American Soviet Jewish activists tried to put the issue of Soviet
Jewry on the public agenda. Efforts focused on educating both the Jewish
community and the public at large about the denial of human rights for Jews
in the Soviet Union. The National Conference began with its constituent members and their local branches including federations, local community relations

councils, synagogues and temples, B'nai B'rith lodges, and Hadassah chapters throughout the fifty states (Shinbaum 1999:178).[131] Internal organizational materials informed members about the conditions of Soviet Jews with individual stories, pictures, names, and addresses. Synagogue movements for example arranged for twinning of Bar and Bat Mitzvah children with children in the Soviet Union. Several organizations manufactured or purchased bracelets with names of Refuseniks which members proudly wore (Bayer 1989).[132]

To raise public consciousness the Union of Councils and NCSJ sponsored speaking tours by Soviet Jewish émigrés across the country. This increased contact between American and Soviet Jews (Orbach 1979:67). The Union of Councils sent over 150,000 greeting cards, made movies and issued pamphlets (Naftalin 1999:230). Modern technology facilitated phoning by American Jews to Soviet Jews and Refuseniks (Gitelman 1999:91).

Orbach (1979:107) notes that after failing in 1964 Jewish activists had the Soviet Jewry issue on both party platforms for the 1968 Presidential elections.[133] Both major candidates spoke out on the subject. Before an American-Soviet summit in 1972 1.4 million persons signed a petition asking President Nixon to raise the issue of Soviet Jewry with his Soviet counterpart.[134] The Liaison Bureau worked to get local Jewish communities and others to have their Congressmen, mayors, city council people, and governors to protest that status of Soviet Jews. The idea was to get resolutions passed and placed in the local press on the assumption that the Soviets had excellent news clipping services that tracked the American media.[135]

The NCSJ and constituent agencies also began to target the elected officials in the nation's capital. Phil Baum (1989) suggested that the task had not been so difficult since many in Congress were already anti-Soviet; this was the height of the Cold War. They could pontificate moralistically to satisfy their Jewish constituents and wave the anti-Communist flag (Also see Orbach 1979:2,3). In Israel Miller's (1990:24) view Congress was very pragmatic as the Soviet Jewry Movement was able to "paint the Soviet Union into a corner of human rights issues" and this was always an American goal and concern. Often on resolutions condemning the USSR other Congressmen wanted to join (Orbach 1979:157,158) "realizing the issue's political promise, rushed to its support with public statements" in the Congressional record. Petitions and calls to Soviet Jewish activists were first class political capital.[136]

NCSJ had Congressmen and Senators adopt Soviet Jewish activists; they established an organization called Congressional Wives for Soviet Jewry and they sponsored seminars on Soviet Jewry for staff and Congressmen.[137] Congressman Ben Gilman organized interested colleagues and staff to meet regularly. The NCSJ ran an orientation for Freshmen Congressmen on the Soviet Jewry issue. It as well as many constituent agencies had full time lobbyists in Washington, D.C.[138] In addition they could urge the members of their constituent bodies to write and visit their Congressmen on the subject of Soviet Jewry.

During John Kennedy's brief term as President, Llewelyn Thompson arranged for Supreme Court Justice Arthur Goldberg and Senators Jacob Javits and Abraham Ribicoff to meet with Soviet Ambassador Anatoly Dobrynin (Rosenne 1989:10; Orbach 1979:13,14; Baum 1989; Pratt 1989; and Chemin 1999:16,17,30–31).[139] During the Johnson Administration (Orbach 1979:156) executive officials inundated Jewish groups with sonorous statements that cost little and satisfied Jewish groups (Orbach 1979:153–156).[140] President Lyndon Johnson cabled support for Soviet Jews to rallies on several occasions.

Activities often snowballed as is evident in the following example of a Jewish student leader at Brandeis in the 1970s which may represent thousands of similar situations (Geller 1989). Following the arrest of Anatole (Natan) Sharansky in March 1977 campus activists at Brandeis sent a bus to Washington, D.C. to protest. They got help from NCSJ, the Action for Soviet Jews (Councils), Helsinki Committee and the SSSJ. In 1978 they sent three buses. In later years this became an annual event bringing thousands of students from around the country to Washington, D.C. and the group became "Student Coalition for Soviet Jewry." During the first Washington visit students met with Senator Edward Kennedy and Congressmen Sylvio Conte and Robert Drinan.[141]

The example of the CJF is also noteworthy. In the 1970s it was a weakly organized non-centralized umbrella organization of Jewish federations throughout the United States.[142] Each year it holds a General Assembly in an American city with thousands of lay and professional participants from hundreds of American Jewish communities. Year after year Soviet Jewry appeared on the agenda with speakers from Israel and the Liaison Bureau, NCSJ and former Refuseniks and "Prisoners of Zion." Key members of Congress and the White House would be invited. Four times a year the CJF holds quarterly meetings, which involve lay leaders and professional staff of executive committees and major federations from throughout the United States. In the early 1970s they began to hold one quarterly in D.C. in order to allow delegates to lobby their Congressmen on Soviet Jewry (and other) issues.

The NCSJ and its constituent agencies and nonaffiliated grassroots organizations demonstrated at Soviet embassies and consulates and at various cultural exchanges (Rosenne 1989:13).[143] They picketed Soviet artists and dance groups. More militant groups broke up performances in major concert halls in Washington, D.C., and in New York City.

Prior to the 1970s two "exodus" marches were held in New York City. A small demonstration probably in 1962 involved a short march and delivery of a written protest at the Soviet UN Mission.[144] A second march in 1969 with over 15,000 persons and led by Theodore Bickel and Rabbi Abraham Heschel focused on national rights for Soviet Jews and not emigration. The Conference and other Jewish groups organized the first protest rally for Soviet Jewry in Washington, D.C., in September 1965 with about 10,000 protesters participating in a vigil in Lafayette Park.[145]

Beginning in 1972 the New York Conference on Soviet Jewry instituted an annual national Solidarity Day march with Soviet Jewry. Within a few years over 100,000 persons participated and the event attracted national media attention. In time the number of non-Jewish speakers increased and in David Geller's view the agenda became more "American" and less "Jewish."

The American Soviet Jewry Advocacy Movement also used the special ties of their leaders and members to broaden and mainstream their protests. The following examples of Eugene Gold, the NSCJ President from 1977 to 1979, Ms Jacqueline Levine, a leader in the Woman's Division of the American Jewish Congress and Richard Maass, the first President of NCSJ are typical of hundreds if not thousands of leaders, activists and members of the Soviet Jewry advocacy movement in the United States.

Brooklyn District Attorney Eugene Gold put the issue of Soviet Jewry on the agenda of the meetings of the National District Attorney's Association of which he was an officer.[146] He later arranged for the Association to visit the Soviet Union and to host a Soviet delegation in the United States. The issue of Soviet Jews and their plight was raised and covered by the media in the various cities in both countries during the visits of the respective delegations.[147]

In late 1971 Jacqueline Levine had members of the Leadership Conference of National Jewish Women's Organizations "adopt" Silva Zalmanson, a Jewish woman trapped and harassed in the Soviet Union. Later that year she led the organization to initiate "National Woman's Plea" which involved annual protests in cities across America on December 10 to mark International Human Rights Day. The first year each of the 9 presidents organized protests in 3 different cities (Bayer 1973:215). By 1989 demonstrations were held in over 100 cities.

Finally, Richard Maass, president of NCSJ, used his contacts in business to further the cause of Soviet Jewry. He influenced General Motors President Murphy to raise the issue of Soviet Jewry at the East West Trade Council. He had similar success with the Philip Morris company.[148] He was unable to move Pullman and Aramco to intervene on the Soviet Jewry issue.

Finally an important function and service of NCSJ, Union of Councils and others involved initiating, organizing and briefing visits by Americans to the Soviet Union.[149] Visitors included individuals, tourists, members of organizations and elected officials from city council members to mayors, governors, members of Congress and their staff and even officials of the Executive Branch of Government. The NCSJ organized trips to the USSR by American citizens and funded some of them.[150] People would bring in materials including books, pamphlets and religious items and make contact with Russian

Jews. Similarly the Union of Councils had its own visitors operation. Religious and secular Jewish organizations sponsored official trips to the USSR. Visits were a shot in the arm to Soviet Jews (Levanon 1999:80; Bayer 1973:231). They also energized American Jews.[151]

A side effect of the visits sparked controversy and tension between the American Jewish establishment and the Liaison Bureau. The large numbers of visits from Americans may have contributed to stimulating Soviet Jewish interest in going to the USA rather than to Israel. The Americans often invited Soviet Jews that they met to visit (Geller 1990 and Pratt 1989). In practice with American visitors less was said about Israel (Jacobson 1990).[152] Regardless, in the long run, the visits gave American Jews direct contact with Soviet Jews and their situation. This lessened their dependence on Israelis for knowledge about the situation in the Soviet Union.

THE JACKSON-VANIK AMENDMENT

The most significant political issue in the Soviet Jewry advocacy movement in the United States in the early 1970s involved the Jackson-Vanik amendment. It sought to deny trade concessions to non-free market countries unless the President assured Congress and provided assurances and evidence of right of free emigration. This would not have stopped all trade but would interfere with subsidized trade and credit (Fosdick 1990:16). At the same time, it was clear to all, that the amendment had the potential of derailing détente between the two super powers (Orbach 1979:viii). Although presented as denying the Soviet Union Most Favored Nation (MFN) status and credits if it did not allow the free emigration of its Jews, in point of fact, the amendment spoke of free emigration and made no reference to Jews.[153] Later, when some American Jewish leaders got cold feet under pressure from Secretary of State Kissinger and President Nixon, Dorothy Fosdick (1990) recalls that Jackson stated: "Listen boys and girls, its not your problem only . . . you can't tell me what to do."[154]

According to Stern (1979:22) the key players along with Senator Jackson were Senate aides Richard Perle and Morris Amitay. Both maintained ties with American Jewish leaders. While heaping praise on the Union of Councils and criticizing the NCSJ at the beginning of her in-depth study, Stern suggests that the NCSJ and its Washington, D.C., staff person June Silver Rogul played a major role among the American Jewish organizations (Stern 1979:55 and Korey 1974:204).

President Richard Nixon preferred quiet diplomacy on the Jewish emigration issue (Stern 1979:13–15). His National Security Advisor Henry Kissinger favored refraining from interfering in the domestic affairs of the Soviet Union. He did not want to endanger détente. He emphasized that we would not appreciate their telling us about race in the United States. At the time a State Department official argued that the United States while deploring Soviet policy on emigration could not be of direct assistance to those wanting to go to Israel.

Before leaving for the May 1972 Moscow Summit President Richard Nixon told a group of Jewish leaders that he would raise the issue of Soviet Jewry with the Soviet leaders.[155] At the summit President Richard Nixon and Party Secretary Leonid Brezhnev signed a Strategic Arms Limitations Treaty (Salt I) and Principles on International Conduct. In July 1972 Commerce Secretary Peter Peterson worked out a comprehensive trade agreement (to be signed in October 1972) involving Soviet repayment of $722m in Lend Lease in exchange for the President seeking MFN status for the USSR. While no document had made reference to Soviet Jews, 14,000 had left in 1971 and almost 30,000 were expected to leave in 1972 (Korey 1999:98).[156]

On August 3, 1972 the Soviets announced an education tax on those emigrating. On August 14 the decree was reaffirmed by "order" of the USSR Council of Ministers (Korey 1974:202–203). Emigrés would have to reimburse the state for education; this involved about $36,000 for a doctorate degree.[157] Salitan (1992:40,41) argues that Soviets instituted the tax to discourage emigration of the well educated.[158]

Buwalda (1997:91) views the educational tax as a Soviet blunder. He argues that Politburo member Mikhail Suslov initiated and got approval for the tax when Leonid Brezhnev and Andrei Gromyko were on vacation. Mikhail Suslov opposed emigration and wanted to stop the emigration of the well educated. It provided Senator Henry Jackson with an opportunity to propose linking trade benefits for the Soviets with emigration for Soviet Jews (Fosdick 1990). Following the issuance of the Soviet educational tax, Senator Jackson asked to meet with the NCSJ Executive Committee which planned a special meeting about the tax in Washington, D.C., on September 25, 1972.[159] Richard Maass, NCSJ president, agreed and Jackson spoke at a meeting on September 25, 1972 (Goldberg 1996:163). He outlined his legislative proposal tying trade benefits to removal of curbs on emigration. At the meeting his aide Richard Perle reminded the audience of the "consequences of official Jewish silence during the Nazi Holocaust" (Stern 1979:32).

The NCSJ executive backed Jackson unanimously but some expressed dissent. Many American Jewish leaders, according to Goldberg (1996:165–167), realized the risk in opposing the President whose support Israel wanted. He argues that the Israeli Foreign Ministry did not want to anger President Nixon. In effect, the NCSJ broke with the official Israeli position. The Union of Councils also supported the amendment. The Greater New York Conference on Soviet Jewry lobbied for the bill. They had the approval of the Liaison Bureau in New York City (Interviews with Zeesy Schnur, August 12, 2002 and Malcolm Hoenlein, February 1, 2001). According to Evans and Novak in the *Washington Post*, Israel's Ambassador Yitzhak Rabin stated that United States interference on the tax would be counterproductive (Stern 1979:22). Yet behind the scenes Nehemia Levanon and other key Liaison operatives worked to get Congressmen and American Jewish organizations to support Jackson-Vanik (Buwalda 1997:93,94).[160] Levanon (1995:397) believed that passage of the amendment would be a breakthrough in American pressure on the Soviet Union on behalf of Soviet Jewry. A defeat of the amendment, he believed, would be a major defeat for the Soviet Jewry advocacy movement. Writing in 1999 he believed that his support helped the movement resist the pressures of the Nixon Administration.[161]

President Nixon had the support of Jacob Stein, President of the President's Conference, and Mr. Max Fisher, President of the CJF and a self appointed spokesperson for American Jewry (Goldberg 1996:170). Friedman (1999:4,5) argues that Nixon and Kissinger argued with Fisher that Jackson-Vanik legislation to "trade off commercial advantages for liberalized Soviet emigration policies would not do the job; that tying Soviet emigration policies to arms control and other issues would be more effective." Some Jewish liberals thought that the amendment would harm détente (Korey 1974:216). Henry Kissinger told both Stein and Fisher that he could accomplish more with the Soviets without the amendment. He indicated to them that the Soviets would drop the education tax and might increase exit visas to 35,000 a year (Goldberg 1996:170).[162]

Charles Vanik introduced the amendment (HR 16705) in the House on September 22, 1972. It would deny Export-Import Bank credits and development loans to any country charging more than $50 exit fee (Stern 1979:30).[163] In early October 1972 Senators Jackson and Ribicoff introduced an amendment to the East West Trade Bill with 32 sponsors.[164] The amendment would refuse non-market economy countries MFN and credits, credit guarantees and investment guarantees if that country denied its citizens the right to emigrate or imposed more than a nominal tax on emigration.

It is important to note that the late submission in 1972, along with the absence of a companion bill in the House, indicated to all that there was little chance of passage during the current session. Therefore, the co-sponsors risked very little. Moreover, in exchange for President Nixon releasing Senate Republicans to co-sponsor the bill, Senator Jackson kept the issue of the amendment out of the November 1972 Presidential elections (Stern 1979:4).

On October 18, 1972, the United States and the Soviet Union signed a trade agreement. The Soviets would repay $722m in Lend Lease and President Nixon would seek MFN from Congress and Export-Import Bank credits for the Soviet Union. On the day of the signing, the Soviet Union let 18 families leave for Israel without paying the educational tax (Stern 1979:43–44).[165]

In February 1973, 238 members of the House co-sponsored a Vanik version of the bill.[166] On March 15, 1973 Jackson reintroduced his bill which now required periodic presidential reports to Congress concerning free emigration. It had 75 co-sponsors. Goldman (1999:147) and Stern (1979) note that many conservatives, including George Meaney and the AFL-CIO supported Jackson in hopes of stopping the development of trade and cooperation between the United States and the Soviet Union.

President Nixon tried to (Goldberg 1996:169) separate Jackson from Jewish supporters by gaining Soviet concessions on emigration. He called in the Soviet Ambassador and warned that the tax would effect American-Soviet relations and could influence Congressional action and bills.[167] He and Kissinger also met with Soviet Foreign Minister Gromyko at Camp David on October 23, 1972. Gromyko told Nixon that the education tax would fade away (Buwalda 1997:93–95). Later that day Secretary of State William Rogers told Jewish leaders that the Soviets were showing flexibility on the emigration issue (Korey 1999:101).

Max Fisher and Jacob Stein brought a delegation of 15 Jewish leaders to meet President Nixon at the White House on April 19, 1973. He told them that the tax was lifted and that the Soviets would permit a rate of 32,000–35,000 Jews to emigrate per year (Stern 1979:73; Orbach 1979:139; Korey 1999:102). President Nixon stated: "You gentlemen have more faith in your senators than you do in me. And that is a mistake. You'll save more Jews my way. Protest all you want. The Kremlin won't listen" (Golden 1992:279). Following the meeting Charlotte Jacobson, vice chair of NCSJ, Jacob Stein and Max Fisher issue a statement in the name of all saying that they saw documents from Henry Kissinger about nonenforcement of the tax. They asked the President to help 100,000 Jews leave the USSR. They also praised the Presidents efforts and made no mention of Jackson or his amendment (Stern 1989:73).[168]

On April 30, 1973, an enlarged NCSJ executive met with the Conference of Presidents on the Jackson-Vanik Amendment. Rabbi Balfour Brickner led those opposed to Stein and Fisher. A majority voted to have Max Fisher, Jacob Stein and Richard Maass sign a document in support of the amendment (Stern 1979:80; Korey 1974:218 and 1999:102).

In April 1973 President Nixon introduced a Trade Reform Bill on which Jackson reintroduced his amendment which provided Congress with the right to withhold MFN status.[169] President Nixon then released a statement by Leonid Brezhnev that the tax would not be reintroduced.[170] Negotiations continued between the Soviets and the Senate via Henry Kissinger to guarantee that a number of Soviet Jews would be allowed to leave each year.

Leonid Brezhnev came to Washington in June 1973 (Korey 1999:104).[171] Whereas he had charmed a group of Congressmen in Moscow on April 23, 1973 on the subjects of trade and emigration, he failed to reassure Senators in Washington, D.C., on the emigration issue (Korey 1974:221–222: Stern 1979:81–84).[172]

The Yom Kippur War in October 1973 and Israel's increased dependence on the United States government for its survival complicated the politics of the Jackson-Vanik Amendment (Orbach 1979:145). The administration used support for Israel as a means to urge opposition to Jackson-Vanik (Korey 1999:107). Kissinger and the White House again asked the Meir government to pressure American Jews but she remained cautious. One White House source explained to Jewish leaders that Israeli interests required cancellation of Jackson-Vanik (Korey 1999:107).[173] The American Jewish establishment retained its support for the Jackson-Vanik amendment.

The House passed the Jackson-Vanik amendment on December 10, 1973 by a vote of 319 to 80 and the Senate thereafter by an overwhelming vote defeated an administration sponsored effort to delete it from the trade bill. Henry Kissinger then sought to deal with Jackson and the other sponsors in hopes of achieving a compromise (Korey 1999:107,108).[174] Kissinger also sought compromise with the Soviets.[175]

Goldberg (1996:172,123) claims that in October 1974 with Gerald Ford in the White House (since August 9, 1974), Henry Kissinger brokered a deal with the Soviets and Senators Jacob Javits, Abraham Ribicoff and Henry Jackson which allowed an annual rate of Jewish emigration at about 60,000.[176] Kissinger was concerned about helping the Soviet Union to save face; it refused to publicly acknowledge a figure on emigration. On August 15, 1974, Kissinger and the Senators agreed to a three letter arrangement between the President and Senator Jackson without direct involvement of the Soviets. In the first President Ford would state that he had assurances from Soviet authorities to permit emigration and end harassment.[177] In the second, Senator Jackson would respond and cite the figure of 60,000 as a benchmark and in the third President Ford or Henry Kissinger would concur on the understanding stated in Jackson's letters (Stern 1979:150–152). In response Jackson would then introduce an amendment to allow the President to waive restriction of MFN and credits for 18 months followed by an additional year to be granted by vote in both houses. On September 30, Kissinger's notification that the administration would not agree to the third letter upset Senator Jackson. Jewish groups intervened and pressured Jackson to meet with Kissinger. At a meeting on October 8, 1974 Kissinger told Jackson that Gromyko had backed away from his previous commitment to 45,000 exits per year (Stern 1979:157). On October 18, 1974 Senator Jackson and President Ford signed the letters and Jackson made the contents public (Korey 1975:162). At a press conference at the White House, Senator Jackson announced that the Soviets had retreated.[178]

It is interesting to note that Senator Abraham Ribicoff did not come with Jackson to the White House on October 18, 1974. It suggests certain sensitivity by a Jewish elected official in the early 1970s. Stern (Stern 1979:161) argues that he "felt uncomfortable as a Jew taking such a conspicuous position on a "Jewish issue." He had been heard to say, "I don't want to be the Jew boy who got the Jew deal."

A week later in Moscow Henry Kissinger found a livid Leonid Brezhnev (Buwalda 1997:105). A few days later, on October 26, 1974, and unknown to others at the time, Andrei Gromyko handed Henry Kissinger a letter which said that the letters of October 18th distorted the Soviet position (Korey 1975:162). Kissinger kept the letter a secret when testifying in December 3, 1974 Senate hearings on the Trade Reform Act. Kissinger testified that Brezhnev, Gromyko and Dobrynin had given assurances but that he could not assert the existence of a formal agreement on emigration because the Soviets considered it an internal matter (Orbach 1979:151; Korey 1999:109,110). The Senate then voted 88 to 0 approving the waiver on provisions.[179]

Both houses passed the amendment and approved the Conference Committee version on December 18, 1974. That day the Kremlin released Gromyko's letter of October 26, 1974 (Orbach 1979: 151,152). On December 20, 1974 both the House and the Senate passed the trade reform act. It became law on January 3, 1975 (Korey 1999:111).

Contributing to the anger of Soviet leaders may have been the passage of a routine U.S. Export Import Bank funding bill with an amendment by Senator Stevenson of Illinois. It limited Soviet import credits to $300m over a five year period, prohibited credits for production of gas and oil and limited gas and oil exploration credit to $40m (Korey 1975:165). [180] This was one fourth of what they were already getting and Soviet leaders had expected that the trade agreement would give them billions in credit.[181] Korey (Korey 1999:111) believes that both Kissinger and American Jewish organizations had not been aware of the implications of this act.

On January 10, 1975 the Soviet Union informed Kissinger that "it had decided to scrap the October 1972 trade agreement with the United States (Korey 1975:170).

There are different opinions about the success of the Jackson-Vanik Amendment. Proponents argue that it focused American and world attention on the Soviet Jewry issue. It placed the issue of Soviet Jewry at the center of U.S.-USSR relations including trade and disarmament (Dominitz 1996:117). Some Jewish activists saw the amendment as the key to letting Soviet Jews emigrate, that it turned the tide in the struggle for freedom. Korey believes that the amendment would "ultimately serve as a powerful lever on Soviet emigration practices" (1999:111). In the late 1970s, for example, the Soviets increased the rate of emigration until the end of the decade possibly to gain favor with the American public and officials (Buwalda 1997:109).[182] In his view (1999:114) the Jackson-Vanik amendment helped liberate 1.250 million Soviet Jews and is a testament to the "determination of America Jews to stand firmly behind the legislation in the vigorous struggle on behalf of their beleaguered Soviet Jewish brethren." Finally, the amendment helped light the spark among Soviet Jews as they came to realize that the American Jewish community had taken up their cause.[183]

Max Fisher believed that it was a mistake. Had it not been passed then tens of thousands of Jews could have left each year. He remained convinced that Henry Kissinger could have brokered a compromise with at least 40,000 émigrés per year. Goldberg (1996:174) concurs with Fisher noting that the Jackson-Vanik and Stevenson bills made future emigration solely the whim of the Soviets. Western bargaining power had been eliminated.

Marshall Goldman also concurs. He (1999:115ff) argues that the amendment proved to be counterproductive. He notes that Bert Gold of the American Jewish Committee and Phil Baum of the American Jewish Congress questioned publicly the need to rethink Jackson-Vanik after the drop in emigration. He suggests that the Soviets might have been willing to negotiate with American Jews in 1978 and 1979. In the final analysis, however, he credits Mikhail Gorbachev and not the Jackson-Vanik Amendment for opening the gates of the Soviet Union for Soviet Jews: "his valiant, if imperfect, effort to liberalize the Soviet Union and reshape it into a hybrid democracy" (Goldman 1999:122).

Goldberg concludes that the struggle on Jackson-Vanik was important for American Jews because they took on both the Nixon Administration and the Kremlin and won. "Jews had proven to the world and to themselves that they could stand up and fight for themselves. The stain of Holocaust abandonment had finally been removed." Hereafter, the American Jewish community would assume a new activism in American politics. For example, they would work to pass legislation against the Arab boycott (1977) and to hunt down Nazi war criminals. Most importantly, they would become politically active in "regulariz(ing) the entry of Soviet Jewish refugees in the United States" (Goldberg 1996:175–179). Friedman (1999:5) concurs. He argues that the struggle over the amendment transformed the Jewish lobby into a Washington powerhouse in the 1970s and later.

Importantly, Stern downplays the importance of the Jewish lobby on the Jackson-Vanik Amendment. She also downplays Israeli influence and importance. She (Stern 1979:210–211) emphasizes that the legislation was "born" in Jackson's office and not in the establishment Soviet Jewry movement; he had to convince them to support and not to desert it. "Throughout the two and one half year battle over the Jackson amendment, Jackson was steering the Jewish groups, not vice versa. Interest groups may have shaped Jackson's policy as he anticipated the constituency for his position. However, lobby groups played a supporting role during the campaign for the amendment" (Stern 1979:210). Nevertheless, the strong and steady support of the NCSJ and Conference of Presidents for Jackson was important. They also played a crucial role in urging him to compromise with Kissinger in 1974. Within these organizations the influence of Levanon and company was most evident. While not controlling them he strongly influenced their positions.

HELSINKI AGREEMENTS

One final event at this time would have important consequences for the issue of emigration of Jews from the Soviet Union. On August 1, 1975, representatives of the United States, Canada, the USSR, and 32 European governments signed the Helsinki Agreements which finalized the European borders established after the Second World War. This was an important achievement for the leaders of the Soviet Union (Spier 1989b:99).[184] The Western nations had incorporated in the agreements a number of humanitarian aims (basket three) including that the signatories "facilitate" and "expedite" approval of exit visas for achieving reunion of families. They also refer to religious and cultural rights and called for an easing of contacts and communication between East and West. This was the first time that "human rights were formally recognized in an international agreement as a fundamental principle regulating relations between states."[185]

Many Soviet Jewish activists were stunned by these humanitarian provisions (Korey 1999b:125,126). According to Buwalda (19997:116) most American Jews only became aware of the document after it was signed. Importantly, the Helsinki Agreements would enable foreign individuals and organizations to become involved in what had previously been considered an internal Soviet matter (Gitelman 1999:91).[186] The Soviet Jewry advocacy movement in the United States and elsewhere and the Liaison Bureau would use the Helsinki Final Act, its Commission on Security and Cooperation in Europe (CSCE) and follow up conferences to promote human rights and emigration of large numbers of Soviet Jews (Friedman 1999:6).[187]

The United States Congress established a Helsinki Commission to monitor implementation, headed by Congressman Dante Fascell of Florida.[188] Members included six representatives each from the House and Senate and one representative each from the Departments of State, Defense, and Commerce. The Commission had close ties to the NCSJ and Union of Councils in Washington, D.C. A former NCSJ D.C. staff member, Meg Donovan joined the staff at the Commission.[189] The United States "pushed" the emigration and human rights issues at the follow up conferences in Belgrade (October 1977–March 1978), Madrid (November 1980 to September 1983), Ottawa (summer of 1985), Bern (spring 1986) and Vienna (November 1986–January 1989). A commission study issued on August 1, 1977 argued that free emigration was implied and thus part of the official United States reports on implementation (Korey 1999b). In contrast the Western Europeans and at times the United States Department of State emphasized détente and arms control in matters relating to the Helsinki Agreements and follow up conferences (Korey 1999b:129–132).

Former Supreme Court Justice Arthur Goldberg headed the American delegation to the Belgrade Conference on Security and Cooperation. While some in the West did not like his abrasive style, he broke the silence barrier on Soviet Jewry (Buwalda 1997:122,123). He raised the issue of human rights by focusing on individual cases of Soviet Jews. NGOs including NCSJ played a role. The Madrid Conference became a magnet for dissidents and human rights groups. Max Kampleman, a skilled diplomat, headed the American delegation. He put on record hundreds of cases of discrimination violations. He was joined by other Western delegates in chastising the Soviets (Buwalda 1997:122). Belgium accused the Soviet Union of anti-Semitism.[190] Avital Sharansky, NCSJ, Union of Councils and the World Conference of Soviet Jewry participated. The Media broadcast reports of Madrid to the USSR.

In 1984 the Commission on Security and Cooperation in Europe held a conference on Confidence and Security Building in Stockholm. In exchange for concessions on disarmament the West demanded speedier family reunification from the Soviets (Buwalda 1997:122). At the Vienna Conference (November 1986–January 1988) (Korey 1999b:132) Secretary of State George Shultz told his chief delegate to link strong Soviet desires for further arms limitation talks and a human rights conference in Moscow to the USSR acceptance of a positive commitment on emigration. The Vienna document removed all obstacles for emigration and included a demand for cultural freedoms and religious rights in the Soviet Union.[191]

CONCLUSION

By the 1970s the Liaison Bureau had achieved considerable success in putting the Soviet Jewry issue on the public agenda in the United States. It had made Soviet Jewry a major and important issue in the American Jewish establishment, second only to support for the State of Israel. As importantly, it had helped establish an organizational structure which both educated and informed American Jewry and the general public about Soviet Jewry and pressured American politicians on all levels to act on behalf of Soviet Jewry. This lobby together with the more autonomous Union of Councils successfully supported the Jackson-Vanik Amendment which pitted the Soviet Jewry issue against the trade and foreign policies of the President of the United States. Clearly, the Liaison Bureau of Israel and American Jews and their supporters had placed the issue of Soviet Jewry and their right to emigrate at the center of Soviet American relations.

In Brussels the Liaison Bureau had established in international body to coordinate and involve national Soviet Jewry advocacy organizations throughout the world. During the early and mid-1970s they directed their efforts to focus on emigration and immigration to Israel, the Jewish homeland.

Within the Soviet Union, the gates had begun to open for the emigration of Soviet Jewry. Rather than hundreds or even thousands there were tens of thousands leaving each year. Nevertheless signs of trouble for an Israeli "game plan" surfaced with the sudden increase, after 1973, of Soviet Jewish émigrés, who upon arrival in Vienna, chose not to continue on to Israel. They preferred to resettle in the West. The Liaison Bureau labeled these émigrés *"dropouts."* Initially, the dropouts received limited assistance and support from HIAS, JDC and the Union of Councils. In a short period of time, however, a broad cross-section of American Jews expressed support for the idea that Soviet Jews should have freedom to choose where to resettle.

It is to this issue of "freedom of choice" that we turn to in the next chapter. It marks the beginning of a break between the Israeli government and its Liaison Bureau and the American Jewish establishment.

NOTES

1. Phil Baum (1989:11,12) of the American Jewish Congress suggests that the initial issue had been national rights. The denial of national rights led to the demand for return to the homeland. Glen Richter (1989:49) recalled that when he set up the Student Struggle for Soviet Jewry he focused on rights and did not envision mass emigration. Also see Orbach 1979:83.

2. At the time he was vice chairman of the Conference of Presidents of Major American Jewish Organizations and a former director of the Greater New York Conference on Soviet Jewry and activist in the Student Struggle for Soviet Jewry (SSSJ). Orbach (1979:18,19) describes an American Jewish establishment unable to involve American Jews in a Soviet Jewry movement. Veteran American Jewish professional Ted Comet (1989:4): "Without them (Israelis) conceptualizing this, energizing this, inspiring us, we wouldn't have had it, certainly not at that time." Similarly Phil Baum (1989:9) says of Meir Rosenne of the Liaison Bureau: "he was "vitally instrumental in kindling understanding of this problem among American Jews."

3. Lawrence (1970:54) puts the toll at 200,000 dead. The Liaison Bureau supplied most of his figures.

4. Salitan (1992:14) refers to limited cultural autonomy between 1918 and 1930 with 116 libraries, 47 reading clubs, 1,000 Yiddish schools, 3 teachers colleges, 5 agricultural institutes, 16 industrial-technical schools and 18 Yiddish theaters. There were even Yiddish language courts and police stations.

5. In 1919 the regime had banned 1,200 Zionist chapters and deported or placed in labor camps 3,000 Zionist leaders (Lawrence 1970:55ff). In 1930 Stalin dissolved the Jewish section of the Communist party (Freedman (1989b:61–65) and Freedman (1989b:61–65).

6. On the fiftieth anniversary of the USSR in 1967 150,000 religious schoolchildren in New York City collected nickels and dimes to pay for a 3 page ad in the *New York Times* asking Prime Minister Kosygin "Is it a happy anniversary for more than 3 million Russians of Jewish faith who are not permitted to have one Jewish school?" (Lawrence 1970:181).

7. They and their offspring would form the nucleus of a post 1967 Zionist movement. See Levanon's (1995:15,16) reference to thousands of graduates of Zionist youth movements and Hebrew/Jewish schools in the Baltic states and Poland now in the Soviet Union.

8. Pinkus (1992:374) notes that in 1947-1948 the Soviet Union had a positive attitude toward Israel accompanied by "a cessation of attacks on Zionism, and no worsening of situation of Jews in USSR." This positive attitude toward Israel channeled some Soviet Jews toward Zionism.

9. On April 8, 1942 Stalin established a Jewish Anti-Fascist Committee of the Soviet Information Bureau headed by Shlomo Mikhoels. Mikhoels visited the United States and spoke at several rallies (Chernin 1999:15 and Lawrence 1970:62,63).

10. Six of the nine doctors arrested on January 13, 1953 were Jewish. The Israeli government considered a public protest. Mr. Ben Locker, head of the World Zionist Organization (WZO), called for Israeli doctors to organize an international conference in Switzerland. The conference was cancelled after Stalin's death (Pinkus 1992:389). Over 1,500 persons attended a Jewish Labor Committee protest against Soviet anti-Semitism in December 1952. A resolution in the United States Senate condemning Soviet anti-Semitism in February 1953 was later changed to include all persecuted peoples in the USSR. Also see Orbach (1979:13,14); Baum (1989) and Pratt (1989). A Jewish Labor Committee affiliate body (Congress for Jewish Culture) got Eleanor Roosevelt to protest the treatment of Jews during a meeting with Soviet Premier Nikita Khrushchev. It also held a protest on the tenth anniversary of Mikhoels death. At the meeting Leon Crystal of the *Forward* called for world wide protest to mobilize public opinion. Nehemiah Levanon of the Liaison Bureau met with Crystal before the rally. While Chernin (1999:23-25) sees the protest as "grass roots" it may have been Israeli "directed."

11. Several sources claim that Stalin planned to deport large numbers of Soviet Jews to Siberia (De Jonge 1986:500-502 and Salitan 1992:20-22). Salitan cites Pinkus.

12. The 1959 census listed 2,267,000 Jews. The number of Jews dropped by 5 percent to 2,151,000 in the 1970 census. However, in 1970 Soviet citizens were allowed to change their nationality. Shapiro (1978:79-82) estimated the 1977 Soviet Jewish population at 2,678,000. The 1979 census listed 1,800,876 Jews. Ten years later there were 1,449,117 Jews in the Soviet Union (Salitan 1992:5).

13. Novick (1999:70) cites Chaim Weitzman's fear that the Holocaust undercut Israel's raison d'être.

14. Isser Harel and Shaul Avigor co-chaired the new group which had the code name "Nativ" (Levanon 1999:71). Pinkus suggest that in the early 1950s Nahum Goldmann supported the policies of the Liaison Bureau (1992:382).

15. The Liaison Bureau had offices in Geneva and Vienna. Shaike Dan coordinated activities in Eastern Europe from Vienna. The Bureau would translate into Russian over 150 books including Uris's *Exodus* (Dinstein 1989:39).

16. According to Pinkus (1992:381) Ben-Gurion saw the possible Soviet immigration as "feeble in the extreme." Dinstein argues that Soviet immigration was not a priority for Ben Gurion (Interview, May 3, 2003).

17. Naftalin (1999:225) refers to a grassroots organization, Magen, in the British Mandate of Palestine organized in 1928 to assist Soviet Jews. It urged Sharret to take advantage of Soviet recognition. He refused; he did not want to upset Soviet Israeli relations. Naftalin also argues that in the 1950s the Israeli government tried

to tone down protests by Diaspora Jewry against the Soviet Union. Schroeter (1974:188) lambastes the indifference of the Israeli government toward Soviet Jewry: "By and large, members of the movement within the USSR had learned that they could expect little help or guidance from Israel. It had been even more difficult before 1967 when Israel and the USSR had diplomatic relations and Israeli diplomatic officials had behaved with (what seemed to the Soviet Jews) maddening propriety."

18. Levanon (1995:330) claims that in the 1960s they broadcast daily in Russian to the USSR. The Soviets began to jam the broadcasts in 1972.

19. Born in Estonia, Nehemia Levanon (Levitan) helped found Kibbutz Kfar Blum. Since the Soviet Union had broken diplomatic relations with Israel over the bombing of its embassy in Tel Aviv, Levanon served temporarily as a diplomatic courier between Stockholm, Olso, Copenhagen and Helsinki where he developed contacts among prominent Jews, newspaper editors and others. He arrived in Moscow in late 1953 (Buwalda 1997:21,22). In 1969 Golda Meir appointed him head of the Liaison Bureau (Levanon 1999:79). He served until 1980.

20. The Lubavitcher (Chabad) movement operated a clandestine religious and educational underground, which fostered Jewish religious identity. It received partial funding from the JDC (Goldman 1995). This may explain the opposition of the Lubavitch movement to active demonstrations against the Soviet Union (Appelbaum 1986:619). Orbach (1979:24) argues that the ultra-Orthodox, non-Zionist Agudas Israel (having United Nations' non-governmental organizational status) disapproved of the open campaign against the Soviet Union. It preferred a *Shtadlan* (quiet diplomacy) approach. Its UN delegate refused to raise the issue of Soviet Jewry.

21. Geula Gil had a tour of 23 concerts in the early 1960s with audiences as large as 2,500 persons (Lawrence 1970:32).

22. Jim Rice referred to a $4m JDC budget for packages in December 1976. (Notes of UAHC Executive in Los Angeles, December 4, 1976). JDC began sending packages to Jews in the Soviet Union (and Siberia) from Iran in the 1940s and 1950s (Interview, Ted Feder, July 20, 1999). According to Levanon the Liaison Bureau got involved with packages in 1954 and the JDC provided the funding. They sent 7 in 1954, 1,284 in 1955 and eventually tens of thousands annually. The Liaison Bureau and NCSJ supplied addresses to JDC (Interview with Jerry Goodman, May 1, 2003).

23. David Harris (Interview, August 8, 2002) claimed that Israeli and Jewish publishers would leave thousands of books behind and tens of thousands of souvenir items. Pratt (interview, October 2002) tells the story of a Polish actor invited to make a movie in Moscow in the 1960s who brought materials in with his entourage.

24. Levanon (1995:160) suggests that some Soviet Jews forged documents to exit with those persons repatriated to Poland. Among them were future employees of the Liaison Bureau.

25. The number of open synagogues dropped from 500 in 1960 to 97 in 1965 while the number of Rabbis declined from 40 in 1965 to 5 in 1977 (Shapiro 1978:81-85 and Freedman 1989b:66). In 1956 a delegation of French Socialists raised the issue of Soviet Jewry with authorities (Pinkus 1992:389). At a 1959 summit President Dwight Eisenhower raised the issue of Soviet Jews with Premier Nikita Khrushchev. At the time several members of the American Jewish Committee met with Anastas Mikoyan. The American Jewish Committee also sponsored an interfaith appeal to Khrushchev

and subsequent petition signed by prominent scholars and clergy "urging repeal of the decrees on so-called 'economic crimes' and the death penalties meted out to a number of Jews in the Soviet Union" (Orbach 1979:17,18). In 1962 Martin Buber, Bertrand Russell and François Mauriac cabled dismay to Nikita Khrushchev over economic executions. On February 28, 1963 the Soviet press published letters and Khrushchev's reply. This made Soviet Jews aware of protests. The protest may have been organized by the Liaison Bureau. Bertrand Russell also wrote Aaron Vergelis, editor of *Sovietish Heimland*, about injustices and forced assimilation of Soviet Jews (Shapiro 1965:427).

26. For example the number of Jews among scientific workers fell from 10.2 percent in 1958 to 7.4 percent in 1968 (Salitan 1992:29). In higher education the percentage of Jews declined from 3.2 percent in 1960 to 2.5 percent in 1964 and to 1.9 percent in 1972. Also see Shapiro 1978:94.

27. *Bar* maintained secrecy, truth in its publications and sought not to endanger Soviet Jews. It operated often indirectly through Western figures, journalists, men of letters, and scientists (Pinkus 1992:389; Dominitz 1996:116; and Gur- Gurevitz 1996:2). In 1955 or 1956 it passed information about the murder of Michoeles to Western journalists (Levanon 1989). Gur-Gurevitz (1996:1) and Dinstein (Interview, May 2003) credit Benyamin Eliav with organizing Bar. At various times Bar had agents in New York City, Los Angeles, Washington, D.C., Mexico City, Buenos Aires, London, Paris, Rome and Stockholm (Gur- Gurevitz (1996:7). Mr. Emanuel Litvinov headed operations in London. He directed the Jewish Library on Current Affairs and published *Jews in Eastern Europe* which later became a monthly called *Insight*. Earlier Meir Rosenne (1957-1960) began Bar activities in Paris. (Orbach (1979:33). Ada Serenyi served in Rome. Levanon (1999:73,74) also established a Liaison Bureau information bureau in Tel Aviv (*Yeda*) which compiled extensive data on Soviet Jewry. Later, it supported the Association for Research on Eastern European Jewry at the Hebrew University whose staff included Professors Shmuel Ettinger, M. Althschuler and Benjamin Pinkus. It published three periodicals—*Newsletter, Jews in Eastern Europe* and *The Jews and The Jewish People* (Pinkus 1992:391).

28. It arranged an ad in the *New York Times* on December 2, 1963 against punishing economic crimes signed by Bertrand Russell, Martin Buber, Linus Pauling, Dr. Albert Schweitzer, Norman Thomas and others (Rosenne 1989:11). In September 1960 Rosenne organized an international conference on Soviet Jewry in Paris. Goldmann of the WJC (WZO) co-sponsored but later changed his mind. Levanon (1999:76,77) thought that Goldmann wanted to show the Soviets that he was a moderate but they refused to meet with him on the Soviet Jewry issue. Participants included Martin Buber, Episcopal Bishop James Pike of San Francisco, and Label Katz of B'nai B'rith. Mr. Daniel Mayer of France chaired. Italian Communist Senator Umberto Teraccini gave support but did not come (Pinkus 1992:391). Eliav had recruited Bertram Russell and Jean Paul Sartre to participate in conferences. Similar conferences were held in Italy in October 1963, France in October 1964 and in Sweden in 1965.

29. Yitzhak (Izo) Rager of the Liaison Bureau joined Litvinov's staff after the Leningrad trials. He initiated the "Organization of 35"—35 English women, all aged 35, who protested the arrest of 35 year old Raisa Palotnik in the USSR. According to Spier (1989b:104) the Thirty Fives were affiliated with the American Union of Councils. Rager claims that organized English Jewry feared the activist protests. One of Rager's activists

set up the Scientific Committee for Soviet Jewry. Dissatisfied with the committee set up by the British Board of Deputies dissidents established the National Council for Soviet Jewry for Great Britain and Ireland (Spier 1989b:105). British Jewry also published "Jews in the USSR" a weekly compilation of news beginning in 1971. The Institute of Jewish Affairs of the WJC published *Soviet Jewish Affairs* (see Buwalda 1997:37).

30. The Liaison Bureau (Pratt 1989) believed that for Soviet leaders, the views of American officials were more important than those of Western European leaders.

31. The Bureau at one time had representatives in NYC, Washington, D.C. and in Los Angeles (Interview, Jerry Goodman, January 10, 2001).

32. They included Benyamin Eilav (1960) who served as the Consul (not Liaison Bureau representative), Meir Rosenne (December 1961–July 1967), Yoram Dinstein (1961–1962 at UN and 1966–1970 as consul), Yehoshua Pratt (1970–1973), Sy Barr, Igo Rager (1975–1978), Sara Frankel (1978–1983), Yeshayahu Barzel and Binyamin Eliav. Peretz (2004:50) lists Uri Ra'anan (1958–1961) and Haim Ber (1975–1978).

33. Baruch Gur-Gurevitch served from 1982–1985, Yehoshua Pratt (Kopel) from 1984–1987 and Jerry Shiran followed him. Peretz (2004:50) also lists Nir Baruch (1969–1973). Levanon, an expert on the Soviet Union, appeared often before Congressional committees, The Council of Foreign Relations and other groups and met with Congressmen, staff and officials at the State Department. He also spoke all over the country. He cultivated persons like Malcolm Toon, Henry Kissinger's adviser Helmut Sonnenfeldt, Max Frankel (whom he may have known from Moscow) of the *New York Times*, Stephen Rosenfeld of the *Washington Post*, Leon Volhoff of *Newsweek*, Zbigniew Brzezinski and others.

34. In a phone conversation (February 2001) he emphatically denied knowledge of the Liaison Bureau. Nevertheless he confirmed his involvement in activities attributed to the Liaison Bureau in the United States.

35. Decter also did a special issue on Soviet Jewry for the American Jewish Congress's *Congress Monthly* (Baum 1989). Appelbaum (1986:615) says of Decters writing in the January 1963 issue of *Foreign Affairs* "Status of Jews in the Soviet Union"— his factual arguments showing special discrimination about Jews "provided the firm intellectual basis on which later activities would be built."

36. Decter remained until 1978. When he left the NCSJ absorbed his activity which was paid for by the "Israelis." Funds sometime were transferred via the WZO, American Jewish Committee (AJC) or private sources. For example, Rosenne suggested (Interview, June 27, 2002) that Sam Rothberg and Joe Schwartz gave Golda Meir, then Prime Minister, $25,000 each annually for Soviet Jewry. A luncheon by Mr. Rafi Recannati in New York City each year raised between $10,000 and $12,000 for the same purpose. (Decter 1989:5,17). Decter aided David Weiss of UCLA to set up the 7,000 member Academic Committee on Soviet Jewry in April 1967 which both Nathan Glazer and Hans Morgenthau later chaired (Orbach 1979:34,88 and Appelbaum 1986:620).

37. The American Jewish Congress did not charge rent. Nahum Goldmann of the WJC provided for payment of the editor's salary. After 1962 Eliav went to see Joe Schwartz (JDC) to arrange for funds to be funneled to the American Jewish Congress to cover Decter's salary and expenses (Decter 1989:31,32). The Anti-Defamation League provided some office staff services.

38. Douglas remained active in the Research Bureau until his health deteriorated. Orbach (1979:89) makes references to a later letter of December 25, 1970, to the *New*

York Times signed by Theodore M. Hesburgh, Arthur Miller, Hans J. Morgenthau, Bayard Rustin, Telford Taylor and 12 others.

39. The conference issued an "Appeal to Conscience for the Jews of the Soviet Union." Meir Rosenne (1989:17,18) credits the American Jewish Committee with getting statements from Martin Luther King, Telford Taylor and Norman Thomas. An ad hoc Commission on Rights of Soviet Jews which included Dr. John C. Bennett, Father George R. Ford, Emil Mazey, Bayard Rustin, Teleford Taylor and Norman Thomas held a public tribunal on Jewish life in the Soviet Union with the involvement of Justice William Douglas, Martin L. King, Jr, Bishop James Pike, Walter Reuther, and Dr. Eugene Rabinowitch, editor of the *Bulletin of Atomic Scientists* (Goodman 1969:117; Orbach 1979:33). Eugene Gold (1990:18ff) accompanied Telford Taylor to a meeting with Len Garment in the White House. At the initiative of Yitzhak Rager, Taylor, a Nuremberg prosecutor, contacted Roman Rodenko, the Soviet General Prosecutor, who also had been at Nuremberg, on behalf of Jewish prisoners of conscience. Taylor agreed to appeal their case on legal grounds provided that the Israelis stayed out. Izo Rager raised the money from Rabbi Haskell Lookstein's contacts and from Noam Shudowsky and hired Alan Dershowitz and Leon Lipson to head a legal team. This led to Taylor's book *Courts of Terror*. They also sent Taylor and a delegation to Moscow.

40. Gunther Lawrence (Phone Interview, July 3, 2003) who then worked on public relations for the Union of American Hebrew Congregations (UAHC) tells of being recruited clandestinely by Meir Rosenne and Yehuda Hellman. His superior at UAHC Maurice Eisendrath agreed to let Lawrence help Rosenne gratis. Lawrence worked to get "pink cables" publicity in the media. Chernin (1999:31) credits Lova Eliav and Meir Rosenne with playing "key roles in influencing leadership and grassroots to put this issue on the agenda of the United States and to encourage a campaign of responsible public protest."

41. At the time Abram was President of the American Jewish Committee. According to Rosenne (1989:18-22) some Israeli cabinet ministers opposed raising the issue out of fear of hurting Soviet Israeli relations. The French, British, Israeli, Australian, Italian and Scandinavian Communist parties as well as the *New York Times* protested the book's publication (Orbach 1979:20,98; Shapiro 1965:426). Levanon (1995:193) hints that Moshe Decter, working for the Liaison Bureau had the manuscript translated into English. Between 1971 and 1979 Rosenne complained to UNESCO about denial of educational rights for Soviet Jews and to the International Postal Union because the Soviets sent back letters from Israel. In the mid 1960s Israel condemned Soviet treatment of its Jews at the United Nations General Assembly and Human Rights Commission. For example, in April 1965 at the United Nations Israel Supreme Court Judge Haim Cohen argued for the right of religious communities to publish texts. The Israelis also appealed for the right to emigrate (Orbach 1979:36).

42. Jerry Goodman and others credit Segal with directing the American Jewish Committee's involvement with Soviet Jewry. In the early 1950s it published Solomon Schwartz's books *Jews of Eastern Europe* and *Jews of the Soviet Union* and Peter Myers *Jews in the Soviet Satellites* (Orhbach 1979:17). It also used *Commentary* to publish articles.

43. Established in 1924, The Synagogue Council of America united the three branches of American Judaism (Reform, Conservative and Orthodox) for contact with

other faiths. They voted to disband in 1995 (Goldberg 1996:61). The Reform move-ment made a movie about Soviet Jewry "Price of Silence" narrated by Edward G. Robinson. Rosenne (Interview, June 27, 2002) claims that this was a Liaison Bureau project. B'nai B'rith became active even though it risked loosing its non-governmen-tal organizational status at the UN. See Orbach 1997:90.

44. Levanon argued that the grassroots leaders did not want to cooperate with him because of his ties to the Jewish establishment. He helped the Cleveland group get funding from Edward Ginsburg. Also see Naftalin (1999:229). From Orbach's (1979:41-43) account of Decter's activities with leaders of the Union of Councils one could con-clude that the Liaison Bureau had infiltrated the Union of Councils. Rosenne also had contact with grassroots groups in Cleveland and with the Student Struggle for Soviet Jewry. Orbach (1979:33) reported that the Cleveland Council on Soviet Anti-Semitism cooperated with the Liaison Bureau, but . . . "less than ten years later, the Israelis at-tempted to destroy the activist movement."

45. Yoram Dinstein clashed with grassroots activists. See Orbach's (1979:39–52). Mr. Louis Rosenblum of the Union of Councils in Cleveland wrote Ambassador Rabin on May 4, 1970 claiming that Dinstein had threatened "I shall see that you are de-stroyed."

46. On October 7, 1963, Rabbis Irving Miller (Synagogue Council of America) and Abraham Heschel met with representatives of major Jewish organizations to marshal resources for "public action and education" on Soviet Jewry (Orbach (1979:20). A subcommittee of presidents of the National Community Relations Advisory Council (NCRAC), the Conference of Presidents, the Synagogue Council of America and the American Jewish Committee developed a program which led to the convening of the American Jewish Conference on Soviet Jewry the following April. (Also see Goodman 1965:313). Rabbi Heschel had threatened that unless bold action was taken "he would begin his own national movement" (Weinstein 1988:601). In February 1964 Heschel spoke before a joint meeting of the Presidents' Conference and the Ameri-can Jewish Committee. The Presidents' Conference voted to adopt his proposal and the American Jewish Committee agreed to participate (Weinstein 1988:202 and Chernin 1999:33). Orbach (1979:23) credits the Synagogue Council of America with initiating the American Jewish Conference on Soviet Jewry. At the 1963 conference Agudat Israel and the Lubaavitcher organization opposed active protest (Orbach 1979:24). Bulwalda (1997:38) is mistaken when he implies Israeli opposition to the American Jewish Conference. While Israel officially kept its distance, its Liaison Bu-reau helped to set it up. He is equally wrong in suggesting that the American Jewish establishment stood on the sidelines until Jackson-Vanik and the establishment of the National Conference for Soviet Jewry (1997:39).

47. Rose Halperin of the WZO threw Rosenne out of her office and complained to Prime Minister Levi Eshkol.

48. Dinstein rejected the idea of the President's Conference serving as an umbrella organization because the American Jewish Committee did not belong.

49. The Israeli ambassador did not attend and other Israelis kept a low profile (We-instein (1988:603).

50. Credit for the initiative is given to Rosenne (by Chernin 1999:35–38) and to the American Jewish Committee (by Dinstein (1989:2,3). Appelbaum (1986:615,616) sug-gests that the poor results of a meeting with Soviet Ambassador Dobrynin led Justice

Arthur Goldberg and Senators Jacob Javits and Abraham Ribicoff to recommend a general conference of Jewish groups to mobilize the community on behalf of Soviet Jews. He also praises the efforts of Rabbi Heschel and Moshe Decter. Also see Chernin 1999:33; Goldberg 1996:165,166 and Orbach 1979:24).

51. A delegation then met with Secretary of State Dean Rusk and later with President Lyndon Johnson and McGeorge Bundy. President Johnson called for a day of prayer for Soviet Jewry (Chernin 1999:36,37; Orbach 1979:26). On June 15 a steering committee named George Maislen, President of the United Synagogues of America as chair of the American Jewish Conference on Soviet Jewry. He would be assisted by professionals on loan from constituent organizations.

52. Some in the Liaison Bureau believed that the CIA provided funding to the Councils because of their anti-Soviet stand (Interview with Jerry Shiran, February 28, 2003).

53. Speech of Irving Miller, *Light on Soviet Jewry: Report of Conference on Jews in USSR* (London: June 15, 1969, Board of Deputies). Dean Rusk once asked Miller whether it was more important to live as Jews or to leave. He replied that the essence was to pass on Jewishness which could not take place within the USSR.

54. According to Appelbaum (1986:618) several establishment groups opposed citing emigration because it might upset the Soviets.

55. The president of AJC served as the first chairman. Later chairmen included Rabbi Herschel Schacter (1970–1971) who was from Mizrachi (Religious Zionists) and Rabbi Israel Miller from the Zionist Council who served for three years. Lewis B. Weinstein of Boston succeeded Rabbi Miller,

56. Later active staff included Jack Baker of the Anti-Defamation League, Yehuda Hellman of the President's Conference and Abe Bayer of the National Community Relations Advisory Council (Goodman 1979:20).

57. Isaiah Minkoff assigned Henry Siegman to serve as coordinator of the Conference. Al Chernin replaced him. (Chernin 1999:43; Abe Bayer 1989 and Goodman 1969:11). In 1966 NJCRAC assumed "temporary responsibility for professional guidance of the Conference."

58. It circulated and reprinted its "Declaration of Rights of Soviet Jewry" (18 points) (Goodman 1969:112). It had 90 Senators sign a petition calling for cultural and religious freedom in December 1966 which it later published in the *New York Times* and other papers.

59. In the summer and fall of 1964 NCRAC initiated rallies in 25 major cities. In October 1964 the American Conference held its first rally in New York City. It held a rally in Madison Square Garden in June 1965. Chernin claims that George Maislen of the Conference opposed protest visits to Washington, D.C., by Jewish religious congregations organized by Meir Rosenne.

60. The Matzoth of Hope had been the matzoth of oppression (Appelbaum 1986:619).

61. Nehemiah Levanon briefed an America Rabbinical delegation in Amsterdam on its way to visit the USSR in 1956 (Levanon 1995:155). In 1961 B'nai B'rith leaders visited. In July 1965 Rabbi Israel Miller took a group of Orthodox Rabbis from the Rabbinical Council of America to visit the USSR. A year later another delegation of 11 persons under the auspices of the Appeal for Conscience Foundation visited. In August 1966, 22 members of the Union of American Hebrew Congregations (Reform)

spent five weeks in the Soviet Union (Lawrence 1970:12,13). Meir Rosenne convinced Hadassah to send a delegation to the Soviet Union.

62. See "Eased Exit Viewed for Soviet Jews," *NYT* December 4, 1966 and "Kosygin Pledge on Emigration of Jews is Praised by Israelis," *NYT*, December 5, 1966. According to Yehuda Dominitz (1996;117), *Pravda* and *Izvestia* also published a statement by Wladislaw Gomulka in 1968 stating that he would allow the emigration of those Jews who see Israel as their homeland. In doing so, Soviet authorities hinted that Russian Jews who categorized themselves similarly might be allowed to leave.

63. Gitelman (1999:89,90). suggests an implicit collusion among Soviet Jews, Israel and Soviet authorities in defining the movement as one for reunification of families, a simple humanitarian aim, and repatriation to the national homeland a stickier demand but applicable to very few groups in the USSR. Between the end of World War II and 1987 the Soviet Union let out about 450,000 citizens; 294,000 Jews, 110,000 Germans and 53,000 Armenians (Heiitman 1989:115–118).

64. According to Gur-Gurevitz (1996:3,4) the Soviets issued 18 exit visas to Jews between 1948 and 1953, and less than 1,000 per year until 1965 when they issued 1,444. In 1966 they issued 1,892. The number dropped to 1,162 in 1967 and only 231 in 1968. It jumped to +3,000 in 1969 and back to 1,027 in 1970. According to Gitelman (writing in 1972:9) 4,667 left until 1964, 750 in 1965, 1,613 in 1966, 1,109 in 1967, 1,109 in 1968 and 2,100 in 1969. The number would drop to 1,000 in 1970.

65. Gitelman (1999:89) argues that the Soviets let several thousand Jews out in 1971 based on a belief that if they let the leaders go the movement would fall apart. They did not understand that allowing some to leave encouraged others to do so.

66. Those wanting to go to the United States needed a similar invitation from American relatives (Memo, Gaynor Jacobson (HIAS) to Cooperating Agencies, March 29, 1971 (JDC files). Buwalda (1979:78,79) reports that for a short time in the 1970s Soviet authorities recognized *vysovs* given by Dutch authorities to Soviet Jewish citizens not able to find relatives in Israel.

67. For a time Israel forced arriving immigrants to write letters to "relatives" in the USSR (JDC Executive Committee, October 26, 1976). Buwalda (1997:47–49) reports from a Liaison Bureau source that both sides understood that no one cared if it was a real relative if they wanted the Jews to leave.

68. Children required documents from schools. Party members needed a reference from the Communist party. All persons required letters from the phone company, housing authority and so forth stating that they had no outstanding debts.

69. This was based on a *Ukase* (Soviet administrative decree) of February 17, 1967. Those few allowed to leave for other countries did not loose their citizenship. In 1970 the cost was 900 rubles overall to leave per person (over 16 years old) which included 360 rubles for exit permit, 40 for application and 500 for rejecting citizenship. Average salary at the time was 185 rubles per month. The Dutch (with Israeli approval and funding) advanced money to those leaving for Israel for travel expenses but when numbers increase in 1971 the Dutch restricted loans to exceptional cases and the demand dropped (Buwalda 1997:80).

70. Before leaving Moscow in 1967 Israeli and Dutch officials in Moscow agreed that there would be no application form, no check on antecedents (i.e. If they had proper Soviet documents), no visa fees, loans for Jewish visas to cover one way air-

fare to Vienna, visas valid for 12 months, and advise emigrants to travel to Vienna where the Jewish Agency would meet them. Later, the Israelis supplied an application form (Buwalda 1997:25).

71. Goldberg (1996:15,16) writes that the Israeli Six Day War victory touched of "a wave of nationalist passion among Jews in America and around the world" and ignited the rebirth of 2 million Soviet Jews which in turn led to a broad based soviet Jewry movement in the USA. Gitelman (1999:85) citing Benjamin Pinkus argues that between 1964 and 1967 Jewish cultural activity, much of it with a Zionists tinge, increased. State of Israel radio broadcasts, discrimination, bans on the baking of matzoth, the gathering of Jewish Youth at Synagogues at Simchat Torah and other holidays and other events contributed to a sense of Jewish identity among Soviet Jews. Orbach (1979:16,17) cites the Ukrainian government's erection of a memorial at Babi Yar without noting the Jewish identity of the victims and the protest by Russian poet Yvgeni Yevtushenko. Sanders (1988:602) refers to the 1968 May essay by Boris Kochuviesky (Kotschubievsky) "Why I am a Zionist." Also on May 15, 1968 26 Jewish intellectuals in Vilna wrote a public letter demanding the right to emigrate to Israel (Sanders 1988:602; Shapiro 1970:466, 467). During 1971 the Samizdat or underground Soviet Journal *Khronika,* principle organ of the Democratic movement, inaugurated a regular section entitled "The Jewish Movement for Emigration to Israel." There was also a Jewish offspring "Ishkod" (Exodus) which had printed on its cover from the Universal Declaration of Human Rights: "Everyone has the right to leave any country, including his own, and to return to his country" (Sanders 1988:604).

72. Levanon and others in the Liaison Bureau opposed joining the general dissident movement because it was anti-Soviet. Another factor was that the Israelis did not trust the non-Jews in the USSR based on a bitter past (Levanon 1995:243-247).

73. Thousands of Soviet Jews registered to leave for Israel (Buwalda 1997:23).

74. Orbach 1979:36,160 and Appelbaum 1986:622.

75. Between 1969 and 1978 more than 5,000 Soviet Jews signed petitions to leave.

76. He also argues (1972:38) that following the new reality of the Six Day War, the occupied territories and the potential demographic problems the Israeli government increased its encouragement of immigration.

77. Pinkus (1992:390–391) refers to Maoz group set up in 1958 to alert Jewish and world opinion to the tragic situation of Soviet Jewry which was critical of the Israeli government. It issued a manifesto in December of 1964 "Let my people go." In 1965 it collected 100,000 names for a petition. The semi official "Public Council on Behalf of Soviet Jewry" was established in Israel by Shaul Avigur and Golda Meir. It was headed by Avraham Harmon (Labor party), Sh. A. Abramov (Likud), Dov Yosefi and Ruth Bar On (Pinkus 1992:398).

78. Some had charged that the Liaison Bureau tried to limit public demonstrations by Diaspora Jewry (Gur-Gurevitz 1996:2) and Freedman (1989b:77).

79. The first Refusenik was Boris Kochubyevski who was arrested in December 1968. Yasha Kazakov renounced his Soviet citizenship on June 13, 1967 and circulated a statement in samizdat to let him leave (Buwalda 1997:29-31). Moshe Decter in New York issued a booklet "A hero for our time" about him (Appelbaum 1986:623). Yasha became Ya'acov Kedmi in Israel and headed the Liaison Bureau in the 1990s (Telephone interview with Benjamin Pinkus, July 2004 and http://1999/infor.jpost.com/ supplements/elections99/articles/article-36.shtml).

80. American Jews also began to lobby for emigration (Appelbaum 1986:623). Yoram Dinstein (Interview, May 3, 2003) notes that in pre-1967 New York most American Jewish organizations did not favor emigration of Soviet Jews. Orbach (1979:155) argues that a more secure Israel allowed American Jews to focus their "Jewish" concerns elsewhere, namely, on Soviet Jewry. He talks about an interactive process whereby the concerns of American Jews moved Soviet Jews to act which in turn led American Jews to do more. Nevertheless, Soviet Jews had become activists long before American Jewish activism on their behalf.

81. Morris Abram (1989:38) believed that "American Jewry would [not] have been the self -confident body of citizens that we are now had it not been for the fact that Israel existed as a unifying force and a strengthening force in our lives."

82. It appeared in French in 1966 and in English in November 1967.

83. Neal Kozodoy translated *Jews of Silence* into English and wrote a "Historical Afterward on Soviet Jewry" which appears in the book. *Kozodoy thanks Moshe Decter "for sharing generously with me the results of his own extensive research into the problem of the Jews in the Soviet Union"* (Wiesel 1966:107). Meir Rosenne (1989:18) "I suggest he go [to the USSR] and I suggest a title." According to Moshe Decter (1990:18) Wiesel went to the USSR "because initiated by the three of us, Binyamin Eliav, Meir Rosenne and me . . . we had to persuade him to go." According to Wiesel (Phone conversation, July 2001) he would have gone, regardless of Liaison Bureau encouragement; as a reporter for Israeli and American Jewish papers said "Soviet Jewry was news." David Geller (1990) says that the American Jewish Committee commissioned the book and that its artists had previously done a poster with the title "Jews of Silence." The Liaison Bureau also assisted Gunther Lawrence in writing his 1970 book which supported the charge against the Soviet Union of the spiritual annihilation of Soviet Jewry. Decter supplied much of the factual evidence and Rosenne and others urged him to write the book (Phone interview with Lawrence, July 3, 2003). The Liaison Bureau also sponsored Ben Ami's (pseudonym for Lova Eliav) *The Hammer and the Sickle*.

84. Jerry Goodman (Interview, May 2003) argues that this view was more prevalent among religious American Jews.

85. Novick (1999:174) says Kahane's "repeated invocation of the Holocaust gave rise to a fear among established Jewish organizations that he was establishing a kind of rhetorical ownership of it. In order to block this takeover bid by the usurper, they themselves began to talk more about the Holocaust." Also see Naftalin (1999:225).

86. The leadership in the Soviet Jewry movement in the United States were second and third generation American Jews. There were some Holocaust survivors including Abe Foxman of ADL and many children of Holocaust survivors.

87. Rabbi Heschel made a connection between the failure to rescue Jews in the Holocaust and the possible saving of Soviet Jewry (Chernin 1999:30). Levanon and Dinstein (1989:28) made similar comments. Morris Abram (1989:38) hoped that the "American Jewish community could redeem some of its failures" including its nonresponse to Roosevelt's inaction to Kristallnacht.

88. The trial of 11 hijackers (9 of them Jewish) opened on December 15, 1970. Ten days later the court sentenced Mark Dymshits and Eduard Kuznetsov to death.

89. For example, most local federations and community relations councils set up Soviet Jewry committees.

90. The press conference led to the establishment of the Ad Hoc Committee of Concern for Soviet Jewish Prisoners whose original members were Leonard Bernstein, Henry Steele Commaner, Robert Penn Warren, Nobel Laureate George Wald, Dwight MacDonald, Alfred Kazin, Telford Taylor, Lionel Trilling and Notre Dame President Theodore M. Hesburgh (Orbach 1979:vii,viii;53).

91. At the time both Houses of Congress passed resolutions about the death sentences. According to Orbach (1979) Israelis told Rabbi Shachter that Henry Kissinger had called Soviet Ambassador Dobrynin. Following international protest the Soviet Supreme Court, on December 31, 1970, commuted the sentences to 15 years hard labor. Also see Buwalda (1997:31), Dinstein (1989), Fosdick (1990), Frankel (1989), Gold (1990), and Weiss (1989).

92. The Lubavitcher Rebbe considered "Brussels" as being dangerous for Soviet Jews (Orbach 1979:57-61).

93. Chernin (1999:59,60) claims that there were 1,500 delegates.

94. According to Levanon (1999:80) Zvi Nezer of the Liaison Bureau ran the technical set up from Tel Aviv. While Chernin writes that Dr. Yoram Dinstein served as a consultant to a five person delegation to present Brussels's resolutions to the Human Rights Commission of the UN he does not mention that Dinstein was a Liaison operative who was the legal adviser to the Brussels Conference (Weinstein 1988:607–609). The presence of Yasha Kazakov and Boris Sperling (despite the opposition of the establishment and Israel who labeled the two "KGB agents" [Orbach 1979:60]) may suggest that the Liaison Bureau did not control the conference with an iron hand. Organizers did not let Meir Kahane participate. Belgian police detained and then expelled him from Belgium (Naftalin 1999:231). Menachem Begin, an Israeli delegate, expressed anger at the exclusion and arrest of Kahane. Yet at the end of his protest talk he stated: "I propose that all the incidents that have taken place here be erased from our memory, let us go back to our homes determined to struggle, despite our differences, for the liberation of Soviet Jewry" (Cohen: 1971:9). Soviet criticism and threats that it would also harm Soviet-Belgian relations gave the conference publicity (Cohen 1971:5). Among the recipients of 255 press cards were *Tass, Novosty, Pravda* and *Izvestia*.

95. Until this time Shaul Avigur, head of the Liaison Bureau, had opposed the participation of Israeli officials in the Soviet Jewry movement (Pinkus 1992:396).

96. Nehemia Levanon handled the resolutions committee. Helping him were Menachem Begin, Abe Harmon and Zalman Abrahamov. Begin drafted the resolutions, Harman checked the English and Abrahmov the French (Levanon 1995:377–379). Jerry Goodman (Interview, May 1, 2003) recalled that the Israelis were not excited about the cultural resolution but were not able to block it. Levanon (1995:376) recalls that in preparing draft resolutions he realized that the extremists among the Soviet émigrés in Israel would only want "Aliyah" resolutions. He was aware of pressure on the issues of freedom of culture and freedom of choice on emigration. He discussed the matter with Shaul Avigur and they decided to add a resolution on condemning anti-Semitism and in favor of cultural rights for Jews in the USSR. Orbach (1979:57) was mistaken when he wrote a strong Israeli influence led to adoption of a pro-emigration policy and neglect of those who did not want to leave (Orbach 1979:57-61).

97. Interestingly, resolutions at the Jewish Agency General Assembly in June 1977 urged freedom for Soviet Jews to leave and "full national, religious and cultural

rights" for those that remained (Len Seidenman to Gaynor Jacobson, July 4, 1977, HIAS files).

98. Korey (1999b:124) writes that the Liaison Bureau office in Tel Aviv coordinates the World Conference on Soviet Jewry.

99. Interview with Jerry Goodman, January 10, 2001; Eugene Gold 1990; Dinstein (1990:2) says of the National Conference on Soviet Jewry "This was essentially our creation."

100. Appelbaum (1986:621-626) argues that grassroots activists were critical of the American Jewish Conference on Soviet Jewry for its lack of budget, permanent staff and minimum local programming. He cites grassroots and student protests at CJF General Assemblies in Philadelphia (1966) and Boston (1969) for more funding for AJCSJ. Also see Orbach (1979:41,48) and (Chernin 1969:62).

101. Its offices were in the building in New York City owned and occupied by the Jewish Agency for Israel. At a meeting with Yehoshua Pratt (1989) and Nehemia Levanon, Yehuda Hellman committed $70,000 a year if the Presidents' Conference took charge of Soviet Jewish advocacy. While Levanon was agreeable Pratt objected; he doubted Hellman's access to funds and argued that the American Jewish Committee did not belong to the Presidents' Conference.

102. Other members included Phil Bernstein of CJF, Yehuda Hellman of the Presidents' Conference, Charlotte Jacobson (WZO) and Isaiah Minkoff of NJCRAC. CJF files, Box 667 has two versions of Lowell's memo—One is dated May 27, 1971 and the second June 9, 1971. The committee held five, five hour meetings; Hellman had not been at the fifth meeting and had not seen the final report.

103. It would have two professionals and secretarial staff and an annual budget of $235,000 of which $75,000 was for staff, $32,000 for operating costs and $93,000 for projects and activities. Constituent agencies would provide $60,000; New York City sources $60,000 and CJF Welfare Funds $125,000 (Memo, Stanley Lowell, May 27, 1971 (CJF files, Box 667).

104. These representatives could be from the local community relations councils if the welfare funds so chose. New organizations could join with the approval of two thirds of the plenum. The plenum would choose a chair, 3 vice chairs and a treasurer. They together with 6 persons chosen by the plenum would serve as an executive committee.

105. It also called for a standing committee of both organizations. The June 9, 1971 version dropped a provision for a special liaison of staff directors and officers of the NCSJ, Conference of Presidents, and NJCRAC.

106. Shinbaum 1999:173 refers to 27 national Jewish organizations in NCSJ. Jerry Goodman (1979) noted that the new name made it easier to involve non-Jewish organizations. There was a proliferation of national and local interreligious councils for Soviet Jewry after 1973. Very active were The National Catholic Conference for Interracial Justice and the American Jewish Committee's Interreligious Affairs Committee which organized the National Interreligious Consultation on Soviet Jewry in Chicago in March 1972 (Orbach 1979:66,93) with over 600 participants, mostly Christian clergy. This was a joint Jewish Catholic venture which promoted Project Co-Adoption which adopted Jews and committed Christians who were being persecuted on the basis of their religious beliefs (Appelbaum 1986:631-632). R. Sargent Shriver became honorary chair and Sister Ann Gillen (Executive Director of the National Council of

Nuns), Executive Director (Bayer 1973:221). The World Jewish Congress did not join until the Bronfman years in the mid-1980s. Sara Frankel of the Liaison Bureau involved Phil Klutznick, President of the World Jewish Congress, in 1979 when Israel Singer, his aide, was encouraged to adopt Prisoner of Zion Yosef Mendelevich (Sara Frankel 1989). Glen Richter (1989:30) argued that that NCSJ excluded the Student Struggle for Soviet Jewry from decision making.

107. Stanley Lowell, former Deputy Mayor of New York City under Robert Wagner Jr., succeed Maass. Those that followed included Eugene Gold, Burton Levinson, Theodore R. Mann, Morris B. Abram and Shoshana Cardin (Shinbaum 1999:174).

108. Minkoff offered Goodman $11,000 left over from the Conference (Interview with Jerry Goodman, January 10, 2001). Yehoshua Pratt (1989:75) claims that most money came from the American Jewish Committee. Glen Richter (1989:25) thought that the Israelis funded a good percentage of its budget.

109. For example, staff did not have a pension fund. Writing in 1979 Orbach (1979:5,6) refers to a budget of $350,000 which he compares this to the $7.5m budget of the American Jewish Committee.

110. It first issue of the NCSJ Newsletter on Jews in the Soviet Union appeared on October 29, 1971. Thereafter it issued a publication called "*Outlook*" (Shinbaum 1999:174; Levanon 1989 and Harris (1989:53).

111. The GNYCSJ handled implementation in New York City. Also see Orbach (1979:6).

112. NCSJ hired Eliahu Bergman as a part time "consultant" in Washington, D.C. in 1972. It hired June Rogul as a part time director of its Washington Office in spring 1973 (e-mail, Jerry Goodman to Fred Lazin, July 3, 2003). Following her were Hjon Totenberg, Marina Wallach, David Harris, Billy Keyserling and Mark Levin.

113. Yehoshua Pratt of the Bureau had recruited Jerry Goodman as the first director (Interview with Goodman, May 1, 2003). In confirming her participation in the NCSJ and Greater New York Conference on Soviet Jewry Sara Frankel (1989:3) commented: "of course . . . it was framed as an international movement under the guidance of Israel."

114. See chapter 7. These funds were not provided either by CJF or by constituent organizations.

115. Peter Novick (1999:148,149) argues that the Six Day War "effected a permanent reorientation in the agenda of organized American Jews. Israel moved to the top of that agenda." By the 1970s ADL wrote that organized American Jewry had become "an agency of the Israeli government, follow[ing] its directions from day to day."

116. Ernie Michel of New York Federation–UJA arranged for Yehoshua Pratt (1989) to brief major donors William Rosenwald and Jack Weiler on Soviet Jewry. They agreed to provide $100,000 per year for Soviet Jewry activity in the city. David Geller of the American Jewish Committee did not want the job so they hired Malcolm Hoenlein. There were some reservations because he was Orthodox and had been active with the Student Struggle for Soviet Jewry. Abraham Bayer (1989) claims that he initiated the New York Conference on Soviet Jewry and that he got Rabbi Lamm to be the first chair. Glenn Richter (1989) says that the Student Struggle for Soviet Jewry co-founded the New York Conference. Orbach (1979:66) argues that the Greater New York group bridged the establishment activist gap. It began with 15 or 16 constituent organizations and a budget of $300,000.

117. Davis and Schnur were children of Holocaust survivors.

118. Rabbi Joachim Prinz, Morris Abram and Robert Kennedy spoke. Yehoshua Pratt wanted President Richard Nixon but Vice President Gerald Ford came and spoke. The day after Nahum Goldmann denounced the event and charged that it had equated Soviets with the Nazis.

119. Zeesy Schnur (1990) claimed that 50,000 persons participated in the first march. According to Ted Comet (interview, March 4, 1999), if the police wanted to make us happy they would always give us a "high" estimate of the number of demonstrators. According to Jerry Goodman, the NCSJ cosponsored the early marches. This stopped later on when he felt that the national organization should concentrate on other matters (interview May 1, 2003). At the request of the Conference of Presidents they organized a 250,000-person protest against Arafat's appearance at the UN (Malcolm Hoenlein, interview February 2001).

120. According to Zeesy Schnur (1990) it received one third of its budget from the UJA–Federation of New York and raised the rest. It also helped Natan Sharansky raise tax-free money in the USA.

121. A group of New York Conference on Soviet Jewry activists along with Borough Presidents Percy Sutton of Manhattan and Elliot Abrams of the Bronx occupied an Island opposite the United Nations' headquarters in New York City during a visit by Leonid Brezhnev. They placed visible signs renaming it "Soviet Jewry Freedom Island." Secretary General Kurt Waldheim protested and Mayor Lindsay dispatched police boats (accompanied by the press). Upon arrival police found that the protesters had a legal right to be on the Island. Later, the New York Conference would send Mayor John Lindsay to visit the USSR. Upon his return he wrote a book on the subject.

122. Meir Rosenne commented that since they could not confront the Soviet Union, they confronted the American Jewish establishment (1989:5). The Cleveland group wrote Prime Minister Levi Eshkol asking what they could do since the local federation had cut their funding.

123. Chernin argues that the Liaison Bureau nurtured this group (see n. 128 p. 69). Levanon (1999:77) prevailed upon Edward Ginsburg to persuade the Cleveland federation to give $10,000 to the Cleveland group, which was the first in a series of grants. The Bay Area Council for Soviet Jewry (BACSJ) got federation funding (Ruby 1999:204 and Orbach 1979:vii).

124. Critics have charged that the Liaison Bureau withheld information from the grass roots groups. Ruby (1999:206) charges that the Liaison Bureau, with the tacit support of some American Jewish groups, wanted to destroy the Union of Councils. Many of these groups and the Student Struggle for Soviet Jewry felt that the Israelis and establishment spent too much time to thwart them (Ruby 1999:204).

125. Gold (1990) felt that the Councils opposed more the constituent member organizations than the NCSJ itself. The Smucklers of Philadelphia, Connie and Joe, very active in the Union of Councils eventually joined the NCSJ. Also see Lowell (1989).

126. Glen Richter, Yaacov Birnbaum, Art Green and James Torcyna founded the Student Struggle. On April 27, 1964 hundreds of students met at Columbia University to hear Mark Brafman of the American League for Russian Jews which called for emigration and improved Jewish life in the Soviet Union (Appelbaum 1986:615-617). Participants decided to demonstrate on May 1, 1964. Over 1,100 marched and the

event made the second page of the *New York Times*. In October 1964 it had a rally on the Lower East Side with 2,000 persons and addressed by Senators Keating and Javits and Presidential Counselor Meyer Feldman. In April 1965 they brought 3,000 to a Jericho March at Dag Hammarskjold plaza. Its Menorah March in December 1965 became an annual event. A subsequent *geulah* (redemption) march in 1966 attracted 15,000 persons. Moshe Decter (1990:13) said of Birnbaum: "He was by far, the most far-seeing, the most perceptive, the most intelligent and the most committed American Jew that I knew of in the cause." Chernin (1999:41) argues that the American Conference on Soviet Jewry had refused to fund the Student Struggle. He suggests that Meir Rosenne probably found them a funding source but Birnbaum denies it. Nehemiah Levanon (1989) helped them get funding. In the 1980s Rabbi Avi Weiss assumed leadership of the SSSJ.

127. Richter (1989) had been active in Herut Zionist and Soviet Jewry activities. In 1966 he volunteered for the Southern Non-Violent Coordinating Committee (SNCC).

128. Jerry Goodman, Interview, January 10, 2001; Orbach (1979:55). JDL protested this action.

129. At the time of the Leningrad trial JDL took over a demonstration of about 10,000 persons in New York City (Orbach 1979:54). JDL began during the Ocean Hill Brownsville school crisis in New York City. In 1969 it adopted a 10 point program to aid Soviet Jews including termination of all Soviet American arms negotiations, an embargo on trade, a boycott; and discontinuation of cultural exchanges. Its members harassed Soviet diplomats and had sit-ins at impresario Sol Hurok's office, World Olympic Committee and Aeroflot. It caused the cancellation of the Bolshoi 1971 visit to the United States. JDL demonstrations in Washington, D.C. in March 1971 led to 1,300 arrests. (Ruby 1999:207). JDL peaked from November 1970 to March 1971. It declined following the arrest of Kahane on arms smuggling and 3 others on bombing charge. Its members threw bottles of ammonia in Carnegie Hall on January 28, 1971. They bombed Aeroflot offices in New York City on November 25, 1970 and a Soviet cultural building in Washington, D.C. in January 1971. A JDL January 26, 1972 bombing at Sol Hurok productions and Columbia Artists Management Inc. injured 14 and killed one (Orbach 1979:55-57,103-105; Bayer 1973:217,218).

130. Interview with Jerry Goodman, January 10, 2001. His followers broke into the offices of the NCSJ.

131. Many Hadassah groups, B'nai B'rith chapters and federations had a Soviet Jewry chair and committee (Jacobson 1990). In the late 1960s Jewish communities around the country began to hold Simchat Torah demonstrations on behalf of Soviet Jews (Dinstein 1989). Abe Foxman (1989) report ADL publish ads in *NYT* in coordination with NCSJ; they also published materials on *Pamyat* and Bornel's Book *I am a Jew* the first reader on Soviet Jewry. The UJA and other constituent organizations encouraged many of its members to visit with Soviet Jews.

132. Both the Union of Councils and the NCSJ had an adopt a family program and twinning of cities (Orbach 1979:112). Also phoned militants in USSR.

133. Both platforms had watered down statements (Chernin 1999:39).

134. Three Baptist conventions also asked President Nixon to intervene on behalf of Soviet Jews. In 1970 Secretary of State William Rogers raised the issue of family reunification of Soviet Jews with Andrei Gromyko. For the first time an American Secretary of State gave his Soviet counterpart a list of names of Soviet citizens, many of them Jewish.

135. The Liaison Bureau prepared a book for President Nixon with names and addresses of Refuseniks. It reached President Nixon via an Assistant Secretary of State that knew Yehoshua Pratt from their days in Moscow.

136. For example, Senator Ribicoff (September 25, 1963) attracted 64 fellow sponsors for a resolution condemning Soviet religious persecution and demanding free exercise of religion and the pursuit of culture by Jews and all others within its borders. The other sponsors often substitute all minorities rather than Jews (Orbach ibid). In the mid 1960s some Congressmen protested the lack of matzoth for Passover in the USSR (Goodman 1965:328,319). Lawrence (1970:184,201) noted that in 1963 and 1964 the State Department pressured Congress to tone down its resolutions. By 1965 there was no pressure to do so.

137. Glen Richter (1989) praises Ted Kennedy, Ben Gilman, Robert Drinan, Mario Biaggi, Ed Koch and Daniel P. Moynihan. This political activity was copied in state capitals throughout the USA. For example some governors "adopted" Refuseniks (Levine 1989 and Frankel 1989). Israel Miller (1990:19) credits Congressman Waxman's wife. Mrs. Henry Jackson was also very active.

138. CJF opened an "action office" staffed by Mark Talisman in D.C. in November 1975. He conducted Harvard University's biennial seminar on the legislative process for newly elected Congressmen. He also conducted the institute for the Assistant Secretary level of staff in the State Department. He was Vanik's staff person who helped prepare the legislation for Jackson-Vanik (September 18, 19, 1976 notes for J.C. Hoffberger, CJF files, Box 697).

139. President Kennedy raised the issue of Soviet Jewry with Andrei Gromyko. Kennedy told Meyer Feldman that he could do little except for private notes (Lawrence 1970:170). His ambassador Llewellin Thompson told Label Katz of B'nai B'rith that direct action on behalf of Soviet Jews would be "counterproductive" (Ibid: 172). In August 1963 Lewis H. Weinstein, chair of NCRAC and JFK friend from Boston talked with Kennedy about Soviet Jewry. Lewellyn Thompson, Kennedy adviser on USSR said America protest would be counterproductive. Senators Javits and Ribicoff and Supreme Court Justice Arthur Goldberg broached the subject with Secretary of State Dean Rusk who favored having an international and not an American group meet with the Soviets (Orbach 1979:13,14).

140. At the Twenty-first Human Rights Commission Session the United States delegation supported draft Convention on the Elimination of All Forms of Religious Intolerance, which permitted the right to publish religious books and maintain schools. This continued under Nixon. In 1971, U.S. delegate to the UN Rita Hauser charged anti-Semitism and a lack of free emigration in the USSR.

141. As a member of the U.S. Helsinki Committee Congressman Robert Drinan played an important role on behalf of Soviet Jews.

142. Elazar (1976:134) wrote that "All Jewish religious, social, welfare and educational institutions (in the United States) are local, both in name and fact."

143. Rabbi Schneier's Congregation Zichron Ephraim was located across from the Soviet Mission to the United Nations. In the winter of 1964 it hung a plague outside commemorating the cry of the oppressed (Soviet Jewry). Robert F. Kennedy spoke and the event made the *New York Times* with a picture.

144. Ted Comet and Phil Baum organized the first march in 1962 which made an inside page of the *New York Times* (Bayer 1989, Comet 1989, Geller 1990 and Richter 1989.

145. Meir Rosenne (1989) initiated the protest and got the American Jewish Conference to support it. Unable to get funding from constituent organizations, he received money from Rabbi Schneir's Synagogue. According to Orbach (1979:26,27) Henry Siegman of American Jewish Conference on Soviet Jewry proposed the Washington D.C. "Eternal Light Vigil" which attracted 6,000 participants. Chernin claims (1999:43) that over 10,000 came. Orbach argues that leaders of the Conference opposed the Washington protest (they wanted to hold it in Philadelphia). They were also angered by the support for the vigil given by the Israeli consul. Levanon (1999:77,78) writes that Israeli Ambassador Avraham Harmon convinced American Jewish leaders to support the demonstration against the objections of Rose Halperin of the World Zionist Organization. He claims that the vigil was successful beyond dreams and that inspired us and American Jewish organizations to work harder. It also had an impact on Capitol Hill and in the State Department. At the end Theodore Bikel of the American Jewish Congress, Rabbi Seymour Cohen, chair of the American Conference, Rev. John Cronin of National Catholic Welfare Conference and Bayard Rustin delivered a petition of protest with one million signatures to the Soviet Embassy.

146. Following the death sentences in the Leningrad trial he led a protest in Foley Square. The number of ordinary people and "Wall Street types" who participated surprised David Geller (1990).

147. Gold coordinated the 1978 visit to the USSR with Liaison Bureau NY consul Yehoshua Pratt and with Nehemiah Levanon.

148. He opposed the proposed boycott of this company by other activists of the Soviet Jewish movement. A threatened protest at a NCSJ dinner to honor Don Kendall of Pepsico led to its cancellation.

149. Levanon flew to the United States to prep Hubert H. Humphrey on a visit to the USSR. Rabbi Israel Miller helped prep Ted Kennedy. All were given names and addresses of Soviet Jewish activists.

150. Jerry Goodman (Interview, May 1, 2003) stated that there were four categories of "visitors to the Soviet Union": (1) tourists whom NCSJ briefed; (2) missions of activists and politicians whom were briefed and sometimes asked to smuggle out documents; (3) special teams (couples), about 10 per year, sent in by Aryeh Krol of the Liaison Bureau (who was in New York) for purposes of "education" of Soviet Jews; and (4) celebrities for whom funding was often provided. In the case of John Lindsay, for example, they would have found someone to fund the ticket. The Liaison Bureau "coordinated" visits of persons "sponsored" by NCSJ. Another group operated by David Hill, President of 999 Kosher Sausages Company, also organized visits (interview with Jerry Goodman, January 10, 2001). Pratt (1989) claimed that he sent Koch and others but did not recall who paid. Charlotte Jacobson sent lists of names and addresses of Refuseniks to Congressmen going to the USSR. Buwalda (1997:40) notes that the Soviets were aware of the "visits" by "tourists" and their contacts with Refuseniks but failed to interfere with them.

151. According to Abe Foxman, leaders in the Soviet Jewry movement were those who had visited the Soviet Union. Rabbi Irving Miller claimed that a visit to the USSR changed his life (Orbach 1979:92,93). At NCSCJ request the American Jewish Congress published a briefing kit on how to find and meet Soviet Jews when visiting the USSR.

152. In her interview with Dorot, Zeesy Schnur (1990), then director of the NY Coalition to Free Soviet Jewry (April 25 and May 1, 1990) stated that Israel made a

serious attempt to cut off the American Jewish community from contact with Soviet Jews. The Israelis were concerned about Americans visiting the USSR and opening doors for Soviet Jews to come to America.

153. Stern (1979 n.25) wrote that the question for Jews was "one of the fuzziest issues in the entire debate." Jackson referred to article 13/2 of the Universal Declaration of Human Rights which holds that "everyone has the right to leave any country, including his own." See Korey (1999:97), Orbach (1979:129-133) and Stern (1979:1) for efforts by the Union of Councils to tie trade legislation to Soviet emigration policy. According to Goldberg (1996:167,168) and Friedman (1999:5) the idea of the Jackson-Vanik amendment came from Brooklyn Democratic Congressman Bertram Podell. Stern (1979:11) suggests that it began with Professor Harvey Lieber and Attorney Nathan Lewin who had ties to the Union of Councils. Podell showed a draft to I.L. Kenen of AIPAC who shared it with Richard Perle on Jackson's staff and with Mark Talisman of Vanik's staff. They in turn worked with Morris Amitay of Ribicoff's staff. Mark Talisman (Interview, October 2002) claims that Representative Charles Vanik of Cleveland had the amendment a year before Jackson. When the Soviets announced the poll tax in August 1972 Richard Perle and Morris Amitay met with Jerry Goodman of NCSJ, Yehuda Hellman of the Conference of Presidents, I. L. Kennen, and David Brody of ADL. They discussed Podell's amendment. A few weeks later Senator Javits made reference to it in a rally in New York (Baum 1989 and Levanon 1989). Israel Miller (1990) says Jackson came to the idea by himself while Mark Talisman probably pushed Vanik. Dorothy Fosdick refers to Scoop as a "cold war warrior" who did not want the Communists to inherit the world "fundamental conviction about the significance of human rights and democracy for the future of humanity." His visit to Buchenwald, three days after its liberation, in her view was the "most profound experience of his life."

154. Phil Baum (1989) makes reference to Jackson rejecting the idea of inserting a clause for free emigration to their homeland.

155. Prior to the trip the NCSJ gave President Nixon a petition signed by 1.5 million persons asking him to make emigration of Soviet Jews a priority of the summit (Bayer 1973:219).

156. Goldman (1989:144) argues that the Soviets allowed more Jews to leave from 1970 to 1972 because they wanted to expand European ties (Fiat factory) and to receive United States trade credits. Buwalda (1997:90) cites a reference to a statement made by Nelson Rockefeller of a rumored tacit agreement of 35,000 Jewish émigrés a year.

157. "Soviet Emigration Law Change May Affect the Exodus to Israel," *NYT*, November 20, 1972. Yitzhak Rager (1990) said pay tax for a few people. Yehoshua Pratt (1989) thought that we could afford to pay due to gap between official and black market ruble rate. He favored payment but Avigur oppose. Shimon Peres said in the cabinet why not let the world know we pay—also would help Soviets with hard currency. Levanon (1995:395) said that Shaike Dan in the Liaison Bureau favored paying it (we did so in Romania in the past). Levanon urged the Conference of Presidents to mobilize the American Congress to fight it. Levanon (1999:81) urged Prime Minister Meir not to pay. Akiva Kohane reported (Memo to Mrs. Loin Mayer, JDC Rome, JDC file, December 12, 1972) that major Jewish organizations in the world decided not to yield to blackmail. He suggested that this was supported by leading activists in the Soviet Union.

158. She notes that of the 140,000 invitations sent by Israel between 1969 and 1972 that one third went to families with a member with a University education. The Soviets also hoped to discourage prospective émigrés from studying. She suggests that the Soviets knew that the Jews could not pay; they expected the West to pick up the tab. Ms. Zeesy Schnur (Interview, August 12, 2002) says that Professor Yirmiyahu Branover was the first and last person to pay a $40,000 tax. Freedman (1989b:74) asserts that the Soviets may have imposed the tax to please Arab states or to get Western money needed for grain purchases or as a means to deter scientists from leaving or as Brezhnev said it was a bureaucratic bungle.

159. Twenty-one Nobel laureates issued a statement of dismay at the tax. They were joined by a protest of 6,000 professors of the Academic Committee on Soviet Jewry who placed an ad in the *New York Times*.

160. Sara Frankel (1989:6) argued that Levanon visited to the USA specially to mobilize support for the amendment. Yoram Dinstein (1989:30ff) suggests that Nehemiah Levanon "masterminded the whole campaign" (in favor of the amendment). Jerry Goodman explained that Levanon assured some doubtful parties that he had spoken with the Prime Minister who urged support for the amendment. Sara Frankel recalls that Levanon was very friendly with Jackson, Perle and staff and that the NCSJ convinced several Senators to support the Jackson Amendment. Yitzhak Rager relates that Prime Minister Golda Meir and the foreign office told us not to interfere. Knowing that Levanon supported the amendment, Rager tried to undercut the opposition of the Conference of Presidents chair Jacob Stein. Another former senior Liaison operative argues that Levanon acted on his own. Levanon (1995:400) says that the prime minister threatened to call him home after she spoke to Jack Stein. Ambassador Dinitz had told Golda that American Jews should support the President on this.

161. Levanon (1999:81) argues that a special tribute must be made to Jackson and his dedicated assistants Richard Pearl and Dorothy Fosdick "for their determination and devotion to the cause of Soviet Jewry."

162. Both Fisher and Stein were Republicans. To get support for Nixon in the 1972 elections Fisher got Louis Pincus of the Jewish Agency to issue a statement saying Jews should "bless President Nixon for the manner in which he deals with the issue of Soviet Jewry" (Golden 1992:272). The Jewish Telegraphic Agency of October 3, 1972 reported that Rabbi Avi Weiss (1989) claimed that Senator Jackson threw Richard Maass, President of NCSJ, out of his office when he tried to convince the Senator to withdraw his motion. Max Fisher and Jacob Stein tried several times to convince the Senator to abandon the issue. Jackson told Fisher he would need a commitment of 100,000 exits per year to call off the amendment (Golden 1992:270,278,295).

163. At the time the Israeli exit fee was over $50. The amendment was dropped later that month.

164. Senator Javits did not sign because he did not want to irritate Nixon (Korey 1999:99). He signed later. Eventually, the bill had 76 sponsors.

165. On December 29, 1972, the Soviets exempted from the tax persons over the age of 55 and gave all persons credit for each year worked. They also published the educational tax regulations in the "Bulletin of Supreme Soviet" which is the equivalent of the *Congressional Record* (Korey 1974:205; Buwalda 1997:96).

166. At the time American Israel Political Action Committee (AIPAC) sent out 1,000 letters in support of the amendment to key supporters to lobby their Senators and

Congressmen (Stern 1979:55). Korey (1999:99) cites a letter writing campaign of the NCSJ, and support by trade unions and several religious groups. Wilbur D. Mills, chair of the House Ways and Means Committee, supported the bill. While Friedman (1999:6) argues that the Holocaust also left an impression on Congressman Wilbur Mills, Stern (1979) shows that Mills vacillated in response to various political pressures from Jewish friends, lobbyists and others. Talisman commented on the 235 cosponsors in the House saying that there was a lot of guilt about the "Nazi Holocaust" (Stern 1979:55).

167. Stern (1979:65–66,74–75) reports that the administration asked for Israeli help but that the Israelis were reluctant to get involved. She says that Yitzhak Rabin, who supported Nixon's reelection, tried to get Perle not to resubmit the amendment. She reports a rumor that when Prime Minister Meir returned in March 1973 from Washington that she no longer supported the amendment. The government made no statement after its meeting on April 30, 1973, but its Minister of Absorption had praise for President Nixon on the Soviet Jewry issue and Golda Meir quoted him.

168. An appeal from over 100 Soviet Jews in support of Jackson-Vanik, with references to the Holocaust arrived on April 23, 1973. In September, 1973 Sakharov would support it as being essential to Détente (Korey 1999:102,105; Bayer 1973:218).

169. The Soviets also targeted big business. In February 1973 the National Association of Manufacturers sponsored an American Soviet Trade Conference. A 15 person Soviet delegation participated. They also visited Congress where an adviser to the Politburo, G. A. Arbatov, Director of the Institute of United States Studies of the Soviet Academy, suggested that the Jackson Vanik amendment might lead to anti-Semitism in the Soviet Union. This angered Senator Abraham Ribicoff who argued that he basically favored U.S.-USSR trade (Korey 1974:206-207).

170. Senator Jackson was unimpressed with Soviet assurances in March 1973 to Secretary George Shultz that the educational tax would not be enforced. Soviet journalist and insider Victor Louis wrote in an Israeli newspaper on March 21, 1973 that the tax would not be enforced (Stern 1979:64; Freedman 1989b:74; Buwalda 1997:98).

171. The Administration asked Max Fisher and Jacob Stein to restrain demonstrations. Orbach (1979:68) reports that Maass, Stein and Minkoff (NJCRAC) pressured the Union of Councils to cancel an anti-Brezhnev candle light march to the Western White House on June 20, 1973. Israel contributed to the effort by not allowing Meir Kahane to leave the country. Instead of demonstrations the NCSJ organized regional conferences (Korey 1974:221). During this visit Max Fisher and Jacob Stein attended a banquet for Brezhnev on June 18, 1973 at the request of President Nixon which angered many American Jews.

172. Buwalda (1997:98-100) claims that Senator Jackson also wanted a guarantee on emigration for non-Jews. In a meeting in Moscow in June, Leonid Brezhnev agreed to no tax and to let 36,000 to 40,000 Jews leave each year.

173. Under pressure from Stein and Fisher Maass of NCSJ with Charlotte Jacobson and Rabbi Arthur Herzberg of the American Jewish Congress asked Congressman Al Ullman to postpone the vote on Jackson-Vanik (Ruby 1999:213). Importantly, around this time Rabbi Israel Miller and Mr. Stanley Lowell replaced Jacob Stein and Richard Maass as heads of the Conference of Presidents and NCSJ respectively. The newer men were more inclined to take a stand in support of the Jackson-Vanik amendment (Stern 1979:119-120).

174. According to Buwalda (1997:100,101) Henry Kissinger told Senator Jackson that his demand for 100,000 Jewish émigrés per year was out of the question. He suggested that the Soviets might consider 45,000 and end harassment. Also see Orbach 1979:148.

175. Since the early 1970s Kissinger urged the Soviets to let more Jews out (Buwalda 1997:44,45). But emigration was down by 40 percent in the first half of 1974. In Cyprus Gromyko suggested 45,000 a year but the Senators wanted 75,000 (Korey 1975:108,160 and Salitan 1992:32).

176. Orbach (1979:149,150) argues that President Ford supported the demand by Senator Jackson and Stanley Lowell (NCSJ) for a Soviet letter of assurances. Kissinger promised to provide a letter from the Soviets. Korey (1999:108) says that Ford had promised a personal guarantee that the Soviets would end harassment and let a significant number leave. Buwalda (1997:101) claims that Dobryinin told Ford that they would agree to 50,000 per year, but not put it in writing. Soviet officials invited Senator Jackson to visit and meet with Brezhnev but when he indicated that he would meet also with Sakharov (privately) they withdrew the invitation. See Orbach (1979:148,149).

177. The October 18 letter from Ford stated that security clearances would be in effect for 3 years.

178. Some, including Buwalda (1997:110) still wonder if Jackson was not motivated by his Presidential ambitions. If he had compromised harassment may have ended and 30,000 to 45,000 a year might have left. Phil Baum (1989) later believed that Jewish leaders at the time were culpable of hubris." When the Jackson-Vanik amendment passed he said they celebrated on the steps of the Capitol as if they had brought the USSR to its knees. This was not true. We had rejected compromise but think "we can get unlimited emigration." Baum emphasizes that there was a lot of pressure on Jewish organizations not to break ranks on Jackson-Vanik. At the time "paranoia about divisiveness in Jewish community" made them not want to make dissent public. Korey (1999:109) notes that excessive optimism was dispelled when in the fall harassment continued and numbers dropped and on November 21, 1974, nine Soviet Jews wrote an open letter to Ford documenting harassment (Buwalda 1997:102-107).

179. At the Vladivostok summit on November 23, 24, 1974 Leonid Brezhnev told President Ford that emigration would go ahead as agreed (Buwalda 1997:107).

180. The President's authority to use the Export Import Bank was to expire on June 30, 1974. Senators Jackson and Stevenson and their staffs decided early on not to add the Jackson Vanik amendment to the bill. Stern (1979:117) writes: "For the rest of the year, the Jewish groups failed to keep up with the developmental bank bill even though it was closely associated with the Jackson Amendment." Korey (1975:168) wrote: "The striking fact that the Jewish organizations, which had fought so determinedly for the Jackson Amendment, were completely unaware that the Stevenson Amendment would, in effect, nullify what they had been striving to realize." Sara Frankel (1989) says that the NCSJ and Israelis were not concerned about Stevenson but saw it as being anti-Soviet.

181. The Stevenson amendment probably strengthened Soviet hardliners that opposed relaxing controls on emigration (Korey 1975:166; Freedman 1989b:76; Goldberg 1996:174; Orbach 1979:152). After the breakdown the Soviets curtailed emigration and arrested Sharansky. Minton Goldman (1995) claims that American Jews

failed to respond to Soviet actions. For example, when the Soviets began to open the gates in 1978 and 1979 the American Jewish organizations, except for the American Jewish Congress, did not favor backing away from Jackson-Vanik. Goldman also suggests that in 1979 that Vanik unlike Jackson was willing to end the ban on MFN for the Soviet Union. He also suggests that the pressure of the Jewish Defense League and Student Struggle for Soviet Jewry made other organizations reluctant to compromise on Jackson-Vanik in 1979.

182. Freedman (1989b:75–77) suggests that the recession in the Soviet Union in 1975 might have led the Soviets to allow more Jews to leave in hopes that they could revive credits in the United States. They also could have been signaling the new President, Jimmy Carter. Secretary of State George Shultz (1993:887) said that he used it in the 1980s to argue for more trade in exchange for more emigration.

183. Buwalda (1997:108) reports that Sharansky and 60 others signed a petition in support.

184. Senator Henry Jackson, Governor Ronald Reagan of California, Aleksandr Solzhenitsyn and the *Wall Street Journal* urged President Ford not to sign (Korey 1999b:125.

185. Buwalda (1997:116–121) claims that Gromyko was shocked by the human rights aspects but believed that the Soviet Union was "covered" by the clause of non-intervention in internal affairs of a country (sixth principle).

186. Soviet dissidents Vladimir Slepak and Anatoly Sharansky organized a public group to oversee fulfillment of the Helsinki Accords in the USSR. According to Buwalda (1997:70–72) Sharansky set up this group with Yuri Orlov and Andrei Amal-rik. Sakharov's wife served on the Soviet Helsinki Watch group (Buwalda 1997:1119); Korey 1999:126). It operated for two years and supplied documents for the meetings in Belgrade and Madrid. The Soviets arrested Orlov in 1977. Sharansky was arrested on March 15 and charged with treason. He was sentenced to 13 years in prison. He was released on February 11, 1986 in Berlin. Shultz (1993:698) claims that several years before he had arranged for the possible release of Sharansky but that the Orthodox Jewish friends who were close to his wife opposed the Soviet condition that he write a letter to Soviet authorities (1993:273).

187. In 1975 and early 1976 HIAS and others feared that the Soviets might use the Helsinki Agreements to limit emigration to those Jews with first degree relatives abroad (Hand memo to files of Carl Glick, September–October 1976, HIAS files; Sarah Honig, *JP*, September 6, 1976. Spier (1989b:100) argues that little was achieved at the follow up conferences.

188. According to Korey (1999b:126,127) Yuri Orlov in Moscow convinced Congresswoman Millicent Fenwick to support the Helsinki Act. On her visit to the Soviet Union the NCSJ arranged for her to meet with Refuseniks. Upon her return she changed the attitude in Congress in favor of the Helsinki agreements. Korey also credits testimony of Jerry Goodman in moving subcommittee chair Congressman Dan Fascell to push for the legislation for the Helsinki Commission which Secretary of State Henry Kissinger opposed. Orbach (1979:73,74) claims the Union of Councils supported Congressional Legislation to set up the commission while the NCSJ was passive. In England the "35s" launched Helsinki Agreement Watchdog Committee.

189. According to Korey (1999b:128) she recommended to Spencer Oliver, the Commission staff director, that immigration be given high priority. The Commission

at the suggestion of NCSJ became a repository of documents on refusals to emigrate from the Soviet Union. Eugene Gold (1990); Memo, Abraham Bayer NJCRAC to member Agencies, July 29, 1976 (JDC files); and Comments by Eugene Gold at November 1976 Summary of JDC Executive Committee (JDC files).

190. Shultz (1993:596) has great praise for him. He later headed the American delegation to the disarmament talks with the Soviets in Geneva. He also developed close ties with high-ranking KGB personnel in Soviet delegations.

191. It also called for an end of the Soviet jamming of Israeli radio broadcasts to the USSR. By this time Gorbachev's Perestroika was beginning to influence Soviet policy. Dobrynin stated that the Helsinki Final Act "generated the fundamental changes inside the Soviet Union and the nations of Eastern Europe that helped end the Cold War" (Buwalda 1997:125). In June 1990 the Copenhagen meeting on racism issued a document opposing racism and pushing minority the rights; right to ethnic, cultural, linguistic and religious identity and use of mother tongue. Shoshana Cardin, head of NCSJ was a member of the American delegation to the Commission on Security and Cooperation in Europe meetings in Paris in November 1990 (Korey 1990b:133,134). The CSCE held a Moscow conference on Human Rights in 1991 (Shultz 1993:1137).

3

Freedom of Choice and the Committee of Eight: Israel versus the American Jewish Establishment

Until 1973 almost all Soviet Jewish émigrés resettled in Israel. By 1975–1976, however, a near majority favored resettlement in the United States and other Western countries. This situation led to a disagreement between the Israeli government and American Jewish leaders over the preferential country of settlement for Soviet Jewish émigrés. While the government of Israel wanted all émigrés to resettle in Israel, many American Jews came to support "freedom of choice"—the right of Soviet Jewish émigrés to choose their country of resettlement.

Windmueller (1999:161) places the freedom of choice debate in the context of two different versions of the future of the Jewish people. One emphasizes the rebirth of a Jewish state and Zionist dream of bringing all Jews to Israel; the other envisions principles associated with an age "where free individuals could make independent choices, allowing them to define their own destinies."

While positions of Israeli officials and American Jewish leaders in the 1976 confrontation on "freedom of choice" partially support his thesis, other events, before and after, do not. For many Israeli leaders other priorities often took precedence over the Zionist objective of settling all Russian Jewish émigrés in Israel. Except for one event in 1987, the Israeli government refrained from formally requesting that the United States (and other Western countries) not admit Soviet Jewish émigrés.[1] As Gur-Gurevitz (1996:6) writes: "It was the feeling in Israel, traceable to the trauma of World War II, that Jews, including the government of Israel, should not ask foreign governments to restrict the free entry of Jews." Moreover, no Israeli government until 1989 denied Israeli exit visas to Soviet Jews unlikely to continue on to Israel (Buwalda 1997).[2] In practice, the Israeli government often exhibited pragmatism. For example, after failing to dissuade American Jews from supporting the resettlement of Soviet Jews in the United States, the Israeli government accepted the American Jewish position. It decided not "to antagonize the American Jewish establishment" whose political support was essential for Israel's interests with the American government (Goldman 1994:14).[3] The development of the Israeli position on freedom of choice, from ideological opposition to one of pragmatism is a theme of this chapter.

Similarly, for many American Jewish leaders freedom of choice did not always take precedence in dealing with Soviet Jewish émigrés. They too had a pragmatic approach tempered by economic and political considerations. In several instances in the early 1970s and later in the 1980s many American Jewish leaders and organizations abandoned the principle. Early on, for example, American Jewish organizations, including HIAS, agreed to stop assisting Soviet Jews who had first gone to Israel and then tried to enter the United States. As early as 1976 several major federations rejected requests to resettle Soviet Jews and by the late 1980s, the majority of American Jewish leaders supported the Zionist position that Soviet Jews should be resettled in Israel. The development and change in the American Jewish position is another theme of this chapter.

DROPPING OUT

Most Soviet Jews left on visas for Israel via a train to Vienna, Austria. Prior to a terrorist incident in the summer of 1973 the Israeli government via the Jewish Agency had legal authority over Soviet émigrés in Austria. Almost all Soviet Jewish émigrés arriving in Vienna continued on immediately to Israel. According to Dominitz (1996:118) during 1969 and 1970 there was not a single dropout case. Only fifty-eight persons dropped out in 1971. Out of the 32,000 Jews who left in 1972 a mere 251 dropped out. In 1973 when 35,000 Jews left, the number of dropouts reached 1,500 (Letter, J.K. Fasick Government Accounting Office [GAO] to Jaynor (sic) Jacobson, October 15, 1976, CJF files).[4] By the end of the decade the dropout rate reached more than two-thirds (see appendix).

Some evidence suggests that until 1973 Israeli authorities influenced or coerced some émigrés to go on to Israel against their wishes.[5] Mr. Charles Jordan, a senior JDC official noted ("Administrative Report," March 1, 1966, JDC files) that some Soviet Jews in Vienna wanted to change their destination. The view of the Jewish Agency, HIAS, and JDC, he stated, was that destination should not be changed so as not to anger the Soviets. He suggested that if they want to go elsewhere they should apply directly to other countries (Johnston, November 9, 1976). According to a report (1976:48) of the U.S.

Government Accounting Office (GAO), "during 1972 and 1973 . . . there was little opportunity to break off (dropout) in Vienna."

Following the 1973 terrorist incident the Austrian government closed the Jewish Agency facilities at the Schoenau Castle and assumed authority over the Soviet émigrés in transit.[6] Chancellor Kreisky closed Schoenau because "emigrants staying there had no choice of where to resettle" (*Jewish Telegraphic Agency Bulletin [JTA]*, March 24, 1977). The Austrian policy arranged for the Jewish Agency to take charge of all persons arriving from the Soviet Union on Israeli visas. Jewish Agency representatives met the émigrés and Liaison Bureau operatives interviewed them (Levanon 1994:436). Austrian government authorities, however, insured Soviet émigrés freedom of choice which mitigated against possible pressure to continue on to Israel. The number of Jewish émigrés not going on to Israel increased.

The Jewish Agency referred all Jewish émigrés not wanting to go to Israel to the American Joint Distribution Committee (JDC) and the Hebrew Immigrant Aid Society (HIAS) for assistance to go to other countries. Both organizations handled very few Soviet émigrés in the early 1970s. For example, in 1971 they handled 57 cases or 0.44 percent of the movement. In 1972, 203 cases (0.64 percent). After 1973 the caseload grew to 1,372 or 4.28 percent. In 1974 the caseload reached 3,726 or 18.09 percent. The percentage almost doubled in 1975 to 35.88 percent (4,745 persons). In 1976 the caseload reached 6,752 or 47.33 percent (Memo, Akiva Kohane "Soviet Jewish Transmigrants in Vienna and Rome," April 13, 1977, JDC files).

The Israeli government and the Liaison Bureau charged that the option of going to the West together with the support of American Jewish organizations provided incentives for Soviet Jews not to settle in Israel. The Israelis, most American Jewish leaders and many scholars assumed that the overwhelming majority of Soviet Jewish émigrés would otherwise prefer to immigrate to Israel. Underplayed at the time was the possibility that many Soviet Jewish émigrés had always preferred to go to the United States.

Ironically, the Israelis may have inadvertently facilitated the dropout process. In 1966 when Soviet authorities allowed a few hundred Jewish citizens to emigrate for reasons of family reunification a few chose not to go to Israel. The Liaison Bureau and the Jewish Agency approached HIAS and JDC to facilitate the transfer of certain "undesirables" to the United States and other countries. The Israelis did not want Vienna filled with Soviet Jewish émigrés refusing to go to Israel. It preferred them to be resettled elsewhere as soon as possible (Interview, Ralph Goldman, November 22, 1996 and Levanon 1995:440).[7]

Probably as part of Liaison Bureau efforts on behalf of Soviet Jewry, in January 1967, HIAS and other American Jewish leaders agreed to join a worldwide campaign to encourage the establishment of contact between Soviet Jews and their overseas relatives (Memo, Eliezer Shavit to Charles Jordan and Gaynor Jacobson, RE: "Decision in Mr. Pincus's office on January 26, 1967," February 9, 1967 JDC files). The parties would act quietly without press and publicity. No appeals would be made to governments for visas; only in concrete problem cases would governments be approached. Both HIAS and the Jewish Agency would provide technical assistance to families with relatives in the United States.

HIAS on its own may have been interested in helping Soviet Jews reach the United States. Almost from the day of Alexei Kosygin's announcement on permitting family reunification in December 1966, HIAS organized a campaign to have American Jews invite their Soviet relatives to join them in the United States. HIAS did not limit its efforts to "first degree" relatives.[8] Later, under pressure from the "Israelis" and in an agreement with the Jewish Agency, HIAS limited its efforts to "*real* family reunion cases of Russian Jews with their families in the United States." It also agreed to refrain from initiating "any large scale campaign for immigration of Soviet Jews to the United States" (Memo, Eliezer Shavit to Haber, May 9, 1972, JDC files).[9] At the time the Soviet Union allowed few Soviet Jews to leave on visas for the United States. Consequently, most Soviet Jews wanting to leave, regardless of their desired final destination, had to (and preferred) to leave on visas for Israel.

In January 1967 HIAS and JDC agreed to only accept and care for Soviet Jewish émigrés in Vienna that were transferred to them in writing by the Jewish Agency. Some Jews and most non-Jewish émigrés used the services of other agencies including World Council of Churches/Church World Service, International Rescue Committee (IRC), Tolstoy Foundation, International Catholic Migration Commission and the Rav Tov organization.[10] The Liaison Bureau viewed the Rav Tov as part of an effort by the Ultra Orthodox Jewish leaders to steer Soviet Jews, many of whom were intermarried, away from Israel. All of the agencies either helped émigrés apply for visas to the United States and other countries and/or provided them with care and maintenance (Fasick to Jacobson, October 15, 1976). As with HIAS and JDC, the United States government contracted with and reimbursed these agencies for services provided to refugees.

JDC provided care and maintenance and HIAS assisted in obtaining visas and coordinated resettlement in the United States and elsewhere. Both organizations, probably in consultation with American authorities and the Liaison Bureau, decided to move the Russian émigrés to Rome where they would apply for visas to the United States and other countries. The United States government covered the cost of the train supplied by the Austrian government to HIAS. The rate of dropouts determined the number of trains per week or month (Conversation with Carl Glick, September 22, 1999 and Memo, Ted Feder to Sam Haber, June 7, 1971).[11] The Israeli Consulate in Vienna provided émigrés with travel documents to continue on their way to countries other than Israel. HIAS, in cooperation with the American Embassy in Vienna, issued a "collective document valid for transit through Rome" for émigrés who lacked transit visas (Buwalda 1997:59,60).[12]

In Rome JDC provided rental housing mostly in Ostia and Ladispoli and a subsistence allowance. Later, schools and social activities were established. JDC involved the Jewish Agency and the Israel Community Center Association in educational and cultural activities in hopes of influencing the refugees to go to Israel. It used Chabbad Rabbis for teaching "Yiddishkeit" and had ORT teach English classes (Memo, Paul Bernick to Max Braude, May 7, 1976, JDC files, and Minutes, JDC Executive Committee Meeting, March 22, 1977, JDC files) HIAS helped émigrés obtain visas. It counseled applicants to emphasize anti-Semitism and persecution as reasons for leaving the Soviet Union (Berman 1991:43). In the words of one former head of the CJF and NCSJ "HIAS trying to get refugee status for unqualified people; they were teaching them to be qualified" (Shoshana Cardin, interview on September 3, 1995 and Berman 1993:43).

With the increase in Jews leaving the Soviet Union in the 1970s, the American Soviet Jewry advocacy movement sought United States governmental aid for refugee resettlement in Israel. In 1973, for example, the United States gave Israel $25 million to help resettle Soviet Jews because that "movement of Soviet Jews from Soviet Union is a matter of United States foreign policy and as such it deserves close support" (Shapiro 1984:74).[13] Through June 1977 the United States Government spent $155m on programs to resettle Soviet Jews with $122m being spent in Israel, $24m to resettle in other countries and $10m for transportation.[14] The United Israel Appeal (UIA), a voluntary tax-exempt agency, incorporated in the United States, administered the American governmental aid via its on site agent, the Jewish Agency. This allowed the Israeli government to direct the use of the funds through its control of the Jewish Agency.[15] As the rate of dropouts increased a larger percentage of the resettlement grant was used outside of Israel for care, maintenance and transportation of Soviet Jewish émigrés.[16]

When the number of Soviet Jews trying to come to the USA increased, HIAS, federations and others worked to facilitate their entry into the United States. They lobbied to have Soviet Jews admitted as refugees (conditional immigrants) or parolees (Goldberg 1996:183,184).[17] Until the Refugee Act of 1980 the United States definition of a refugee mostly involved persons fleeing Communist regimes, which was the case with Soviet Jewish émigrés.[18] The definition since 1980 stipulated that a refugee was any person who was outside his/her country "and who is unable or unwilling to return to . . . because of persecution, or a well-founded fear of persecution, on account of race, religion, nationality, membership of a particular social group, or political opinion" (Reimers 1985:191). Therefore, Soviet émigrés had to prove to an immigration officer in Rome that they had a well founded fear of persecution (Zolberg 1995:138 and Goldberg 1996:265). Most managed to do so until the late 1980s; United States policy was to accepted all Soviet Jews as refugees (Bayer 1991:140–141). Few were rejected. David Reimer (1985:240) writes that "whereas the main problem for German Jews in the 1930s was finding a home to escape Hitler, forty years later Russian Jews had little difficulty being admitted to the United States."

Another option involved Parole.[19] It allowed the Attorney General to permit the entry of political refugees without specific quotas provided a sponsoring agency took responsibility for the parolee (Windmuller 1999:164). It was less advantageous than refugee status because recipients and their sponsors received less resettlement aid and it was more difficult to obtain permanent residency and citizenship. Between 1972 and 1975 about 2,739 Soviet Jewish émigrés entered the United States under parole. Most Soviets involved in parole were processed in third countries.[20] In 1976 when the visa process backup in Rome stranded many Soviet émigrés Mr. Max Fisher, then chair of the CJF, intervened with the Republican administration which had Attorney General John Mitchell parole thousands of Soviet Jews to enter the United States (Memo, Gaynor Jacobson to Cooperating Agencies "Backlog of Soviet Jews in Rome," November 30, 1976 CJF files, box 710).[21] In August 1976, a HIAS staff person recommended that the Jewish community pressure officials in Washington, D.C. for direct parole, that is, that visas be issued in Moscow and not in "third countries" in order to save money (Memo, Ann Rabinowitz to Gaynor Jacobson, re: "Use of Parole . . ." August 6, 1976 HIAS files).

The Soviets, however, were unwilling. They severely limited direct visas to Soviet Jews wanting to join relatives in the United States. The Soviets preferred Third Country Processing (TCP) for family reunification cases to the West.[22] Eligible persons received Soviet passports to travel to the West based on a family reunion invitation. American consuls were very cooperative.[23] Interestingly, the Immigration and Naturalization Service (INS) found that only 5 percent of the 1,767 TCPs from the USSR in Rome in 1974–1975 had close enough relatives "to permit issuance of immigrant visas on the basis of relationship." Therefore, they authorized conditional entry (refugee) to the United States.[24] As noted, Soviet exit policy, therefore, influenced most Soviet Jews to apply for visas to Israel rather than to the United States. The odds of success were much greater.

With the increase in Soviet Jews coming to the United States, HIAS and CJF lobbied their government for financial assistance for resettlement. While Goldberg (1996:182) refers to this effort as being "audacious" Reimers (1985:65,158) documents the American tradition of aiding the resettlement of Hungarian, Cuban and Vietnamese refugees in the 1950s and 1960s. Moreover, at least since the Migration and Refugee Assistance Act of 1962, the United States provided aid for refugees outside the United States (Reimers 1985:158). Importantly, aid for Soviet Jewish refugees was "not a hard sell"

(Goldberg 1996:182). The American Congress had supported freedom for Soviet Jews. When domestic resettlement expenses increased after 1975 "to ease the burden, Talisman proposed getting the federal government to match the Jewish community's expenditures" (Goldberg 1996:182) (Goldberg 1996:182).[25] Mark Talisman, the CJF lobbyist, working with Stuart Eizenstat of the White House, initiated and drafted legislation and nursed it through Congress. Daniel Inouye of Hawaii sponsored the bill in the Senate.[26] Phil Bernstein (1983:75) suggests that the bulk of the cost of maintaining and transporting refugees was met by the United States government.

Behind closed doors in 1979 an interesting event occurred which presages later conflicts between advocates of Soviet Jewish refugees and other American refugee aid groups (see Chapter 8). At a meeting in his office with representatives of several refugee support organizations including HIAS, Senator Daniel Inouye expressed concern "about the difference in the treatment of refugees."[27] He asked why we should give $2,400 to help a Soviet Jew in Israel, $600 to assist a Cuban in the United States and only 50 cents per person to help a Vietnamese in Southeast Asia." Why, he asked, "should we give so much assistance to Soviet physicians but nothing to a Cambodian who may have a medical degree from Paris?" He felt that the Soviet Jews "were in competition with the Cambodian refugees for assistance." Later speaking of refugees, the Senator stated: "85 percent are Jews and represent a big cost. Many people automatically assume they are assisting Soviet Jews to go to Israel. The Americans are not aware that the bulk of these refugees are coming to the United States." He asked the HIAS representatives "when is your doomsday? When do you shut your doors? Someone from HIAS responded angrily that they would never shut the door on Jews (Notes by Carl Glick, Meeting in office of Senator Daniel Inouye, January 23, 1979, HIAS files).[28] Within a year or two, HIAS would agree to close the door on Russian Jews who had first settled in Israel. Within ten years when Gorbachev would open the gates of the Soviet Union and most Soviet Jews wanted to come to the United States, the American Jewish establishment would be willing to partially close the gates to Jewish refugees.

The federal block grant in the late 1970s which provided as much as $1,000 per person improved the resettlement situation (Bernstein 1983:80–82). Refugees and their sponsors became eligible for financial support for transportation, baggage, maintenance, visa processing fees, and resettlement in the United States. As we shall see below, the block grant was given to the CJF and not to HIAS to administer. CJF, in turn, provided HIAS and Jewish federation reimbursement of tens of millions of dollars for the care, maintenance and resettlement of Soviet Jews in the United States. Federations matched much of the aid from Washington.

Federal financial support for refugee assistance made HIAS and to a lesser extent JDC dependent on federal funding for their work with Soviet Jewish émigrés (Carl Glick, form letter to HIAS Board, April 22, 1977, HIAS files and Karl Zukerman [1990]).[29] While federal funds were a boon to both organizations, the federal government often left HIAS and JDC without federal reimbursement for long periods of time.[30]

The federal government reimbursed HIAS for the care and maintenance and resettlement of Soviet Jewish refugees as well as other Jewish and non-Jewish refugees.[31] HIAS also received considerable funding from the American Jewish community. For example, in 1976 HIAS spent $6.5m of which $1.1m came from the UJA-Federation of New York, $600,000 from UJA and approximately $2.5m from the United States government (Memo, Irving Kessler to UIA Board of Directors, re: "Agenda February 2, 1977," January 25, 1977, HIAS files). Because there was no formal allocation agreement with the UJA, the UIA and JDC had to approve the annual allocation for HIAS.[32] In the fall of 1974 UIA and JDC agreed to additional funding annually for HIAS during a period of increased Soviet Jewish immigration to the United States and other countries.[33]

Dependence on the UIA and JDC weakened HIAS and may have partially restrained its freedom to challenge Israeli policy on Soviet Jewish émigrés. Both organizations had close ties to Israel. The UIA professionals and executives sought to serve the interests of the government and people of Israel. While the JDC was more independent of Israel, the Israeli government and Liaison Bureau had considerable influence on JDC professionals and lay leaders. When the Israelis became upset because the additional funding for HIAS was deducted from UJA monies earmarked for Israel, the UIA announced that they were obligated to discuss with the Jewish Agency leadership any change in funding arrangements in the United States which may have reduced transmissions to Israel (Memo, Irving Kessler to UIA Board of Directors, March 21, 1977 and Letter, Irving Kessler to Leon Dulzin and Eliezer Shavit, March 11, 1977 HIAS files).

In contrast to HIAS, UJA allocated funds to the JDC according to a set formula. While this gave JDC greater financial stability and independence, it too suffered from dependence on federal funding. The United States government reimbursed over 90 percent of its JDC care and maintenance expenses in Europe. Fluctuating dropout figures and late federal reimbursements often caused budgetary nightmares. For example, when the dropout rate in Vienna jumped from 3 to 6 percent to over 20 percent in 1973 JDC almost doubled its budget for transmigrants from $1,170,000 to $2m (JDC Executive Report, September 4, 1974 JDC files).

CJF in coordination with HIAS set up an advisory committee on Soviet Jewish Resettlement—National Professional Planning Committee (NPPC). Jim Rice of the Chicago Federation served as the first chair. Participants included representatives of local federations, HIAS, Jewish Welfare Board, National Council of Jewish Women, UJA, National Association of Jewish Vocational Services, and Association of Jewish Family and Children Agencies (Meeting of CJF Advisory Committee on Soviet Jewish Resettlement, June 11, 1976, CJF files, Box 710 and Bernstein 1983:78). The body and its subcommittees facilitated regional allocation formulas for distributing immigrants throughout the United States. Where applicable, the NPPC strove to settle refugees near relatives. It sent about half to the New York City area to be resettled by the New York Association of New Americans (NYANA) and the rest to federations throughout the United States.[34] This may confirm the finding by Portes and Rumbaut (1996:33) that "the early locational patterns of political refugees and seekers of political asylum are often decided for them by government authorities and private resettlement agencies." Despite efforts to resettle them throughout the United States, however, the overwhelming majority resettled (or later moved) to New York City, Chicago, Boston and its North Shore, Miami, Los Angeles, and San Francisco.[35]

To meet the increase in Soviet refugees in 1976 which was expected to reach about 5,000, CJF and HIAS organized an emergency resettlement effort via NYANA and federations in 134 cities throughout the United States (Phil Bernstein and Gaynor Jacobson, CJF Council Paper to Federation and Executives and Family Service Agencies re: "Emergency Resettlement of Soviet Jews in Next Two Months," December 15, 1975, JDC files).[36] They decided that the federations would take primary responsibility for resettlement and asked them to accept the quota set down by HIAS and CJF which had increased by about 25 percent over 1975 (Bernstein 1983:79).

With the increase in Soviet Jewish émigrés arriving in the United States each year after 1975, the Jewish federations had a very difficult time funding the absorption of these destitute newcomers. By the summer of 1976, HIAS reported that six of the 12 communities with Jewish populations above 75,000 and several medium size Jewish communities, "restricted their acceptance of new refugees to those people who have first-degree relatives in that community." This created a problem for those persons not having first-degree relatives and for those with special vocational, psychiatric and medical needs. In addition, a problem of coordination between HIAS in Rome and the federations in the United States which reflected the unwillingness of federations to accept certain refugees delayed refugee departures from Rome (Memo, Gaynor Jacobson to Cooperating Agencies, August 31, 1976, JDC files).[37] This suggests that early on some federations and communities were having second thoughts about resettling Soviet Jews. It also indicated early grassroots dissent for support for freedom of choice.

In guidelines issued in May 1977, the NPPC tried to standardize services and limit aid by federations to assure conservation of funds, uniformity in equitable treatment and acceleration of immigrants' independence.[38] In September 1976 most federations gave refugees outright grants while the New York Association of New Americans gave loans (CJF, "Advisory Committee

on Soviet Jewish Resettlement," September 17, 1976, CJF files).[39] While the
NPCC may have striven for uniformity in resettlement policies, actual practices were far from uniform. Each federation set its own policies. Importantly, federal resettlement funds also stipulated that aid be given as a grant
and not as loans (Memo, Ralph Goldman to file, April 20, 1976, JDC files).[40]
HIAS monitored and supervised resettlement for six months and did post migration work to help legalize the immigration status of refugees.

SOVIET *YORDIM**

Prior to the major confrontation over dropouts between American Jewry and
the Israelis an altercation occurred involving several thousand Soviet Jews in
the 1970s who after having settled first in Israel wanted to immigrate to the
United States. The response of the leadership of both HIAS and JDC was far
from defense of the principle of freedom of choice.[41] Many had problems
leaving Israel because they owed authorities money for their transportation
and initial absorption. They also faced a complex and hostile Israeli bureaucracy which withheld cooperation and tried to prevent more from leaving.
One journalist suggested that the difficult plight they faced in Europe after
leaving Israel was intended to serve "as deterrent for all who want to leave Israel" (Luise Rinser, "Who leaves Israel is left (by Israel)," *Der Spiegel,* April 4,
1977; Carl Glick, hand notes, September 2, 1976, HIAS files). They also had to
pay an exit tax which would have been in violation of the original Jackson-
Vanik limit for nations seeking MFN from the United States (see chapter 2).

In August 1973 American Jewish leaders from HIAS and JDC met in
Jerusalem to discuss the subject of Russian immigrants leaving Israel with Is-
raeli officials from the Liaison Bureau and Jewish Agency. Aryeh Dulzin, then
treasurer of the Jewish Agency, explained that although they could not stop
Russian Jews from leaving they could limit the action by having American
Jewish organizations not provide them with aid and assistance. He noted that
Prime Minister Golda Meir was "au courant and endorsed this position"
(Meeting in Jewish Agency, Jerusalem, August 23, 1973, HIAS files).[42]

Aryeh Dulzin proposed a six-month trial period of no aid from international
Jewish organizations for Soviet Jewish émigrés leaving Israel. The proposal
would be reevaluated after three months. The group, including HIAS and JDC,
decided that as of September 9, 1973, those Russian immigrants leaving Israel
on Laissez Passers would be told that if they intended to use the document for
emigration and not as a transit visit "international Jewish organizations in Rome
were no longer assisting returnees from Israel." There would be no official an-

---

*Hebrew for Jews who emigrate from Israel.

nouncements; the policy would be spread by word of mouth among Soviet Jewish circles. Both the Israelis and HIAS supported this position. HIAS did not want to publicize that it would no longer be helping Israeli-Russian émigrés in Rome. Uzi Narkiss of the Jewish Agency commented that it is one thing to publicize a policy and another to have a document issued by Israeli authorities that would be seen as an obstacle "officially endorsed . . . being put into their way" ("Meeting in Jerusalem Office of Uzi Narkis," August 26, 1973; Letter of Carl Glick to Aryeh Dulzin, January 7, 1974).[43]

As a result of this agreement the IRC and not HIAS handled Russian émigrés in Rome who had left Israel. This troubled several HIAS leaders who feared that the IRC might appeal to Jewish federations to support their efforts to aid Soviet Jewish émigrés.[44] The number of Russian Jews leaving Israel did not decrease (Letter, Eliezer Shavit to Aryeh Dulzin, November 11, 1973). No review of the policy took place by the end of 1973 due to the Yom Kippur War of October 1973. By January 1974 HIAS distanced itself from the agreement and continued (resumed) to handle Soviet Jewish émigrés who had come from Israel (Letter, Carl Glick to Aryeh Dulzin, January 7, 1974, HIAS files).[45]

The issue resurfaced as more and more Soviet Jews left Israel and came to Rome and Vienna and sought the help of HIAS and JDC (and other organizations) to enter the United States as refugees. From 1974 to April 1976, 3,634 received United States funded assistance from voluntary agencies while awaiting resettlement in other countries (GAO 1976:49).[46] A problem facing many was their sojourn in Israel. If they had received Israeli citizenship or had been permanently resettled in Israel for more than a year they were ineligible to enter under conditional entry (refugees). However, a ruling by the INS's General Counsel Samuel Berenson of January 6, 1975, stated "in the absence of an overt act signifying acceptance of Israeli nationality, its involuntary acquisition neither precludes a Soviet Jew from conditional entry eligibility nor constitutes evidence in itself of firm resettlement. Further . . . admission into Israel as an immigrant upon the individual's application creates a presumption of firm resettlement, that the presumption is rebutable and that a conditional entry applicant who claims that he can prove that he has not firmly resettled should be given an opportunity to present his evidence." He concluded that the burden of proof lay with the Immigration and Naturalization Service to prove ineligibility (Letter, INS, United States Embassy Rome, to Evi Eiller, HIAS Rome, February 10, 1975, CJF files and JDC Executive Committee, April 3, 1974, JDC files).

Immigration and Naturalization Service and State Department policy on issuing visas to émigrés who had gone first to Israel wavered over the next year or two. The major problem group concerned those that had been in Israel longer than a year, possessed Israeli passports and had obtained Israeli citizenship.[47] In March 1976 Carl Glick referred to several thousand Soviet Jews (who had left Israel) in Europe who could not get visas nor be resettled in Europe. He urged them to return to Israel. Thousands of these persons held a strike in HIAS and JDC offices in Rome in July 1976. Eventually most found entry into the United States or permanent settlement in Europe (Letter, Carl Glick to Cong. Joshua Eilberg, March 9, 1976; Memo, Gaynor Jacobson to CJF Advisory Committee on Soviet Jewish Resettlement, CJF files, box 710; Telex, Ralph Goldman to Ted Feder [#1362], June 23, 1976, CJF files, Box 710).

THE DROPOUT CONTROVERSY

Even before the monthly figure rose above fifty percent in March 1976, the dropout situation alarmed the Israeli government and Jewish Agency (Letter, Akiva Kohane to Ralph Goldman, March 15, 1976). Their concern focused on support given dropouts by HIAS and JDC in Europe and by Jewish federations in the United States. As early as 1976 the Jewish Agency and the Israeli government pressured HIAS and JDC to limit their efforts on behalf of those Soviet Jews who chose not to go to Israel. For example, Nehemiah Levanon of the Liaison Bureau told the JDC Executive Committee that both American and Jewish organizations should tell Soviet Jews that if they dropout and they would not get aid. JDC President (elect) Don Robinson told him that was a threat. Levanon replied that he did not mean it that way because he lacked the courage to say so (Ralph Goldman notes, JDC Executive Committee Meeting, April 19, 1976, JDC files).

In the confrontation over dropouts all parties assumed that most Soviet Jewish émigrés would prefer to settle in Israel. Understated was a position articulated later by Gitelman (1989, 1997), Salitan (1992:7) and others that most émigrés after 1973 preferred the United States with its perceived greater economic opportunities. Gitelman (1989) suggests that those Soviet Jews with stronger Jewish identities from the Baltics, Moldavia and Georgia went to Israel while most assimilated Jews from the heartland preferred the West.[48] Most Soviet Jewish Zionists who only wanted to immigrate to Israel had done so by 1973.[49] The overwhelming majority leaving after 1973 were motivated more by economic betterment than by Zionist ideology. Many saw Israel as a very small market with fewer opportunities (Harris interview August 8, 2002).

Interestingly, writing years later (1999:82) Nehemia Levanon admitted that it was hard to sell Israel because most Soviet Jews saw the United States as paradise and Israel as a poor, hard country with serious military problems. "We could not reach the Jewish masses. With all our efforts, including those of American Jews, we reached very few Jews out of the millions of Soviet Jews. The mass of Jews were very different from the Refuseniks and activists with whom Jews from the West met."

In the debate over the dropout phenomenon the Israelis presented many arguments both explaining and condemning it. Some were pragmatic but many ideological. On the other side many American Jews also explained and justified the dropout issue. Eventually, freedom of choice became an ideological justification for American Jewish support of dropouts.

The Israelis initially blamed HIAS and JDC for "stealing" Soviet Jews by directing them to the United States. According to Dominitz (1996:121) Israeli public opinion believed that HIAS is "agitating for emigration to countries other than Israel and actually 'kidnapping' Jews to North America."[50] HIAS always denied these charges (Dominitz, interview, July 3, 2001).[51] Many Israeli officials assumed these agencies wanted more clients and that the federations wanted more Jews. While Nehemia Levanon, Yehuda Dominitz and other Israelis blamed only HIAS and not JDC for recruiting Russian émigrés, the Israeli press and Knesset often did not make a distinction. Levanon (1995:441,442) saw JDC and Ralph Goldman as allies and partners on the dropout issue despite JDC support for dropouts. Levanon claimed that JDC lacked the power to overcome CJF and HIAS on this issue.

The Israelis argued that without requests by American Jews to admit more Soviet Jews and assistance from American Jewish organizations in Europe and the United States fewer persons would have dropped out (Frankel 1989:23).[52] Not mentioned had been the fact that originally the Israelis had approached HIAS and JDC to help care for the dropouts and to facilitate their migration to some other country.[53]

Leading the attack against American Jewish support for dropouts, often on an ideological level, were several Israeli Prime Ministers including Golda Meir, Yitzhak Rabin (during his first term) and Yitzhak Shamir in the late 1980s (Ralph Goldman, "Records of meeting with Nehemia Levanon, July 4, 1976). While committed to the principle of settling Soviet Jews in Israel, Prime Minister Menachem Begin exhibited greater flexibility; he often placed matters of family reunification above the interest of homeland. Nevertheless, after expressing their positions, most Israeli politicians exercised restraint. They needed the support of American Jewish leaders for other areas including U.S.-Israel relations, United States government aid and peace in the Middle East. Through the early 1980s, Jewish Agency Treasurer and later Chairman of the Executive Aryeh Dulzin, became the Israeli hard liner. He vigorously chastised American Jewish leaders and organizations. He publicly attacked them and engaged them in debate. In sharp contrast to the late 1960s, by 1975–1976, Israeli politicians could no longer tell American Jews what to do.

In defense of aiding dropouts HIAS emphasized that should it cease its activities without dropouts that other voluntary organizations, eligible for federal government reimbursements, would assist them to enter and resettle in the United States. Moreover, HIAS argued that Soviet Jewish émigrés being aided by non-Jewish and anti-Zionist organizations would bring shame upon the American Jewish community. Gaynor Jacobson, the director of HIAS told

Yehoshua Pratt (1989:44) that if we (HIAS) bring them to the United States they will remain Jews, but if the Tolstoy Foundation does, we will lose them.

A second set of explanations for the dropout phenomenon concerned conditions in Israel versus those in the United States. There existed excellent communication by telephone and mail between Soviet Jews resettled in Israel and the United States and their relatives and friends in the Soviet Union. While reports from Israel focused on problems those from America were much more promising.[54] Soviet émigrés in Israel wrote about inadequate housing, few job opportunities for professionals, bureaucratic red tape characterized by conflicts between the government and the Jewish Agency, terrorism, military conscription and negative public attitudes toward Russian immigrants (Memo, Irving Kessler (UIA), December 10, 1976, CJF files, and Gitelman [1989:163–166]).[55] Many émigrés after 1973 who were motivated to improve their economic well-being felt Israel was too small for them; many believed that the United States would enable them to continue their careers in arts and academia (Kohane, "Memo on Soviet Jewish Transmigrants," April 13, 1977, JDC files). Israel's security situation meant that all men and women did compulsory military service at age 18 and most male immigrants up to age of 40 had to do some military service. In David Harris's words (Interview, August 8, 2002) "Israel was a hard sell."

Many blamed the Jewish Agency and the Israeli government for poor, disorganized and insufficient immigrant absorption polices. It began with unqualified, poorly trained, ill prepared and often too few emissaries in Rome and Vienna.[56] Ironically, in 1975 the Agency's absorption budget was cut from $133m to $90m "creating the hardships of denial of some services and lengthened waiting periods."[57]

Finally, some argued that Soviet Jews had no real information about Israel which prevented them from making a rational choice as to where to go. Soviet Jews knew little about Israel and what they knew was negative. The Soviet press was very anti-Israel, always playing up the failures and problems (Interview with David Harris, August 8, 2002). Also, after 1972 the Soviets jammed the Voice of Israel.[58]

Other explanations focused on conditions in Vienna. Some argued that dropouts had preferential treatment in comparison to those going to Israel. After 1973, the latter would be taken to a "refugee center" and fly out to Israel the next day. In contrast dropouts often remained in apartments or hotels until transferred to Rome where they received housing and support and assistance in obtaining refugee status to the United States and elsewhere. After arriving in the country of their choice they could still declare willingness to go to Israel (Ralph Goldman at JDC Executive Committee Meeting, April 29, 1976; letter, Paula Temza to Yehuda Dominitz, May 10, 1976; Don Robinson at JDC Executive Committee Meeting, May 27, 1976, JDC files).

Another factor involved mixed married couples who preferred the West due to fears of the rabbinical establishment in Israel (Ralph Goldman notes, April 19, 1976, JDC files).[59] Intermarriage among Soviet Jewish émigrés in the 1970s ranged from 15 to 30 percent. In addition, the Soviet Government exiled non-Jews via visas for Israel. For example, not wanting to set a precedent for Slavs, the KGB solution was to have Pentecostal Christians apply and leave on visas to Israel (Schifter 1999:156).[60] Also, some non-Jews married Jews in order to leave the Soviet Union (Clara Falcone, "Inquiry on the Jews Staying in Rome," *Il Tempo*, February 13, 1975). Other non-Jews had bribed the KGB to get out (Yehoshua Pratt, 1989).[61] These latter groups had no desire to go on to Israel. Before 1973 JDC and the "Israelis" conducted "short conversions" for non-Jewish spouses in Vienna in the interest of facilitating acceptance in Israel. The practice stopped when the Lubavitcher Rabbi of Brooklyn objected (Herzberg 2002).[62]

The Israelis and their supporters argued that Israel needed these immigrants for its survival; the large number of Soviet Jews would help in the demographic struggle between a declining Jewish majority and very fertile Arab minority.[63] They emphasized that these immigrants were highly educated and had skills in medicine, technology and many other areas. They could make an important contribution to Israel's economic development. "We need the rich human resources which only Russian Jews can give us" (Decter: 1990:36). Israelis also emphasized that in the past the country had absorbed many poor and uneducated Jews from Arab lands.

Unstated most of the time was the fact that most Soviet Jews (it was assumed) were Ashkenazim (European), a declining minority amongst Israeli Jews. An Ashkenazi establishment had ruled and dominated Israel since its founding. A large Soviet Jewish influx would reestablish the Ashkenazi majority.[64] Over the years several government, Jewish Agency and American Jewish leaders made mention of this. Gitelman (1972:32) refers to tensions in Israel between Russian immigrants and Oriental Jews, some of whom saw the Ashkenazi establishment wanting to maintain power by encouraging Soviet immigration to whom they gave benefits. He blamed Golda Meir and the Israeli media for "having extravagantly dramatized the Soviet immigration in the first months of its appearance" and implied that the generous benefits for the Russians angered poor Oriental Jews. Later these benefits were "regulated" (1972:40,41).[65]

While many American Jewish leaders sided with the Israelis on the issue of need, a few did not. Jim Rice, Executive Director of the Chicago Federation and former head of HIAS represented a position supported, often not publicly, by some Jewish professionals and lay leaders.[66] He is probably as much as Carl Glick the ideologue behind the "freedom of choice" position among American Jewish leaders.[67] He conceded that Israelis could make a case for receiving educated Soviet Jews because they previously absorbed

Holocaust survivors and "illiterate and disease ridden people from the Mellahs and primitive villages and caves of North Africa." American Jewry, however, he argued, had a similar case for demanding a maximum number of Soviet Jews because anti-Semitism and restrictive immigration policies had kept out Jewish immigrants until the present (Comments of Jim Rice at Union of American Hebrew Congregations Board of Trustees, Los Angeles, December 4, 1976).[68]

In addition, the Israelis and many of their supporters emphasized the issue of Jewish identity and continuity. Both Israelis and leaders of the Soviet Jewry advocacy movement in the United States agreed that the Soviet Jews were being rescued in part to rejoin the Jewish world. They thought that Israel offered the best opportunity for their re-immersion into Jewish culture and a Jewish way of life (Gitelman 1989:180–182 and Levanon 1999:82). They assumed that many going elsewhere and especially to the United States would assimilate and be lost to the Jewish people. Moshe Decter (1990:36,37) argued that those in Israel want to save them "Jewishly . . . they wanted Aliyah both for the sake of Soviet Jews and for the sake of Israel." Those leaving had a moral obligation to try it. "They have a historic obligation to Jewish history and to the Jewish people, whose struggle on their behalf was a Jewish struggle, not a humanitarian struggle, and it was a Jewish struggle with Jewish dimensions significantly delineated from Israel and by Israelis." Activist Rabbi Avi Weiss asserted that since were being lost our Jews to American culture, to bring Soviet Jews here was to lose them en masse to assimilation. The apparent early trend of many Soviet Jews not to affiliate with the organized American Jewish community strengthened this argument. Rice and others disagreed.[69]

The Liaison Bureau also charged that the dropouts undermined the long struggle of Soviet Jews for national rights. It claimed the right to emigration and the Soviet willingness to allow Jews to leave was based on family reunification in the national Jewish homeland (Israel).[70] In going to the United States, the arch-capitalist enemy of the Soviet system, the dropouts negated the justification for their special status (Jerry Goodman, "FYI "Soviet Jewish Emigration: Questions and Answers," November 24, 1976, CJF files).[71] Moreover, since the Soviets limited the number allowed to leave each month, those going West were taking the few places that could be used by the Zionists and Jews in the Soviet Union who desired to go to Israel.[72] Related to this issue were a set of arguments concerning the ethical issue of leaving the Soviet Union on Israeli visas and then dropping out. Some considered this dishonest and an insult to Israeli sovereignty.[73] Israel charged that the Soviets might use this deception as an excuse to close the gates (Maass 1989 and telex, Len Seidenman to Gaynor Jacobson, April 20, 1976, HIAS files).[74]

Several American Jewish leaders disagreed. They justified the deceptive use of Israeli visas by dropouts since an Israeli visa was the only way for a Jew to leave the Soviet Union. Some Israelis including Liaison Bureau personnel understood this (Dominitz, interview, July 3, 2001). Many American Jews argued that the highest priority was to get a maximum number of Jews out of the Soviet Union which justified the "misuse" of Israeli visas (Telephone interview with Leonard Fein, June 12, 2003). Others ridiculed Israeli concern over deception in the use of its visas saying that we had falsified documents for hundreds of years to save Jews.[75] They also had doubts about the misuse of visas causing the Soviet Union to close its gates. They suggested that Soviet authorities may have manipulated exits to insure a high dropout rate in order to show Arab allies that Soviet Jews were not going to Israel.[76]

FREEDOM OF CHOICE

Many American advocates for Soviet Jewry favored the principle of Soviet Jews going to Israel. Once they realized that many Soviet Jews preferred not to do so, then they favored freedom of choice (Shiran interview, February 28, 2003). According to Abe Foxman (1989), the *aliyah* movement, which called for repatriation to the homeland, was based on the Refuseniks and Prisoners of Zion. It disappeared with the appearance of dropouts. Whereas on most issues involving Israel, American Jews felt inferior to Israelis whose children served in the army, this was not the case with the dropout issue. "There was a strong gut reaction against it" (Comments by Rabbi Wolf Kelman as reported by Malka Rabinowitz in the *JP*, January 1977, HIAS files).

Underpinning freedom of choice was the collective memory of the American Jewish experience during and after the Holocaust. They recalled their helplessness when the American government kept shut the gates of the United States to Jewish refugees trying to flee Hitler's Third Reich. Jim Rice (letter to Leon Jick, June 1, 1976, JDC files) asked: "Shall American Jewish organizations put themselves in the position of going to our government to say: "We want this door closed to Jews?"

Freedom of choice found support in traditional American liberal and civil libertarian positions which held that you cannot force people to go anywhere they do not want to go. "They want to come to the United States? It's too bad, we don't like it, but it's their basic right to make the choice" (Decter 1990:34).

The position also had roots in the Jewish tradition of rescuing those in danger (*Pidyon Shvuim*). The Soviet Union was, is or could be a place of danger and even death for Soviet Jews. To restrict emigration only to Israel might result in many not leaving (Letter, Frank Reiss to Len Seidenman and Irving Haber, August 30, 1976, JDC files and Minutes, Executive Committee JDC, February 22, 1977, JDC files). Who could predict what the future would bring for them in the USSR? Nehemia Levanon (1989:68) would argue that he always believed that the Soviet Union was not Nazi Germany; there was no physical threat at present. The future, however, could be different. Failure to aid would be abandonment of "traditional Jewish humanitarian principal of helping rescue oppressed Jews" (Comments of Morris Fine, American Jewish Committee, at National Executive Council Meeting on December 5, 1976, December 6, 1976, CJF files).[77]

Finally, many American Jews were self-conscious about forcing others to go to Israel while they lived in the United States. This bothered many Jews who were Zionists and strong supporters of Israel. Many retell the account of an American Zionist who encouraged a Soviet émigré in Ladispoli to go to Israel; the émigré retorted "*und Du?*" (and you?).

Frank Lautenberg, President of UJA at the time, opposed freedom of choice. In contrast to the 1930s, he argued, Israel existed and the Soviet Union of the 1970s was not the Germany of the 1930s. To be sent to Israel (which you could leave) was not to be sent to Auschwitz (JDC, Summary of Executive, November 16, 1976, JDC files). Other Israeli and American Jewish opponents often responded that since the establishment of the State of Israel that it was not the responsibility of the Jewish people to help Jews move from one Diaspora community to another (Goldman 1995:22).[78]

THE COMMITTEE OF EIGHT

In the winter and spring of 1976 when the monthly dropout figure approached 50 percent Israeli and American Jewish leaders became alarmed. JDC implemented policies in Vienna designed to reduce dropouts. It ceased employing dropouts (and urged HIAS to do the same), recommended that potential dropouts be housed separately from confirmed dropouts, urged moving all dropouts out of the city within 72 hours, and pressured the Israelis to work harder on influencing potential dropouts to go to Israel (Ralph Goldman, Notes for Executive Committee Meeting, JDC, June, 30, 1976 [typed]).[79]

Rumors floated about an Israeli plan to close HIAS and JDC operations in Rome, to move émigrés to an obscure place and to keep them in camps and not apartments or hotels.[80] Meetings between officials of the Liaison Bureau, HIAS, CJF, JDC, UJA and UIA in April 1976 failed to reach a consensus on what to do (Draft memo, Carl Glick to HIAS Board of Directors, December 7, 1976, CJF files). In a revealing memo a JDC official reported that he had met with senior leaders of the Liaison Bureau who offered no practical solution to the dropout problem (Memo, Akiva Kohane to Ralph Goldman, May 6, 1976, JDC files). Frustration prevailed in many quarters.

In June 1976, the Jewish Agency began to refuse to transfer to HIAS/JDC Soviet émigrés with relatives in Israel and none in the West. It had previously refrained from implementing this policy (Memo, Akiva Kohane to Ralph Goldman, June 15, 1976). Under the earlier Pincus agreement HIAS/JDC only accepted and aided dropouts referred to them in writing by the Jewish Agency (Memo, Ellen Lewis to Ralph Goldman, "Requests for Actions made, October 9, 1980, JDC files).[81] A senior JDC official argued that if the Agency had instituted this policy from the start then there might not have been a dropout problem (Memo, Akiva Kohane to Ralph Goldman, June 18, June 1976 and Ralph Goldman, hand notes of JDC meeting, April 19, 1976, JDC files).

Each year in June many American Jewish lay leaders and senior professionals attend the Jewish Agency Board of Governors meetings in Israel. This allowed for an exchange of ideas with Israeli governmental leaders including the Prime Minister, whose party controlled the Executive of the Jewish Agency. At the June 1976 meetings the Jewish Agency placed the issue of dropouts on its agenda. The discussions were held within the context of the Coordinating Committee for Immigration and Absorption, a joint Israeli government–Jewish Agency body established in 1954 (Dominitz 1996 and Stock 1988:72,73).[82]

An opening meeting on July 15, 1976 of the Coordinating Committee brought together a larger group of Israeli and American Jewish leaders. Participants included Max Fisher, Chairman of Board of Governors, Mel Dubinsky, Irving Kessler (Executive Director of UIA), Frank Lautenberg (UJA lay person), Irving Bernstein (Executive Director of UJA), Phil Bernstein (Executive Director of CJF), Jerold Hoffberger (CJF lay person), Jack Weiler (JDC Board member), Don Robinson (President, JDC), Ralph Goldman (Executive Director of JDC), Carl Glick (President, HIAS), Gaynor Jacobson (Executive Director HIAS), Charlotte Jacobson (WZO), and Ray Epstein.[83] On the Israeli side were Prime Minister Yitzhak Rabin, Deputy Prime Minister and Foreign Minister Yigal Alon, Ministers Shlomo Rosen and Gideon Hausner, Yosef Almogi (Chairman of Executive of Jewish Agency), Nehemiah Levanon, Zvi Netzer and Shaike Dan of Liaison Bureau, Moshe Rivlin, Yehuda Dominitz (Jewish Agency) and Yehuda Avner (adviser to the Prime Minister).[84]

Fisher presented a previously prepared American position which recommended that émigrés who exited the USSR on Israel visas and dropped out should not be aided (Max Fisher, "Problem of Soviet Jews Emigrating with Israeli Visas" [draft], July 11, 1976 and Summary of meeting of American Jewish organization leaders, July 1976, JDC files). This policy would go into effect once Soviet Jews had sufficient time to learn about the details. Those not wanting to go to Israel would have to apply in the Soviet Union for visas to other countries on the basis of family reunification. American Jewish organizations would pressure their government for visas for family reunification and provide aid to the refugees coming to the United States. They would discourage non-Jewish American refugee support organizations from helping dropouts. They would also find permanent resettlement as soon as possible for dropouts presently in Rome. Fisher wanted secret deliberations by a committee of eight persons to work out the details for a unified Israeli-American Jewish policy.[85] Fisher proposed giving the Committee of Eight 90 days to prepare a detailed operational proposal.

Clearly, Fisher proposed that American Jewry cease aid to the dropouts. This may suggest his close collaboration with either or both the Liaison Bureau and Ralph Goldman of the JDC.[86] He did not mention freedom of choice. Nevertheless, he did suggest that those who applied for visas in the Soviet Union for the United States and elsewhere on the basis of family re-unification would be aided by American Jewry upon arrival in the United States. After reading reports in the press, Jim Rice, the executive director of the Jewish Federation of Metropolitan Chicago, wrote Phil Bernstein of CJF (July 23, 1976) suggesting a strong response to the reports that leave "a clear and incorrect impression that various American organizations are accepting the point of view that there should be active discouragement of Soviet Jewish immigration to the United States."

In the discussion that followed participants accepted most of the American ideas. On one issue, however, the Israeli position won out. Both sides agreed that American Jews should not embark on a *campaign* to get visas for those not wanting to go to Israel (Notes of secret meeting on *Noshrim*, July 15, 1976, JDC files). Prime Minister Yitzhak Rabin reiterated that: "we succeeded in opening Russian gates on the assumption that the Jews are leaving for Israel and Israel only. . . . Had we departed from that, we would never have obtained the Soviet consent to Jewish emigration." He argued that dropouts in Vienna jeopardized the entire emigration effort. Therefore there was a need for a unified Israeli and Jewish Agency policy supported by world Jewry (Hand notes of Ralph Goldman, JDC files). Deputy Prime Minister Yigal Alon supported this position yet he added that an important goal was to get the maximum number of Jews out of the Soviet Union. If Soviet Jews want to change their destination Alon proposed they do so in Israel. In sharp contrast Dulzin argued that the "first duty is not to save Jews, we must save only those who will go to Israel" (Hand notes of Carl Glick at this meeting or a possible continuation of the meeting, HIAS files).[87] Dulzin reiterated that in principle the Jewish Agency would care for Jews leaving the Soviet Union in Vienna; those dropping out would receive no aid from HIAS. Fisher responded that this decision should be left to the Committee of Eight (notes of Carl Glick). When Jerold Hoffberger commented that a Russian Jew should have the opportunity to come or not to come to Israel Yitzhak Rabin retorted that Israeli visas would be used only to go to Israel. He did not however want to punish dropouts. He stated that they would not use force against those who asked not to come.

Prime Minister Yitzhak Rabin appointed a committee of eight professionals to develop within 90 days recommendations for the joint government

Jewish Agency Coordinating Committee. Nehemiah Levanon of the Liaison Bureau and Ralph Goldman of JDC co-chaired. Other members included Yehuda Avner (Office of Prime Minister) Uzi Narkiss (Jewish Agency), Zeev Szek (Foreign Office and former Ambassador to Austria), Phil Bernstein (CJF), Gaynor Jacobson (HIAS) and Irving Kessler (UIA).[88] HIAS, JDC and CJF were to be party to an eventual agreement. The need for consensus gave each organization a potential veto over the proposals. The committee planned to meet in Geneva from August 12 to 15. Until such time as a new policy would be announced, Max Fisher, Chairman of the Board of Governors and/or Joseph Almogi, Chairman of the Executive, would handle all inquiries.[89]

In the Geneva meetings from August 12–14, the members of the Committee of Eight first examined the situation in the Soviet Union. They discussed how to handle non-Israel bound requests, contacting potential immigrants, the Dutch Embassy, Soviet government reaction to the new policy and the possibility of direct flights to Israel (Hand notes of Ralph Goldman, in CJF files and typed notes "Committee of Eight" meeting August 12, 13, and 14, 1976 JDC files).[90] Next they dealt with matters concerning *Vienna* including the potential response of Austrian authorities to the proposed policies of not providing Jewish communal aid for dropouts and withholding documents of the émigrés (Notes of secret meeting . . . July 15, 1976, JDC files and *Baltimore Sun*, August 18, 1976).[91] They considered having Austrian authorities relocate all dropouts in a refugee camp where Jewish Agency staff of the highest quality would try to persuade them to go to Israel. They discussed reducing the staffs of JDC and HIAS and expanding the number of Jewish Agency personnel in Vienna. They wanted to prevent dropouts from going to non-Jewish organizations who were eligible to be reimbursed by the United States government. Specifically, they discussed having Max Fisher get Washington to stop reimbursing the International Rescue Committee so that it could not assist Jews from the Soviet Union to resettle in the United States (Notes on Geneva of Ralph Goldman, CJF files).

Nehemia Levanon proposed moving HIAS activities and third country processing of Soviet émigrés (TCPs) from Rome to Athens or elsewhere (Irving Kessler, Note to file, June 29, 1976, JDC files).[92] They discussed clearing all dropouts out of Rome as fast as possible under the present policy. This required pressure we put on the United States government to admit more refugees from Rome. They also wanted to expand Jewish content in educational activities for émigrés waiting in Rome.

Conditions of absorption in *Israel* were also a central subject. Nehemia Levanon hoped for tangible improvements within limits. They called for improved coordination at the airport between the Jewish Agency and the Ministry of Absorption. They recommended that the Jewish Agency reform its loan policy by making transportation to Israel and support for the first six months a grant.[93]

In a discussion on reporting their findings, participants proposed that the boards of JDC, HIAS, CJF, UJA and UIA be convened as soon as possible. Phil Bernstein suggested that he *telephone* each organization and explain the proposed plans. Also, they intended dealing with the American government at the highest level concerning the new policy; this probably meant having Max Fisher contact President Gerald Ford with whom he had personal ties.[94] They wanted the American government to influence the Soviet Union to allow direct immigration of Soviet Jews to the United States; cease reimbursement of non-Jewish organizations aiding dropouts; issue necessary visas; find sites other than Rome for third country processing (TCP); and provide funds for direct flights from the Soviet Union to the United States. Finally they discussed resettlement in the United States. HIAS, JDC and UIA would try to minimize the role of non-Jewish refugee agencies with dropouts. They would also try to make NYANA's resettlement practices standard for the entire country and on a par with support and benefits provided Russian immigrants in Israel.

Gaynor Jacobson absented himself from the session in which the participants worked on the final draft. One participant claims that this was intentional as Jacobson doubted that HIAS lay leaders would support the proposed document.[95]

The Committee of Eight proposed that HIAS and JDC cease to aid dropouts in Vienna (Letter, Nehemia Levanon to Ralph Goldman with "Draft Agreement," August 30, 1976; Document received by Ralph Goldman from Nehemia Levanon, n.d.; Letter, Ralph Goldman to Phil Bernstein, Gaynor Jacobson and Irving Kessler, "The implications of the drop-out problem for the future of Soviet Jewish emigration" September 7, 1976, CJF files).[96] On February 1, 1977 Soviet Jews would be informed of the following changes. Once in possession of a *vysov* from a relative in Israel, Soviet Jews wanting to go to Israel would go to the Dutch Embassy in Moscow to obtain a visa. They would then leave for Vienna where they would be met by representatives of the Jewish Agency who would aid them to continue on to Israel.

Soviet Jews wanting to resettle outside of Israel would have to apply in Moscow for visas to those countries. This would require a *vysov* from relatives in those countries and approval by Soviet authorities. In effect Soviet Jews would have freedom of choice within the Soviet Union. This required the cooperation of the Soviet Union. HIAS and JDC would provide assistance and maintenance and then help with resettlement for those arriving in Vienna with a visa for another country in which they had relatives. Jews who came out on Israeli visas but changed their mind would receive no assistance. Levanon later indicated that he expected that the local Viennese Jewish community might provide short term assistance to the dropouts (Document, n.d., JDC files). The Committee of Eight expected that the new policy would end the dropout phenomenon. The Committee hoped to make an announcement between September 5–10, 1976 and the new policy would go into effect three months thereafter.

Several problems were evident to the Committee members. First, it was unclear whether the Soviets would permit Jews to leave for family reunification in countries other than Israel. At the time it allowed a minimum of its Jewish citizens to leave on visas to the United States. Second, Israel's absence of diplomatic relations and direct flights with the Soviet Union required the use of Austria as a transit site. Here the Israelis would have to abide by Austrian law and the policies of Chancellor Bruno Kreisky. Until now he had insisted that Israeli authorities guarantee émigrés entering Austria freedom to choose where they wanted to go.

On August 26, 1976, Gaynor Jacobson sent a confidential memo to Ralph Goldman stating, "I personally, nor do I feel my organization, could accept" some of the positions of the summary of the Committee of Eight (JDC files). Many of Jacobson's reservations were technical. For example, he was bothered that the document did not include references to the danger of the Rav Tov and other non-Jewish refugee aid organizations replacing HIAS and JDC. He doubted the ability of Jewish and non-Jewish organizations "to persuade the United States Government to adjust its financial assistance to the concept underlying this new policy," that is, not to reimburse other organizations handling the resettlement of Soviet Jews. Most importantly, he did not believe that financial assistance from the United States government should be denied to stateless Jews even if they had end visas while they were in asylum countries. He felt that this could also be financially damaging to efforts by HIAS, JDC and the Jewish Agency to conduct programs in asylum countries. He also opposed closing down Rome. In response, Ralph Goldman altered many of the proposals to meet Jacobson's technical objections.[97] HIAS and JDC personnel met with government officials in Washington, D.C. They had the impression that the government would not change its visa policies due to the upcoming elections (Memo, Irving Kessler to Max Fisher, September 28, 1976).[98]

Representatives of the organizations of the Committee of Eight met with Max Fisher in Israel in early September (about the 12th), 1976. They made no decisions (Carl Glick hand notes, non-*Noshrim* box #6, HIAS files).[99] According to Carl Glick, Ralph Goldman reported that the Austrians had accepted the program in principle.[100] Nehemia Levanon announced that Prime Minister Yitzhak Rabin had intervened to provide more housing and jobs for potential immigrants. Finally, Max Fisher announced that he had yet to obtain American agreement on visas. He wanted to first clear out the refugees already in Rome. Phil Bernstein (CJF) and Irving Bernstein (UJA) emphasized that Israel should not hinder anyone from leaving by denying an Israeli exit visa. A sharp exchange occurred between Max Fisher and Carl Glick of HIAS.[101] Fisher charged HIAS with trying to sabotage the Committee of Eight.

Gaynor Jacobson in turn argued that the Israelis had already instituted new policies restricting freedom of choice for those leaving the Soviet Union. Yitzhak Rager denied this. He claimed a decrease in exits reflected Soviet policy.

Max Fisher remained firm in his desire for consensus and a united stand on actions in the United States.[102] Yitzhak Rager requested a meeting very soon but Max Fisher suggested that the contacts in Washington, D.C. would take about a month. He called the next meeting for this group on or about October 12, 1976. Finally they decided to tell certain key federations including Chicago to hold up on decisions until the Committee of Eight finished its work.

The proposal of the Committee of Eight reached the various organizations in September, 1976, and rumors of the cutting of aid to dropouts followed (Memo, Leonard Seidenman to Gaynor Jacobson, September 22, 1976, JDC files and *JP*, September 22, 1976).[103] In mid-September, CJF President Jerold Hoffberger announced that no action had yet been taken by Max Fisher and the Committee of Eight (Notes for J Hoffberger at Board of Directors of CJF, September 18, 19, 1976, CJF files, box 697). He emphasized that the high drop out rate could result in "drastic action by the Soviet Union to cut back emigration."[104]

At the time some of the American participants on the Committee of Eight retreated. At a JDC Executive Committee Meeting on September 21, Ralph Goldman reported that the Committee of Eight had been guided by the following principles: to maintain freedom of choice for all perspective immigrants; to assist every Jew who needs help to leave the country of emigration and go to the country for which he has a visa; and to bring out the maximum number of emigrants from the Soviet Union. Goldman hinted at problems with the Dutch, Austrians and Italians. He indicated that Max Fisher was optimistic about getting additional entries for Soviet Jews wishing to emigrate directly to the United States.[105] At the same meeting Phil Bernstein emphasized that it was important to help every Jew in the USSR: "nobody wants it on his conscience that Jews who otherwise could have gotten out were kept behind because of his failure to help." He felt Israelis wanted to help "anyone get out of the Soviet Union. Nor do they want to limit the freedom of choice of every Jews to go where he wants to go" (Ralph Goldman report, JDC Executive Committee, September 21, 1976).

Expressing a HIAS position at the time, Gaynor Jacobson argued that the Committee of Eight wanted to guarantee maximum Soviet Jewish emigration regardless of destination. The question was whether they should exercise freedom of choice in the USSR or in Vienna ("Soviet Emigrants who dropout to U.S. stir dispute in Israel," *Washington Post*, September 26, 1976).

Public discussion about the Committee of Eight focused on the issue of whether or not to cut aid to dropouts. It also involved Soviet Jews in the

USSR and in Israel. There existed no consensus. While much of the response of Soviet Jews was spontaneous and reflected their own perceptions of the situation, each side in the freedom of choice debate encouraged their "Soviet Jews" to speak out. For example, former Prisoners of Zion Mark Dymshiits and Josif Mendelovitch strongly opposed aiding dropouts in Vienna (*JP*, September 22, 1976).[106] Sylva Zalmanson and Dr. Mark Gelfand warned if Israel became the only option fewer would leave (Letter from Rechovot [Sylvia Zalmanson et al. to American Jewish community], November 1, 1976, HIAS files).[107] In the blunt "Lunz" letter, 11 recent Soviet immigrants to Israel charged that cutting aid would abet the KGB efforts to reduce Jewish emigration.[108] In contrast, a group in the Soviet Union argued that those dropping out should not be aided with Jewish communal funds. They had a right to drop out but on their own. They warned that dropouts could end emigration (Letter from Soviet Jews received by phone by V. Lazaaris et al. from Tallinn, Leningrad, Riga, Vilna and Kiev addressed to Nahum Goldmann et. al., September 22, 1976, JDC files).[109] In a visit to Chicago sponsored by NCSJ, Dr. Vitaly Rubin, a noted Soviet professor who had immigrated to Israel told the Chicago Jewish Federation that "to withhold the means of saving a man's life just because he does not want to go to where we want him to go" is wrong (Interview with Dr. Vitaly Rubin, *JTA*, August 30, 1976 and *JTA*, December 3, 1976).

Israelis too were divided. A Gallup Poll in fall 1976 found that 46 percent of Israelis favored freedom of choice while 43 percent opposed (Carl Glick, draft memo to HIAS Executive, December 1, 1976, HIAS files). Former Israeli Foreign Minister Abba Eban attacked efforts to coerce people to come to Israel. He argued that immigration to Israel was incompatible with coercion (Abba Eban, "Soviet Jews-Persuasion not Coercion," *JP*, November 22 1976).[110] Joseph Tekoa, President of Ben Gurion University and a leader of an organization of Soviet Jewish immigrants blasted Eban. He argued that dropouts took limited places of Soviet immigrants to Israel. Tekoa charged that service arrangements for dropouts in Vienna, sponsored by HIAS and JDC with the cooperation of the Israeli government and Jewish Agency, "encourage, legitimize and increase the flow of dropouts." He predicted the Soviets would use this as an excuse to close the gates (Quoted in Jewish Immigrant Aid Services of Canada Information Bulletin, January 3, 1977, CJF files).[111]

Many diverse Jewish organizations in the United States supported freedom of choice at this time. The consensus of a special task force of the Synagogue Council of America coordinating body of Reform, Conservative and Orthodox Rabbis concluded that "the traditional Jewish concept of *Pidyon Shvuim* (redemption of captives) imposes an overriding moral obligation to assist all Jews who have managed to leave the Soviet Union. Moreover not to assist may undermine the entire moral basis of our struggle on behalf of Soviet

Jews, which is based on the principle of reunion of families and the right of free movement of population grounded in the United Nation Universal Declaration of Human Rights." Rabbi Alexander Schindler, Chairman of the Conference of Presidents, also favored freedom of choice (Memo from Rabbi Wolf Kelman to Synagogue Council of America [SCA] Plenum, November 26, 1976 and *JTA*, December 31, 1976).[112]

Probably representative of the Union of Councils, Si Frumkin, of the Council of Soviet Jewry in Southland, opposed all limitations on entry into the United States (*Southwest Jewish Press*, September 3, 1976 and October 29, 1976).[113] In the fall of 1976 the Jewish Defense League sat in at HIAS's office charging treachery and perfidy and betrayal of Soviet Jewish refugees. They argued that dropouts were foolish and weak but should not be abandoned. They referred to the Committee of Eight as a "latter day *Judenraat*." (*Kahane: The Magazine of the Authentic Jewish Idea*, Volume 1, #7 [November 1976] and "Jewish Defense League Pamphlet," "Treachery and Perfidy," HIAS files). In late October the American Jewish Committee opposed unofficially the proposed implementation of the Committee of Eight proposals on grounds that they would deny freedom of choice (Letter, Bert Gold [AJC] to Ralph Goldman, Gaynor Jacobson et al., October 28, 1976, JDC and CJF files).[114]

Many American academics criticized the Committee of Eight proposals and supported freedom of choice. For example, the Committee of Concerned Scientists and the American Math Society supported the position not to alter aid to dropouts (Letters, Committee of Concerned Scientists to Gaynor Jacobson, February 2, 1977, JDC files and American Math Society to Carl Glick, November 15, 1976).[115] Marshall I. Goldman of the Harvard Russian Research Center advised that the key to the exodus of Soviet Jews was Soviet American relations. He thought that dropouts would not be important unless there was considerable publicity about their arrival in the United States. He predicted that a cessation of aid for dropouts by HIAS in Vienna would cause an uproar (Letter, Marshall Goldman to Steve Spiegel, December 20, 1976, JDC files).[116] Robert O. Freeman (Memo, "The Advisability of Aiding the Soviet Jewish 'Drop-outs,' n.d., JDC files) argued that the Soviets wanted to please the American government and did not care where the émigrés settled; in fact going to the United States helped the Soviets with the Arab States.

In a press conference in September 1976 Chancellor Bruno Kreisky let it be known that he opposed coercing émigrés to go to a particular country. He objected to any restrictions, which would hinder freedom of choice for Russian Jewish émigrés in Vienna. He responded following a meeting in which Israeli representatives tried to convince the Austrian Minister of Interior to guarantee that all Soviet Jews arriving in Austria with Israeli visas would be sent on to Israel (Telex, JDC to Ralph Goldman, September 30,

1976 and Memo, Leonard Seidenman to HIAS, September 30, 1976).[117] In early October, Kreisky promised that all émigrés admitted to the country would be given "right to choose the country to which he wants to go" (*Das Juedische Echo*, October 4, 1976 and Telex, Akiva Kohane to Ralph Goldman, October 5, 1976, JDC files). A few weeks later the Vienna paper *Kurier* reported that Kreisky opposed an Israeli proposal to fly all Soviet Jews arriving in Vienna to Israel ("Kreisky Bars Plan to Cut Vienna Drop-Outs" *JP*, October 24, 1976).[118]

In October, the Committee of Eight became the Committee of Ten with the addition of NJCRAC and NCSJ. More importantly, the body became a technical subcommittee for a CJF sponsored "all American" policy making group named the Interorganizational Committee. Headed by Max Fisher, it consisted of presidents and executive directors of CJF, JDC, HIAS, UJA and United Israel Appeal (Memo, Carl Glick to HIAS Board, December 7, 1976 and Carl Glick hand notes, HIAS files).[119] In effect the American Jewish organizations dealing with the dropout phenomenon became officially independent from their Israeli counterparts. Nevertheless, many leaders and organizations continued to refer to the Committee of Eight proposals.

Initially the new committee supported the Israeli and Committee of Eight position on not aiding dropouts. It met on October 26 and endorsed the two principles of freedom of choice and a maximum number leaving the Soviet Union (Summary of JDC Executive Committee, November 16, 1976, JDC files). Soviet Jews would exercise their right of freedom of choice in Moscow. According to Max Fisher the Interorganizational Committee wanted to insure freedom of choice "to be exercised when the prospective immigrants apply for their exit permits and to help every Jew get to the country of his choice" (Note, Max Fisher to HIAS, October 25, 1976, HIAS files). The new committee operated on the premise that nothing was to be done to interfere with Jews leaving the USSR regardless of destination. It decided that HIAS would limit their help to those with visas for other countries (Jerry Goodman, "Paper on Situation, NCSJ," November 24, 1976).[120] In other words, aid to dropouts in Vienna would cease.

Phil Bernstein told the Executive Committee Meeting of NJCRAC (October 24 or 25, 1976) that they would give Soviet Jews 100 days warning before implementing the new policy. He suggested that the new process would not prevent anyone from emigrating from the Soviet Union (Stated at NJCRAC Executive Meeting, October 25, 1976, JDC files).[121] He indicated that he expected the necessary number of visas to be available to other countries including the United States and that the Dutch would cooperate.[122] Uncertainty remained as to whether the Soviets would let Jews apply to go to other countries.[123]

HIAS's President, Carl Glick, attacked the Interorganizational Committee's proposal to cut aid to dropouts beginning on February 1, 1977 (Memo, Emergency Meeting, October 26, 1976, HIAS files). He traveled all over the United

States speaking in favor of freedom of choice. He argued that since the Soviets would probably not allow Jews to leave on American visas then only
the Israeli option remained. This might result, he feared, in some Jews not
leaving. Glick and others suggested that Soviet Jews might face physical persecution in the future. At the same time he argued that with an Israeli commitment not to refuse anyone a visa, Soviet Jews could continue to drop out
as before and receive assistance from non-Jewish and anti-Zionist organizations who would replace HIAS.[124]

Max Fisher publicly supported the Committee of Eight (Ten) proposals. He
received assistance from the Israeli government who sent over Nehemia Levanon to work for their adoption by American Jewish organizations. Levanon
and other members of the Liaison Bureau and staff and lay leaders of the
NCSJ spoke before Jewish federations throughout the country in favor of cutting aid to dropouts (Rager 1990 and Gold 1989:32).

Regardless of Glick's position, HIAS sought to cooperate with Max Fisher
and the Interorganizational Committee.[125] The HIAS Board of Directors met
on October 26, 1976 and passed a resolution stating that HIAS "will join in the
search for a means by which Israeli visas would be used for Jews going to Israel; and American, Canadian and other visas would be used by Jews who
wish to go to these countries (JDC files, n.d., c. August 1976).[126] It urged that
"nothing be done that will reduce the outflow of Jews from the Soviet Union
or subject Jews in the Soviet Union to unnecessary risk" (Resolution, HIAS
Board of Directors, October 26, 1976, JDC files). HIAS recommended "sending of invitations or affidavits into the Soviet Union for those Jews who wish
to come to countries other than Israel for family reunion"; and proposed that
HIAS, JDC, and the Jewish Agency monitor the situation to see if Soviet Jews
were using non-Israeli visas, whether the Soviet government honored them
and whether the United States and other governments provide visas. In effect,
HIAS gave qualified support to the Committee of Eight proposals.[127]

At a meeting on October 16, 1976 the Executive Committee of the JDC endorsed the Committee of Eight proposals. JDC lay leader Jack Weiler later commented that few came and that discussions were "heated. They were tense, the
subject was very controversial and they were not ordinary discussions" (Minutes of JDC Executive Committee Meeting, November 16, 1976, JDC files and
Summary of Executive Meeting of JDC, November 16, 1976, JDC files). The
JDC Board had yet to approve the proposals.

At JDC Executive Committee meeting on October 26, 1976 members discussed Glick's objection to a 90- or 100-day implementation date on
grounds that there would be insufficient time for American Jews to arrange
for affidavits and invitations for their relatives in the Soviet Union (Summary
and Minutes of special meeting of JDC Executive, October 26, 1976, JDC
files).[128] Since it had taken the Israelis at least two years or more to set up
the invitation and affidavit process some argued that it would take as much

time to organize invitations to the United States, a difficult bureaucratic process involving at least five stamps (approvals) on an affidavit (Memo, Phil Bernstein to Ralph Goldman "Next steps on emigration of Soviet Jews," October 29, 1976, JDC files).[129] Some also referred to Glick's point that an overloaded system and lack of visas for the United States stranded 2,300 persons in Rome.[130]

Phil Bernstein told the JDC Executive that the Committee of Ten had not set a date for implementation (Summary of Special Meeting of Executive Committee of JDC, October 1976, JDC files). He reiterated the concern for maximum exit and freedom of choice. He talked of the need to get more visas for entry into the United States, the need for additional consultations in Washington, D.C. and the need to determine what would happen in the Soviet Union. The meeting passed a resolution that "every effort should be made to develop such procedures to assure that maximum number of Jews wanting to leave the Soviet Union will be helped to do so."

Those present at the JDC Executive Committee meeting on October 26, 1976 endorsed the Committee of Eight proposals. They favored, however, a step-by-step approach rather than setting a date to begin implementation of the entire plan. They wanted to see what worked and what did not and adjust accordingly (Summary of Executive Committee Meeting of JDC, November 16, 1976 and *JP*, November 5 1976).[131]

The JDC Executive Committee next met on November 16, 1976. Its newly designated President elect Donald Robinson endorsed the cessation of aid to dropouts. He feared that unless American Jews acted that the Soviets might close the exit gates. He believed more visas to the West would be granted. Those present discussed the issue of setting a date to begin implementation. Nehemia Levanon argued that once they set a date for cutoff of aid that it could be changed if problems occurred. He also felt that Soviet Jews would not apply for American visas until they realized that dropouts would not be aided! For the same reasons he opposed a step-by-step approach which the JDC had endorsed at its last Executive Committee meeting. For example he felt that visas would materialize only when there were requests.[132] The overwhelming majority favored a resolution (two persons opposed) that the Interorganizational Committee goes forward with a date as soon as possible (Minutes and Summary of Executive Committee Meeting of JDC, November 16, 1976, JDC files).

While it appears that Nehemia Levanon's efforts were bearing fruit, his qualified success with JDC did not last long.[133] Prior to the last JDC Executive Committee Meeting, the CJF General Assembly in Philadelphia derailed the Committee of Eight (Ten) proposals.

Many had looked forward to a decision being made at the 45th Annual General Assembly of the CJF which was held in Philadelphia from November 9 until November 14, 1976. The Israelis sent Nehemia Levanon of the

Liaison Bureau and Yehuda Avner of the Prime Minister's Office to lobby for the Committee of Eight proposals (*Time*, November 22, 1976). At the meetings Max Fisher reported on the work and proposals of the Committee of Eight and the Inter-organizational Committee. Some suggest that he delivered a poorly prepared and ineffective speech. Carl Glick spoke in opposition. A person in the audience, probably Leonard Fein, gave a powerful emotional address favoring freedom of choice. He made mention of the Holocaust and recalled American gates being closed to Jews wanting to flee Hitler's persecution. His moving comments together with Glick's efforts increased significantly the opposition to the Committee of Eight proposals. Sensing this, Max Fisher decided not to have a vote on the proposals at the General Assembly.[134] The lack of a vote meant that the all important CJF, representing almost all Jewish federations throughout the United States, had not endorsed the Committee of Eight proposals to have HIAS and JDC end aid to dropouts that did not have relatives in the United States. The status quo remained in force.

The *JP* of November 15, 1976 reported that at a proposed meeting that day of the Committee of Eight in New York City both HIAS and JDC would support the proposals that the Jewish agency aid those leaving on Israeli visas and HIAS and the JDC those leaving on visas for other countries. Dropouts would not be aided. Both organizations, however, would ask for a delay in implementation of non-aid for dropouts until such time as more visas were available. Later HIAS (and possibly JDC) asked for a further extension to allow sufficient time for a campaign to recruit people in the United States to write letters of invitation to relatives in the Soviet Union.[135] Israeli critics of HIAS felt they were stalling. Others charged that the HIAS position reflected their need to remain in the absorption business in order to survive (*JP*, November 5, 1976, Sarah Honig and Eugene Gold [1990: 30]).[136] For the time being both HIAS and JDC would continue to aid dropouts.[137] Importantly, the percentage of dropouts increased until the gates of the Soviet Union closed in 1982.

CONCLUSION

Clearly, the American Jewish establishment led by the CJF had resisted Israeli pressure and rejected an Israeli proposal to stop aiding Jewish émigrés who left the Soviet Union on Israeli visas but chose to resettle in the United States. Orbach (1979:76) referred to the defeat of the Committee of Eight proposals as "an American Jewish Declaration of Independence" from Israel. It clearly signified an independent position on the Soviet Jewry issue. Freedman (1989b:79) saw this as the first time the American Jewish establishment opposed "an Israeli policy preference on Soviet Jewry."

Many have believed that HIAS led and dominated the American Jewish opposition to Israel on the dropout issue. At that time and until the present day many Israelis and American Jews consider Carl Glick as the personification and spokesperson for freedom of choice. Yet the evidence presented here suggests that HIAS at times did not support the position of its President, Carl Glick, of total opposition to the Committee of Eight proposals. Importantly, both Glick and HIAS lacked the influence to sway the American Jewish establishment on the freedom of choice issue. First, HIAS was a relatively small organization with a few thousand supporters throughout the country. Second, HIAS depended upon UJA, with the approval of JDC and the UIA, for an important part of its funding. The UJA and UIA supported the Israeli government on the freedom of choice issue (as did many in JDC). This led the organization to follow a course of restraint; it repudiated Glick's proposals to reject outright the Committee of Eight proposals.

More significant was the response of the federations that made up the CJF. Many of their leaders revolted against the national CJF leadership on the issue of freedom of choice. From around the country lay leaders of various federations opposed cutting aid to dropouts on the grounds of freedom of choice and the Jewish tradition of rescuing prisoners. In the minds of many American Jews was the memory of the Holocaust when the United States refused entry to Jewish refugees fleeing first persecution and later the gas chambers of Hitler's Final Solution. While evidently some leaders and communities had reservations about freedom of choice, those favoring it carried the day.

The findings support an important insight articulated best by the late Dan Elazar (1976). He preferred a non-centralized as opposed to either a centralized or a decentralized model of organizations to describe the structure of American Jewish organizations. His insight explains how the CJF operated in a loosely connected organizational system.[138] It was a loose confederation of many independent and powerful local federations. Many of them exerted considerable influence on national policy. To a great extent the leadership of local federations scuttled a proposed Israeli solution to the problem of dropouts, which many "national" Jewish leaders supported.[139]

Ralph Goldman (1995:21,22) places much of the blame of the failure to block support for dropouts at this stage on the Israeli political leadership.[140] He believes that in autumn 1976 it was possible to stem the dropout phenomenon. At the time there were no American visas available for thousands of Soviet Jews waiting in Rome. Max Fisher "was pressured to request special Parole Visas from the United States government." Fisher, according to Goldman, was willing to withstand pressure but wanted the support of the Israeli government. Prime Minister Rabin was "not enthusiastic about such pressure being brought to bear on the United States Government" and sought the support of the opposition leader, Menachem Begin. Begin urged

Prime Minister Rabin to postpone for six months the Committee of Eight proposals to cut aid to dropouts. He wanted time to consult with Soviet immigrants who opposed ending aid (*Maariv*, October 6, 1976).

While the events described here do not fit the Windmueller thesis of the two divergent views of the future of the Jewish people, most Israeli leaders and the American Jewish establishment took opposing views on freedom of choice. Within a decade these divergent views would converge when Mikhail Gorbachev decided to allow free emigration of Soviet Jewry.

NOTES

1. Israeli officials and many American Jewish leaders referred to émigrés who chose not to go on to Israel upon their arrival in Vienna as "dropouts" (*Noshrim*). In a letter to Gaynor Jacobson on July 6, 1977 (HIAS files) Leonard Seidenman reported that Zvi Netzer of the Liaison Bureau told him that the new Israeli government considered telling the American government that it objected to the United States considering Russian Jews as refugees. Seidenman did not take the threat seriously. Netzer added that the American government had asked Israel to make this request "in order to reduce pressure of American Jewish organizations."

2. An Israeli government official refused a request from the American State Department to provide Israeli visas for Soviet Jews who might not be able to receive American visas in Moscow after October 1, 1989 (Interview with Princeton Lyman, February 12, 2004). See chapter 8.

3. Levanon (1995:444) admits that after years of struggle he accepted his government's pragmatism on dealing with American Jews. Dinstein (Interview, May 3, 2003) claims that Levanon always restrained himself on freedom of choice because he was never sure he was 100 percent correct.

4. The letter contained a draft report "US Assistance Provided for Resettling Soviet Refugees." From 1971 through April 1976 19,285 (16.1 percent) refugees leaving USSR chose not to resettle in Israel. About 82 percent (12,807) including some who later left Israel, resettled in the United States and 1,000 went to Canada (see apendix).

5. A former senior Liaison Bureau operative confirmed (Interview, 2002) that "probably no option to drop out before 1973."

6. The Austrian Red Cross opened a new transit facility for use by the Jewish Agency.

7. Yoram Dinstein (Interview, May 3, 2003) blames Liaison Bureau people in Vienna who recommended asking HIAS and JDC to get the drop outs out of the city. The Liaison Bureau in Tel Aviv approved this rather than pursuing a "Romanian" option which would have sent all émigrés via Bucharest to Israel. This would have involved a fee but insured no dropouts. In the 1960s about 3 percent of Romanian Jewish emigrants passing through Rome on the way to Israel dropped out. Then, the Jewish Agency asked HIAS to assist Romanians with first degree relatives to reach other countries in the West (Dominitz 1996:120).

8. Levanon (1995:211) comments that American Jewry woke up to the idea of family reunification to the United States after Kosygin's speech. HIAS promised to forward

the invitations and supporting documents to the State Department for transmission to the American Consul in Moscow. Letter of Gaynor Jacobson to local cooperating agencies, December 9, 1966. (JDC files). Later HIAS offered to subsidize families to bring over their relatives (Gaynor Jacobson to cooperating agencies, March 29, 1971).

9. In 1973 HIAS had 6,000 applications on file. HIAS Annual Meeting Report "Emigration from the Soviet Union" March 11, 1973, (CJF files). In 1976 it had 10,000 applications from relatives in the United States and Canada. Only a few communities reach out to new comers to counsel them on how to transmit letters of invitation to USSR relatives (Gaynor Jacobson to Cooperating Agencies, December 3, 1976, HIAS files); Gaynor Jacobson (memo to Phil Bernstein et. al., January 1977, JDC files) reported that during the last 6 months of 1976 the rate of invitations had increased 3 fold. Levanon (1995:445) believed that the HIAS effort failed because American Jews were not excited to invite their relatives.

10. Soviet authorities expelled some non-Jews including Pentecostal Christians on visas for Israel (Letter, Fasick to Jacobson, October 15, 1976, HIAS files). Rav Tov was associated with the anti-Zionist Satmer Rebbe. HIAS and other American Jewish groups tried unsuccessfully to prevent its 1976 accreditation by the State Department (Letter of Carl Glick to Congressman Joshua Eilberg, March 9, 1976, HIAS files); Minutes of JDC Executive Committee, February 22, 1977; *JTA*; and Memo, Eliezer Shavit to Charles Jordan, RE: "Decision in Mr. Pincus's Office on January 26, 1967," February 9, 1967 (JDC files). Irving Kessler (UIA) received a report from Molly Tatel of Robert R. Nathan Associates (November 12, 1976) on Rav Tov (HIAS files). Initially, Rav Tov dealt mainly with Jews leaving Israel. Later, HIAS would help Rav Tov resettle some of its clients in the United States. Albert Einstein helped set up the International Rescue Committee in the 1930s to rescue Jewish refugees from Germany. While once focusing on Jewish refugees by the 1970s it had become non-sectarian (http://www.theirc.org/, July 15, 2004). After World War II the IRC received some funding from the anti-Zionist American Council of Judaism's Philanthropic Fund. During the period studied here it had no ties to the American Council of Judaism (Interview, Al Kastner, IRC, July 2004).

11. IRC and Tolstoy–Foundation sponsored refugees also traveled on the HIAS train (undated hand notes of Ralph Goldman, JDC files). Ralph Goldman argued that Israel had a long standing agreement with Austria on transportation of refugees which it delegated to HIAS. In a June 1976 hand note Akiva Kohane noted that HIAS reimbursed the Jewish Agency for the transportation to Rome (JDC files).

12. HIAS listed the names of person on plain paper with a letter on letterhead stating persons "are transiting Italy for the purpose of pursuing applications for entry into the United States or third countries."

13. At the time, Soviet Jews were the only refugees who moved with the full financial support of the American government. Irving Kessler (UIA document, December 10, 1976, CJF files) credited Senator Edmund Muskie and Congressman Jonathan Bingham for the grant. Max Fisher met Senators Javits and Muskie and Congressman Bingham about the proposed legislation (Golden 1992:276). Previously, the United States provided some en route care and maintenance for Soviet Jewish émigrés under the Migration and Refugee Assistance Act of 1962 (PL 87–510).

14. The State Department administered these funds while the Inter-governmental Committee for European Migration (ICEM) funded transportation. (GAO 1977 and

Johnston (November 9, 1976). According to GAO (1977) American aid allocated $52m or 43.2 percent for expansion of Israel's absorption infrastructure; $66.1m or 54.8 percent for assistance and services to individuals, and $2.49m or 2 percent for maintenance en route. Funded projects include absorption centers, 1,355 apartments, hospital wings and clinics and absorption of academics $6,8m. The Agency of International Development (AID) provided $100m in loan guarantees from 1972 to 1976 for private American financing of mortgages for low cost housing in Israel.

15. According to GAO the (1977) Jewish Agency spent or allocated $1,872m to carry out its absorption functions from 1972 to 1976. During this time United States aid covered 5 percent of the Jewish Agency's receipts.

16. For FY 1977 Congress stipulated that the $15m appropriation could be spent only in Israel, Johnston (November 9, 1976).

17. Importantly, since the 1960s the United States government worked with non-governmental organizations (NGOs) including HIAS to resettle refugees in the United States. Much of Congressional funding for refugee aid and resettlement went to these NGOs (Reimers 1985:156). In practice, individual applying for refugee status had to be sponsored by one of a select group of non-profit agencies which would be responsible for their initial housing, medical care and language training. The federal government would cover a share of non profit agency cost. Several other refugee groups (sectarian and nonsectarian) participated in these arrangements including the International Refugee Committee and church groups.

18. The Hart Celler Act of 1965 replaced the national origins quotas with preference system based primarily on a reunification of families and needed skills. Reimers (1985:120) credits NGOs including HIAS and the AJC for its passage. Freeman 1995 study argues that elite groups and elected officials shape the policy on immigration. It exemplifies client politics with well organized groups outside the public view. The Act listed the following preferences (Liskofsky 1966:172) "*first preference* (up to 20 percent for unmarried children over 21 of US citizens; *second preference* (up to 20 percent) for spouses and unmarried children (regardless of age) of alien residents; *third preference* (10 percent) for prospective immigrants who are members of professions or who possess exceptional abilities in science and/or the arts; *fourth preference* (up to 10 percent) for married children of US citizens; *fifth preference* (24 percent) for brothers/sisters of US citizens; *sixth preference* (10 percent) for persons capable of performing skilled or unskilled labor not of a seasonal nature; *seventh preference* (6 percent) for refugees because of persecution or fear of persecution on account of race, religious or political opinion have fled from any Communist or Communist dominated area or any country in Middle East. Recipients not to be given immigrant visas but allow to enter USA conditionally for 2 years then status can be adjusted to permanent resident; '*non-preference*' '*immigrants*' '*aliens*' who cannot qualify for one of the preference classes' admitted on first come first served basis."

In the 1970s only a few Soviet Jews would enter the United States as immigrants (Buwalda 1997:57,58). On May 5, 1975 the State Department announced procedures to process prospective conditional entrants as non-preferential immigrants. Through September 1975 about 1,329 refugees (145 Third Country Processing [TCP] and 1,184 breakaways [dropouts] and returnees [*yordim*] granted admission under this category (See Fasick to Jacobson, October 15, 1976 (CJF files) and Memo, Gaynor Jacobson to Max Fisher, September 15, 1976 (HIAS files).

19. Sec 212(d) (5)) "The Attorney General may in his discretion parole into the U.S. temporarily under such conditions as he may prescribe for emergency reasons or for reasons deemed strictly in the public interest any alien applying for admission to the U.S." This included persons fleeing Communist countries, the Middle East, Asia, and Cubans (Letter, Fasick to Jacobson, October 15, 1976). During the 1980s the Attorney General paroled over 1 million persons, mostly Cubans and Vietnamese (Reimers 1985:155,161,172).

20. On July 30, 1973 the Attorney General announced use of 800 paroles for Soviet émigrés in Rome (including some from Israel). See note 22.

21. The first Soviet parolee arrived in Rome in December 1971 (Memo, D. Horowitz to Sam Haber, December 30, 1971). HIAS brought the Feldmans (first parole family to arrive in the United States) to meet Attorney General Mitchell. Congressman Ed Koch had proposed a bill to admit 30,000 Soviet Jews (HIAS file "Message from President of HIAS at 88th Annual Meeting, March 12, 1972). The State Department opposed the bill and others because they would antagonize Soviets (internal matter) (*JTA*, October 15, 1971). Koch and 150 supporters from House and Senate agreed to withdraw. Orbach (1979:117–122) argues that many Jewish groups opposed because they wanted Soviet Jews to go to Israel; Kuch withdrew when the Attorney General said he would help Jews leave the Soviet Union.

22. This required a prior invitation (*vysov*) from an American relative and an OVIR exit permit. Eligible were spouses and children, parents, brothers and sisters of American citizens or permanent resident aliens. The recipient petition could not include the entire family. Often, beneficiaries would go to an interim country to seek TCP entry for other family members. (Memo draft, Carl Glick to HIAS Board of Directors, December 1, 1975 (CJF files). Akiva Kohane, memo on Soviet Jewish Transmigrants in Vienna and Rome, April 13, 1977 (JDC files). There were 5 TCPs in 1971; 239 in 1972; 424 in 1973; 575 in 1974; 572 in 1975; 671 in 1976 and 95 in first quarter of 1977—total 3337. During this same time 134,945 left on visas for Israel.

23. In 1976 most TCP cases in Rome were Armenians from Beirut. Soviet Jews made up 20 percent of the Rome TCP caseload (Memo, Akiva Kohane to Ralph Goldman re: Armenian TCP(s), November 17, 1976; USSR Desk of U.S. Department of State memo "Emigration of Soviet Emigrants with Exit Visas for U.S., June 29, 1976 [JDC Files]."

Chart Soviet emigrants with exit visas for USA processed by U.S. Embassy Moscow (exclusive of dual US USSR citizens: 1970: 230, 1971: 287, 1972: 494, 1973: 758, 1974: 1,019, 1975: 1,162, 1976 thru May: 1,020 (mostly Armenians)

Armenian and Jewish Soviet emigrants (excluding dual citizens) processed by U.S. Embassy in Moscow:

	1973	1974	1975	1976 (Jan–May)
Armenians	185	290	455	661
Jews	502	622	585	305

Kohane also reported (memo, June 14 to Ralph Goldman) that Soviet citizens could leave USSR on Soviet passport except if they went to the Republic of South Africa, Rhodesia and Israel. TCP Visa holders did not have to renounce citizenship and did not have to pay extra fee.

24. Since 1972 only 2 or 3 TCP cases had been denied visas (Fasick to Jacobson, October 15, 1976).

25. American aid to resettle Soviet Jews in Israel also served as a precedent.

26. Karl Zukerman of CJF in New York City worked with Talisman on this effort in the late 1970s. The legislation provided a block grant to CJF which allocates a per person fee for refugee resettlement to federations.

27. Senator Inouye was chairman of the Subcommittee on Foreign Operations of the Committee of Appropriations. Bruce Leimsidor (re: minutes of National Professional Planning Committee [NPPC] to members of HIAS/CJF September 11, 1979) reported on block grant to CJF for refugees and pressure in Congress from William Jordan, Senator Inouye's chief of staff, to standardize aid for all refugees. Talisman believed this would hurt Soviet Jews (JDC files, early May 1978 Transcript conference call RE: U.S. government funding of Transmigrant Operation, JDC files).

28. Also see "Summary of Washington Consultations, January 23, 24, 1979" (HIAS files). Present at the meetings for HIAS were Carl Glick, Mark Talisman and Daniel Maccoby. Other organizations represented were the American Council for Nationalities Service, American Fund for Czech Refugees, JDC, Church World Services, International Rescue Committee, Lutheran Immigration and Refugee Service, Polish American Immigration and Relief Committee, Tolstoy Foundation, United States Catholic Conference of Bishops, and ACVAFS. Also see letter of Margy-Ruth Davis to Sara Frankel et. al., January 26, 1979 (HIAS files) and Summary of Washington Consultations January 23–24, 1979 (HIAS files).

29. In 1979 HIAS spent $20.9m. It received $4.7m from CJF, $400,000 from JDC and $16.1m from the federal government (Bernstein 1983:87).

30. A September 2, 1974 memo of Julian Breen, JDC Headquarters to JDC Rome, re Russian transmigrants reported that United States Refugee Program (USRP) funds for 1974 would soon be exhausted. Ralph Goldman urged pressure on Congress but "felt that we as a Jewish organization should maintain a low profile as far as this sum is concerned" (JDC Executive Committee, March 24, 1974, JDC files). Gaynor Jacobson (letter to David H. Lissy, Associate Director of Domestic Council, White House, September 28, 1976 (HIAS files) reported that there were no funds available for refugee emergency programs. On November 9, 1976 the President authorized an additional $2m for Refugee Emergency Fund to bridge gap until Congress enacts the supplemental budget proposal. In a letter to Mark Talisman of January 15, 1977, Joel E. Fisher reported that no funds had been budgeted for Calendar Year for reception and placement of Soviet refugees in USA nor for movement of their personal effects and household goods. He reported a request of $8.3m for supplemental appropriation for Refugee Emergency Fund use in 2nd and 3rd quarter of 1977. Fisher also report that budget officers from OMB and State *indicated displeasure at an attempt to limit reception and placement funds and baggage funds only to Soviet Refugees.* On February 25, 1977 Representative Sidney R. Yates wrote Jim Rice that the Foreign Operations Appropriations Subcommittee appropriated full amount of $3m that requested for settlement of Soviet Jews (HIAS files). *A condition of U.S. government support was freedom of choice, that is, that Soviet Jews have the right to choose in which country to resettle regardless of the visa they possessed. Memo, Ralph Goldman to file, April 20, 1976* (JDC files).

31. In the 1970s HIAS resettled through Jewish federations tens of thousands of non-Jewish political refugees for the American government (Bernstein 1983:101). For example in 1972 it resettled in 26 communities 62 Asian families expelled from Uganda by Idi Amin.

32. From 1962 through 1977 UJA allocated HIAS funds (up to $400,000 per year) to offset annual budget deficits. UJA gave HIAS $650,000 in 1975 and $595,000 in 1976. The UIA rejected a request by HIAS for an additional $195,000 for baggage and a larger case load in 1976. UIA accounting study found no baggage deficit. It claimed that HIAS wanted the funding for an overall deficit account reserve for overseas emergencies (Minutes, Board of Directors UIA, March 25 and May 19, 1977, HIAS files). Later HIAS complied with UIA recommendation to impose a 750 kg limit for baggage per family that it would reimburse.

33. Moreover, the UJA sometimes supported HIAS's financial needs. For example in response to a 1974 HIAS request for additional funds, UJA and CJF let HIAS retain $300 for reception and placement from federal funds. HIAS signed an agreement with the State Department in April 1974, which gave it $300 for each Soviet refugee (GAO, June 20, 1977). It transferred these funds to cooperating agencies through August 31, 1974. Thereafter HIAS retained about $3.1m of reception and replacement funds through September 1976.

34. In 1955 HIAS gave up its resettlement activities. NYANA took over resettlement in the New York area and federations supervised it throughout the country. In 1973 NYANA's budget was less than $1m; it jumped to $4m in 1975. Two years previously the organization had almost been phased out (JDC Executive Committee Report, September 4, 1974).

35. Upon arrival in Rome HIAS prepared an individual dossier on each Soviet refugee, which it then transferred to Jewish federations in the United States.

36. Five voluntary agencies resettled 9,644 Soviet refugees in the United States from 1972 through June 1975. HIAS handled 7,907 or 82 percent including. 1,790 Soviet émigrés who had come from Israel. The other resettling agencies included World Council of Churches/World Service 1,181 or 12.2 percent; Tolstoy Foundation, 419 or 4.3 percent; International Refugee Committee 128 or 1.3 percent; and International Catholic Migration Committee 7 or 0.15 percent. Letter, Fasick to Jacobson, October 15, 1976; GAO 1977. Later, HIAS handle 15 122 or 80 percent including 3049 from Israel (GAO, 1977). HIAS report from 1974 to September 30, 1976, 44 percent resettled in the New York area with large numbers also in Los Angeles, Philadelphia, Chicago and Detroit.

37. Mr. Robinson at JDC Executive Committee of September 21, 1976 reported a mixed American reaction toward Russian Jewish refugees. Ralph Goldman, notes on trip to Vienna and Rome, June 23, 1976 (JDC files); Telex 1361, Feder to Ralph Goldman, June 23, 1976 (CJF files, box 710); CJF Advisory Committee on Soviet Jewish Resettlement, June 11, 1976 (CJF files, box 710).

38. For example, it proposed a buddy system whereby larger federations provided support services for smaller communities who agreed to absorb Soviet immigrants (Advisory Committee meeting (addendum report on New England regionalization program, June 11, 1976, CJF files, box 710) and "CJF Guideline Statement on Grants and Loans for Resettlement of Soviet Jewish Immigrants," May 1977. Also see memo of S.R. Weber on Association of Jewish Federations and Children's Agencies guidelines, April 5, 1977; JDC Executive Committee May 27, 1976; and Memo, Irving Kessler to Rivlin, June 25, 1976 (JDC file). JDC file report on NYANA program for settlement that relatives in USA have responsibility to assist in resettlement. See Memo, Herbert Bernstein (NYANA) to Judge Simon H. Rifkind, June 24, 1976. (See: CJF Advisory

Committee on Soviet Jewish resettlement, June 11, 1976 (CJF files, box 710; and letter, Fasick to Jacobson, October 15, 1976). U.S. government cover cost of transportation to United States which it considers a loan. Refugee families required to sign agreement to pay HIAS who in turn reimburses the American government. U.S. government expects HIAS to collect 60–65%; if fall below agency expected to make up difference with community funds (CJF guideline statement on grants and loans for resettlement of Soviet Jewish immigrants, May 1977, CJF files).

39. Soviet Jewish refugees that entered either as refugees or parolees were eligible to public relief and assistance including AFDC, Medicaid, food stamps, and rental supplements (letter, Fasick to Jacobson, October 15, 1976) but most voluntary agencies refrained from using these except for hardship cases. They believed that to accept public assistance might jeopardize refugee application for permanent residence for public charge.

40. It reported that cities with about 80 percent of the Soviet Jews have implemented the proposed loan/grant policy.

41. Reimers (1985:120) writes on Israelis immigrating to the USA "many American Jews were embarrassed by the presence of these immigrants in their midst and the implications of emigration from Israel. The GAO 1977 report says 7,000 Soviet Jews had left Israel. Earlier at Jewish Agency meeting of Board of Governors Bodies (September 30–October 3, 1975) Ray Epstein reported that 5,000 of 106,000 Soviet Jewish immigrants had left Israel. *Haaretz* of June 15, 1976 reported that 8,000 of the 116,000 Soviet Jewish immigrants in past 5.5 years had left.

42. One participant thought that cessation of aid might be misunderstood since Max Fisher had arranged for some Russian émigrés from Israel to enter the United States on parole visas. Liaison and Jewish Agency officials, with the exception of Yehuda Dominitz supported Dulzin. Dominitz feared that the Italians would object to policies that denied émigrés freedom of movement. Memo to file, Ralph Goldman, February 15, 1974 (JDC files). According to Sara Frankel (interview June 26, 2002) an agreement was reached after Prime Minister Golda Meir met with leaders of HIAS and JDC. Frankel recalls that at the time she told Jewish Agency officials about HIAS/JDC aid to dropouts in Vienna. When she said it had to stop they told her that they had just settled the issue of Soviet émigrés who had left Israel and couldn't fight another issue. A HIAS official warned that if they did not aid these émigrés that other organizations would. In response, one liaison person stated that most Jews would not apply for aid from non-Jewish organizations.

43. The Glick letter may not have been sent. It referred to an August agreement involving HIAS.

44. The Executive Committee of the JDC on April 3, 1974 reported that IRC was caring for about 400 Russian Jews in Rome who had previously settled in Israel. It also noted that HIAS was negotiating with the IRC to handle the resettlement of these refugees in the United States. Leonard H. Marks of IRC wrote Congressman Joshua Eilberg (March 2, 1977) asking his help to include 300 Russian refugees as parolees since that Immigration and Naturalization Service rejected them for having been in Israel for over a year.

45. Haber of JDC thought that the issue remained unresolved (JDC Executive Committee, April 3, 1974.). Feder reported (JDC Executive Committee, September 4, 1974) that Jewish communities in Brussels and Paris resented the fact that Soviet Jews

who had left Israel (Yordim) are being taken care of by non-Jewish organizations. "On the whole it was felt that it was better not to encourage the Russian Jews to go to Israel if they wished to settle elsewhere, for cost a lot to integrate them in Israel and would be wasted if leave."

46. In 1976, 4,000 received aid which was limited to assistance for resettlement, documentation and transportation (GAO 1977).

47. On September 30, 1976 the State Department discontinued eligibility to Soviet refugees traveling on Israeli passports who departed after October 1, 1974. Some exceptions were made for family reunion and if provide evidence of refugee status. Then on October 15, 1975 the State Department announced that all returnees who reside in Israel less than one year were eligible for United States refugee assistance, family reunion cases remained the exception to the one year criteria provided one or more family members already declared eligible for assistance and were awaiting final resettlement and that family reunion took place before final resettlement of already eligible member. If they failed to meet these they would have to provide convincing evidence so as not to be resettled in Israel. From October 1, 1975 through February 13, 1976 INS in Rome rejected 51 cases which State Department had accepted for refugee assistance. GAO 1977 reported that State Department was still processing persons contrary to an INS ruling.

48. Gitelman (1989:163–168) argued that most Soviet Jewish émigrés going to Israel have a high level of Jewish consciousness while most going to the United States are assimilated and from the Slavic heartland. The great majority of Georgian (94 percent) and Central Asian Jews (87 percent) went to Israel as well as most of the Jewish émigrés from the Baltics and other areas absorbed by the Soviet Union between 1939 and 1944. Only about 30 to 35 percent of those from the European heartland came to Israel. Eighty-seven percent of Soviet Jewish émigrés in the United States were from Russia, Ukraine and to a lesser extent Byelorussia. Overall, seventy five percent of émigrés from Russia and Ukraine did not go to Israel.

49. Soviet authorities hoped to end the "Zionist" protest by letting (encouraging) the Zionists to leave (Salitan 1992:32). She does not deny the influence of negative letters from Soviet Jews in Israel, the Yom Kippur War and the security situation (1992:49). Shapiro (1978:99 writes: "It is important to distinguish between Jewish dissidents, most of whom are right-wing Zionist orientation and the larger Jewish emigration movement, which is essentially motivated by non-political considerations."

50. He believed this to be "an oversimplification of the problem." He argued that "the existence of available support services made the road to other countries easier and in certain cases tipped the scales in the personal decision-making process."

51. Sara Frankel (Interview, June 26, 2002) claims she saw HIAS personnel try to convince Soviet Jews to go to America. Judy Siegel noted: "Israeli study shows HIAS helps increase Soviet dropout rate," *JP*, April 27, 1977. Hand note in HIAS file says Phil Bernstein doubts there is a study. The Liaison Bureau may have "used" the well-known American-Jewish academic Prof. Leon Jick of Brandeis University. On returning from a 16-day visit with Refuseniks he wrote in a letter to Carl Glick (May 20, 1976) and American Jewish communal leaders that "a universal opinion in the Soviet Union" was that HIAS officials exert influence on immigrants to come to the USA. Jick argued (telephone interview on July 29, 2003) that he took the initiative on his own. He explained, however, that Israelis helped set up his trip and instructed him how to act in the USSR. Yehoshua Pratt (1989); Judy Siegel, "6000 Jewish immigrants to the

US," *JP*, August 27 1976.; Dan Margolit, "The place of Russian Immigrants is in Israel and not in California" *Haaretz*, December 1, 1974. Also see "The Joint and HIAS help drop outs and emigrants" *Haaretz*, June 15, 1976. Goldman (1995) wrote "to . . . link JDC with HIAS on issue of Neshira (dropouts) is erroneous and misleading. HIAS invoke slogan freedom of choice and encourage Soviets who come out on Israeli visas to go to America. JDC oppose and fight against dropping out. JDC accept dropouts after Jewish Agency (representing government of Israel) approve their transfer "[JDC] had no choice but to continue its historic role to help Jews in transit."

52. Gitelman (1989:167) writes that impressive resources of both immigrants and the United States Jewish community "combine to provide for a generally smooth resettlement." Nehemia Levanon (1989:72) asserted that despite the desire of American Jews that Soviet Jews go to Israel, their actions did not match their words. Morris Abram commented that Soviet Jews received the "benefits of being refugees: payments of cash, money and medical service and other things." Rabbi Avi Weiss (1989:48) expressed shame that American Jews provided incentives for Soviet Jews to come here. He believed that there could not be freedom of choice if our streets are paved with gold. Even without this aid it was apparent to many that Israel had a tough time competing with the United States, the wealthiest nation on earth.

53. Nehemiah Levanon confirmed this at JDC Board, November 16, 1976.

54. Evidently, those Russian émigrés wrote less about their negative experiences in the United States; most saw the United States as a land of freedom and economic opportunity. Gitelman (1989:168) argues that in Israel the government is involved in absorption so it is blamed while in America resettlement responsibility is more diffuse. He also cites an Israeli "folklore of immigrant complaints" whereby immigrants compete to outdo each other in terms of negative immigrant experiences.

55. Dominitz (1996:122–123) referring to a study by Elazar Leshem in 1975–1976 on reasons for dropping out found that location of relatives, expectations of finding work in their profession and orientation toward Israel to be most important. Writing in 1972:13 Gitelman argued that although many letters of Soviet immigrants in Israel were negative they did not discourage others from wanting to come; it made them more realistic. He also argued that most Soviet immigrants were pleased with their decision and that despite the costs and problems Israel was on its way to "successfully absorbing the immigrants" (1972:42).

56. Party affiliation determined the appointment of many Agency absorption personnel including emissaries ("Max Fisher speaks out," *Israel Star*, July 23, 1976); *JP* clipping c. July 1976 reported that Raphael Kotlowitz was to hire Russian speaking American immigrant Israelis to work in Europe to dispel the image of American streets paved with gold. Most emissaries were former Russians who are not believed by Russians leaving USSR. Memos, Akiva Kohane to Ralph Goldman, June 15, 1976 and June 18, 1976. David Harris (interview, August 8, 2002) said that the Agency's use of American immigrants as emissaries in Vienna often proved problematic. Their emphasizing that they gave up the good life (materialism) for Israel did not go over well with Soviet émigrés. Yoram Dinstein (interview, May 3, 2003) made the same point.

57. UJA reported on cutbacks in housing for immigrants (UJA document to members of executive re: "Notes on Executive Committee, Retreat, May 22–25, 1975," June 30, 1975, CJF files, box 658). GAO (1977) refers to vacant apartments built in wrong places in Israel. Dominitz (1996:123) admitted to shortcomings in material absorption

(housing, jobs) but commented that in some professions including medicine Israel provided better opportunities.

58. In a May 1976 *Jerusalem Post* article Mikhail Agursky claims that the Soviets did not jam Kol Israel until 1972 because they wanted to get rid of Jews. David Shipler ("Soviet Drive Against Dissidents and the Carter Response," *NYT*, February 12, 1977) reported that the Soviets stopped jamming Voice of America, British Broadcasting Corporation and others three years before in full bloom of détente. As early as 1966 American Jewish Conference on Soviet Jewry got Voice of America to increase broadcasts to the USSR. Later Senators Barry Goldwater, Edwin Muskie and George McGovern pressured Voice of American to increase its weekly 10 minute broadcasts to Soviet Jews to two and later three times per week (Orbach 1979:111,157). He notes that such broadcasts may have resulted in a greater dropout rate.

59. In Vienna, HIAS and JDC often disagreed as to who was a Jew. HIAS personnel believed that colleagues at JDC feared (in light of the post 1968 Polish exodus) that many non-Jews assumed Jewish identity to flee. Usually, having one or more Jewish parents was sufficient for HIAS and JDC officials (Memo, Ted Feder to Loni Mayer, July 10, 1973, JDC files). Those not meeting this criteria would be decided on a case-by-case basis. JDC used Rabbi Eisenberg who facilitated conversions (Memo, Len Seidenman to Gaynor Jacobson, July 3, 1969, HIAS files). A study by Gitelman (1989:172–175) found that more non-Jewish spouses went to the United States than to Israel.

60. Once this policy had been clear the Pentacostals set up a *vyzov*-manufactring office in Rome where people could call to get a *vyzov*. KGB gave out the Rome phone number.

61. Ralph Goldman (notes of July 9, 1976) reported that the Russians were sending out 18 percent non-Jews. Robert O. Freeman memo "The Advisability of Aiding the Soviet Jewish "Drop-Outs" December 1976 (JDC files).

62. A former Liaison Bureau official (interview with J. Shiran, February 28, 2003) claimed that ultra-Orthodox wanted Soviet Jewish émigrés to be resettled outside of Israel because of questions of their "Jewishness." Yehuda Dominitz (interview, July 3, 2001) claimed that opposition to conversations came from the Ultra-Orthodox in Antwerp, Belgium. He recalled conversions in Vienna involving 60 to 70 persons and Rabbis Steinmetz, Kleinfeld and Eisenberg. Rabbi Untermeyer, the chief Ashkenazi Rabbi of Israel approved the setting up of a Rabbinical Court for conversions in Vienna. Those undergoing conversion remained in Vienna a few weeks.

63. Israel settled few Soviet immigrants in the territories with the exception of East Jerusalem. In 1990 5,830 Soviet Jews resided in East Jerusalem. According to Cohen (1991) most Soviet immigrants chose not to settle in the West Bank and Gaza. Out of 180,000 immigrants during 1968–1989, 1,800 settled in the West Bank and zero in Gaza. In 1989 184 out of 13,000 and in 1990 2,500 out of 200,000 went to the West Bank and 500 to the Golan. Minister of Housing Ariel Sharon did not settle Russian immigrants in the territories in order not to sabotage their emigration. Even Minister of Science Yuval Neeman, from the settlement party, "went so far as to declare that Soviet immigrants should not be settled in the territories. Gorbachev had enough problems with the Arab countries on the subject of aliya (immigration to Israel)" (Gur-Gurevitz 1996:24).

64. At a closed meeting in Jerusalem in the early 1990s Simcha Dinitz told Jewish Agency staff involved in flying Soviet Jews to Israel via Eastern European cities that

we not only brought the musicians to play in our new orchestras but the audiences as well.

65. Irving Kessler at a December 10, 1976 meeting, for example, commented that 64 percent of Soviet Jewish immigrants were European. After 1989, the Israeli government provided some of the married children of poorer veteran Israelis access to some of the housing built for Soviet immigrants.

66. When working for HIAS in the 1950s Jim Rice assisted in clandestine operations which brought North African Jews to Israel (see Szulc 1991:261).

67. Active in national UJA and the Greater New York Federation-UJA, Glick was a banker and partner in a New York Stock Exchange firm. He was also very active in American Israel Cultural Foundation and JDC. He served as President of HIAS 1972–1977 (letter, Carl Glick to Prime Minister Begin, September 29, 1977, HIAS files).

68. He also took umbrage with the term "dropout." While he understood why the Israelis used it, in this country, he argued, "we see them as refugees requiring assistance and as future citizens and members of our Jewish communities." He chastised Ralph Goldman's negative description of dropouts as being more tourists than people escaping from persecution. Most in fact had relatives so this involved "family reunion." "One can want to help Israel and be concerned without describing them in such a way "as to create a lack of sympathy for them and confusion in the mind of the American Jewish community." (Letter, Jim Rice to Jerry Goodman, June 28, 1977, HIAS files); Letter, Jim Rice to Ralph Goldman, December 13, 1976 (HIAS files). HIAS and other groups consistently argued that family reunification justified Soviet Jews coming to the United States as refugees. In a letter to the *New York Times* of September 28, 1976, James Rice referred to 80 to 90 percent as being "family reunion cases." Gaynor Jacobson referred to 80 percent (Letter to Colette Shulman, February 25, 1977, HIAS files). Also see letter of Jim Rice to *NYT*, October 8, 1976.

69. Karl Zukerman claimed this was not true. He cited a 10-year survey showing Jewish affiliation of Soviet Jews in the United States. Some federations emphasized "Jewish programs" in local absorption. According to Ted Comet (1989:22,23), most active were the Federations of San Francisco, Chicago and to a lesser extent Los Angeles. Gitelman (1989:180–182) also questions the assumption of non-affiliation.

70. Dinstein (1989:36–38) wrote that the dropouts could jeopardize the entire movement; if Jews do not go to their homeland then their situation is not unique. Levanon (1995:442–444) suggested that only on the basis of a return to homeland had the Liaison Bureau received the support of World Jewry. A memo probably prepared by Carl Glick (to HIAS Executive, December 1, 1976, CJF files) admitted that it was easier for Soviet authorities if émigrés went to Israel because they tell the rest of the population that Jews are outsiders and are returning to the homeland.

71. Goodman argued that the movement in the Soviet Union had struggled for the right of "Jews to settle in Israel and live according to their culture and traditions."

72. Writing in the late 1980s Friedgut (1989:4) argued that the overwhelming majority of activists in the USSR were involved in a movement in the "name of aliyah, immigration to Israel, as Zionists devoted to their people's return to its homeland." They become angry and frustrated at dropouts who get growing percentage of few exit permits. Even if they support the principle of freedom of choice, they are bitter. This was clearly ideological. *JTA* of January 21 attributes this position to Golda Meir.

73. Goldman (1995:21) criticized HIAS for using Israeli visas rather than conducting a campaign for invitations from the USA.

74. Later (see below) the Liaison Bureau and others would cite Soviet diplomatic sources. Buwalda claims (1997:167) that all these sources were lower level with the exception of the Soviet Ambassador to France.

75. Nehemiah Levanon told the JDC Executive Meeting of November 16, 1976 that the policy of his government was to send false papers to every Jew in the USSR even though they knew that they were dropouts and would misuse them.

76. Soviet authorities decided who received an exit permit; they knew that almost all Jews from Georgia, Moldavia and the Baltic areas went to Israel while most Jews from Moscow, Kiev and Leningrad went to the United States. See JDC Executive Committee Meetings, October 30, 1974 and May 27, 1976 (JDC files); Memo, Akiva Kohane to Ralph Goldman, March 15, 1976, "Transmigrants in Rome,"(JDC files); and Sarah Honig, "KGB organizes drop-out of Soviet Jews in Vienna," *Jerusalem Post (JP)*, October 21, 1976. Jerry Goodman wrote Eugene Gold of the American Jewish Committee that a high State Department official reported that there was no evidence to suggest that dropouts bothered Soviet officials. Carl Glick (memo draft to HIAS Board, December 1, 1976, HIAS files) reported that Leonid Brezhnev told Armand Hammer that he could care less about dropouts. Some would later (Ralph Goldman; Glick to Board, August 7, 1976, HIAS files) say that the Soviets preferred they leave on Israeli visas for fees twice as high as other visas and have to renounce citizenship

77. Supporters of freedom of choice also believed that an effort could be made to make the absorption in the United States focus more on Jewish identity and values.

78. Goldman claims that an agreement was worked out with Prime Minister Begin concerning Iranian Jews who would be helped regardless of where they wanted to resettle. In cases of Iranian Jews in Vienna who wanted to go to the United States, JDC would contact their relatives to cover the cost of travel. If relatives were unable to help, the refugees took loans from Hebrew Free Loan Societies.

79. Ralph Goldman (Note on trip to Rome and Vienna, June 23, 1976) suggested only to employ dropouts as interpreters and only while being processed for visas. Uzi Narkiss (letter to Gaynor Jacobson, January 5, 1977) protested HIAS hiring dropouts in Vienna (and Rome). Earlier, Gaynor Jacobson claimed that HIAS "never employed Soviet Jewish drop-outs for operational work in its Vienna office." He said two women dropouts were employed to type forms required by the Italian and Austrian governments (JTA, January 26, 1977).

80. In a telex to Gaynor Jacobson (April 20, 1976), Len Seidenman claimed that Don Robinson of JDC supported these ideas.

81. Harold Friedman argued that some accused him of selling out to the Israelis when he committed HIAS to the Pincus agreement.

82. The Prime Minister and head of the Jewish Agency Executive co-chaired. Diaspora representatives on the Jewish Agency Board of Governors participated. Some argued that the Israeli government used this Committee to tell Jewish Agency officials and Diaspora leaders what was expected of them (letter of Chiam Zohar, October 30, 1984).

83. Max Fisher chaired the Jewish Agency Board of Governors from June 1971 until 1982. Jerold Hoffberger succeeded him. Earlier he had chaired the UJA (1965–1967), UIA (1968–1971) and the CJF (1969–1971, Golden 1992).

84. Louis Pincus served as Chair of the Jewish Agency until his death in 1973. He was succeeded by Pincus Sapir who died in 1975. Yosef Almogi served from 1975 to 1978. He was succeeded by Leon Dulzin. Simcha Dinitz later replaced Dulzin in December 1987 (Golden 1992:255).

85. Ralph Goldman claims that he suggested the idea of a Committee of Eight to Prime Minister Rabin (Shachtman 2001:124). Many American Jewish communal leaders preferred to conduct sensitive matters in secrecy. For example, in a letter to Carl Glick (October 10, 1977) Phil Klutznick wrote that we both agree "better if there was not this difference of opinion expressed publicly, even though people can differ privately as much as they wish."

86. Fisher consulted frequently with Nehemia Levanon. Later he would use Ralph Goldman to draw up an "American response" to the Prime Minister's proposals on drop outs (see Chapter 4).

87. At the second meeting Nehemia Levanon even suggested withholding documents from dropouts so that HIAS would "break its neck."

88. Grisha Feigin, a leader of Russian immigrants in Israel, protested his exclusion from Committee of Eight (*Daily News*, July 7, 1976); Agenda, Committee of Eight, July 15, 1976 (JDC files); JDC Executive Committee Meeting, September 21, 1976. Dominitz may have replaced Narkiss.

89. Prior to meeting in Geneva, the Americans (possibly with some of the Israelis including Nehemia Levanon) held two working sessions in the United States. They had received a basic plan prepared by Nehemia Levanon. Ralph Goldman, Gaynor Jacobson and Phil Bernstein prepared an 18 item agenda. (Memo, Ralph Goldman to Jack Weiler, August 20, 1976, JDC files); Executive Committee Meeting JDC, August 11, 1976. Agenda, Committee of Eight, July 15, 1976 (JDC files); *Jewish Post of NY* A new Lay Committee Studies dropout issue" December 3, 1976; *Chicago Tribune*, "Israel Eyes Penalties to keep Soviet Jews" July 20, 1976.

90. Sarah Honig in the *JP* of August 17, 1976 reported that the Committee of Eight rejected a proposal (suggested by Ralph Goldman) to limit invitations to certain areas of the USSR. He also asked Levanon to cease practice of Israeli emissaries of collecting names of potential émigrés from dropouts ("Notes for David" June 22, 1976, JDC files). Frank Reiss (Leonard Seidenman and Irving Haber, August 30, 1976, JDC files) say still sending letters of invitation to persons in USSR that they know will drop out.

91. Johnston (November 9, 1976) reported that the Committee proposed to send dropouts to Vienna without documents or money (while bags went to Tel Aviv) and to close offices of HIAS and JDC in Rome and Vienna. At this time Fisher met with United States officials and learned that 20,000 visas were available for Russians and that they would be liberal on interpretation of family reunification. During the meetings in Geneva, Ralph Goldman consulted with Max Fisher (Ralph Goldman to record, n.d. : Letter, Ralph Goldman to Jack Weiler, August 20, 1976, JDC files).

92. He noted that the American government had built transit-housing facilities in Greece and about 100 persons from Romania had gone there from Israel (wives not Jewish). Goldman suggested using Germany ("Notes on trip to Vienna and Rome" June 23, 1976, JDC files).

93. They failed to reach a decision on baggage subsidies and weight limitations. Someone noted that many émigrés take things out that they later sell.

94. Golden suggests that Fisher reached the height of his power and influence with Gerald Ford in the White House (1992:300).

95. Gaynor Jacobson had worked with Israeli authorities at the end of World War II to help them move Holocaust survivors to Israel. He later cooperated with them to bring North African Jews to Israel (Szulc 1990). He claimed (1990:20) that he wanted Soviet Jews to go to Israel but without coercion.

96. The Levanon document begins: "From the outset, the moral imperative and political drive of the struggle on behalf of Soviet Jewry have been founded upon the principle that Soviet Jews shall not be deprived of their right to emigrate and to unite with their brethren in Israel if they so desire." It goes on: "This service, rendered on behalf of the American Jewish community and with American Jewish public funds, actually encouraged the drop-out rate."

97. For example, instead of Rome being closed as "a center" it would be eliminated as "the center" for Third Country Processing cases (TCPs).

98. Gaynor Jacobson with Herbert Katzki of JDC and others met with Frank Armitage, Deputy Secretary of State for European affairs who advised that the Strategic Arms Limitation Talks may prevent "démarche with the Soviet Union on Soviet Jewry." He felt that the Soviets would demand trade off if we request more visas for direct movement to the United States. He did not see a problem to issue visas in Moscow provided they could guard against KGB agents. He also expressed the view that the Soviets were pleased with dropouts since it helped them with Arab nations. They also met with James C. Wilson of the State Department's Bureau of Humanitarian Affairs, an aid to Congressman Joshua Eilberg, and with Mark Talisman. Also see handnotes of Carl Glick, Carl Glick files, folder #20 *Noshrim* (HIAS files). He report that James Wilson and James Carlin did not want rash actions because they had just got over the budget hurdle and needed Congressional action by October 2.

99. Carl Glick also has hand notes of this meeting in HIAS files, non *Noshrim* box #6.

100. Yitzhak Rager of the Liaison Bureau gave an optimistic report about his contacts in Austria and in the Netherlands and on measures Israel took to improve absorption.

101. According to Windmueller (1999:166) and Glick (interview, September 22, 1999) Fisher had stated: "we have to give Golda what she wants." Many criticized HIAS for circulating the Lenz letter (see below) opposing the proposed policies of the Committee of Eight.

102. He indicated that he would contact Henry Kissinger and that contacts would be made with Congress. While emphasizing the need to work from below, he stated that if need be he would see the President and Attorney General Edward Levi. Fisher indicated that Gaynor Jacobson would coordinate the work in Washington, D.C. Quiet contacts would begin with various American Jewish organizations.

103. For example Leonard Seidenman of HIAS reported to his NY office that Dulzin on returning to Israel stated that "with a clear conscience . . . they should only be helped (to immigrate to Israel) even if this means that others cannot get out of the country . . . says that his position of no assistance to dropouts is supported by leaders of Diaspora Jewish community."

104. Ralph Goldman told the JDC Executive Committee on October 12, 1976 that he expected a report by the Committee of Eight in a week. He suggested that success depended on the willingness of the American government to admit Soviet Jews. He

warned "for the sake of policy, we don't want to use any kind of quota . . . because that's a very disturbing kind of thing for all of us."

105. He also hoped to get additional Third Country Processing visas. The *Jewish Week-American Examiner* of October 26, 1976 reported that President Gerald Ford told a delegation of 150 Jewish leaders in Washington, D.C. that he "would make every effort with Congress and the Soviet Union to get broader opportunities for Jews to leave for Israel and the United States."

106. Telex, JDC Israel to Ralph Goldman, September 20, 1976, report that Israel Russian Immigrant Committee in favor of cutting aid in Vienna to dropouts and that 13 members resign claiming that the organization is a rubber stamp for Jewish Agency.

107. In contrast the *Maoz* group in Israel felt it wrong to force people to come to Israel; they favored aiding dropouts. They also felt that HIAS and JDC should not be made scapegoats for Israeli failure in absorption.

108. Alexander Lunz letters to Mr. Jacobson, Yitzhak Rabin et. al. mid September 1976 (JDC files) say Soviet émigrés suffer but should not cut aid; Open letter to Committee of Eight, Lunz et al., August 18, 1976, discredit Leon Jick letter which stated that Soviet Jewish activists oppose aid to drop outs. Also Luntz letter, November 9, 1976; and Johnston (November 9, 1976).

109. Others claimed that aid attracted Soviet Jews to the United States (Letter of M. Azbel et. al from Vilna and Gorky, received by phone, September 27, 1976, JDC files).

110. Ralph Goldman thought Eban's statement "regrettable" (Notes, Executive Committee JDC, December 8, 1976). Jonathan Frankel of the Hebrew University (*JP,* "Free Choice for Soviet Jews" September 23, 1976) said coercion would discourage many from leaving and bring to Israel many more who would want to leave. He said that basically the policy was designed to force people to come to Israel. He felt that the Soviets let Jews go because of pressure from the West and that they did not care where they went (see "Soviet Jews' Flow to US Worrying Israeli Government," *NYT,* September 26, 1976; *Washington Post,* H. Greenway "Soviet Emigrants Who 'Dropout' to U.S. Stir Dispute in Israel," September 27, 1976).

111. The *JTA,* December 1, 1976 report that *JP* favor Committee proposals and *Haaretz* opposed them. See S. Zalman Abramov "The Crux of the Drop-Out Issue," *JP,* December 9, 1976.

112. Kelman headed the SCA Task Force on Soviet Jewry. The 400 strong Orthodox Rabbinical Alliance of America as well as the Union of Orthodox Jewish Congregations endorsed and recommended continuation of aid to Soviet émigrés even if they chose America (*Jewish Week-American Examiner,* November 28–December 4, 1976). *Time* (November 22, "Soviet Jews") reported that Irving Howe and Moshe Decter favored freedom of choice. On November 30, 1976 (CJF files, box 710) Agudat Israel's convention passed a resolution opposing financial pressure being applied by Jewish organizations against dropouts.

113. HIAS files contain many documents supporting freedom of choice. For example, the Jewish Community Council of Greater Washington, D.C. (letter to Carl Glick on December 27, 1976) voted to favor the right to emigrate and settle in the country of choice.

114. In mid-December the American Jewish Committee again criticized a recommendation of the Committee of Ten not to aid dropouts arguing that this violated the

original principles and objectives of the Committee of Eight. The American Jewish Committee ("Statement," December 15, 1976, HIAS files) doubted that the Soviets would allow Jews to immigrate directly to the United States. The Jewish Labor Committee (Draft Resolution, December 13, 1976, HIAS files) also argued that Jewish communal organizations had an obligation to help Jews resettle in the country of their choice.

115. In 1972, the Committee for Concerned Scientists supported Moscow seminars for Soviet Jews. The Bay Area Council on Soviet Jewry encouraged American scientists at artificial intelligence convention in September 1975 in Soviet Georgia to demand that Dr. Benjamin Lerner attend. They escorted him from Moscow (Orbach 1979:101,102 and Buwalda, 1997:62,63).

116. Spiegel forwarded this to Ralph Goldman on February 2, 1977 (HIAS files). Spiegel of UCLA collected views of fellow academics for JDC and others. He gave Goldman a copy of Elihu Bergman's (Harvard) analysis of Prof. Percy Tannenbaum's (UC Berkeley) study that found most Soviet Jews decided on their destination before they left the USSR (also see *JP*, December 9, 1976).

117. Ralph Goldman reported that Austrian Minister of Interior would cooperate but that Prime Minister Bruno Kreisky opposed the plan. Eliahu Salpeter writing in the *Israel Star* of February 22, 1977 "Soviet Emigration: the Operation that Failed" argued that American Jewish leaders were reluctant to press politicians in Washington DC for American visas. At this time Max Fisher might have asked Larry Eagleburger in the State Department if there was something that could be done to prevent Soviet Jewish émigrés from coming to the United States (Interview with Larry Eagleburger, July 12, 2003).

118. Some Israeli officials feared that bringing reluctant immigrants to Israel against their will would demoralize the country. At the JDC Executive Meeting on December 8, 1976 Ralph Goldman reported that Yitzhak Rabin had met with Bruno Kreisky in Geneva and that Kreisky agreed to cooperate on dropouts.

119. At this time at a CJF Board meeting (no date, HIAS files) Max Fisher spoke of the Committee of Eight and its goals of getting the maximum number out of USSR and freedom of choice. He did not mention Israel.

120. Goodman noted that the Committee of Ten expected that the federations would resettle all those who reached their communities. Based on Soviet authorities allowing 900 Armenians and 200 Jews to leave in 1976 on American visas, he argued ". . . *the Soviet Union has accepted the principle of direct visas,* mostly based on family reunion."

121. In late October NJCRAC executive did not vote on the Committee of Ten proposals but decided to consult with constituent bodies (Phil Bernstein to Ralph Goldman, Irving Kessler and Gaynor Jacobson, October 25, 1976). Bernstein wrote Fisher (December 23, 1976) that if a vote had been taken that NJCRAC would have voted overwhelmingly against HIAS cutting aid to dropouts.

122. Johnston (November 9, 1976), reported that the Immigration and Naturalization Service regional office in Rome cut by 50 percent the number of U.S. visas granted Soviet Jews in Moscow, Rome and Vienna. In a memo to cooperating agencies on November 30, 1976 (CJF files, box 710) Gaynor Jacobson talked about the serious problem of a back up of dropouts in Rome. Also see Executive Committee JDC of December 8, 1976. Memo, Nahum Barren to Max Fisher (December 21, 1976). On

December 1, 1976 Gaynor Jacobson wrote Max Fisher (HIAS files) that there were more refugees than 10,200 yearly conditional entry numbers. He urged Max to convince Attorney General Edward Levi to grant more parole visas. Gaynor Jacobson on March 7, 1977 sent a version of this letter to Mrs. Joyce Starr of the White House (JDC files). In early 1977 Attorney General Griffen Bell extended Parole to some Soviet Jews in Rome (*American Israelite,* "HIAS Will Help Jewish Emigrés Who Skip Israel" April 7, 1977).

123. "Canadian Jewish Congress Weekly Summary" (November 12, 1976) reported that Secretary of State for External Affairs of Canada Donald Jamieson was "coolly rebuffed" when he raised the issue of reunification of families in his recent talks in USSR. Mr. Walter M. Lipppman, Executive Vice President of Australian Jewish Welfare Societies wrote Phil Bernstein (December 8, 1976, HIAS files) that due to unemployment our government did not encourage immigration but we get a steady flow of permits. We favor maximum to Israel but believe have to help those that come here. Lippman wrote Gaynor Jacobson (January 11, 1977, CJF files) that idea of letters to invite relatives would not be worthwhile since Australian law includes only parents and dependent children for family migration. He did not favor a change in the law because authorities were sympathetic to our requests.

124. As early as 1969 HIAS warned the Jewish Agency that the International Rescue Committee could appeal to federations for aid in resettlement. It also warned that it would be harmful to have anti-Israeli Israeli émigrés (Soviet Jews and others) being taken care of by the International Rescue Committee (Meeting on cases of questionable Jewish Identity, July 25, 1969, HIAS files). In a *NYT* ad of January 13, 1977 Rav Tov wrote: "Is it not to deal thy bread to the hungry? Claimed that established Jewish organizations were not helping hungry Jewish refugees in Europe who chose not to go to Israel. This is totally contrary to the charitable and humane traditions of the Jewish people. Where is the conscience of world Jewry?" They asked for donations for food packages for Ostia.

125. Herbert Katzki of JDC (Telex to JDC Jerusalem, October 22, 1976) instructed JDC staff in Israel that Ralph Goldman and Max Fisher wanted them to get the Prime Minister to talk to William Rosenwald to convince him to support the Committee of Eight and to send his thoughts to HIAS before the Tuesday meeting (JDC files).

126. Max Fisher, Jerold Hoffberger, Frank Lautenberg and Richard Maass planned to meet with leaders of HIAS to get them to agree.

127. The *JP* reported (October 29, 1976) that Glick failed twice to have the HIAS board reject the Committee of Eight proposals outright. Bernard Postal (*Jewish Week,* November 14–20, 1976).

128. Harold Friedman argued that family reunion was a fiction. He believed that Soviet Jews had no real or immediate family in the United States, only distant relatives who in the past had refused to sign affidavits. In a memo to Leonard Seidenman and Irving Haber (August 30, 1976 JDC file) Frank Reiss reported that Soviet authorities feared Ukrainians and others would want similar opportunities and that to leave with citizenship in tact (on American visa) that would allow return. Gaynor Jacobson argued (letter to Mrs. Joyce Starr, March 8, 1977 (JDC files) that 90 percent of those who left USSR for USA believed "it was necessary to use Israeli invitations and visas to secure their USSR exit." Ralph Goldman reported (Meeting of JDC Area Committee on

Eastern Europe, June 20, 1977) that the experiment on direct visas to USA and Canada or other countries did not work.

129. The Committee of Eight expected that some persons who arrived in Vienna and who had relatives in the USA would begin to apply for an affidavit from the USA. This clearly could not be completed in 90 days.

130. Someone also referred to Glick's complaint that the Committee had decided to wait until after the U.S. election to determine the Soviet position.

131. The *JP* claimed that HIAS and JDC reject proposal that after February 1, 1977 Russian Jews would to spend 6 months in Israel and then leave without any support. In a note to be passed on to Nehemiah Levanon (Phil Bernstein to Ralph Goldman, October 29, 1976, JDC files) "next steps on emigration of Soviet Jews', Phil Bernstein emphasized problems in Rome, DC (with State Department) and the need to consult with more American Jewish leaders and leaders of the Brussels Conference. He also argued that the Ford administration was dubious about changing visa and immigration policies. Also see Johnston (November 9, 1976).

132. He also confirmed that he told the Dutch Foreign Minister to issue visas to all applicants including persons not intending to go on to Israel after exiting the Soviet Union.

133. At the end of October Max Fisher and others remained optimistic that the details could be worked out in the near future (Memo, Phil Bernstein to Ralph Goldman "Next steps on emigration of Soviet Jews" October 29, 1976, JDC files). Phil Bernstein wanted to determine what to do now rather than wait until February.

134. Glick claims that the General Assembly delegates voted down the Committee of Eight proposals. Richard Jaffe ("Long Debate Due Before Action in Soviet Dropouts," *Jewish Week*, November 21–27, 1976) reported that no decision was reached at the General Assembly.

135. It received a $250,000 grant from UJA to hire staff to implement a plan to encourage Soviet Jews who wished to go the United States to apply for American visas (*JP*, November 22, 1976).

136. At a meeting on November 9, Rabbi Schindler, President of the Presidents Conference called for a "unified position that would avoid polarization in the American Jewish community between American Jewry, world Jewry and Israel." Fisher claimed that the dropout problem was "untruthfully reported" (*Jewish Week*, November 20, 1976). Charlotte Jacobson, chair of the American Section of the WZO, told UJA of Canada that a 100 day information campaign would soon begin to tell Soviet Jews that holders of Israeli visas would be told either to go to Israel or to forfeit organized Jewish aid.

137. In "Soviet Jewish Emigration, Questions and Answers" December 21, 1976 (CJF files) Goodman explained that HIAS and JDC assistance to dropouts would be maintained for the time being.

138. The Presidents of Major American Jewish Organizations was a non-centralized body par excellence.

139. The major contributors to the United Jewish Appeal (UJA) dominated the leadership of the American Jewish community and its federations since the Second World War. Gone from the scene were Rabbis Stephen Wise and Abba Hillel Silver. Importantly, the local federations raised about 80 percent of UJA monies (Golden

1992:76). Over the years many federation and CJF Presidents became active in the national UJA (Silberman 1985:212). They served on the boards of the UIA, UJA, Joint Distribution Committee (JDC), HIAS, and the Board of Governors of the Jewish Agency. Many also served on the boards of B'nai B'rith, Anti-Defamation League, American Jewish Committee and American Jewish Congress.

140. On the issue of dropouts JJ Goldberg wrote that an enraged Israeli government. "was unprepared to deal with the American Jewish community as an equal partner, much less as a rival" (Goldberg 185,186).

4

Round Two of the Freedom of Choice Debate: The Israelis Fail Again

In the first round of the struggle over freedom of choice for Soviet Jewish émigrés, lay leaders and professionals in American Jewish federations and HIAS defeated the government of Israel, its Liaison Bureau and the Jewish Agency. American Jewish leadership refused to acquiesce to the Israeli demand to cease helping Soviet Jewish émigrés, who exited on visas for Israel, to enter and resettle in the United States. Memories of political inaction and impotence in the face of closed American gates during the Holocaust together with a commitment to freedom of choice, the Jewish tradition of rescuing prisoners, organizational interests and a desire by some to rejuvenate the American Jewish community explain the refusal of American Jewish leaders to accommodate Israeli demands.

Until the Soviets closed the gates to Jewish emigration in 1982 the Liaison Bureau and its American Jewish allies continued to pressure the federations and HIAS to lessen their support for helping Soviet Jews resettle in the United States. A revised Liaison Bureau position emphasized three components. First, it favored a guarantee of freedom of choice for all Soviet Jews within the Soviet Union; Jews not wanting to go to Israel would apply in Moscow for visas to other countries. This proved problematic because the Soviet Union continued to limit the direct immigration of its citizens to the United States and other countries while being more accommodating toward requests for family reunification in Israel. Second, it agreed to American Jewish organizations aiding and resettling dropouts having first degree relatives in the West. Finally, while it pressured HIAS and JDC to cease aiding dropouts in Vienna and Rome, it consented to federations resettling Soviet Jews who arrive in their communities under the auspices of other, mostly non-Jewish refugee assistance organizations.

Two American Jews, Mr. Max Fisher, chairman of the Board of Governors of the Jewish Agency and a lay leader of enormous political stature in the Jewish community with close ties to Republican Presidents and Ralph Goldman, the Executive Vice President of JDC played key roles in mobilizing American Jewish support for the revised Israeli position. Both men, in principle, remained committed to the Committee of Eight position of cessation of American Jewish aid to Soviet Jewish émigrés who chose not to settle in Israel.

In this round, in contrast to the earlier period, the CJF, and its President, Mr. Morton Mandel of Cleveland, Ohio, played a more active role in the freedom of choice debate. Unlike Max Fisher and Ralph Goldman, who saw eye to eye with the Israeli leadership and Liaison Bureau, Morton Mandel held an independent view. While deferential and sympathetic to the Israeli position, he and other CJF leaders were often more concerned about freedom of choice and the need for consensus within their own organization (Phone interview, Morton Mandel, August 6, 2001).[1]

This chapter follows the second round of the struggle over freedom of choice. It documents the important role of CJF leaders in limiting Israeli influence on the Soviet Jewry advocacy movement in the United States. CJF leaders also checked and limited efforts of American Jewish leaders who supported the Israeli position. It reveals, however, that as an increasing number of Soviet Jews resettled in the United States several federations began having second thoughts about aiding and accepting them. In the long run the federations would become more sympathetic to the Israeli position of having a maximum number of Soviet Jewish émigrés settle in Israel.

INCREASED ACTIVITY IN VIENNA AND ROME

In early 1977 the situation remained unchanged for Jews in the Soviet Union. While allowing almost 15, 000 Jews to leave for Israel, the Soviet authorities permitted very few to leave for the United States and denied most requests to emigrate (Comments of Nehemia Levanon at JDC Executive Committee, July 26, 1977 and Letter, Gaynor Jacobson to Phil Bernstein, July 28, 1977, JDC files).[2] HIAS sought to secure additional invitations to the United States and Israel tried to improve its absorption policies. While Israel turned many loans for immigrants into grants, some American Jewish federations turned refugee grants into loans (See letter of Gaynor Jacobson to Jim Rice July 11, 1977, HIAS files).

The increase in dropouts and a slow issuance of American visas resulted in a backup of Soviet Jewish émigrés in the Rome area. By October 1977, the presence of over 3,000 Russian Jewish émigrés and another 1,000 or more Russian and Armenian migrants "stuck" in Rome turned into a crisis (Letter of American Council for Nationalist Service, American Fund for Czech Refugees, Church World Service, HIAS, IRC; Lutheran Immigration and Refugee Services, Migration and Refugee Services–United States Catholic Conference, and Tolstoy Foundation to White House, October 25, 1977, HIAS files). Over 5,000 were expected by the end of the year. In mid-March 1978 JDC predicted a shortage of about 12,500 visas by September 1979. It expected some recent arrivals to wait up to three years to obtain a visa (JDC Planning Department, "Projected Soviet Jewish Immigration to the USA, 1978–1979," March 28, 1978, JDC files). Pro-refugee groups complained about hardships for émigrés and argued that the situation both embarrassed the United States and could jeopardize the further exodus of Soviet Jews. They pinned their hopes on parole.[3] On June 14, 1978, the United States government authorized 12,000 parole visas to be used before May 1, 1979, for persons fleeing from Communist countries who feared persecution on the grounds of race, religion or political opinion (Gaynor Jacobson to cooperating agencies, June 21, 1978, HIAS files. Press release, Department of Justice, June 14, 1978, HIAS files). The number of Soviet Jewish émigrés in Rome reached 9,100 in March 1979. In May Attorney General Griffin Bell approved 25,000 parole visas for East European refugees, most of whom would be Soviet Jews (Ralph Goldman reports from the field, May 9, 1979, JDC files). Expecting the Rome caseload to reach 18,500 by the end of FY 1979, Jerold C. Hoffberger had asked for an additional 12,500 parole entries (Letter to Secretary of State Cyrus Vance, April 10, 1978, HIAS files and Transcript of JDC Executive Committee Meeting, March 21, 1979, JDC files).[4]

The cost of supporting and maintaining an increasing number of dropouts in Europe and resettling them in the United States became a major burden for the organized American Jewish community. Despite federal reimbursements, JDC and HIAS officials remained in an almost continuous state of concern about federal funding (Minutes of JDC Executive Committee, July 26, 1977, JDC files).[5] In addition JDC spent at least $4m per year to fund a Liaison Bureau project of sending relief packages to Jews in the Soviet Union (Shachtman 2001:175 and Transcript, JDC Executive Committee Meeting, February 7, 1979, JDC files).[6]

In December 1977 HIAS had estimated that it would provide assistance to 10,000 Soviet Jewish émigrés (8,800 to the United States) in 1978 at a cost of $8,118,000. By January 1978 it revised the figures to 14,000 (12,000 to the United States) and support for 6,000 in Vienna and Rome at a cost of $11.2m. By the end of the year it predicted the arrival of 24,000 Soviet Jews in 1979 (Letters, Gaynor Jacobson to Cooperating Agencies, June 21 and November 21, 1978, HIAS files).[7] Whereas JDC had its funds covered almost automatically by UJA, HIAS was in a more precarious position. Israeli pressure on the UIA and JDC, who had to approve UJA allocations to HIAS, often made funding a problem (Comments by Jerold Hoffberger at special meeting of UJA in

New York City, February 20 1978 (CJF files, box 658; Carl Glick to Board Members February 28, 1978, HIAS files).[8]

The large number of Soviet émigrés also created logistics problems in Europe for HIAS, JDC and the Jewish Agency. The émigrés flooded the understaffed offices in search of direction and assistance. Interviews by Israeli emissaries were often hurried ("Observation of interviews by Jewish Agency *Shlichim*," October 20, 1978, JDC files). For example in April 1979 when the Soviet exodus increased Ralph Goldman had doubts about HIAS and JDC Vienna being able to transport and then house additional persons in Rome. He rejected a suggestion from INS that non-Jewish organizations help with the Soviet Jewish caseload (Memo to file, Ralph Goldman, October 25, 1978, JDC files). He also doubted access to sufficient visas and had reservations about the ability of the federations to resettle 1,000 persons per week (Ralph Goldman, Report from the Field, March 9, 1979, JDC files).

The lack of visas explained only part of the problem. Other troubles included the cumbersome and time consuming processing procedure in Rome (Letter, Gaynor Jacobson to Len Seidenman, May 23, 1978, HIAS files; JDC, Executive Committee Meeting of April 5, 1978, JDC files). Émigrés had to fill out forms for INS, JDC and HIAS. It took the United States authorities almost 42 days to conduct a security clearance for a single refugee applicant (Comments of Ralph Goldman at JDC Executive Committee, September 22, 1977 JDC file).[9] The longer the process, the greater the expense for JDC and the United States government (Transcript, JDC Executive Meeting, February 7, 1979, JDC files).[10] By October 1979 the average length of stay of an émigré in Rome was 66 days; 62 for those going to the USA and 123 days for those going elsewhere (Memo, Feder to Ralph Goldman, October 17 1979, JDC files).

HIAS coordinated the match up between refugees and local CJF federations and welfare funds throughout the United States and with NYANA in the greater New York City area. Federation involvement reached 154 communities in 42 states and D.C. in 1979 (Edelman 1981:159). HIAS and CJF allocated a quota of Soviet refugees to each federation. Yet as early as 1977 and 1978 some federations were unable to act quickly enough to absorb visa ready refugees in Rome.[11]

The United States government provided aid on several fronts. First it helped fund the resettlement of Soviet Jews in Israel (UIA, "History of UIA-US Government Grant Funds [1973–1995], September 24, 2001; United States State Department, Bureau of Public Affairs "Soviet Jewish Immigration" July 1977).[12] Funding by the United States Government indicated the unique status of Soviet Jews in American refugee policy. Except for Soviet Jews in Israel, the United States had not funded the resettlement of refugees outside of the United States. The Cold War explained a great deal; the Soviet Jews were fleeing persecution in a Communist country. CJF and other groups also conducted a successful lobbying effort. For some in the Administration and Congress settling Soviet Jews in Israel may have been preferable to bringing them to the United States.

Second, the government of the United States provided reimbursement for the care and maintenance of political refugees, including Soviet Jews in Europe who applied for entry into the United States (Letter, Gaynor Jacobson to Al Chernin, March 1, 1978). It funded 85–93 percent of JDC refugee operation budget and 60–65 percent of HIAS budget (Bruce Leimsidor, "Minutes of NPPC," September 11, 1979, JDC files).[13] In practice, however, as in the early 1970s, funding proved problematic especially in the short term.[14] Finally, in 1978 Congress provided a block grant to CJF to help federations and HIAS resettle Soviet immigrants in the United States (Mort Mandel [CJF], form letter, March 30 1979, HIAS files).[15] The United States Department of Health, Education and Welfare administered the federal program (Letter of Department of Health, Education and Welfare to Carl Glick, October 3, 1978, HIAS files).

THE STRUGGLE BETWEEN ISRAEL AND AMERICAN JEWISH LEADERS CONTINUES

HIAS continued to help Russian Jews who had left Israel to obtain entry into the United States. In response to Israeli criticism, Gaynor Jacobson explained that "we have been quietly requested by American government officials to assume responsibility for processing these individuals and thus avoid developments which are undesirable for Israel, the United States and the American Jewish community" (Letter, Gaynor Jacobson to Uzi Narkis, November 1, 1977, HIAS files; Memo of Leonard Seidenman to Gaynor Jacobson, January, 27, 1978; *JTA*, April 4 1978; and Telex, Trobe to Ralph Goldman, April 4, 1978, JDC files).[16] The Helsinki generated United States Commission on Security and Cooperation in Europe had recommended bringing 300 Soviet Jews who had left Israel to the United States. The commission feared that the Soviets might exploit their plight to show the United States refusing to accept Soviet Jewish refugees (Memo, Jerry Goodman to Gaynor Jacobson et. al., August 22, 1977, CJF files); Memo from David Blumberg, October 7, 1977 (CJF files); Letter of Charles J. Tanenbaum, October 28, 1977 and *IRC Annual Report of 1980*, HIAS files).[17]

Leaders of HIAS at the time believed that Aryeh Dulzin of the Jewish Agency and the Liaison Bureau were trying to limit the entry of Soviet Jews to the United States. For example, Mr. Shmuel Adler, adviser to Absorption Minister David Levy, told Congressman Joshua Eilberg and his staff from the Subcommittee on Immigration, Citizenship and International Law that Soviet émigrés were not political refuges and that HIAS and others conceal true

costs of absorption in the United States (Letter, Gaynor Jacobson to Ralph
Goldman, April 13, 1978, HIAS files). Carl Glick called Adler's actions criminal (Letter to Elie Wiesel, April 20, 1978, HIAS files), *JTA*, February 22, 1978;
and Memo, Carl Glick to Elie Wiesel, February 23, 1977 (HIAS files).

Congressman Joshua Eilberg, however, defended HIAS. He issued a report
which argued that émigrés decided on final destination before leaving the
Soviet Union. A review of this report in the Israeli newspaper *Haaretz*
blamed the dropouts on a "bankrupt" and outdated Israeli absorption system
(Press release from Congressman Eilberg, February 1, 1978, and Habib Ke-
naan, "HIAS, Migration without Zionism," *Haaretz*, February 10, 1978).[18] At
the end of May 1978 Aryeh Dulzin warned that the dropout rate might reach
70 percent and urged HIAS, JDC and world Jewry to stop helping dropouts.
He argued that inside the Soviet Union "activists [were] . . . fighting for aliyah
to Israel, not for emigration to the United States" (*JTA*, May 31, 1978).[19] He
wanted HIAS and JDC to shut their offices in Vienna and for the Jewish
Agency to take over their activities.

In response Carl Glick issued a public statement: "The Jews of the Soviet
Union are in great danger . . . critical that all USSR Jews who wish to leave
be enabled to leave whatever there destination. {Essence of Jewish morality
that all Jews in need} . . . are provided with such help by their fellow Jews.
. . . [T]he Holocaust has provided a lesson on the need to provide help without questions. We do not agree with Mr. Dulzin that the choice should be to
stay in Russia or to go to Israel. . . . Over 80 percent of the Soviet Jews who
come to the United States or Canada are being reunited with their families
. . . major rationale for permitting to Jews to leave the Soviet Union is for the
purpose of family reunion. . . . [If close HIAS and JDC in Europe] their activities would be taken over . . . by other American voluntary agencies authorized and funded by the US government to provide help and assistance to
refugees" (HIAS news release June 6, 1978, HIAS files).[20]

In May 1977, Menachem Begin became Prime Minister of Israel. While his
party had often criticized the Liaison Bureau for its restraint vis-à-vis the Soviet
Union's treatment of its Jews, Begin did not immediately alter Liaison Bureau
policies. Moreover, he often disagreed with other Israeli leaders on the issue of
freedom of choice. He was much more tolerant and accepting of the primacy
of family reunification. In principle he opposed asking any country to prevent
the entry of Jews as refugees (Gur-Gurevitz 1996:7). He told an American Jewish audience in November 1976 that while he wanted Soviet Jews to go to Israel in principle, ". . . Nevertheless, there are human problems involved and in
my opinion. . . We cannot just abruptly cease helping our brethren who do not
go to Israel. That we cannot do" (Dialogue Rabbi William Berkowitz and Prime
Minister Menachem Begin, Institute of Adult Jewish Studies of Congregation B'-
nai Jeshurun, NY, 1977, HIAS files).[21]

While the new Prime Minister was willing to compromise, many of the American Jewish supporters of freedom of choice were not. At the April 11, 1978 meeting of the Coordinating Committee in Jerusalem he stated that the group could not decide that HIAS should stop helping dropouts (Jerold Hoffberger, Notes of Coordinating Committee meeting, April 11, 1978, CJF files, box 710).[22] Significantly, he stated that "we" might influence the dropouts but have no right to order them to come to Israel. While all Israelis agreed that all Russian Jews should come to Israel they also believed that no Jew should be let down. He ordered the Liaison Bureau to work with the Dutch to have their embassy convince Russian Jews that it was their moral obligation to come to Israel if they left on Israeli visas. He called the entire issue a national dilemma that needed time to be worked out. He called for consultation with HIAS and a dialogue if necessary.

The debate continued at the June 1978 Jewish Agency Board of Governors in Jerusalem. When the Israelis suggested direct flights, someone raised the problem that many Russian Jews might want to leave after arriving in Israel. The body took no action. Rabbi Israel Miller of the United States asked whether the Jewish Agency could assume HIAS and JDC activities in Vienna. Yehuda Dominitz of the Jewish Agency explained that the Austrian authorities would not allow it. At the end of the Board meetings Max Fisher announced that American Jews would not end aid to Soviet Jewish dropouts. He said that most American Jewish leaders supported this view. This indicated a clear split between Israeli and American Jewish leaders.

Despite the apparent policy disagreement on dropouts, the Liaison Bureau, HIAS, JDC, and the Jewish Agency agreed to a high-level professional consultation team to suggest ways to increase Soviet Jewish immigration to Israel and to reduce the drop out rate (*JTA*, June 19, 1978). The team met in Israel from August 23–28, 1978. They discussed changes in absorption in Israel and resettlement in the United States and then focused on Vienna and Rome. HIAS and the Jewish Agency agreed to end a practice of allowing émigré families to split up with the elderly going to Israel and younger persons to the United States. When children prefer the United States and parents Israel HIAS would not service unless the parents have other children in Israel. Participants also agreed with a Jewish Agency request for more time with the émigrés in Europe believing "that if [they] knew more about Israel, and what Israel has to offer them and their children, many more of them would choose Israel" (Ralph Goldman hand notes, August 24, 1978, on *Noshrim* Committee of functional agencies and "The *Noshrim*," summary minutes, August 27, 1978, JDC files).[23] This would eventually lead to joint counseling of émigrés in Vienna by the Jewish Agency, HIAS and JDC and a "Naples Plan" which proposed having the dropouts spend two weeks in Italy under the auspices of the Jewish Agency before their arrival in Rome.

Members of the team proposed keeping the discussions and proposals quiet (Ralph Goldman notes to file August 27, 1978).[24] They decided not to submit the proposal to the Coordinating Committee ostensibly because neither HIAS nor JDC officially participated in the Coordinating Committee. The real reason for this decision, however, may have been the participation of representatives of the CJF on the Coordinating Committee. The CJF had rejected the previous proposals of the Committee of Eight. Nehemia Levanon feared that CJF might torpedo any effort to strongly influence more Soviet Jews to go to Israel. Ralph Goldman warned that the Prime Minister needed to make a strong case in order to win over the American Jewish community (Ralph Goldman to file, August 28, 1978, JDC files). For example, at the time Phil Bernstein of CJF argued that what actions other Jewish organizations should take on dropouts were outside the power of the Jewish Agency (Letter, Phil Bernstein to Rafael Kotlowitz, September 21, 1978, JDC files). Nevertheless, Goldman reported that federation professionals accepted the proposed changes but had to sell them to their lay leaders (Ralph Goldman to file, August 28, 1978 and September 12, 1978).

A series of meetings of this team held in Vienna on or about October 18, 1978 are revealing. The Liaison Bureau expected that two thirds of the expected 36,000 Soviet Jewish émigrés in 1979 would drop out (Memo "re: *Noshrim*, Vienna, Rome and Ostia) 15–17 October" October 25, 1978, (JDC files).[25] Not wanting Rav Tov and other non-Jewish refugee agencies to meet the trains arriving from the Soviet Union the team members agreed to limit access only to Jewish Agency emissaries who would now meet all the trains. Until this time, manpower limitations permitted Agency emissaries to meet only some of the trains (Ralph Goldman to files "Meeting of Team" October 18, 1978 and "Train visits," October 19, 1978, JDC files).[26] The team also called for additional visas to the United States and a speeding up of processing in Rome (JDC Executive Committee, November 2, 1978, JDC files).[27]

The team wanted to bring all immigrants and dropouts under one roof in Vienna and to have the Jewish Agency spend about two weeks with them. This required either expanding the existing hostel or adding another in Vienna. When this became impractical the group focused on Italy and the *Naples Plan. Yehuda Dominitz and Nehemia Levanon hoped that the plan would increase immigration to Israel by 5 to 7 percent.*[28]

Under the Naples Plan the Vienna offices of HIAS and JDC would become non-operational. The Jewish Agency would transport all Soviet émigrés within 72 hours of their arrival in Austria to Naples where they would be under its supervision for about two weeks.[29] Thereafter, those going to Israel would be flown there and all others would be transferred to JDC, HIAS and other organizations in Rome (Ralph Goldman notes, "Additional Processing in Italy Team," October 25, 1978).[30] The Jewish Agency secured 600 beds in the Grand Hotel in Pinotamore, Italy. Then Yehuda Dominitz informed the others that the Agency would need at least six months to prepare the program in Naples. Shortly thereafter, he informed Ralph Goldman that a committee representing the Jewish Agency, Liaison Bureau and Israeli government decided not to proceed with the Naples plan (Ralph Goldman to file "Phone talk with Dominitz," November 2, 1978, JDC files).[31] HIAS and JDC continued their activities in Vienna (Ralph Goldman, "Jewish Agency Program for Extended Screening," October 27, 28, 1978. JDC files).[32]

While these efforts were taking place, in November 1978, a Knesset Committee charged HIAS and JDC with encouraging Soviet Jewish émigrés to come to the United States rather than to Israel. The Committee called on the Israeli government and Jewish Agency to cease cooperation with JDC and HIAS, explore the possibility of granting citizenship to Russian Jews in Moscow, work for direct flights from Moscow, and revoke foreign ministry documents covering transportation of Soviet émigrés from Vienna to Rome. This angered Ralph Goldman. He argued that HIAS "encourage[d] those who came out of the Soviet Union with Israeli visas to go instead to the West, . . . JDC . . . oppose[d drop outs and fought] the issue in the halls of policy and opinion makers" (Ralph Goldman to file, "Phone Conversation with Dominitz," November 2, 1978).[33] Nevertheless, JDC provided dropouts with care and maintenance. Ralph Goldman called on Aryeh Dulzin to disassociate himself from the Knesset decisions. Dulzin refused.

For the moment Ralph Goldman broke ranks with the Israelis on the issue of dropouts. He later told a Liaison Bureau friend that he had no quarrel with the Knesset but "I do question the moral basis and courage of the government and Jewish Agency leadership when they do not want to take responsibility for the dropouts but instead prefer to place the blame on JDC and HIAS . . . [who have been] . . . asked to carry out services which we all had agreed should be handled by the Jewish Agency, only because today it is politically uncomfortable for the Jewish Agency leaders to take the step" (Ralph Goldman to file "Phone with Shaike [Dan]," November 4, 1978; Goldman 1995:20).[34]

In March 1979 Rafael Kotlowitz and Aryeh Dulzin met with American Jewish leaders about the 76 percent dropout rate. A month later, Jewish Agency Treasurer Akiva Lewinsky complained that UJA funds raised for Israel were being used to absorb Soviet Jews in the United States (Ralph Goldman to Aryeh Dulzin [telegram] November 14, 1978; *JTA*, March 22, 1979; and Ralph Goldman telex #653 to Don Robinson, April 1979, JDC files).

Meetings with American Jewish leaders and the Prime Minister were planned for June (1979) in Jerusalem. In the interim Nehemia Levanon made new suggestions for reducing the dropout rate which were similar to those proposed by the Committee of Eight. Levanon urged that HIAS and JDC only handle dropouts with first-degree relatives in the United States. He wanted American Jews to contact recent Soviet arrivals and have them send invitations to their relatives to join them. He also felt it might be necessary to close HIAS and JDC operations in Rome. Finally Levanon stated that if the drop out mess were solved then there would be concerted effort by government and Jewish Agency to improve absorption in Israel (Letter, Nehemia Levanon to Ralph Goldman May 8, 1979, translated from Hebrew).[35] At the time Aryeh Dulzin considered flying all Soviet émigrés from Vienna to Israel.

Ironically, the proposals of Levanon and Dulzin would meet more opposition from Yehuda Dominitz, a Jewish Agency professional, than from the Americans. He doubted that the Austrian government would allow the proposed flights. Moreover, this would create complications for Soviet Jews who would then want to continue on to the United States. Israeli law grants citizenship automatically to stateless Jews arriving on immigrant visas. To withhold citizenship for a year required new legislation. Dominitz warned that granting housing and tax breaks to these "temporaries" would create resentment among Israelis. He doubted that temporary residents, lacking the motivation of immigrants, would overcome the problems of absorption including a serious shortage of housing and absorption facilities. Israel would become a transition camp rather than a center of absorption which would cause havoc and influence others to leave ("Dominitz Report," May 9, 1979, JDC files).

THE GOLDMAN COMMITTEE AND A MORE ACTIVE CJF

Max Fisher asked Ralph Goldman to head a professional committee to prepare a position paper on the dropout issue. It would serve as the basis for a meeting of American Jewish leaders and then for Fisher's recommendations to Prime Minister Begin and his cabinet (Memo, Phil Bernstein to Ralph Goldman and Joan Wolchansky, "re: statement on Soviet Jewish Migration," JDC files, and Summary of Comments on Meeting on Soviet Jewish Emigration, May 30 1979, JDC files). Ralph Goldman consulted with fellow professionals in American Jewish organizations. Importantly, representatives of the Liaison Bureau and the Jewish Agency participated.[36] The Committee met several times in May and June. In a draft the Committee declared that for Israel Soviet Jews are a source of immigration while for American Jewry "the increased numbers of Soviet Jews seeking to settle in the United States and Canada present economic, social, and ideological problems" (Ralph Goldman, hand notes and "Summary of all Options Presented to Professional Committee," May 17, 1979, JDC files).[37] Its stated principles were maximum exit from the Soviet Union, maximum number to Israel, individual's right to choose country of settlement, minimum time to settle and minimum cost. It wanted to reduce dropouts without reducing emigration.[38] It hoped to reduce the drop out rate by 10 to 15 percent thus returning it to about 50 percent. Those holding Israeli affidavits would be assisted to travel and settle only in Israel. The committee decided that "An exception would be made for humanitarian reasons in the case of first degree relatives (father, mother or children) who hold Israeli visas but opt to go to the United States." The committee suggested direct flights via Bucharest but had yet to consider specific proposals. The Israelis feared that with direct flights up to 50 percent of the émigrés would want to leave upon arrival (Memo, Phil Bernstein to Goldman and Wolchansky, May 23, 1979, JDC files). It considered a possible center in the United States to clear and process Soviet émigrés as was done with the Hungarian refugees in 1956 (Ralph Goldman, Notes of May 17, 1979, JDC files).[39]

The committee discussed the pros and cons of limiting the issuance of Israeli visas by the Dutch Embassy in Moscow. They rejected for legal and moral reasons an option to send all with Israeli visas to Israel for one year with option to leave during that year.[40] While Irving Bernstein and Sara Frankel favored cutting aid to those with Israeli visas who went to the West, Phil Bernstein explained that the CIF's "constituency doesn't accept it." The revised report refers to reducing aid to dropouts in Vienna and Rome.[41] At the May 30th meeting of the Goldman Committee, Jerold Hoffberger stated that there would be an "unimaginable uproar" in the United States if one Jew exiting on an Israeli visa would not be allowed entry into the United States.[42] The Committee argued that American Jewish leadership "*is not prepared at this stage to reduce aid to those with Israeli visas who opt to go to the West*" (Working document revised or second draft, May 17 or 25, 1979, JDC files).

On June 8, 1979, Max Fisher brought a delegation of American Jewish leaders to the White House to meet with Ed Sanders and Stuart Eisenstadt about the plight of Soviet Jewry.[43] Fisher explained that the American Jewish community wanted to change the current situation of a 68 percent dropout rate. He proposed United States affidavits in Moscow for Soviet Jews who wanted to go to the United States thus guaranteeing freedom of choice in the Soviet Union and direct flights (via Romania) to Israel for those holding Israeli visas. He asked for affidavits for all émigrés with first-degree relatives (including non-citizens) in the United States.[44] Dick Clark responded favorably to affidavits but indicated that an increase would require additional funding from Congress.[45] William Farrand cited Soviet reluctance to grant visas to the United States to any Soviet citizen.[46] In summarizing Dick Clark emphasized that if the Soviets cooperated and allowed more Jews to come to the United States that the United States could handle the increase. He had trouble, however, understanding how all of this would induce more Soviet Jews to go to Israel. He commented that the Soviet government might even favor resettlement in the West because it placated the Arabs.[47]

Mr. Max Fisher convened a meeting of American Jewish leaders with Ralph Goldman and the professional committee at LaGuardia Airport in New York

City on June 9, 1979. Liaison Bureau and Jewish Agency personnel participated.[48] Max Fisher explained that he planned to present ideas to the Prime
Minister in hopes of developing a single unified Jewish (American)–Israeli
approach to dropouts (Ralph Goldman to file "Inventory of Items to be Followed up by Committee Members . . . . June 8, 1979, JDC files and Highlight
of Meeting on Soviet Jewish Emigration [draft], June 9, 1979, JDC files).

Fisher defended the ad hoc nature of the Goldman committee despite the
calls by Mort Mandel of CJF and others to create a permanent body with professional staff. Participants discussed the need to reach Jews in the Soviet
Union, a single central absorption authority in Israel, Jewish affiliation of Soviet Jews being resettled in the United States, changes in American Jewish attitudes toward where Soviet Jews should be resettled and motivation of Soviet Jews to go either to Israel or to the United States. Morton Mandel argued
that there was a great deal of ambivalence in the American Jewish community. Fisher asked whether their goal was saving Soviet Jews for Judaism or
saving Soviet Jews as people (Ralph Goldman to file "Inventory . . . ." June 8
1979 and Slater, hand notes on LaGuardia, June 9, 1979, JDC files).

Fisher summarized stating that they had reached a consensus on the need
to follow up on a package of affidavits and direct flights. Ironically, while insuring freedom of choice within the Soviet Union, Fisher's endorsement of
direct flights denied émigrés the option of dropping out once they left the
Soviet Union. Fisher urged Israel to deal more effectively with absorption.[49]

On June 29, 1979, Max Fisher presented Prime Minister Menachem Begin the
recommendations of the Goldman Committee, at a meeting with Israelis and
American Jewish leaders ("Notes: meeting with Prime Minister" June 29, 1979;
"Working document for the meeting with the Prime Minister June 27, 1979;
Ralph Goldman hand notes, meeting with Prime Minister, June 27 1979, JDC
files). The Committee had reached a consensus on the need to reduce the
dropout rate while not hindering the maximum number of Jews leaving the
Soviet Union. It wanted to give Jews freedom of choice within the Soviet
Union which required affidavits for family reunion from countries of destina-
tion. It decided that those émigrés with American visas (and invitations from relatives there) would be eligible for assistance from American Jewish organizations (Ralph Goldman, "Summary of all options presented to Professional
Committee," May 17, 1979; "Notes: meeting with Prime Minister," June 29, 1979;
"Working document for the meeting with the Prime Minister June 27, 1979; and
Ralph Goldman hand notes, meeting with Prime Minister, June 27, 1979, JDC
files).[50] The Committee had yet to consider specific proposals. Fisher believed
it would take time to work out details and to reach agreement. He urged improvement and changes in absorption in both countries. He wanted to save
Jews as Jews.[51]

At the meeting Morton Mandel of CJF reported that most federation leaders would welcome a legitimate process to discourage going to the United

States and encourage coming to Israel. Frank Lautenberg acknowledged that there is only one place of refuge, Israel. He urged Israeli leaders to provide direction.[52]

Aryeh Dulzin questioned whether the American government would intervene with the Soviets on the issuance of visas. Even if they did, he doubted that the Soviets would agree. After all, he noted, there were millions of Ukrainians who could ask for the same thing. He also argued that there was no such thing as a Jewish refugee today since Israel existed (Ralph Goldman, Hand notes, Meeting with Prime Minister, June 27, 1979, JDC files; *JTA*, June 18 and 19, 1979).[53] This was to become a major component of the position of the Israeli government and the Jewish Agency. Later, many Jewish activists in the Soviet Union and the United States supported this position.[54]

Prime Minister Begin responded by referring to the tragedy of the dropouts. He hoped to reach a consensus with the Americans. He praised the work of HIAS and JDC and recognized their dilemma. He argued that Israel is prepared to receive every immigrant.[55] He declared that we are all for freedom of choice; whomever has first-degree relatives in the United States (or the West) would be helped to go there. All others would be aided to resettle in Israel. This would be referred to as the Begin Plan. He proposed that in the near future they make known this new policy.

Max Fisher responded that he wanted a policy that his constituency would follow; he needed the consensual support of American Jewish communal leaders. Evidently, many of the Americans presented opposed restricting activities of HIAS and JDC (*JTA*, June 29, 1979). They believed that they had an obligation to help those that chose to come to America. Aryeh Dulzin took a compromising position. While opposed to "transporting" dropouts to the United States, he did not object to federations aiding them upon their arrival (*JTA*, July 11, 1979). Later, Prime Minister Begin would support this position. Prime Minister Menachem Begin told Max Fisher that he would not rush him; he proposed a reasonable time to work out a consensus. A few months later Ralph Goldman noted that some had referred to Begin's proposal as the "quota proposal" which in American Jewish immigration history is synonymous with restrictive measures against Jews. He doubted that American Jewry was ready for a decision because "I do not as yet see a strong and determined leadership telling the people where they stand" (Memo, Ralph Goldman to Akiva Kohane, re: "Movement of Russian Émigrés," October 3, 1979, JDC files).

THE CJF TAKES CHARGE

By the summer of 1979 the situation in Rome became more problematic. Only 11,000 of 25,000 allocated parole visas had been used; the remaining

14,000 had to be used by the end of September 1979. HIAS, however, processed only 700 persons per week. At the expected arrival rate of 3,500 a month the INS and Ralph Goldman expected a backlog of about 9,000 émigrés in Rome at the end of September. The expectation that there would not be additional visas issued before January 1, 1980 meant that the refugee caseload in Rome might soon reach 15,000 (Ralph Goldman notes and report to JDC Executive Committee [dictated in Rome], July 11, 1979, JDC files).[56]

The American Jewish leaders and Israelis met again on "dropouts" on August 23, 1979 (Ralph Goldman to file, August 23, 1979, JDC files).[57] Morton Mandel assumed the role of lead negotiator with the Israelis. He reported that Phil Bernstein was preparing a statement to be presented to the CJF Executive Committee and Board, which would meet at O'Hare Airport on October 21, 1979. He noted that many people favored the federations giving resettlement aid only to persons with relatives in the specific community. He doubted, however, whether a consensus could be reached by the O'Hare meeting. He did not expect a vote at that meeting. In the interim CJF would conduct an elaborate consultation process on the issues involving many federations, their executives and various CJF committees (CJF "Background Information for CJF Discussions" "Soviet Jewish Emigration to Israel and Elsewhere: The Problem of Their Destination," September 20, 1979).[58] Jerold Hoffberger urged caution rather than optimism; he did not see the troops forming to support the proposal. He suggested that American federations reduce aid. He believed it wrong to overspend and compete with Israel. Max Fisher noted that money being raised for Israel was being spent on Soviet Jewish resettlement in the United States. Fisher wanted to develop enough consensus so that leaders could stand up, feel convinced and project that conviction. He proposed using Nehemia Levanon to help convince lay leaders (Ralph Goldman hand notes to file, September 14, 1979, JDC file; CJF Executive Committee, New York City, September 15, 1979).[59]

Another issue which surfaced and would continue to be a problem was the resettlement rate of émigrés by American Jewish federations (Transcript of conference call, "U.S. Government funding of Transmigrant Operation" [early May 1978], JDC files).[60] Several flights from Rome to the United States were cancelled because "communities were slow in providing assurances for people or were refusing to receive refugees when scheduled for arrival." HIAS urged the federations to be as "cooperative as possible in receiving" the expected large numbers ("Minutes of NPPC," September 11, 1979, JDC files). JDC criticized the lack of coordination between the agency that arranged for transportation to the United States and HIAS (Transcript of JDC Executive Committee Meeting, March 21, 1979, JDC files). Evidently the decision of at least seven federations to restrict resettlement to those with first-degree relatives in their community hindered and slowed the resettlement process in the States (Memo, Jim Rice to various federations, August 31, 1979, HIAS files).

CJF Executive Committee met at the O'Hare Hilton on October 21, 1979 to provide guidance in formulating a constructive response on the issue of destination of Soviet Jewish émigrés. Max Fisher and Prime Minister Menachem Begin had invited their response. Sixty-three persons representing 25 communities and 86 percent of the settling communities and leaders and professionals of UJA, CJF, HIAS, JDC and UIA attended.[61] Mort Mandel emphasized that they had come to hear opinions, did not want a split, would take no formal action and that there would not be a press release. Max Fisher stated that they agreed on the need for all to leave the Soviet Union, freedom of choice and maximum to Israel. A decision involved risks.[62] Jerold Hoffberger proposed giving aid to dropouts with first-degree relatives in the community. He emphasized, however, that each community should decide its own policy.

Several federations including Los Angeles, Miami, Philadelphia, Detroit, St. Louis and Dallas announced various degrees of restrictions; most limited acceptance to persons with first degree relatives in the community. Los Angeles, for example, made implementation dependent on "certain actions in Israel" ("Statement with Regard to the Issue of Soviet Jewish Immigration," October 15, 1979, in JDC files). Others including D.C., Cincinnati, Chicago, and Atlanta reconfirmed no restrictions. Harvey Kruger of Bergen County in New Jersey reaffirmed the right to self determination but proposed not financing those who came to the United States for funds were for Israel and local federation needs.

At O'Hare only 25 percent favored the first-degree relative stipulation; the majority opposed the idea of restricting aid (Ralph Goldman to file, October 21, 1979, CJF files; CJF agenda of O'Hare Hilton Meeting, CJF files, box 710) and Notes on Expanded Executive Committee (same date).[63] In summarizing the meeting, Morton Mandel argued that he found many communities troubled by the "first degree" issue. He believed that he did not have a mandate for action.[64]

Many of the key American Jewish leaders met a week later in Israel on October 27, 1979.[65] Morton Mandel reiterated the consensus on a maximum to leave the USSR and to go to Israel. He argued that most communities were looking for guidance for change. He called for sensitivity in dealing with federations. He reported that CJF was working on guidelines that would sharply reduce expenditures for resettlement in the United States. He believed that news of this change would filter back to Jews in the Soviet Union. He hoped that the CJF would get more federal government funding (from $24m this year to $36m next year). Similarly he urged the UJA to raise more funds. He asked the Jewish Agency to do more educational work within the Soviet Union and to improve its absorption practices. As he often stated: "Israel needs to pull people." He explained that he needed more time before providing a final answer to Prime Minister Begin.

Max Fisher commented on the number of communities who wanted to restrict absorbing dropouts (without first degree relatives).[66] He surmised that
once Soviet Jews realized that they could not go somewhere else, they
would come to Israel. Nevertheless, he urged that information on community restrictions not be made public.

Most interesting were the comments by Jerold Hoffberger from Baltimore.
He was disturbed by what he heard. He commented that at O'Hare they had
gathered to make an American decision. He expressed surprise at the rein-
troduction of the Israelis in the process. Moreover, he castigated Max Fisher
for suggesting that Russians who dropped out and had no place to go would
be left in Rome to fend for themselves.

On October 29, 1979, American Jewish leaders met with Menachem Begin
in Jerusalem (Ralph Goldman notes to file, October 29, 1979, JDC files).[67]
Mandel reported on CJF plans for a drastic change in community practices
which would make coming to USA less attractive. He emphasized, however,
that the CJF was giving guidance and not direction.[68] The expected reduction
in costs and savings would be transmitted to UJA (and to Israel). He repeated
his call for the Jewish Agency to provide more Jewish education in the Soviet Union and in Rome and for improved absorption services so as to provide a pull to Israel.

Frank Lautenberg made reference to six communities that restricted the acceptance of Soviet Jews. He also suggested that while some criticized Israeli
interference with Soviet Jews, others, who had not been heard, said we gave
money to establish Israel as a place of refuge. He stated that we are being
asked to demonstrate leadership. In contrast, Jerold Hoffberger reiterated
that no solution could be imposed on the federations. Dulzin called for an
announcement that Los Angeles and other communities would take only
first-degree relatives and he wanted a public debate.

Rafael Kotlowitz urged Begin to support limiting aid to first degree relatives. Max Fisher demurred. He told Kotlowitz that politics is the art of the
possible. He denied that there was a public debate in the United States.
When Dulzin asked about changes in Rome, Don Robinson of JDC responded that JDC was an American agency and as such would be guided by
the American Jewish Community.

Nehemia Levanon argued that Mandel's proposed policy did not give a
clear-cut message to Soviet Jews. He agreed that a policy could not be bull-
dozed but at the same time did not want to loose momentum. He was bothered by the fact that there were already 20,000 Soviet Jewish families in the
USA. Kotlowitz argued that since Max Fisher's request for more time in
June an additional 10,000 dropouts had come to America, thereby increasing
the pool of "first degree relatives" in the United States.[69]

In a public statement issued a few days later Max Fisher indicated that the
American Jewish leaders had resisted pressure from Prime Minister Begin to

restrict aid to dropouts. He emphasized a unified American Jewish commitment to provide maximum help for Jews to leave the Soviet Union and for a maximum number to go to Israel (Irwin S. Field to UJA officers, "Statement of Max Fisher," November 2, 1979, JDC files). He noted that the CJF was working with community leaders to consider major changes and develop new approaches for the resettlement of Soviet Jews. He also noted that Israel would take steps to attract more Soviet Jews. He reported that there would be steps taken to make assistance in both Israel and United States comparable and provide more funds for Israel.[70] He added that all agreed that "the time has come for a dramatic change in community practices" which will be brought before the forthcoming CJF General Assembly (GA) in Montreal.

At the CJF General Assembly in Montreal, participants debated the issue of funding resettlement in the United States and elsewhere. The delegates tabled a resolution by a hand vote (60–40) submitted by Bergen County, New Jersey, to limit resettlement aid in the United States to those émigrés with first-degree relatives. Many saw this as a rejection of the Begin plan (which was not voted on) (*JTA*, November 19, 1979; Jonathan Braun, "Dulzin's Criticism Fails to Move NY View on *Noshrim*," and *Jewish Week*, December 16, 1979, CJF files, box 697).[71] The General Assembly endorsed the principles that every Jew should be allowed to emigrate from the Soviet Union and that a maximum number should go to Israel. Morton Mandel focused on the implications of dropouts and resettlement for fund raising in the federations. He advised that if a community did not achieve its campaign goal because of local resettlement needs, then its allocation to UJA for Israel should not be further reduced because Israel needed funds for absorption.[72] He expected that proposed CJF guidelines for resettlement would reduce community costs. Those Soviet Jews wishing to come to the United States for reunion with families in cities where those families were now located would be aided by HIAS, JDC, and federation (if own families can't help). Others, without family, would be aided by HIAS and JDC in Europe and would continue to be received by communities to the extent possible. He hoped to make clear to the American government the full Jewish commitment to carrying out human rights principles and hoped for a maximum United States government block grant. Again he urged the Israelis to do more to attract Soviet Jewish émigrés.[73]

Meeting in early December Max Fisher, Morton Mandel and others failed to formulate a strategy on dropouts to present to Prime Minister Begin (Ralph Goldman, Notes on Meeting, December 7, 1979, JDC files, and Edwin Shapiro, Memo, Board of HIAS, December 14, 1979, HIAS files). Max Fisher reported that Prime Minister was sending Nehemia Levanon to build support for the Israeli position among American Jews. Interestingly, Robert Hiller, the CJF Executive Vice President, objected to Levanon's activities in the United States. He asked Max Fisher "that he not send Levanon over to work on this issue. The issue really is being resolved very well . . . by our practical actions.

The continuation of raising the specter of an issue by the Israelis is coun-terproductive" (Memo, Robert Hiller to Marvin Mandel, December 21, 1979, CJF files, box 697).[74] Morton Mandel remained concerned about federations only accepting first-degree relatives. By late February 1980, 32 communities including 10 of the 13 big communities had limited intake; 12 accepted only first-degree relatives and 20 family reunion individuals (Ralph Goldman on *Noshrim* in Jerusalem, February 26, 1980, JDC files).[75] He feared that this could overburden the NYANA and deny Soviet Jews freedom of choice. He emphasized that the NYANA would have to be more efficient; it would have to either enforce fiscal restraint or limit intake. (Letter of Albert D. Chernin, Executive Vice-Chair of NJCRAC, to Jim Rice, July 31, 1979, HIAS files).

At a February 1980 meetings of the Coordinating Committee during the Jewish Agency Board of Governors meeting in Jerusalem, Aryeh Dulzin, with the support of Minister David Levy, renewed criticism of American Jewish aid to Soviet dropouts. Dulzin charged that every Jew who dropped out prevented others from leaving (Meeting of Coordinating Committee, February 27, 1980, held in Knesset).[76] He objected to calling dropouts refugees. He along with Akiva Levinsky, Jewish Agency Treasurer and La-bor Party representative, proposed closing down HIAS in Vienna. He wanted to transfer all dropouts within hours to Rome where it would be easier for Jewish Agency to influence them. Max Fisher attacked both men and stated that their telling American Jews what to do was counterproduc-tive (*JTA*, April 11 and 14, 1980). HIAS responded that implementing Dulzin's proposals would lead to the Austrian government closing down the entire "rescue" operation in Vienna. Max Fisher still talked about im-plementing the Begin plan of aiding only dropouts with first-degree rela-tives (Ralph Goldman on *Noshrim* in Jerusalem, February 27, 1980, JDC files).

At a second meeting of the Coordinating Committee Max Fisher added Aryeh Dulzin, Rafael Kotlowitz and David Levy to the American professional committee dealing with dropouts (Ralph Goldman on *Noshrim*, February, 28 1980, JDC files) and Memo from Max Fisher to Members of Jewish Agency Assembly . . . re: Report on . . . Board of Governors . . . February 1980 (HIAS files). The Coordinating Committee also formed a joint Israeli Diaspora com-mittee to work on the dropout problem. Dulzin again proposed referring to all Soviet Jewish émigrés as Israeli immigrants and not refugees. Gaynor Ja-cobson of HIAS objected.

Following the meeting Jacobson attacked Dulzin's position in a letter with copies sent to most leaders in the American Jewish establishment. He argued that both the United Nations's protocol which Israel signed and the United States Refugee Act of 1980 defined a refugee as one having a well founded fear of being persecuted for reasons of race, or religion (March 4, 1980, HIAS files).[77] He noted that the protocol of 1980 did not make a person less a refugee if he left a country with a visa for another. A person remains a refugee as long as she/he does "not acquire a new nationality and has [not] been firmly resettled in the country of his new nationality."

Yehuda Avner, adviser to Prime Minister Begin, answered Jacobson (March 12, 1980, HIAS files). He conceded that according to American law that a Jew leaving the Soviet Union is classified as a refuge. He argued however that Dulzin had been taking a "moral Jewish position. With Israel, a Jew on the road has the address in his pocket and the key to the door of his own homeland. He is not homeless and needs no one to intercede on his behalf in search of a place to unpack his bags. Therefore, he is not a wandering refugee. *It is this philosophical difference of approach that underlies the debate we have been conducting for four years. If I perceived matters otherwise I would not be a Zionist"* (Letter, Irving Bernstein to Gaynor Jacobson, March 26, 1980, JDC files). In the words of Jewish Agency absorption official who often sided with the American critics of Israeli policies, the dropout phenomenon signified a failure "even an act of betrayal . . . an offense" (Dominitz 1996:118).

Aryeh Dulzin also replied (Letter to Gaynor Jacobson with brief, March 27, 1980, JDC files). He wrote that "those who are continually offering material inducement to Jews leaving the USSR with Israeli visas to emigrate to the United States (and this in the face of repeated express warnings of the probable consequences), cannot escape a heavy moral responsibility of what has happened." He charged that HIAS was interested in maximizing the flow of Soviet Jews to the United States ("*Olim* Could be Refugees in the United States," *JP*, March 31, 1980).

In the spirit of the Zionist position the Coordinating Committee on February 28, 1980, passed the following resolutions regarding Russian dropouts: "*The Coordinating Committee stresses the historic truth that with the establishment of the Jewish state an end has been put to Jewish refugee homelessness and calls upon all olim [Immigrants to Israel] from the Soviet Union to return to Israel. The Coordinating Committee views with the utmost gravity the dropout of olim from the Soviet Union. The Coordinating Committee calls upon all the authorities and agencies involved in aliyah and its absorption from the Soviet Union to act in coordination, so as to bring about a reduction of the dropout rate and its termination so that the olim from the Soviet Union return to Israel.*"

In spring 1980 Prime Minister Menachem Begin visited the United States. Aryeh Dulzin had urged him to discuss with President Carter and American Jewish leaders the Refugee Act of 1980, which made it easier for Russian émigrés to enter the United States as political refugees and provided financial aid for their resettlement. Dulzin proposed that American Jews either amend the law or make it clear that it did not apply to "Soviet Jews who have Israeli visas." Prime Minister Begin took no action at this time. He may well have been sensitive to the wishes of the American Jewish establishment. According to Howard Squadron of the American Jewish Congress the Israelis like Dulzin were asking us to repudiate "the values we have always stood for and fought for (*JTA*, April 17, 1980; *JP*, March 30, 1980).[78] More importantly, Begin opposed in principle the idea of asking a foreign country to close its gates to Jews.

In June 1980 the Coordinating Committee's subcommittee on Soviet migration, consisting of a group of senior American Jewish professionals, Jewish Agency professionals and members of the Liaison Bureau met in New York City (Report, Subcommittee of the Committee on Jewish Migration from the USSR [3 sessions], June 5–8, 1980, JDC files).[79] In a prepared position paper, Nehemia Levanon described a crisis in emigration and in dropouts ("A Grave and Dangerous Development," June 2, 1980, JDC files). He explained that the Soviet Union had allowed fewer Jews to leave and requests for *vyzovs* declined. A newly enforced Soviet policy of requiring invitations from first-degree relatives in Israel resulted in Soviet émigrés in the United States "trapping" their relatives within the Soviet Union. He was worried that the changed situation did not spark a protest among Jews in the Soviet Union; they accepted the situation in silence. Levanon argued that we could only protest to the Soviets on the basis that they denied the right of Soviet Jews to rejoin their families "in a Jewish homeland." Denials made to individuals wishing to go elsewhere, he argued, "denied the outside Jewish world and the State of Israel a basis for continuing our protest and appealing to world wide public opinion" (Report . . . June 5–8, 1980). This clearly reflected the "Zionist" position of the Israelis. The subcommittee urged American Jews to give a clear public message on the priority for movement to Israel. Nevertheless, it called for continued JDC and HIAS operations in Vienna and Rome and an increase in visas to the United States.[80] The subcommittee formulated two operational options but adopted neither.

Option one involved a revised "Naples" plan. Upon arrival in Vienna all émigrés would be housed in the Red Cross hostel.[81] Those going to Israel would leave as soon as possible. All others would be transferred to a hotel outside Rome for 8–10 days where Jewish Agency emissaries would try to convince them to go to Israel. In one version of the "Naples" plan HIAS and JDC staff would join the Jewish Agency emissaries in counseling the émigrés to go to Israel. Those dropouts without relatives in the West would be informed that they would get no aid. Those with close relatives would be referred to HIAS/JDC in Rome. The committee hoped to present this option before the CJF Quarterly meetings in September. They perceived problems with the Soviet and Austrian governments, the émigrés, American officials and other refugee agencies that could assist those not receiving aid from HIAS and JDC.

Option two, which was not elaborated on, would have HIAS, JDC and the Jewish Agency granting assistance only to "those proceeding to Israel or the country for which they have a visa." In other words HIAS and JDC would cease aiding drop outs who left the Soviet Union on visas for Israel. The members of the subcommittee concluded that the situation had become so grave that "drop outs could endanger the future of the entire Soviet Jewish emigration." They encouraged no public discussion while these proposals were being considered and then implemented. At Max Fisher's discretion exploratory steps could be taken in Vienna and Italy. The subcommittee decided that HIAS, JDC and the Jewish Agency would review the proposal with their respective "governance groups" and that *CJF leaders would be informed* (Ralph Goldman to file, June 26, 1980 (JDC files).

In Jerusalem at the end of the month Robert Hiller informed Max Fisher and the others that CJF wanted to bring the subcommittee's proposals to its Board (*Ibid.*). Fisher resisted CJF pressure and Nehemia Levanon supported him. At a larger forum that day Morton Mandel of CJF said that he would be willing to accept the plan. He remained uncomfortable with the solution, however, because other relief agencies might help the dropouts. Until there was a specific plan to help those not to be aided he intended to vote against it (Ralph Goldman to file, June 28, 1980, JDC files).[82]

By the end of the summer HIAS, JDC and the Jewish Agency agreed to the new Naples plan which would become operational by October 15, 1980. It limited HIAS/JDC aid to dropouts with first degree relatives in the United States but allowed federations to resettle dropouts not aided by HIAS and JDC (Memo, Akiva Kohane to Ralph Goldman, August 19, 1980, JDC files; Carl Glick, hand notes about August 21, 1980, Glick non *noshrim* folder #33 HIAS; also see "Movement of Soviet Jews: Proposal for Consideration," August 28, 1980, JDC files; Memo, hand notes of meeting of NPPC, October or November 1980, CJF files).[83] The émigrés would be placed in one site in Vienna and then go either to Israel or to a hotel in the area of Naples, Italy where the Jewish Agency, HIAS and JDC would conduct joint counseling.[84] The Jewish Agency would again handle transportation from Vienna to Rome (Ralph Goldman to File, July 3, 1980 and Mort Mandel, Memo to CJF Board of Directors, August 11, 1980 (CJF files, box 660). Transfer of émigrés from the Jewish Agency would take place in Rome and not Vienna. HIAS and JDC would close up shop in Vienna and their staffs would be transferred or seconded to the Jewish Agency. The parties did not yet agree on a definition of a first degree relative.

The Liaison Bureau had apparently won over American Jewry to its position on dropouts. A satisfied Aryeh Dulzin praised the cooperation between the Jewish Agency, HIAS and JDC. He commented that "HIAS in the work of Jewish rescue is a brilliant chapter in contemporary Jewish history" (Telex, Tadmor to Edwin Shapiro and Irving Kessler, August 25, 1980, JDC files). HIAS and JDC, however, wanted to consult with CJF before implementing.

Before being able to do so, the Israeli press broke the story that HIAS was stopping its aid to dropouts who did not have first-degree relatives in the United States (Telex to HIAS from HIAS Israel, August 28, 1980).[85] The *JP* predicted that the dropout out rate would not decline and that the stubborn Russian Jews who preferred America would turn to non-Jewish organizations: *"if the majority of the Jews leaving the USSR at the present time are not really Zionist, is that a reason to remove the help of the organized Jewish community? Does the Jewish Agency have the right to demand that the official organ of American Jewry stop fulfilling its mission just because they (the Soviet Jews) refuse "for the time being" to go to Israel?"* Sad business but no less sad if HIAS closes its doors in Rome and Russian Jews turn to non Jewish organizations"* (*JP*, August 27, 1980 and Telex, H. Halachmi, HIAS Israel, to HIAS [NY], August 28, 1980, JDC files).

In early September the CJF Executive Committee reviewed the proposal. CJF President Morton Mandel explained that JDC, HIAS and the Jewish Agency wanted to share it with CJF but did not want a formal CJF decision. He explained that the General Assembly in Montreal of November 1979 had committed North American Jewry to a maximum number of Jews leaving the Soviet Union and a maximum number to Israel. Now, the Soviets had changed the rules and cut emigration so JDC, HIAS and the Jewish Agency wanted to change procedures (Notes, CJF Executive Committee, September 4, 1980, CJF files, box 695). He referred to the Naples Plan and withholding of aid to Soviet émigrés not going to Israel and not seeking family reunification in the West. Many felt that withholding Jewish emigration services in Europe would have little effect since non-Jewish agencies would supply support. *Therefore, the Executive decided that "such withholding of services has too many risks for its potential value."* Some felt that the proposal was based on assumptions that the American Jewish community would not accept. The test would be by federations assisting émigrés brought in by non-Jewish organizations. The Executive wanted CJF and the federations to evaluate proposals before implementing. Morton Mandel would review the situation before he consulted the Board on September 7, 1980 (Hand notes of Carmi Schwartz or Robert Hiller, Executive Meeting of CJF, September 4, 1980, CJF files, box 695 and Kohane memo "The Problem of Neshira" November 17 1981, CJF files).[86]

At the CJF Board on September 7, 1980 in New York City, Mort Mandel explained that the proposed intensive joint counseling and new system that "might also involve the withholding of HIAS and JDC services to Soviet Jews not involved in family reunion, subsequent to the counseling procedures." Edwin Shapiro, HIAS President, emphasized that HIAS, JDC and the Jewish Agency all agreed to the proposals. Several board members wanted more information before reaching a decision. Some thought that CJF should not adopt position that would restrict the action of other independent agencies. There was almost unanimous sentiment in support of federations settling Soviet Jewish émigrés whether HIAS or non-Jewish organizations sponsored them (CJF memo to members of CJF ad hoc Committee on Soviet Jewry, "Arthur Brody Analysis" September 17, 1980, JDC files).[87] Mort Mandel called for the appointment of a CJF special Committee on Soviet Jewry made up of board members and professional leaders to evaluate all views expressed and implications and to issue a report as soon as possible. He also asked the CJF-HIAS NPPC to look at the issue (CJF Board of Directors, September 6,7, 1980, CJF files, box 660; Memo of Stephen Solender and Melvin Zaret to members of NPPC re: HIAS JDC proposal; Memo Carmi Schwartz to Ralph Goldman, Robert Hiller, GH Stephen Solender re: "Processing HIAS JDC Proposal," September 8, 1980, JDC files).

The ad hoc committee, chaired by Arthur Brody, met at LaGuardia Airport on September 22, 1980 (Ralph Goldman notes on meeting on *Noshrim*, September 22, 1980, JDC files and Carmi Schwartz notes, CJF file 710).[88] Its stated purpose was to advise and consult with HIAS and JDC. Steve Solender, chair of the NPPC, opposed the plan because it might not achieve the desired results of getting more Jews out of the Soviet Union and more to Israel. He questioned the moral issue of not aiding Jews in need. He advised that the implications for local communities had not been thought through. Steve Nasatir, head of the Chicago Federation, had recently written Steve Solender that Jewish tradition mandated federations to aid those arriving not via HIAS. This in turn might cause problems for block grants. He noted that it was ironic that the American Jewish community "champion of liberalized immigration laws, the rights of refugees and human rights, suddenly withdraws from participation in resettling selected Jews in the United States because we want them to live in Israel" (Letter, Steve Nasatir to the NPPC, September 18, 1980, JDC files).[89] Finally, he feared that the element of coercion might have a negative impact on campaign funding and on the American government. He proposed that émigrés be moved to European Jewish communities for counseling rather than to Naples. Others favored the proposals.

The chair, Arthur Brody, summarized: "The Committee suggests that the migration agencies should consider other possible options than the one suggested in their proposal which might lead to the discontinuation of services. It is therefore recommended that HIAS and JDC continue to provide migration services to all Soviet Jews" (Letter, Morton Mandel to Donald Robinson, JDC, September 29, 1980, JDC files and draft memo, Robert Hiller to Mort Mandel about September 22,1980, CJF files, box 710). By November 9th 1980, *HIAS leaders stated that they would not change their policy of aiding all dropouts to come to the United States* (*JTA*, October 9, 1980; "Scheme to Cut Soviet Dropouts Runs into Snag," *JP*, October 10, 1980).[90] Again, the CJF had blocked an Israeli initiative on dropouts. All along Nehemia Levanon, Ralph Goldman and others felt that the CJF should not be asked to vote on

changing policies of supporting dropouts who did not have first degree relatives in the West. Their fears had been justified.

The JDC Executive Committee met again on the subject around October 1,
1980. Don Robinson reported that the JDC officers had supported him on
this new policy on August 28, 1980. The Executive Committee now endorsed
this stand. They decided not to have a show of hands. Robinson promised to
discuss the issue again. It is unclear whether those present voted to cease
aiding those dropouts without relatives (Memo, Ellen Lewis to Ralph Goldman "Requests for Actions Made," October 9, 1989, JDC files).[91] They would,
however, go ahead with all other points of the Naples plan.

In 1991, Carmi Schwartz, Executive Vice President of CJF in the early 1980s
wrote that in 1980 CJF almost got an agreement from HIAS to cease aid in Vienna for three months. He claimed that if a vote had been taken in CJF "we
would have won in an open vote at Council of Jewish Federations by 4 or 5
to one." He credits the Chicago Federation with preventing a vote by arguing that in CJF decisions are made "by consensus and not majority rule." He
further argued that the leadership of CJF and UJA and the Jewish Agency
agreed to a three month cut in aid but "they couldn't bring their constituency,
the federations, along with them" (Schwartz 1991:6,7).[92]

At meetings in Jerusalem in October 1980 Prime Minister Menachem Begin asked American Jewish leaders for an opportunity to meet with them on
the subject of aid for Soviet Jewry and dropouts. He wanted "to share his
point of view, but also to hear first hand how they feel about this problem."
Morton Mandel invited him to address the General Assembly in Detroit in
November and to later meet with the CJF Executive Committee (Memo, Mort
Mandel to CJF Exec Committee, October 21, 1980, CJF files, box 695).[93]

Prime Minister Begin gave a moving address to the thousands of delegates at
the General Assembly. He did not, however, focus on Soviet Jewry. He began
with remarks on the peace process, defense and security. He next spoke about
persecuted Jews in Syria. He framed the Soviet Jewry issue in terms of *Aliyah*
(immigration) to Israel. He called on the "mighty Jewish community in the
United States [to] raise its voice again for the Aliyah from the Soviet Union." He
charged that dropouts impede immigration to Israel. He inserted comments on
the Holocaust, noting that Soviet troops liberated Auschwitz. He suggested that
in the future Soviet Jews who did not have first degree relatives in Israel would
not be given permission to leave the Soviet Union. In a compromising tone he
hoped that the General Assembly would find a solution "accepted by all—by
Israel and the great Jewish community in the United States. . . . A practical solution accepted by all, which will help us renew the days when there was a permanent flow from the Soviet Union to the historic homeland of the Jewish people" (Begin 1980). No formal proposal was made and no vote was taken.

The Prime Minister then went to a meeting of the members of the CJF Executive Committee. Fisher and other past CJF Presidents joined the group of

about 40 CJF leaders. Morton Mandel told Prime Minister Begin that CJF bodies and federations decided "their communities would receive and resettle Soviet Jews regardless of the migration service bringing such migrants to their community" and that communally funded international Jewish migration agencies should continue to provide migration services to Soviet Jews (Notes for Mort Mandel at Executive Committee, November 14, 1980, CJF files, box 695). CJF vice president Marvin Citrin explained that there did not exist a consensus in favor of the new policy and he argued that consensus was "the engine of our effectiveness" (Hand notes of meeting with Nehemia Levanon and Prime Minister, CJF files, box 710).

Prime Minister Begin tried to convince them to support the Jewish Agency Naples Plan. He made a plea for a change in policy. He favored compromise. He told them that when the Jewish émigré comes to your community "you behave as a Jew" (Minutes of CJF Executive Committee, October 21, 1980, Plaza Hotel Detroit, CJF files, box 695).[94] For Israel and the Jewish People, he argued, the problem is with the stage in Vienna. Following his words Joe Ayn, a Holocaust survivor with tears streaming down his face, said in an "emotionally electrifying" voice: "I was rescued by this country. Don't ask us to shut the door to any Jew" (Phone interview, Morton Mandel, August 6, 2001). The minutes report that all agreed after discussion that the maximum number should leave the Soviet Union and that all hoped that the new cooperation between the Jewish Agency, JDC and HIAS would be productive. No policy change was made. It may be noteworthy that in Morton Mandel's prepared presidential address at the General Assembly he made no mention of Soviet Jewry (Mandel 1980).

The Jewish Agency still planned to begin "Italian" operations in Naples on December 15, 1980. Between November 24 and 25, 1980, an earthquake caused considerable damage to the area near the leased hotel (ALR to Ralph Goldman and Akiva Kohane, telephone dictation, November 28, 1980; Memo, Seidenman to Gaynor Jacobson, December 1, 1980; and Telex, Akiva Kohane to Ralph Goldman, December 2, 1980, JDC files).[95] In late December 1980 the Italian government objected to the Jewish Agency project (Notes on Meeting with Italian Minister of Interior, January 7, 1981, JDC files).[96] Regardless, after the additional efforts at joint counseling HIAS would assist "any Soviet Jew who insists on going to the US." By spring 1981, the Jewish Agency, HIAS and JDC had a single reception site in Vienna (*JTA*, January 12, 1981).[97]

DULZIN ACTS ALONE

A decline in Soviet emigration after 1979 affected the CJF-HIAS operations for resettlement.[98] Its Soviet Jewish Resettlement Program cut its staff from

13½ to 9 positions and many smaller communities were urged to use local consultants. The more refugees from the Soviet Union the larger the number of fixed grants from the American government. For example in 1979 the United States government covered well over 70 percent of HIAS total costs. In 1980 it dropped to 60 percent and in 1981 to less than 50 percent. This in turn increased the burden on federations and UJA funds which in turn led to tension with interests that favored more funding for Israel (HIAS Board of Directors, September 20, 1981, HIAS files).[99] Mort Mandel addressed this issue: "And we dare not damage this fragile state of balance . . . between how we allocated locally and nationally overseas, and you are going to be under great pressure in your community from people who care very deeply with legitimate concerns to try and make up this local shortfall of some of these federal funds out of the annual campaign. . . . And you are also going to likewise pressure for national agency advocates and international need advocate, . . . as Federation leadership we have . . . to show how good we are, by not damaging by not doing violence to this equity, ...We are gong to be called on to be world-class Jewish leaders . . . it is very important that we remember this Board of Trustees has to think locally, nationally and internationally if we are to be the kind of Jewish community we need to be and want to be" (CJF Quarterly Board Meetings, April 11–12, 1981, CJF files, box 660).[100]

Then in mid-August 1981 Aryeh Dulzin took unilateral action. He refused to sign over to HIAS and JDC Soviet émigrés not wanting to go to Israel who did not have first-degree relatives in the United States. His definition of first-degree relatives included spouses, parents or children but excluded siblings.[101] JDC initially cooperated with the new policy; it honored an earlier commitment from 1967 only to accept Soviet émigrés transferred in writing by the Jewish Agency (Ralph Goldman to file, August 26, 1981, JDC files and see chapter 3). The Executive Committee of HIAS voted 8 to 3 on August 24, 1981 that it "fully understands and appreciates the motivation of the Jewish Agency's efforts to increase emigration to Israel. HIAS as a world Jewish organization shares these endeavors and recognizes its responsibility to help achieve such a goal . . . HIAS , however, is not prepared to refuse its services to Soviet Jewish emigrants who have not been specifically referred by the Jewish Agency. The HIAS tradition is to serve every Jewish refugee in need, anywhere in the world, with compassion and understanding" (Reported at HIAS Board of Directors, September 20, 1981, HIAS files).[102] It would also continue joint consultation in Vienna with the Jewish Agency and JDC (Edwin Shapiro to Board members, August 25, 1981, HIAS files; Notes, HIAS Board of Directors, September 20, 1981, HIAS Files; Memo of Edwin Shapiro to Board Members of HIAS, August 18, 1981; and *JTA*, August 26, 1981).[103]

According to Windmueller (1999:167) Dulzin's actions "turned off" many of Israel's supporters in the United States.[104] Take for example Max Fisher's response. He expressed hurt at not being "consulted . . . maybe I should have pressed? I was told this was an ultimatum. I don't like ultimatums."[105] Frank Lautenberg of UJA called the American Jewish–Jewish Agency partnership tenuous if matters were handled this way. Morton Mandel objected strenuously to the manner in which Dulzin disregarded process of Jewish Agency decision making. The United States State Department expressed anger at not being consulted and reiterated that "U.S. policy has always been and will continue to be that Soviet Jewish refugees arriving in Vienna should have freedom of choice with regard to where they wish to resettle. Once the Soviet refugees have arrived in Vienna, we see no reason why they should be obliged to go to Israel if there are other countries willing to offer them refuge" (*JTA*, August 27, 1981).

Within a few days and following consultations with the Jewish Agency and Israeli government officials, however, many American Jewish leaders expressed support for Dulzin's unilateral action. The National Conference of Soviet Jewry chastised HIAS and came to the aid of the Jewish Agency: "We regard ourselves as Israel's partners in this great endeavor. Yet, our partner has not been able to move the partnership for many years, because our communities . . . have vetoed the change our partners have asked for" (NCSJ form letter, August 27, 1981, and letter, Ted Mann [President, NCSJ] to Edwin Shapiro, August 27, 1981, JDC files).[106] Mort Mandel indicated that what is decided by the Jewish Agency, HIAS and JDC will be carried out by us (Ralph Goldman hand notes, meeting on August 30, 1981, JDC files; and Carmi Schwartz notes in CJF files, box 710, no date).[107] He would let the process and change take hold and only discuss the issue at the next quarterly. He thought some communities would accept it for a fait accompli. He argued that the Jewish Agency has the right to make decisions it made but that the American Jewish community must figure out what it means for us in our own communities. In mid-September he noted that the decision had been made on the basis of information that exit visas "for Soviet Jews are being curtailed due to the high rate of movement to the West" (Carmi Schwartz notes of CJF meeting, August 31, 1981, CJF files, box 710, highlights CJF Board, September 17–20, 1981). He probably had been briefed by the Liaison Bureau.

HIAS demanded that the Jewish Agency agree to joint counseling and to include brothers and sisters as first-degree relatives. In response, Nehemia Levanon suggested they try the original formula (no brothers and sisters) but that in some compassionate cases a change could be made (Ralph Goldman, hand notes, August 31, 1981, JDC files).[108] The next day Aryeh Dulzin and Max Fisher issued a joint statement saying that "a great degree of understanding" has been reached between the Jewish Agency and HIAS-JDC on the Jewish Agency's recent decisions "related to the dropout of Soviet Jews arriving in Vienna with exit visas good for travel to Israel only." They were in the process of working out the details (Dulzin and Fisher Issue Statement,"

September 1, 1981 (JDC files). *JTA* (September 3, 1981) reported that HIAS had accepted unofficially Dulzin's plan which would be reevaluated at the end of the year. Notes from HIAS meetings contradict this. On September 15, 1981 HIAS Executive Committee reaffirmed (without taking a formal vote) its resolution of August 24 "that no Soviet Jew seeking our assistance would be turned away" (Notes, HIAS Board of Directors, September 20, 1981). Within a few days all parties agreed on a joint consultation process in Vienna and periodic monitoring after 30, 60, 90, and 120 days.[109] Initial reports of the new policy indicated an increase in those going to Israel (*JTA*, September 11, 1981).[110] At the same time Rav Tov handled almost 25 percent of migrants versus its 3 percent share the year before (Notes from HIAS Board of Directors, September 20, 1981, HIAS files).[111]

In Vienna joint counseling continued while HIAS still accepted Soviet Jews who did not receive a referral from the Jewish Agency. In these cases HIAS also provided care and maintenance, which bothered JDC (Telexes from Stern [Vienna] to Ralph Goldman, September 21, 1981 [JDC files] and, Report of JDC Executive Committee, September 23, 1981.)[112] By September 25, 1981 the Jewish Agency and JDC conducted joint counseling in Vienna without HIAS (Abraham Raveh, "The New Program" [translated from Hebrew] October 12, 1981, JDC files).[113] In mid-October a Jewish Agency representative reported from Vienna that about 25 percent of Soviet Jewish émigrés were going to Israel, that HIAS received about 50 percent and that Rav Tov 25 percent (David Harris to Jerry Goodman, October 22, 1981, JDC files).[114] Aryeh Dulzin attacked HIAS for aiding Rav Tov, an anti-Zionist organization that does "everything humanly possible to prevent Jews from going to Israel" (Letter, Leon Dulzin to Max Fisher, October 28, 1981, JDC files).[115]

Morton Mandel pressed for a unified American Jewish position. He and others pressured HIAS to agree to the Agency plan. As long as Rav Tov remained active HIAS refused to agree (Carmi Schwartz, hand notes at meeting between CJF, UIA, JDC, and HIAS, November 2, 1981, CJF files).[116]

Prior to resolution of this issue Edwin Shapiro (HIAS) and Henry Taub (JDC) met with Israeli Prime Minister Menachem Begin in Israel on November 22, 1981 (Record of meeting of Prime Minister with Presidents of HIAS and JDC, November 22 1981, recorded by Yehuda Avner, JDC files).[117] Begin explained that Soviet leaders were unhappy with Soviet Jews resettling in the USA.[118] Begin told his guests that "HIAS cannot claim to pursue its activities outside the consensus of the American Jewish leadership." To this Shapiro responded that he doubted that most had approved Dulzin's plan and those that did might not represent the majority of American Jewry. He even suggested that Begin had been misled. Begin admitted that CJF had rejected his position in Detroit and although a majority may not have approved he argued that they were now "ready to acquiesce." When Shapiro indicated that HIAS would follow the lead of CJF several of the Americans emphasized that the September CJF Quarterly had agreed to cooperate with the plan. The Prime Minister then asked for HIAS to support it for one year; Shapiro mentioned that the original plan had been for three months, Begin responded that this was too short a period. Begin asked him to bring this to his Board on December 1, 1981 and to emphasize that if the present situation continued aliyah and emigration from USSR may cease and thus deny Israel a mass immigration it so needed. He again proposed trying the plan for one year. Shapiro said he would recommend this to his board.[119]

The Executive Committee of HIAS voted 8–4 on December 1, 1981 that "HIAS would, at the specific request of Prime Minister Begin, confine assistance to Soviet refugees exiting with visas for Israel to those who are referred to us by the Jewish Agency for Israel." According to the Jewish Agency only parents, children or spouses of people living in countries other than Israel would be referred to HIAS (HIAS Board of Directors, December 8, 1981, HIAS files). The HIAS Executive Committee stipulated that there be compassionate consideration on a case by case basis for émigrés with siblings (not covered by Jewish Agency policy), daily monitoring and joint counseling. It planned to reconsider continued implementation or termination after 90 days. The HIAS Board on December 8 endorsed the December 1 policies by a vote of 25 to 13 to cooperate on a trial basis for three months.

The Austrian government looked upon the new HIAS position as one which denied freedom of choice. It informed all voluntary agencies working with Soviet émigrés that "all those in Red Cross center who wish not to go to Israel will be given possibility to contact your organization." They placed a sign informing émigrés that if they did not want to go to Israel they could get in touch with the assistance of the Austrian Red Cross with other listed organizations including Rav Tov.[120] They also allowed Rav Tov to meet every plane and train arriving with émigrés from the Soviet Union (Hand notes c. December 29, 1981, CJF files, box 710; Memo, Stern to Slater, December 30 1981; and "Israel Immigration Unit Curtails Vienna Efforts," January 7, 1982, probably *NYT*). The Jewish Agency told the Austrian Interior Ministry that its new policy violated an agreement between the Red Cross and the Jewish Agency and that world Jewry was upset at the entrance of missionary groups into the hostel. He claimed that the Austrian government had leased the facility exclusively to the Jewish Agency (Telex, HIAS Geneva to Len Seidenman, December 30, 1981, CJF files, box 710; Carmi Schwartz hand notes, December 31, 1981; and Memo, Slater to Ralph Goldman, December 31, 1981, JDC files). He also charged that the Austrian government violated an agreement giving the Jewish Agency exclusive access to Soviet Jews arriving in Vienna on Israeli visas. In protest Rafael Kotlowitz moved the Jewish Agency operation from the hostel to hotels. The Austrian Government offered to change this policy if HIAS agreed to accept all who did not want to go to

Israel. After negotiations the Austrians removed the sign and informed émigrés by word of mouth of the several options. All going to Israel or Rome
signed a document that it was being done voluntarily. Many refused to sign
(Hand notes of Carmi Schwartz, January 6, 1982, CJF files, box 710). [121]

Many Israeli and American Jewish leaders felt that the three-month period
would be too short to evaluate the effectiveness of the new policy. Nehemia
Levanon prepared a memo proposing a longer experiment time. He argued
that it would take several months for Soviet Jews to hear of the new policy
and begin to apply to leave. Those leaving during the next three months had
begun the process several months before (Letter, Nehemia Levanon to Len
Seidenman, December 21, 1981, CJF files, box 710; Memo of Meeting in Vienna, December 18, 1981, JDC files). [122]

The HIAS trial period was to end on March 31, 1982. The HIAS Executive
Committee met on April 13 1982 and voted 22 to 0 to resume "our historic
role of offering HIAS services to any Jew in the world who is in need" (Minutes, HIAS Board of Directors, April 26, 1982). Prime Minister Menachem Begin had asked them to table the decision until after Brussels III which would
be held on October 25, 1982 in Paris. HIAS offered a compromise; it would
not accept dropouts in Vienna but only in Rome. This would allow them to
accept those cared for by Rav Tov. The Jewish Agency rejected the compromise. Prior to an April 26, 1982 board meeting of HIAS the Presidents of JDC,
CJF, UIA, UJA and Chairman of the Board of Governors of the Jewish Agency
asked them to postpone Executive Committee vote on the resolution. After a
discussion the HIAS Board voted 40 to 12 to approve the earlier resolution
providing services for all Jewish émigrés. Edwin Shapiro explained to friends
of HIAS that "we could not continue with our policies and/or procedures
that not only were ineffective in reaching stated goals, but were in performance harmful to the refugees and World Jewry" (Memo, Edwin Shapiro to
Board Members, July 16, 1982, HIAS files." [123]

The tension between HIAS and the Jewish Agency complicated matters for
JDC. In April 1982 HIAS requested that JDC provide maintenance for Jewish
émigrés under its care who had not been referred by the Jewish Agency. At
a JDC board meeting the organizations solidarity with Israel on the drop out
issue cracked. Henry Taub, JDC President, felt that JDC should remain faith-
ful to its agreement with the Jewish Agency and refuse the HIAS request. He
found it "hard to repudiate the position taken by the Prime Minister of Israel." He also noted that the small number of refugees did not warrant split-
ting the community. Mr. Herbert Friedman (former HIAS President and JDC
board member) disagreed. He retorted "This is not Israel but America; The
American JDC is not the Jewish Agency! We all support Israel but differences
of opinion may exist." He urged accepting HIAS's offer and for JDC to return
to its fundamental principle of taking care of any Jews who needed help and
could be rescued. He also reported that several top federation leaders prom-

ised to fund HIAS at the expense of the UJA. Mr. Edward Warburg added that although he respected statements by the Prime Minister of Israel, "the JDC is the American Joint Distribution Committee." Former JDC Executive Vice President, Mr. Samuel Haber, supported Friedman on condition that Dulzin was wrong in suggesting that dropouts contribute to closing the gates of the Soviet Union. The JDC committee voted to continue to support the policy of only providing care and maintenance for all Jewish transmigrants with Israeli destination visas that are referred to HIAS by Jewish Agency until the end of the forthcoming Brussels Conference. Thereafter the policy would be reevaluated (Minutes, JDC Officers and Area Committee Meeting, May 11, 1982, JDC files) and Memo, Ralph Goldman to file, May 26, 1982 (JDC files).[124]

The internal dissent continued. At an Executive Committee Meeting of JDC in July 1982, Dr. Cherkasky of JDC Europe and Mr. William Rosenwald of New York City favored JDC helping all Jews who wanted to come to the USA. Cherkasky opposed coercing people to go to Israel. Others also questioned the JDC position. Ralph Goldman and JDC President Henry Taub put off a vote on the issue (Minutes, JDC Executive Committee, July 21, 1982 first draft, JDC files). The following year in June 1983 JDC staffer Joan Wolchansky wrote Ralph Goldman that a majority of American Jews sided with HIAS on the issue of aiding all Soviet Jewish dropouts and freedom of choice. She warned that some might shift UJA contributions from JDC to HIAS. Others might see JDC as allying with Israel and not with American Jewry. Moreover, she noted that the government and State Department of the United States also favored the HIAS position. This could influence future United States governmental funding. Finally she reminded Goldman that the policy of only accepting dropouts with first-degree relatives in the United States contradicts JDC historic mission of rescue relief and rehabilitation (Memo "*Noshrim*," Joan Wolchansky to Ralph Goldman, June 16, 1983, JDC files). Finally, others in the JDC as well as American governmental authorities were concerned about duplication; both HIAS and JDC provided care and maintenance to dropouts ("Noshrim," June 16, 1983; Akiva Kohane to Ralph Goldman, July 7, 1983, JDC files). One United States and Refugee Program official warned that "there may be problems" if JDC did not take over care and maintenance for all Soviet Jewish émigrés (Memo on *Noshrim*, Akiva Kohane to Ralph Goldman, July 29, 1983).

Officially, JDC continued to support the Jewish Agency position of refusing aid to dropouts not having first-degree relatives in the United States.[125] Goldman and Kohane reiterated that the Israeli government and Prime Minister should have the final word on dropouts since the subject was of such great importance (Memo, Akiva Kohane to Ralph Goldman, September 6, 1982, JDC files). Three years later both HIAS and JDC were still providing care and maintenance in Vienna. It proved very costly and Washington was raising questions about duplication (Letter, Heinz Eppler to Jerold Hoffberger, May

25, 1985, JDC files).[126] Clearly JDC wanted to provide care and maintenance for all Soviet Jewish émigrés regardless of destination and whether they had relatives in the West. It justified this position to the Israelis by arguing that non-Zionist and even anti-Zionist groups filled the shoes of the JDC in Vienna and Rome (Letter, Heinz Eppler and Saul Cohen to Chaim Aharon and Yehuda Dominitz, July 11, 1985, JDC files).[127]

By January 1982 if not before it was clear to all that the Soviet Union was "closing" its gates to Jewish emigration. This situation and the resulting reduce flow of émigrés reduced the importance of the issue of aiding dropouts (*JTA*, January 28, 1982).

CONCLUSION

Once again the American Jewish establishment led by CJF refused to go along with the Israeli government and its Liaison Bureau on the dropout issue. They rejected the compromise proposed by Prime Minister Begin to assist only dropouts with first degree relatives in the United States while permitting federations to resettle any émigrés who arrived in their communities regardless of which relief organization sponsored their entry into the United States. It was assumed that refugees sponsored by IRC or Rav Tov probably did not have first degree relatives in the United States.

As in the earlier period the federations lay and professional leaders spearheaded the opposition in support of HIAS and against the Liaison Bureau. Again, the memory of the Holocaust and inaction of American Jewry as well as the Jewish tradition of freeing captives, commitment to freedom of choice and organization interests played a role in the motivation of American Jewish leaders in opposing the Israeli request to limit aid to Soviet Jewish émigrés.

At the same time there were signs that some federations and especially lay leaderships were shifting their support from freedom of choice. Several communities felt inundated and overburdened by Soviet Jewish émigrés. They passed resolutions to limit resettlement to those with close relatives in the community. This clearly indicated that should the number of émigrés increase a potentially significant number of American Jews on the federation level might abandon support of freedom of choice (Letter, Mrs. Lawrence Jay Weinberg, President of Jewish Federation Council of Los Angeles, to Irving Kessler, August 31 1976, HIAS files).[128]

When Aryeh Dulzin of the Jewish Agency took unilateral action, CJF and JDC led by Ralph Goldman and a supportive lay leadership acquiesced to the Israeli position. Under pressure HIAS reluctantly went along and then reneged after a three month trial period. These events proved insignificant as Soviet authorities were about to close the gates on Soviet Jews wanting to emigrate.

As in 1976 Max Fisher supported the Israeli position. Here too he found himself checked by CJF leaders who questioned Israel's needs. For this reason he brought in Ralph Goldman (as Rabin had done in the Committee of Eight in 1976) to develop an American Jewish response to freedom of choice, which he hoped would support the needs and interests of Israel. Goldman vehemently opposed freedom of choice from the start and worked with the Liaison Bureau to defeat its supporters in the American Jewish community.

Goldman represented an American Jewish professional completely committed to the Israeli position. He identified with Israel's goals of wanting all Soviet Jews to come as immigrants. His only reservations were about Israel's pragmatism in dealing with American Jewish leaders. A native Bostonian he had spent his earlier professional career serving the Israeli government and its political leaders. Before 1948 he worked in the United States to secure manpower and weapons for underground Jewish forces in Palestine. After 1948 he served in the Israeli consulate in New York City as a representative of Prime Minister David Ben-Gurion. In 1951 he accepted a position in Israel to head the Technical Assistance Department of the Office of the Prime Minister where he administered the Point Four Program (Shachtman 2001:30–41). He became Executive Vice President of the JDC in 1975. He ran many of the JDC activities in Europe and the Soviet Bloc countries in consultation with the Liaison Bureau (Ibid.:69).

It is noteworthy that the JDC served as a conduit for the American Jewish community's UJA to fund many of the activities of the Liaison Bureau (Ibid.: 108,178). For example, it funded a Liaison Bureau computer project at a cost of about one half million dollars (Ibid.:183). The JDC admitted publicly to budgeting the package program which was either a Liaison Bureau project or else a joint Liaison Bureau–JDC project. In an interview (June 26, 2002), Yehuda Lapidot, director of the Liaison Bureau from December 1980 through January 1985, suggested that its budget was funded half by the government and half by the Jewish Agency. Two thirds of the latter's budget comes from the UJA in the United States.[129]

While most professionals in federations and Jewish organizations had emotional ties to Israel, some did not share Goldman's loyalty and commitment to the Israeli cause. Nevertheless very few expressed objections to the pressure and participation of the Liaison Bureau emissaries in the American Soviet Jewry advocacy movement and its decision making process. An exception may have been Robert Hiller of CJF who opposed the activities of Nehemia Levanon within the CJF. Arthur Hertzberg (2002:361,362), then President of the American Jewish Congress and a committed Zionist expressed shock at Nehemia Levanon explaining to him in 1963 what the policy of the American Jewish Congress should be on Soviet Jewry. He suggests that Levanon expected him to obey.

Clearly, many federation lay and professional leaders committed themselves to freedom of choice over Israel's needs for Soviet Jewry. They funded
the resettlement of Soviet Jews in their communities. Ostensibly this rein-
forces Feingold's (1981) contention that in the post-Holocaust reality both Israel and the American Jewish community were in competition for Jews. Yet
evidence here suggests that although they defended freedom of choice
against Israeli demands in the 1970s to have all Soviet Jewish émigrés resettle in Israel, only a minority of federation lay leaders and professionals favored bringing a maximum number of Soviet Jews to the United States. By
the late 1980s the federation leadership and professionals along with other
American Jewish organizations would abandon freedom of choice when
faced with a potential of a million Soviet Jewish émigrés. Ironically, the new
generation of American Jewish leaders of the late 1980s, while favoring an
American Jewish interest as distinct from that of Israel would come to view
Israel as the preferable destination for most Soviet Jews.

Writing in 1989 (1989:4) Friedgut asserts that if one views the Soviet Jewry
movement as an Israeli initiated effort than the dropout phenomenon marks
Israel's loss of control and diminished influence over the movement and its
people—Jewish émigrés.

By 1982, the Soviet Union closed the gates to Soviet Jewish emigration.
Many experts believed it reflected a lull in relations between the United
States and the Soviet Union. With the closure of the gates the issue of Soviet
Jewry began to shift to the Refusenik issues and the release of Prisoners of
Zion, Jews who had not been allowed to leave despite requests to do so
(Gur-Gurevitz 1996:12).

NOTES

1. Mandel believed that Max Fisher was always careful and did what the Israeli
Prime Minister expected of him. He also believed that Fisher was very practical—"he
read the tea leaves."

2. During the first six months of 1976 the Soviets allowed 401 Soviet Jews to leave
on visas to the United States. In the same period in 1977 only 238 left. HIAS provided
1,432 letters of invitation for 3,722 persons from July 1, 1976 through July 30, 1977.
Ralph Goldman (memo to file on meeting with Jim Carlin, September 12, 1978) reported that Rav Tov also sent invitations to Soviet Jews. In the early 1980s when Soviet authorities made it more difficult to file an invitation from the United States, Max
Kampleman of the United States delegation to the Madrid Conference, at the behest
of HIAS, intervened and the Soviets backed down (Memo of Bruce Leimsidor, February 5, 1981, HIAS files).

3. The State Department asked the Attorney General to use his parole authority to
permit the entry of 5,000 Jews and others from the Soviet Union during a six-month
period ending May 1, 1978 (Letter, Deputy Secretary of State Warren Christopher to

Attorney General Griffin Bell, November 10, 1977 (HIAS files) and Memo dated November 23, 1977, "Commissioner of INS Lionel Castillo to agree to request by Deputy Secretary of State to Parole 5000 Soviet Jews in Italy" (HIAS files). The Attorney General had previously paroled 2,250 persons from August 1972 to May 1974 and another 4,000 persons in early 1977. Attorney General Griffin Bell wrote to Congressman Eilberg on December 7, 1977 (HIAS files) that he supported INS opposition to open-ended use of parole visas.

4. Senator Ted Kennedy introduced a bill proposing open-ended parole for two years.

5. JDC expected to double its maintenance costs in Europe in 1978. JDC increased its budget for Rome from $11m to $16m and expected it to reach $21–22m by the end of the year. The United States government reimbursed almost 80 percent. At the time the American government owed JDC $3.1m. (Minutes of JDC Executive Committee, November 8, 1977). Per person cost estimates rose from $2,200 to $3,000. (Ralph Goldman, memo, "On Medical Expenses," October 23, 1979, JDC files).

6. In a memo to file on September 22, 1981 Ralph Goldman refers to sending 33,800 packages at a cost of $5,480,000. A day later (Executive Committee Meeting of September 23, 1981) JDC President Henry Taub referred to sending 45,000 packages this year. JDC partially funded a Lubavitch package program (Shachtman 2001:113). In September 1985 the Liaison Bureau's Tel Aviv office took charge of European warehouses and decided on what to ship and to whom. JDC would supply the funds, purchase contents and monitor the shipments and responses (Executive Committee of JDC, September 19, 1985 (JDC files). See Shachtman (2001:107ff.,175ff) for a discussion of Relief in Transit package program which JDC began in World War II. The Liaison Bureau took charge in the early 1950s and JDC continued to fund and participate in the operation.

7. According to a draft letter of Carl Glick to the HIAS Board (after July 1977) (HIAS files) HIAS expected a $2.5m deficit. In FY 1978 the HIAS budget was about $8m of which $4m was reimbursed by the United States government (Minutes of JDC Area Committees on Eastern Europe and Relief in Transit of December 6, 1977, JDC files).

8. Dubinsky said that Max Fisher will stay firm against HIAS appeal (Hand note, Mel Dubinsky to Irving Kessler, September 23, 1977, HIAS files).

9. In June 1978 HIAS claimed that INS agreed to conduct the security checks in 15 days (Gaynor Jacobson to Cooperating Agencies, June 21, 1978, HIAS files; Memo, Ralph Goldman to Phil Bernstein and Gaynor Jacobson, November 21, 1978; Ralph Goldman, Aide Memoire, meeting with Jim Carlin, June 16, 1978). Carlin told Goldman that the Moscow Embassy would handle Third Country Processing paperwork which would speed up the process in Rome.

10. A reduced processing time in Rome from three to one month would save $4m a month. By 1978 INS used computers (rather than the diplomatic pouch) to expedite clearances by FBI and CIA (Ralph Goldman Aide Memoire, June 16, 1978, JDC files).

11. Jim Rice (Memo to NPPC members, November 21, 1978 (HIAS files) proposed that the UJA develop a national plan "to finance this major rescue program." A resolution at the CJF General Assembly in San Francisco on November 12, 1978 (HIAS files) called for more equity between federations in absorbing. CJF discussed national funding, distribution, standard services and Steve Solender talked of fair share (Carl

Glick hand notes in file #23 1978, probably CJF meeting in November/December 1978). CJF Board of Directors Meeting, September 6–7, 1980 (CJF files, box 660) noted that disabled persons over 65 were eligible for Social Security Insurance at 100 percent federal expense.

12. United States government aid covered en route care and maintenance, construction, acquisition and maintenance of absorption centers, construction of medical facilities and vocational training (Transcript of conference call, "United States Government Funding of Transmigrant Operation," early May 1978, JDC files). The following chart shows the annual allocations between 1973 and 1993:

United States Grant Funds to Israel for the Resettlement of Soviet Jews*

Year	Amount	Year	Amount	Year	Amount
1973	44	1980	25	1987	25
1974	30.5	1981	25	1988	25
1975	34.1	1982	12.5	1989	28
1976	12	1983	12.5	1990	29.5
1977	14	1984	12.5	1991	51
1978	18.5	1985	32.5	1992	80
1979	25	1986	12	1993	80

*figures in $m. Source: UIA, "History of UIA-U.S. Government Grant Funds (1973–1995)." Israel also received $80m in 1994 and 1995.

13. In September 1979 Mark Talisman noted that the government had reimbursed HIAS to compensate for shortfalls in previous appropriations and might also have included payment for interest on loans that HIAS had to obtain to cover expenses.

14. Federal funding ran out for reimbursements for refugee efforts in Europe in fall 1978 and again in March 1979 (Letter of John McCarthy, American Council of Voluntary Agencies to President Jimmy Carter, November 7, 1978, HIAS files); Letter of Gaynor Jacobson to Stuart Eizenstat (Assistant to the President), November 17, 1978 (HIAS files); and Christopher Dickey and Warren Brown "Refugee Surge, Erratic US Policies Strain Voluntary Agency Resources," *Washington Post*, January 6, 1979.

15. He reported on federal grant of $16m for CJF to distribute to federations and others to assist settlement of Soviet Jews ($943 per person). Some costs of resettlement including religious education would not be reimbursed (Edelman 1982:160). Bernard Manekin at CJF Board meeting on January 20, 1980 reported that $18,374,000 of total federal block grant of $25,200,00 had been received (CJF files, box 660). They expected a supplementary $5m grant (CJF Board of Directors, June 7–8, 1980 (CJF files, box 660). At the HIAS Board Meeting of June 4, 1980 (HIAS files) Edwin Shapiro reported that Jewish communities would receive $18m ($1 for every $2 spent). Shapiro succeeded Glick as President of HIAS in March 1979.

16. At the February 1978 World Zionist Congress many charged HIAS with encouraging Soviet Jews to "drop out."

17. B'nai B'rith quietly moved some Soviet Jews who had left Israel to Canada and IRC helped settle them in the United States. David Harris of the International League for Human Rights wanted to assist them.

18. In defending HIAS, Phil Klutnzick suggested that Israel's failure was not in absorbing immigrants but in attracting them (May 23, 1979, CJF files, box 710).

19. Dulzin called *Neshira* (dropping out) a national sin (memo, May 18 1978, JDC files). Also see *JTA*, May 31 and June 7, 1978.

20. Nahum Goldmann of the World Jewish Congress wrote Gaynor Jacobson (June 14, 1978) that he "fully agree(s) with the position of HIAS." On June 20, 1978, Rabbi Moshe Sherer, Executive President of Agudath Israel praised Glick's position as being "in the full spirit of compassion and Tzedaka [charity]." At the time the Rabbinical Council of America adopted a resolution in support of the Jewish Agency policy and critical of HIAS.

HIAS used a 95 percent figure of Soviet Jews joining relatives in the United States until February 1978. In June 1979 Jim Rice claimed that 85–95 percent joined relatives. Two months later Len Seidenman referred to 80 percent (memo to Gaynor Jacobson, August 14, 1979, JDC files). Joan Wolchansky (memos to Ralph Goldman, August 30 and 31, 1979, JDC files) claimed that NYANA had taken "an educated guess" in calculating the percentage of émigrés with relatives in the United States. Sherwood Slater (memo to Wolchansky, September 7, 1979, JDC files) reported that in a sample survey in Vienna 28.7 percent of those going to the United States had close relatives there (parents, children, siblings, grandchildren). A survey of 759 families who arrived in Vienna between August 28 and September 11, 1979 indicated that 35.7 percent had first-degree relatives in America. Mort Mandel of CJF reported on a 43 percent rate of those with first degree relatives who came to the United States and or the West (Ralph Goldman on *Noshrim* February 26, 1980, JDC file). Ralph Goldman wrote Sanford Solender (February 12, 1981) that Joseph Edelman of HIAS had found that only 35 percent of those coming here had first degree relatives.

21. He thought there should be a year or so transition period before changing the system of aid.

22. At the meeting someone reported that all efforts on direct flights failed. Carl Glick, hand notes (HIAS files). Katzki of JDC Geneva wrote Ralph Goldman (August 2, 1978) that Rafael Kotlowitz of the Jewish Agency favored flying all Soviet Jewish émigrés from Moscow to Israel (JDC files).

23. They proposed that the Jewish Agency send Russian speaking American immigrants to work in Vienna and that HIAS, JDC and ORT recruit Israelis for their Rome staff.

24. The new head of the Jewish Agency's Absorption Department Rafael Kotlowitz dissented. He argued that the situation was like that of the Holocaust with Jewish lives at stake.

25. Ralph Goldman (in hand notes of meeting with Nehemia Levanon on October 18, 1978) reported that expect increased emigration after Armand Hammer met with Leonid Brezhnev. Levanon wanted to discuss with CJF their contact with State Department. *He also opposed unilateral HIAS action with State Department on visas.*

26. Goldman noted that a single emissary could not deal with thirty persons on one train. Jewish Agency emissaries in Vienna managed to "rescue" between 50 and 75 persons a month from HIAS (note, Yehuda Dominitz to Ralph Goldman, November 5, 1979). Meetings with Agency emissaries were optional since April 1979. In 1981 Len Seidenman (Minutes of HIAS Board of May 28, 1981) reported that Rav Tov boarded trains to Vienna and tried to attract refugees assigned to HIAS. He claimed

Rav Tov secured accreditation because of its support for the election of President Carter. Len Seidenman (in telex #8553 to Gaynor Jacobson, April 26, 1978) viewed (for the moment) Rav Tov in Vienna and Rome more a nuisance than a threat (HIAS files).

27. Ralph Goldman refers to Eagle Visas (via satellite) that reduce processing from 42 to 15 days (Ralph Goldman meeting with Sam Villanova, INS, October 25, 1978).

28. The Israeli Ambassador in Vienna (note in JDC file on October 20, 1978) informed the group that the Israeli government could not ask the Austrians for a larger camp for Soviet émigrés.

29. Until this time HIAS/JDC operated the train between Vienna and Rome. JDC coordinated the number of trains with American Embassy staff (Memo, Akiva Kohane to Ralph Goldman, December 20, 1979). After the Jewish Agency (Liaison Bureau) obtained biographical data, JDC brought its charges to 2 hotels where it conducted eligibility checks and health screening while HIAS did an initial registration, assigned numbers, collected brief biographical data and set travel arrangements.

JDC preferred processing in Rome since it allowed the Jewish Agency more time to influence potential dropouts (Ralph Goldman, Memo to files, September 12, 1978). When Rome backed up and the Italian Government was reluctant to increase the numbers, the team considered other sites including Paris, Athens, Genoa and Naples (Akiva Kohane, memo to Ralph Goldman, "Movement of Russian Émigrés" October 16, 1979, JDC files). HIAS limited the baggage allowance to 750 kilo (as of July 1, 1976) per family. HIAS reduced reimbursement for shipping costs, storage, etc. to a maximum of 500 kilo per family, as of July 1, 1979, to 350 kilos in October 1979 and 100 kilos effective June 1, 1982 (Memos, HIAS Vice President Harry M. Friedman to Cooperating Agencies, January 1979 and Minutes of Board Meeting of April 26, 1982).

30. Ralph Goldman obtained approval for the Naples Plan from Sam Villanova of INS.

31. In the minutes of HIAS Board of Directors meeting of April 26, 1982 someone reported that HIAS presented the idea of the Naples Plan of 1979 to the Jewish Agency. In the end the Jewish Agency failed to get the approval of the Italian Ministry of Interior for the Naples Plan.

32. The parties proceeded with joint counseling in Vienna. A CJF ad hoc committee which studied the Naples Plan approved joint counseling but refused to endorse HIAS's withholding services from any Jewish refugee in need (Letter, Yehuda Dominitz to Edwin Shapiro, December 26, 1979, JDC files).

33. A November 1979 Jewish Agency report on dropouts: "Neshira: Exodus . . . ." prepared by Amnon Hadari and others partially blamed HIAS and JDC operations in Rome for influencing émigrés to dropout. Some Knesset members criticized the policies of the Liaison Bureau and the Israeli Government. Orbach (1979:30) reports on the Israeli based *Maoz* society which chided Israel and World Jewry on their inaction on Soviet Jewry. It was identified with the Herut movement. Active were Geula Cohen and other right wing Knesset members as well as recent Soviet immigrants (Interview, Benjamin Pinkus, June 5, 2002). It submitted a petition with 97,000 signatures asking the Knesset to consider the Soviet issue openly. It charged Israel with being too concerned about its interests at the expense of Soviet Jews. For example in 1971 Israel cut support for a Russian language magazine in Israel when it published a *samizdat* from the democratic movement (Orbach 1979:9). The Likud once charged that Labor was too tame vis-

à-vis Moscow because of émigré support for the Likud (Ibid:10). Israeli establishment (Liaison Bureau) set up the Israel Public Council for Soviet Jews with Israelis and activist émigrés from Union of Former Prisoners of Zion and Association of Immigrants from USSR (61). Freedman (1989b:96) argues that prior to Gorbachev only fringe Israeli politicians had embraced the Soviet Jewry issue. By 1986 Moshe Arens became involved along with Natan Sharansky. They pressured the Israeli government to take a harder line on the issues.

34. Goldman also learned that the Jewish Agency would not be willing to handle transportation from Vienna to Rome. See telex Trobe to Ralph Goldman of April 4, 1978.

35. In February 1979 the Jewish Agency approved a plan for a joint government Jewish Agency authority for absorption. Unfortunately, nothing ever came of this recommendation (Meeting of Coordinating Committee, February 27, 1980, Hebrew). Previously, in November 1976 the Jewish Agency had approved the Horev Report recommendations for a single absorption authority but the government took no action (Judy Siegel, "Unfulfilled promise," October 26, 1978, *JP*).

36. Present at the May 25, 1979, meeting of Professional Committee were Yitzachak Bar On of Jewish Agency, Irving Bernstein of UJA, Phil Bernstein of CJF; Sara Frankel Israeli consulate (and Liaison Bureau), Ralph Goldman, Gaynor Jacobson, Irving Kessler (UIA) and JDC staff.

37. CJF expected resettlement costs to double in 1979 while the federal block grant would remain the same (SPG to Phil Bernstein, "Current and Prospective Costs of Russian Jewish Migration to the United States," March 21 1979, JDC files). CJF expected a possible HIAS deficit which the federations would have to cover (Phil Bernstein to Ralph Goldman and Joan Wolchansky May 23, 1979). Ralph Goldman proposed that Israel not send Israeli invitations to Kiev and Odessa.

38. The second draft reported that in 1976 HIAS assisted 746 individuals arriving in USA via American affidavits (660 were processed via third countries [TCP].

39. He referred to Fort Dix as a possible processing center. The revised document recommended better-trained and more professional (rather than political appointees) Jewish Agency personnel in Vienna. It suggested that former Prisoners of Zion serve as short-term emissaries. It recommended that the Agency set up an open line in Vienna for émigrés to call Israeli relatives. It opposed the hiring of former Israelis in Vienna and Rome. It urged greater "Jewish" enrichment of programs in Rome and efforts to get émigrés to visit Israel (at the participant's expense). It called for an upgraded and unified absorption authority in Israel.

In November 1979 the Jewish Agency had 3 emissaries working in Rome. They ran a Tarbuth (culture) Club (Memo Ralph Goldman to Yehuda Dominitz November 5, 1979, JDC files). They also conducted a 12-day visit to Israel for dropouts. ORT operated schools and offered English classes. Many émigrés studied English at the Baptist Missionary (Memo, Akiva Kohane to Ralph Goldman, July 26, 1977, CJF files). In 1979 the JDC gave the Israel Community Center Corporation responsibility for education (socialization and rediscovery of Jewish roots) among émigrés in Rome (memo of Joan Wolshansky "Yiddishkeit" August 28, 1980).

40. An earlier version called on making Israel more attractive and improving absorption services while making the USA less attractive (grants versus loans). It also proposed trying to change Soviet Jews' view of Israel and the West.

41. The revised report favored making all aid given by federations a loan. It is noted, however, that a United States government bloc grant can be used only to match voluntary funds for grants and not loans.

42. The negatives cited in the report focused on HIAS/JDC losing a source of government revenues and limiting freedom of choice. Fisher also asked rhetorically whether they were saving Soviet Jews for Judaism or just saving people.

43. Participants included Irving Kessler (UIA), Charlotte Jacobson (World Zionist Organization), Gaynor Jacobson (HIAS), Don Robinson (JDC) and Edwin Shapiro (HIAS). Government participants included Dick Clark, Special Ambassador on Refugees, William Farrand, U.S. Counselor of the USSR; Marshall Brement (National Security Council), Doris Meisner, Deputy Associate Attorney General, and Norman Anderson, aide to Ed Sanders. Summary of Meeting at White House, June 8, 1979 (JDC files). Prior to the LaGuardia meeting of June 9th, Fisher intended to consult with Mort Mandel, Jerold Hoffberger, Don Robinson, Frank Lautenberg, Edwin Shapiro and Phil Klutznick, Chair of the President's Conference.

44. Using Romania, a Communist dictatorship and police state, instead of Austria, would deny émigrés the option of dropping out.

45. He reported that INS had assigned 5 more staff to Rome and was trying to get another 5. They process 500 applications per week. The staff increase should reduce processing time to 3 weeks for INS and 3 weeks for HIAS. He expected a backlog of 4,500.

46. Doris Meisner had doubts that medical screening could be done in the Soviet Union. William Farrand also doubted that the Soviets would allow HIAS to operate in Moscow.

47. Clark thought that the Soviets wanted to "help" the United States because of *SALT* talks. Also see "Aide memoir draft to the Honorable Edward Sanders" RE: Soviet Jewish Emigration," June 9, 1979 (JDC files).

48. Participants included Max Fisher, chair, Yitzhak Bar On (Jewish Agency), Phil Bernstein, Sara Frankel (Liaison Bureau), Ralph Goldman, Charlotte Jacobson, Gaynor Jacobson, Irving Kessler, Akiva Lewinsky (Jewish Agency), Nehemia Levanon (Liaison Bureau), Morton Mandel, Don Robinson, Edwin Shapiro, and JDC staff. Absentees included Irving Bernstein, Irwin Field, Jerold Hoffberger, Frank Lautenberg and Bernard Mannekin.

49. Sherwood Slater of JDC (Memo to Ralph Goldman, "Comments of Options Concerning Soviet Jewish Emigration," May 30, 1979, JDC files) argued that most Soviet Jewish émigrés now preferred the United States for economic and social reasons. Sara Frankel rejected Fisher's criticism of the Jewish Agency. When one has a free ticket to Austria, Italy and the United States, she argued, then why come to Israel? Irving Bernstein, Executive Vice President of the UJA wrote Max Fisher (June 5, 1979, JDC files) that unless Israel improved significantly its absorption practices the situation was hopeless. Dominitz of the Jewish Agency concurred. See Chinitz telex to Irv Kessler, November 25, 1977 (JDC files).

50. Second draft suggested that American visas may become more attractive because the cost was less and did not involve loss of citizenship. At UIA meeting on May 30, 1977 (Ralph Goldman, hand notes) Edwin Shapiro of HIAS noted that the Soviets got lots of money for Israeli visas and none for American visas.

51. Joseph Waxman writing in *Maaariv*, June 29, 1979 reported that 94 percent of dropouts in Los Angeles had severed ties with the Jewish community. See Ritterband 1997 for a discussion of a survey on Jewish identity among Soviet Jewish immigrants in the United States. Stephen Gold (1997) has written that by the late 1980s most Soviet Jews in the United States "were interested neither in religion or in joining American Jewish life at least in the way that the American Jewish community had envisioned" (1997:162). Many joined synagogues (40 percent, mostly reform) and sent their kids for some Jewish education. (1997:280). *Reform Judaism* 8 #2 (November 1999).

52. Earlier deliberations of the Goldman Committee decided that only the Israeli government could make the decision that everyone with Israeli visas would be helped only to travel to and settle in Israel.

53. In a note to Ralph Goldman, Joan Wolchansky ("On refugee status," July 13, 1979, JDC files), argued that Dulzin had only taken this position since May. While Eli Eyal of the Jewish Agency Executive quoted a 1973 United Nations High Commissioner for Refugees ruling that Soviet Jewish emigrants who reach Vienna not have refugee status because they are "protected" by Israel, *JTA*, (July 12, 1979) explained that United Nation High Commissioner for Refugees had adopted the view of Dr. Paul Weis that Jews from Eastern Europe are "not ordinary refugees, but are to be regarded as refugees."

54. The November 1979 Jewish Agency report on dropouts (Hadary et al.) argued that the real question is "whether World Jewry is obligated to finance the decision once made."

55. When Mort Mandel raised the issue of housing problems in Israel, Prime Minister Begin responded that "housing doesn't create Zionism, Zionism creates housing."

56. HIAS gave a more optimistic report in a memo to its members and CJF (Bruce Leimsidor re: "Minutes, NPPC," September 11, 1979, JDC files).

57. Participants included Max Fisher, Leon Dulzin, Jerold Hoffberger, Sara Frankel, I. Baron, Phil Bernstein, Morton Mandel, Irving Bernstein; Edwin Shapiro, Nehemia Levanon, CJ, and Yosef Shapira.

58. The memo argues that Israel was created for Jewish refugees and that dropouts negate and affront Israel. It suggests that Israel needed the dropouts who would assimilate in the West while the Soviets might use dropouts as excuse to close gates. "There is substantial agreement that those who do have first degree relatives in other countries should be reunited with them, even with Israeli visas." The document argues that many prefer the United States because "more generous treatment and assistance . . . personal warmth of reception." Underlying principles: 1. to enable every Jew who wants to emigrate; 2. freedom of choice *within Soviet Union* to country they prefer; 3. maximum to Israel (no coercion). Need for Israel to "pull" Soviet Jews to it. Agreement to get visas to other countries, direct flights, strengthen services in Vienna and Rome and effort to convince to go to Israel; not make resettlement elsewhere more attractive than in Israel; emphasize Jewishness in resettlement programs; trips to Israel; and better use of international media to inform Soviet Jews about Israel.

59. CJF's International Affairs Steering Committee to meet in Chicago on October 21, 1979 to advise Mort Mandel (CJF files, Box 695). NJCRAC President Theodore Mann agreed that HIAS should support only those dropouts with first degree relatives

but allow federations to resettle all other Jewish dropouts upon their arrival in the United States. Mann also supported Ralph Goldman's suggestion for Israelis not to send invitations (*vyzovs*) to areas like Odessa where few émigrés settled in Israel. The Liaison Bureau refused to do so because it might result in fewer Jews leaving (Letter of Theodore Mann to Al Chernin, September 19, 1979, CJF files, box 710).

60. In 1978 and 1979, 12,265 and 28,794 Soviet Jewish refugees respectively arrived in the United States. Gaynor Jacobson noted that at the time the *NYANA* had received only 33 percent of the national share, down from its quota of between 45–50 percent. In 1979 HIAS resettled 9,000 Indochinese with the United States government providing $500 per person ($100 to national HIAS and $400 to federation). In FY 1980 HIAS resettle 5,800 Indochinese and the government asked HIAS to sponsor another 4,800 in FY1981. The American government funded HIAS program to resettle some non-Jewish Ethiopians in United States. HIAS also handled 1,300 Cuban refugees in Miami in 1980 (Minutes of HIAS Board of Directors meeting, January 20, 1980, June 4, 1980 and May 28, 1981, HIAS files).

61. Robert Hiller (CJF) (memo to Ralph Goldman, September 26, 1979, JDC notes) argued that it was more expensive to absorb in Israel. Gaynor Jacobson (letter to Philip Zinman, January 13, 1977, HIAS files) argued it cost $5,000 to absorb a family of three in the United States while it cost ten times this to settle them in Israel. Kessler claimed that the Israelis had "thrown in the kitchen sink" in estimating costs of absorption (hand notes for Kessler and phone conversation, May 9, 11, 1979 (JDC files). The more expensive absorption the more the Israelis could request from UJA and the United States government.

62. He reported that President Carter had not raised the issue of Soviet Jewry with Brezhnev (Gitelman 1999:91). According to Buwalda (1997:129–132) the Soviets let more Jews leave in the second half of 1977 while cracking down on dissidents. They wanted the United States to go ahead with Salt II (signed in Vienna in June 1979) and were dependent on American grain. President Carter proposed to Congress waiving part of Jackson-Vanik but dropped the matter when Senator Jackson and Jewish groups opposed. The Soviets were angered because in 1979 they had allowed 60,000 citizens to emigrate (Jews, Germans and Armenians). One Liaison Bureau official argued that at the time Nehemia Levanon did not have the courage to favor waiving Jackson-Vanik for one year in response to the Soviets letting 51,000 Jews leave in 1979 (Bulwarda 1997:134–139; Dinstein at General Assembly 1984; Goldman 1999:118–120; Interview, Jerry Shiran, February 28, 2003).

63. Ralph Goldman (memo to Akiva Kohane October 3, 1979) reported that HIAS gave each federation a quota.

64. Carmi Schwartz (hand notes at O'Hare, October 21, 1979, CJF files, box 710) suggested that if the community was short on funds for resettlement then it should cut back on all needs proportionally. They discussed fair share plan on cost and resettlement between all federations. In Carmi's notes reference to Israel's efforts to attract more Ashkenazim from Soviet Union.

65. Participants included Max Fisher, Morton Mandel, MD, Chuck Hoffberger, Edwin Shapiro, M. Sacher, Irving Kessler, Phil Bernstein, Robert Hiller, Irving Bernstein, GS, Ralph Goldman (Ralph Goldman to file, October 27, 1979, *Noshrim* folder at JDC). In November 1979 Mort Mandel commented that if the Soviets were to let out 50,000 persons, 5,000 would be of mixed marriages and prefer to go to the West (Min-

utes of CJF Executive, November 14, 1979 (CJF files, box 695). JDC document estimated 10 percent of marriages of émigrés mixed (c.November/December 1979). At the October 21, 1979 meeting (Ralph Goldman to file, JDC) someone estimated more than 30 percent.

66. *JTA*, October 30, 1979 reported that Bergen County and Jewish Community Council of Oklahoma City opposed aiding dropouts with Israeli passports who wanted to come to the United States. Also see Judy Siegel "U.S. Jewry Still Not Backing Begin's Plan to Cut 'dropouts,'" *JP*, October 30, 1979; *NY Post* of October 31, 1979, reported that "US Jews in Move to Curb Entry of Soviet Brethren."

67. Present were Menachem Begin, Max Fisher, Marvin Mandel, Ralph Goldman, Irving Kessler, Phil Bernstein, Aryeh Naor, Yehudah Avner, Yitzhak Rager Irving Bernstein; Frank Lautenberg; Don Robinson, Edwin Shapiro; Gaynor Jacobson, Rafael Kotlowitz, Yehuda Dominitz, Nehemia Levanon, Akiva Levinsky, Sacher, Charlotte Jacobson, Jerold Hoffberger and LD.

68. Mort Mandel later noted that some federations could not cope financially with resettling dropouts (Minutes of Meeting of Jewish Agency Executive, CJF files, box 602). Frank Lautenberg stated that "it was not freedom of choice to travel to the U.S. with funds that were essentially raised with Israeli impetus and with the Jewish Agency as the central theme of the fundraising campaign."

69. Later, David Geller of the American Jewish Committee would note that the more than 50,000 Soviet Jews who had arrived in the United States before 1989 could serve as a basis for a demand for family reunification (Geller 1990:26).

70. He added Edwin Shapiro and Gaynor Jacobson of HIAS to the committee formulating policy on the dropouts.

71. Report that New York Federation reject proposal not to aid *noshrim*. Richard Cohen in *Tribune Juive* of 30 November–December 5, 1979, stated that Oklahoma City and Bergen County, NJ decided to end aid to dropouts (Minutes of CJF Executive Committee in Montreal, November 14, 1979, CJF files, box 695). Rabbi Joseph Sternstein, President of the American Zionist Federation, endorsed Begin's plan only to aid dropouts with first-degree relatives in the United States (*JTA*, January 17, 1980). The Workmen's Circle (Press release of November 6, 1979, HIAS files) urged American Jewish community leaders to reject proposals limiting freedom of Soviet Jews to choose immigration to the United States.

72. *Maariv* (November 15, 1979) claimed that $40m (*JP* $30m) had been cut from UJA due to resettlement costs in the USA (Memo, Ralph Goldman to Milton Steinberg, March 13, 1980, JDC files).

73. He urged them to expand Jewish education in the Soviet Union and Rome, provide more accurate information on Israel, upgrade emissaries in Vienna, sponsor trips to Israel for émigrés, and improve absorption services, especially housing and jobs. Aryeh Dulzin accepted partial blame for dropouts due to Israel's poor housing situation (*JTA*, June 19, 1979). The *NYT* ("Many Russian Jews 'Drop Out' in Vienna," April 12, 1979) reported that an Israeli emissary in Rome claimed that Jews in Russia knew that Israel was unprepared for Soviet immigrants.

74. Hiller served as Executive Vice President of CJF from September 1, 1979 until September 1, 1981. Carmi Schwartz succeeded him.

75. Dulzin claimed leaders in 16 cities including Los Angeles, Cleveland and Miami accepted Begin's proposal of aiding only those with first degree relatives.

76. Both Prime Minister Begin and Deputy Prime Minister Yigal Yadin participated. HIAS Board Meeting of June 4, 1980 (HIAS files) states that Soviet authorities did not accept letters from distant relatives in Israel.

77. In June 1980 Ed Shapiro reported that Gaynor Jacobson would resign and stay on until a replacement was found (Ed Shapiro to HIAS board, June 16, 1980). Karl Zukerman was appointed Assistant Executive Vice President, effective October 1, 1982.

78. In a confidential memo to Nehemia Levanon, Hymewitz (March 28, 1980, JDC files) wrote that it was in the interest of the American Jewish community to avoid overreactions in the press to the refugee act. He noted that the Refugee Act of 1980 admits no more than 50,000 refugees of all ethnic groups in any one year unless President goes to Congress before beginning of FY to request greater numbers. CJF, he explained, wanted no change in the present system of block grants and matching funds.

79. Participants included Max Fisher, Sara Frankel, Irving Bernstein, Yehuda Dominitz, Ralph Goldman, Bob Hiller, Gaynor Jacobson, Nehemia Levanon, Irving Kessler and Shlomo Tadmor.

80. It also called for improved immigration services in Israel.

81. The Dutch would inform applicants in Moscow of the policy one month before it began. The plan also proposed use of Israeli travel documents (instead of American) for émigrés to go from Austria to Rome (Minutes of JDC Executive Committee, February 4, 1981, JDC files).

82. Present were Max Fisher, Jerold Hoffberger, MD, M. Sacher, Irving Kessler, Nehemia Levanon, HB, IF, Robert Hiller, Irving Bernstein, Morton Mandel, Don Robinson, Z or LC, Ralph Goldman Frank Lautenberg and Gaynor Jacobson.

83. JDC, HIAS, and Jewish Agency sign an agreement on the Naples plan (Akiva Kohane to Ralph Goldman, August 19, 1980, JDC files). HIAS Board of Directors meeting September 3, 1980 vote 18 in favor of plan, 9 oppose and 8 abstentions. JDC was unanimous (meeting held in JDC office notes, September 3, 1980). Yehuda Dominitz reported up to 600 beds in Naples. Jewish Agency would not transfer to HIAS non-family reunion cases; they would be left for IRC and Rav Tov. A meeting with Austrian officials did not bear fruit. The Minister of Interior insisted that those going to Israel were to be separated from the others. He also hinted that any change in the status quo would require consultations with Chancellor Bruno Kreisky and with other refugee relief agencies involved including Rav Tov (Ralph Goldman to file "Soviet Émigrés . . . Austrian Government," July 15, 1980, JDC files).

84. Parties discuss document/plan and report that Austrians have not yet given ok for worry that Russians may not agree to enter hostel. Intend to consult with Chancellor and answer in September. Decide to rent hotel (Jewish Agency to cover cost) (Ralph Goldman notes on August 27, 1980 meeting). Thereafter, Gaynor Jacobson, Edwin Shapiro, Robert Hiller and Morton Mandel would "sell" it to the federations and Nehemia Levanon would instruct the Dutch in Moscow to have all leaving sign a document that they are aware of changes in Vienna (Ralph Goldman to file, July 14, 1980, revision of June 29, 1980 document, JDC files). HIAS to fill out a United States Refugee Program (USRP) registration card for each transmigrant in Vienna which is basis of USRP refund. Under new plan some sent to Naples may then go to Israel. Open question if United States Refugee Program would pay cost of detour and the maintenance at hostel.

85. Dominitz failed to get *JP* and *Haaretz* to deny the story.

86. Kohane quotes Rabbi Rosen of Bucharest: "Where is the justification to use Jewish, UJA money to bring a Jew all the way from Russia to this country so that he could get assimilated in Pittsburgh instead of Charkov."

87. Later, on April 14, 1981, Zibbell of CJF wrote Ralph Goldman (JDC files) "that no Federation may receive reimbursement from the CJF Resettlement Program unless the immigrant has been brought to the United States under HIAS auspices."

88. Gaynor Jacobson reported that Rav Tov asked HIAS to help resettle people outside of New York City. Two years later a top CJF official refused to meet with Rav Tov in New York (Letter of Marvin Citrin [CJF] to Leopold Lefkowitz [Rav Tov], January 4, 1982, CJF files, box 710).

89. He also criticized HIAS for acting without consulting with the NPPC. He doubted more dropouts would go to Israel. They could declare themselves non-Jews in Vienna and avoid joint counseling. He noted that Rav Tov and Chabad and Agudas (both have applications pending with State) would fill the void.

90. According to the *JP* ("US Jews May Accept Dropout Plan," October 15, 1980) HIAS had agreed to the plan but CJF opposed it. Morton Mandel said he personally favored; all North Americans at Board of Governors favored. Said CJF opposition not final. *JP* of October 16, 1980 reported that a new Russian immigrant group headed by Grisha Feigin to fight HIAS aid to dropouts. In a letter to Robert Hiller (October 31, 1980, HIAS files.) Bertram H. Gold expressed AJC opposition to cutting aid to dropouts not going to Israel and not having relatives in the West.

91. At the early October JDC Executive Meeting Harold Friedman implied that HIAS had endorsed off the record cutting aid to dropouts above Glick's objections. He emphasized however that this was to be a test and that they would not allow Jews to wander all over Europe without aid.

92. Weinstein (1988:610,611) refers to a meeting of the CJF Board of Directors in the late 1970s at which "the incumbent president and several former presidents urged the board to adopt a resolution to deprive Soviet emigrants who were not bound for Israel of any support . . . with financial assistance going only to those who continued to Israel. I knew the importance of immigration into Israel (*Aliyah*), but I was shocked . . . [would have been the first time in history] when Jews declined to help other Jews escape from tyranny to freedom merely because the escaping Jews chose to go to one area of freedom (the United States) and not to another (Israel)." The resolution was tabled. Edwin Shapiro explained to his board (May 28, 1981) that HIAS had agreed not to aid dropouts without relatives in the West on the condition that JDC and CJF approve. He explained that JDC had never voted on the plan and that a special CJF ad hoc committee had rejected it (HIAS, Office of President to Board members, April 28, 1981, HIAS files).

93. Begin would address the General Assembly in Detroit on Friday, November 14, 1980 from 8 to 10 a.m. At the time it was not customary for the Prime Minister of Israel to address the General Assembly.

94. Nehemia Levanon also spoke.

95. Seidenman (note to Gaynor Jacobson, December 5, 1980) doubted Yehuda Dominitz's report of December 3, 1980 that the Ministry of Interior had approved the Naples operations. Mr. Ottolenghi, President of the Jewish Communities Council of Italy (Telex to Don Robinson, President JDC, November 10, 1980, (JDC files) opposed the Naples Plan arguing that it would be too great a burden for Italian Jewry

and a disaster for those stranded in Europe. HIAS became angry that the empty rooms had not been offered to earthquake victims. Later, the Jewish Agency made the rooms available for earthquake victims.

96. Mort Mandel claimed that the opposition of the Italian government killed the Naples plan. He also noted that CJF modified the plan as presented by HIAS, JDC and JAFI in that it decided that if counseling failed: "HIAS continue to serve Soviet Jews" (Mort Mandel notes prepared for him, CJF board on September 19–21, 1981, CJF files, box 660, *Maariv,* January 11, 1981).

97. In the meantime Dulzin appointed a subcommittee of the Brussels Presidium to look into the issue of dropouts. Fearing that subject might destroy the scheduled fall Brussels III conference he postponed the meetings until May 1982 (Ralph Goldman hand notes of meeting on June 24, 1981, JDC files).

98. In 1981 HIAS expenditures were $10,045,523 for 1982 assuming it would move 10,000 persons including 5,300 Soviet refugees, 3,700 Indochinese and 1,000 others (total budget of $7,623,000). The minutes of HIAS Board of Directors of December 14, 1982 report estimated 1982 budget at $5,434,000.

99. In 1979 federations covered 9.41 percent of HIAS budget. In 1981 it was projected to be 13.6 percent. At the request of the American government HIAS resettled 4,000 Indochinese in FY 1981 and assisted 3,000 non-Jewish Cubans from April to October 1980. Also see Minutes, Annual HIAS Board of Directors March 10, 1982 (HIAS files). HIAS deficit at time was $564,000. With federal cuts HIAS give more federal funds (per capita fee) to local resettlement communities.

100. A year earlier Mandel stated on March 16, 1980 at the CJF Board of Directors (CJF files, box 660): "As far as I am personally concerned, next to CJF's primary mission which is service to communities, increasing our fundraising achievement is our single highest priority, . . . Our whole Jewish machine is fuelled with dollars and we need more dollars, locally, nationally and overseas."

101. Mort Mandel reported (Notes for Mandel on Soviet Jewish Emigration at Board of Directors of CJF September 19–21, 1981, CJF files, box 660) that before acting Dulzin consulted with Jewish Agency treasurer, Head of Department of Absorption, Prime Minister and leader of Israeli opposition and with special Brussels III committee of 15 members. Dulzin met with Edwin Shapiro and Len Seidenman on August 17, 1981 and with Mort Mandel on the 18th. The new policy went into effect on August 19, 1981. He also met with JDC officials, Howard Squadron of Presidents Conference; Edgar Bronfman of WJC; Theodore Mann of NCSJ; Dr. Seymour Lachman, Chair of GNYCSJ; and Charlotte Jacobson, Chair of WZO, American Section (*JTA,* August 21, 1981).

102. HIAS executive met again on September 15 and reaffirm its August 24 resolution (Leimisdor to members and observers of NPPC, October 22, 1981, HIAS files).

103. *JP,* editorial on August 26, 1981, "A new priority" wanted "to persuade the United States government to revoke the refugee status of Russian Jewish emigrants who bear visas to Israel." A NCSJ form letter (August 27, 1981) said that NCSJ had no position but wanted to let Jewish Agency try the change.

104. Friedgut (1989:14) argues that Dulzin's action tarnished "Israel's image."

105. Fisher asked Dulzin to postpone action until after the Jewish Agency Board of Governors meeting at the end of August (notes, HIAS Board of Directors, September 20, 1981). Also see letter, Leon (Aryeh) Dulzin to Len Seidenman for Edwin Shapiro, August 21, 1981 (JDC files).

106. Leon Hadar ("Confidential Cross Fire" *JP*, September 13, 1981) argued that American Jewish support might be influenced by the threat of Yitzhak Shamir raising with the United States government denial of refugee status to Soviet Jews. Contrary to report of Bernard Gwertzman in *New York Times*, August 26, 1981, Hadar wrote that the Israelis thought that the American government would give favorable consideration to Israeli arguments on this issue.

107. Verbatim transcript of the JDC Executive Committee (September 23, 1981). At a meeting of American Jewish Leaders on August 27, 1981 Americans asked the Jewish Agency not to participate. At a second meeting that night called by Max Fisher, attending were JDC, HIAS plus Aryeh Dulzin, Yehuda Dominitz, Rafael Kotlowitz and Akiva Lewinsky of the Jewish Agency. Jewish Agency refuses to accept siblings as first-degree relatives. Others disappointed but Max Fisher worked out consensus. Agreed to proceed for trial period of 90 to 180 days. Edwin Shapiro said HIAS to accept Soviet émigrés without referral. Also some thought that lack of American government initial response might mean that they wanted Soviet émigrés to go to Israel (Carmi Schwartz hand notes of meeting on August 27, 1981, CJF files, Box 710). Dulzin explained that although the Austrians did not give an answer he took a risk for numbers were low. He believed that if Austria closed down the Dutch would open up their country for passage of émigrés.

108. Dulzin noted that 24 percent of cases involved brother/sister relations (Summary Report of CJF Board of Directors, September 19, 20, 1981). Mort Mandel reported a Jewish Agency revision in the definition of first degree relatives to include brothers and sisters "where appropriate" for compassionate and humanitarian reasons. He also noted that the Jewish Agency would provide basics for those émigrés not transferred to HIAS and not going to Israel.

109. Mort Mandel (notes for him, September 19, 21, 1981, CJF files, Box 660) reported that whether or not a Soviet Jew arrives under HIAS or is eligible for block grant assistance he expected that Jewish communities would behave "Jewishly" and " . . . render aid and assistance to a Jewish brother or sister in need." Akiva Kohane (Memo to Ralph Goldman, September 12, 1981, JDC files) noted HIAS guidelines follow instructions on siblings from Edwin Shapiro and Len Seidenman: a. if transmigrant have sibling in USA and in Israel should go to Israel and not eligible for JDC/HIAS aid b. same applies if have sibling in States only but has other sibling of children in USSR c. if sibling only in Israel has to go to Israel. d. if aged or incapacitated person has sibling only in U.S. then HIAS expects partners will agree for compassionate reason to send to United States. In a memo to Goldman on September 12, 1981, Kohane reported on a meeting in the Jewish Agency offices with JDC and HIAS in Vienna on September 10, 1981 (JDC files). While the Jewish Agency did not include siblings as first degree relatives it was understood that under exceptional circumstances and on an individual basis they might be considered. The parties agreed to joint counseling to start on September 11, 1981.

110. Of the 201 Soviet Jews who had left in the previous 3 weeks the majority went to the West. 31 percent went to Israel up from 15 percent before.

111. In September 1981 Israeli and Soviet Foreign Ministers Yitzhak Shamir and Andrei Gromyko met. Shamir told the JTA that the thaw in Soviet Israeli relations would persist with regards to Jewish emigration. He understood that Gromyko opposed "mass Jewish emigration that ended up in the United States." *JTA*, September 28, 1981 and Hebrew press reports dated September 27 1981 (JDC files) reported that Gromyko was not willing to discuss increased emigration but he said all could leave.

Moscow Chief Rabbi told Rabbi Goren of Israel that if Jews left to go elsewhere Soviets would not let them out! Said Gromyko not opposed to direct flights.

112. HIAS and JDC often clashed over performance and policies on the dropout issue. This may have reflected a clash of organizational interests; JDC handled care and maintenance while HIAS dealt with immigration and resettlement in the United States (letter, Gaynor Jacobson to Ralph Goldman, June 19, 1978, HIAS files; Memo, Len Seidenman to Gaynor Jacobson, May 2, 1978, HIAS files; Memo to file, Ralph Goldman "Armenian movement," May 30 1980). From August 19 to September 21, 402 persons arrived in Vienna; 138 went to Israel, 160 to HIAS JDC and 104 to Rav Tov. At meeting Irving Kessler reported that the State Department mission in Israel praised Dulzin's decision. The Jewish Agency provided those not being aided with pocket money (Ralph Goldman to Akiva Kohane October 1, 1981).

113. Joint counseling worked until HIAS NY told HIAS Vienna to accept all émigrés on September 21, 1981 (letter, Dominitz to Irving Kessler, October 16, 1981, JDC files). Len Seidenman also said that no dropouts applied to HIAS as Rav Tov got message to Soviet Jews that our Vienna office was closed. This is contradicted by November 3, 1981 Telex #1206 from Berger in Vienna to HIAS NY. Berger cites HIAS cases of persons not referred by Jewish Agency.

114. Harris reports how Rav Tov had those it helped write others in Soviet Union that there were alternatives to the Jewish Agency. Ironically Rav Tov in Rome made it easier for its clients to tour Israel than did HIAS. Ralph Goldman notes to file, October 30, 1981 (JDC files); Berger to Len Seidenman, October 12, 1981 (HIAS files); Yehuda Dominitz to Irving Kessler, November 2 1981; Telex 1206 Berger to HIAS NY, November 3, 1981 report that about 10 percent disappear (go to Germany?).

115. He reports that HIAS transported Rav Tov clients to Rome. Also see Bruce Leimsidor minutes for HIAS Advisory Committee of Family Agencies meeting of December 8, 1980, February 5, 1981. Leimsidor discussed having HIAS resettle Rav Tov cases outside NY which would be registered as HIAS cases and eligible for block grants. Rav Tov approached CJF to coordinate the resettlement of dropouts in the United States (Letter from Leopold Lefkowitz, President of Rav Tov to Marvin Citrin, President of CJF, CJF 710). It offered to assign to HIAS the Department of Health and Human Services Block Grant monies. Carmi Schwartz (hand notes of December 29, 1981, CJF files, Box 710) reports that Rav Tov now operated in a hostel in Vienna with free use of phones and transportation. This was a result of a new Jewish Agency policy on dropouts which angered the Austrians.

116. Edwin Shapiro argued that the Jewish Agency cooperated with Rav Tov in Vienna and in Rome. Edwin Shapiro had said that he had agreed to the Dulzin proposal (not a plan) but he "took it to the Executive Committee (on August 24, 1981) and it was rejected." (Ralph Goldman hand notes at same meeting, JDC files; Memo, Edwin Shapiro to friends of HIAS, November 5, 1981, HIAS files).

117. Prime Minister Begin had invited them (Letter, Menachem Begin to Henry Taub, November 5, 1981, JDC files). Also present were Kotlowitz, Dov Shilansky, Ralph Goldman, Len Seidenman, Shmuelovitz, Nehemia Levanon, Porat and Yehuda Avner. Also see Dominitz (1996:121).

118. Edwin Shapiro argued that at a previous meeting Begin had agreed to include siblings as first-degree relatives. Shapiro complained that Rav Tov's share had in-

creased almost ten fold. In Avner's notes reference is made to Max Fisher working to get Rav Tov eliminated from receiving United States funds. An official in the Office of Refugee Affairs who would investigate Rav Tov suggested to the author that Max Fisher had brought him to D.C. to work for the government (interview with Richard Krieger, February 7, 2004). One of the Israelis suggested that HIAS support of Dulzin's policy might help Fisher get funds for Rav Tov cut. Kotlowitz noted that to exclude siblings would bring neshira back to 75–80 percent. Ambassador for Refugees Howard Eugene Douglas told Ted Kanner (Letter, Ted Kanner to Ralph Goldman et al., April 21, 1982) that he was in the process of decertifying Rav Tov due to apparent fraud. As of October 1, 1982 Rav Tov was no longer considered an accredited migration Agency by the State Department (Minutes, HIAS Board of Directors, December 14, 1982, HIAS files). Also see Minutes of HIAS Board, May 28, 1981, and letter, Edwin Shapiro to Carmi Schwartz and Mark Handelman, July 27, 1981 (CJF files, Box 710).

119. Henry Taub said that he would have to have the JDC board extend its approval from three months to one year (Note, Yehuda Dominitz to Ralph Goldman, November 26 1981 and Yehuda Dominitz to Len Seidenman on November 17, 1981, JDC files). In January 1981 Edwin Shapiro and Len Seidenman went to Vienna to try to convince Austrian officials to accept the new Jewish Agency policies (Memo, Edwin Shapiro to HIAS Board, January 21, 1982, HIAS files).

120. Seidenman was upset that the Austrians would allow Rav Tov into the hostel. (Letter, Len Seidenman to Irving Bernstein, Ralph Goldman, Irving Kessler and Carmi Schwartz, JDC files). Joint counseling began on December 21, 1981. In a letter to Slater in NY (December 30, 1981) Stern of JDC in Vienna reported that HIAS wanted the Jewish Agency to wire Jerusalem on each case with sibling, thus joint counseling could not reject them. Parties had agreed that if they could not agree on a compassionate case then it would be transferred to organizational headquarters.

121. The *JTA* (February 1982) reported on accord between Austrian government and Jewish Agency affirmed that Austrian law give all "right to choose his or her country of immigration freely." Immigrants told of this on bus or train to Jewish Agency camp. Those wanting to dropout left Jewish Agency premises and went to the nearest police station where they received detailed information about Jewish and non-Jewish aid organizations to help them go West. Jewish Agency moved back to the hostel by January 6, 1982.

122. Len Seidenman (note to Akiva Kohane, December 22, 1981) refused to sign minutes of the December 18 meeting.

123. He claimed support from federations (Boston, Chicago, San Francisco) and B'nai B'rith International. Prime Minister Menachem Begin met in June in New York City with Bobbie Abrams, William Rosenwald and others He told them that Gromyko told him that emigration depend on U.S.-USSR relations.

124. In fall 1982 Yehudah Dominitz issued a report which questioned whether Dulzin's policy change in 1981 had reduced the drop out rate. He believed that there were too many unknowns in Soviet policy to reach a decisive conclusion. He called for a reconsideration of the plan (JDC memo, "Comments on Dominitz Report," December 28, 1982, JDC files).

125. JDC President Henry Taub circulated a report prepared by Akiva Kohane, which argued that dropouts anger the Soviets and influence their emigration policy (JDC Meeting on Soviet Emigration List and Summary, August 23, 1982, JDC files).

126. He noted that he held his board in check on this subject but that the leadership was questioning that we abandon our care and maintenance responsibilities.

127. Saul Cohen replaced Ralph Goldman as JDC Executive Vice President. Following his resignation, Goldman resumed the post for another two years.

128. Windmueller says that Glick claimed that 95 percent of the federations wanted freedom of choice. Carmi Schwartz told him that the majority of federations support Israel but that choice won out because of "Chicago federation's leadership on behalf of the *noshrim* proved to be a significant factor in sustaining the policy of choice " (1999:171). The evidence cited in this chapter suggests that both Glick and Schwartz erred.

129. Irving Kessler (interview, August 21, 2001) suggested that the U.S. government regulated UIA much tighter than it did JDC. He believed that JDC had several "illegal" partnerships.

5

The 1980s: The Soviet Jewry Advocacy Movement Is Kept Alive

This chapter surveys the relatively quiet period in the Soviet Jewry advocacy movement from 1982 when the Soviet Union closed its exit gates to Soviet Jewish émigrés until the coming to power of Mikhail Gorbachev in March 1985. During this time security for Israel following the invasion of Lebanon became the major political concern of the organized American Jewish community. The issue of Soviet Jewry shifted more to the subject of persecution within the Soviet Union as fewer and fewer Soviet Jews left their country.

During this period Israeli efforts on behalf of Soviet Jewish emigration focused on three areas. First, the Liaison Bureau approached American political leaders and officials in an effort to deny Soviet Jews refugee status in the United States. The CJF and other American Jewish organizations used their Congressional allies to block these efforts. Interestingly, these organizations would also defeat proposals by the United States Coordinator for Refugee Affairs to make entry of Soviet Jews as refugees more difficult in order to resettle them in Israel Second, the Israeli government through the Jewish Agency revived negotiations with HIAS and JDC over the dropout issue and proposed direct flights and joint counseling in Europe. Again, the Israelis tried to reduce American Jewish aid for dropouts in Europe. The overwhelming majority of the few Jews that managed to leave the Soviet Union preferred the United States and other countries to Israel. Finally, under Prime Minister Menachem Begin, the Israeli government took a more public role in the world wide Soviet Jewry advocacy movement when it decided to hold the Third Brussels Conference in Jerusalem in March 1983. At the same time Begin's appointment to replace Nehemia Levanon of the Liaison Bureau indicated a possible lack of deep commitment to the struggle of bringing Soviet Jews to Israel.

The Soviet Union "closed" it gates to most Jews wanting to emigrate in 1982.[1] Some officials in the Jewish Agency, Liaison Bureau and several American Jewish groups blamed the dropout phenomenon for the "closed gates"; Soviet Jewish émigrés who left on visas for Israel but ended up in the United States, they argued, embarrassed and angered leaders of the Soviet Union (Friedgut 1989:5–6; memo, "Some Remarks by Soviet Officials on Jewish Emigration from the USSR," May 1982 [With letter, Richard Krieger to Carmi Schwartz, August 24, 1982, CJF files Box 710]; memos, Akiva Kohane to Ralph Goldman, August 1, September 20, and November 23, 1982, JDC files; and Report of Akiva Kohane, August 23, 1982, JDC files). Other Israeli officials including several Liaison Bureau operatives (off the record) and most American Jewish leaders believed that the deterioration in U.S.-USSR relations explained the change in Soviet emigration policy (Heitman [1989:134–136]; and JTA November 20, 1984).[2] According to Cullen (1986:257–262): "The Soviets have allowed high levels of Jewish emigration in periods when they felt they had a reasonable chance of getting arms control, trade agreements or both with the United States. When those hopes evaporated, so did the flow of Jews out of the Soviet Union." The Soviet invasion of Afghanistan in December 1979 and the American response "signified the end of détente" (Shapiro 1981:230). It "brought an end to hopes for ratification of the Strategic Arms Limitation Treaty (SALT) entered into by [General Secretary] Brezhnev and President Carter" (Shapiro 1981:232; Friedgut 1989:6).[3]

In the early 1980s the situation of Jews in the Soviet Union worsened as Soviet authorities increased harassment and persecution of those wanting to leave as well as those active in preserving and disseminating Jewish culture (Orleck 1999:63,64 and "Summary and Projection, NCSJ 1983–1984" presented by NCSJ to Large City Budgeting Conference (LCBC), November 15, 1983, CJF files, box 593).[4] At the end of 1982 HIAS reported on a bleak atmosphere in the Jewish community in the Soviet Union with few applying to leave. During the 18 months of Yuri Andropov's rule from November 1982 to February 1984 anti-Semitism increased (Buwalda 1997:139 and Stenographic notes, JDC East European Committee Meeting, March 8, 1984, JDC files).[5] For example in April 1983 Soviet authorities set up the Anti-Zionist Committee of the Soviet Public (AKSO) which equated Zionism with Nazism.[6] Many believed that it had been set up to fight emigration by Jews (Orleck 1999:66 and Korey 1999:26). Writing in 1983 Leon Shapiro (1983:245) commented that "the current attitude of the authorities created a sense of hopelessness among 'Refuseniks.' Many Refuseniks thought that America no longer cared (Minutes, HIAS Board of Directors, December 14, 1982, HIAS files).

Soviet policy may have backfired as the oppression kindled more interest in Jewish culture and identity among the young (Salitan 1992:63–64). Moreover, the closing of the gates gave the Refusenik community stability of leadership and allowed them to raise a generation of children with Jewish identity. Eliahu Essas set up a Yeshiva and Moscow Refusenik Scientists set up a seminar (Friedgut 1989:8–15).

The sharp decline in the number of Jews allowed to emigrate demoralized and frustrated the Soviet Jewry advocacy movement in the United States. It confirmed fears that their own efforts on behalf of the Soviet Jews had been less than effective. Some questioned whether they could really influence Soviet policy. Clearly in the 1980s the movement suffered from fatigue.[7] As early as 1975 there were signs of boredom and lack of enthusiasm. The focus had gone from active rallies and protests to the bureaucratic routine of keeping up contact with Refuseniks and lobbying Congress (Appelbaum 1986:627).

Finally, Israeli political leaders were concerned about their loss of control and ability to direct the movement in the United States.[8] In the opinion of Yoram Dinstein, the Liaison Bureau could almost dictate Soviet Jewry policy to American Jews from 1967 until 1977. Thereafter, it became much harder to do as American Jewish organizations developed their own ideas and positions. They were less willing to defer to the Israelis for advice and instructions (Interview, Yoram Dinstein, May 3, 2003).[9] The issue of control over the movement would concern the Liaison Bureau throughout much of the 1980s.

THE EARLY 1980S

In response to the changed situation the NCSJ tried to keep alive the Soviet Jewry issue among American Jews, the general public, members of Congress and the Administration. Via its 40 constituent organizations including the three major synagogue movements and 200 local community relations councils and federations it publicized the problems of Jews in the Soviet Union (Theodore R. Mann to Citron, July 1, 1982, CJF files, box 660).[10] It also expanded its travel programs to the Soviet Union; it hoped to stimulate greater interest among Americans while indicating to Soviet Jewry that America and American Jews cared about their plight. It encouraged tourism, organized tours and visits and briefed visitors before their trips. Participants included activists, elected officials, organizational professionals and Jewish and non-Jewish groups.[11]

Throughout the period NCSJ, representing the American Jewish establishment suffered from an inadequate budget and staff (CJF LCBC, Highlights at Plenary Session #2, November 15–16, 1983, CJF files, box 593 and Spier 1989b: 103).[12] This may have reflected the lower priority that Soviet Jewry advocacy had in reality when it came to budget allocations within the American Jewish establishment organizations. This limited the effectiveness of

NCSJ. For example, in 1982 it did not have a public relations person on staff. Its Washington office had problems meeting the increasing demands made by Congressmen and the Administration for information and assistance on the Soviet Jewry issue.[13] Under the auspices of the Congressional Wives for Soviet Jewry it held a conference of Parliamentary Spouses for Soviet Jewry in Washington, D.C. on April 2–4, 1984 with participants from Great Britain, Canada, the Netherlands and Israel (Shinbaum 1999:179). NCSJ also had a Helsinki monitoring commission that worked with the U.S. Commission on Security and Cooperation in Europe ("Summary and Projection of NCSJ, 1983–1984, September 11–14, 1983, CJF files, box 659).[14]

During this time, the NCSJ became even more dependent on CJF and the federations for funding. In 1982 CJF covered 41 percent of the NCSJ budget. If one deducts the expense for the Soviet Jewry Research Bureau, a Liaison Bureau operation not funded by CJF, then CJF funded about 60 percent of the NCSJ budget.[15] The CJF, in turn, demanded more input into NCSJ policy. By the late 1980s the CJF had the power to make or break the NCSJ. In 1989, for example, CJF would mediate the power struggle between NCSJ and the NJCRAC over control of the Soviet Jewry advocacy movement in the United States (see chapter 7).

Importantly, the Israelis had much less influence with CJF than they had with the NCSJ. During this period Liaison Bureau personnel in the Israeli Consulate in New York City and the Embassy in Washington, D.C. continued to participate in staff, executive and board meetings of the NCSJ. The Liaison Bureau had no similar role in CJF where some lay leaders and certain professionals favored keeping the Israelis at a distance. At the same time, the majority of lay leaders and much of the senior CJF and federation staff had strong ties and sentiments toward Israel. In addition, the Liaison Bureau made every effort to cultivate cooperation with CJF leaders and professionals. For example, in the 1980s, CJF Executive Director Martin Kraar met either weekly or monthly with the Liaison Bureau and NCSJ on the subject of Soviet Jewry (Interview, Martin Kraar, October 1, 1996).

While the NCSJ remained in charge of coordinating establishment policy and contacts with the White House and the Administration on Soviet Jewry matters the CJF role in the Soviet Jewry movement grew in importance. Soviet Jewry advocacy, however, remained one of the many concerns of the CJF. In the early 1980s the issue of Soviet Jewry sometimes disappeared from the agendas of the CJF Quarterlies (Memo, CJF to Board Members and National Committee Members, July 23, 1982, CJF files, box 659).[16] For example, when CJF and other Jewish leaders met with Secretary of State George Schultz on September 2, 1982 Lebanon was the issue. No mention was made of Soviet Jewry (Memo from Ted Mann to file "Meeting with Secretary of State Shultz on September 2, 1982, September 3, 1982, CJF files, box 660). In meeting with Congressmen on April 1983, CJF President Martin Citrin spoke about Israel and peace and the social welfare needs of elderly American Jews. He did not mention Soviet Jewry (Notes for Martin Citrin for Congressional Reception in D.C. April 14, 1983, CJF files). Neither did his successor, Shoshana Cardin in her 1985 address to a CJF Board institute meeting (Cardin 1985).

Nevertheless, most CJF Quarterlies and General Assemblies in the 1980s discussed the issue of Soviet Jewry. At the September 1982 CJF Quarterly, for example, Ted Mann of NCSJ urged federations to push the Soviet Jewry issue in their communities (Highlights of CJF Board and Committee meetings, September 11–12, 1982, CJF files, box 659).[17] The CJF also had a very effective lobbyist in D.C., Mark Talisman who helped CJF and NCSJ in their dealings with Congress (Letter, Jerry Goodman to Carmi Schwartz, July 9, 1983, CJF files, box 660).[18] He also served CJF's strong pro-immigration stance which opposed a cap for total immigration and favored the current system with its provision for "unlimited family reunification" (CJF Memo on "Issues in Immigration Reform," January 26, 1984, CJF files, box 695 and "Highlights of CJF Board and Committee meetings September 5, 1984," CJF files, box 659). Simultaneously, hundreds of federations around the country pursued their own Soviet Jewish advocacy and resettlement policies (Letter, David S. Goldstein, chair Jewish Federation of New Orleans to Mr. Abraham Bayer, NJCRAC, May 13, 1983, JDC files).

The Reagan administration responded to Leonid Brezhnev's crackdown on dissidents in a manner which the American Jewish establishment supported. To "underscore concern with Soviet human rights and restrictions on Soviet emigration" President Reagan met with Josef Mendelevitch who had been involved in the Leningrad hijacking and a Prisoner of Zion and with Avital Sharansky whose husband was in a Soviet prison camp. In February 1983 President Reagan publicly stated that the "issue of Soviet Jewry is of high priority to the administration" (M. Goldman 1995:347).[19]

Similarly, when George Shultz replaced Alexander Haig as Secretary of State in 1982 he met with Avital Sharansky and focused on the issue of Jews and human rights before his first meeting with Soviet Foreign Minister Andrei Gromyko (Shultz 1993:121).[20] When he met Andrei Gromyko at the United Nations he began with human rights "problems of Jews, dissidents and families divided by Soviet refusal to allow emigration." He objected to Gromyko's calling these concerns a 10th rate issue (Shultz 1993:122,123).

Clearly Shultz did not neglect human rights issues including Jewish emigration in dealing with the Soviet Union. He told a meeting of the Senate Foreign Relations Committee on June 15, 1983, "We have made clear that human rights cannot be relegated to the margins of international politics" (Shultz 1993:278).[21] Yet, in the early 1980s Shultz was cautious. In a memo to the President of March 1983 Shultz urged that on human rights issues when appropriate "quiet diplomacy leading to results, not counterproductive public embarrassment of Moscow" (Shultz 1993:265). And in October 1984 he made his view known that it was not a good idea to link the issue of Soviet Jewish emigration and arms reductions. He favored addressing each "issue on its merits: We would press on what was right for Soviet Jews whether things were going well or poorly on other issues of concern" (Shultz 1993:488).

At the Madrid meetings (1980–1983) to the Conference on Security and Cooperation in Europe, the follow up of the Helsinki Agreements, Mr. Max Kampleman, the head of the American delegation, had the Administration's endorsement to push human rights (Levanon 1995:406). He constantly brought up the issue of Soviet Jews (Buwalda 1997:122). Unfortunately, the meetings had little effect on the Soviet Union (Salitan 1992:59ff).[22]

With the change in Soviet policy on Jewish emigration in the early 1980s, the refugee activities in Vienna and Rome soon ground to a halt. While 2,692 Jews left the Soviet Union in 1982, the number dropped to 1,314 in 1983 and a mere 721 in 1984. Seventy four percent (1961 persons) dropped out in 1982, 71 percent (927) in 1983 and 67 percent (483) in 1984 (Memo, Secretary General of Jewish Agency to Members of Coordinating Committee, October 24, 1984 [Jewish Agency archives] with document, "The Plight of Soviet Jewry").[23]

After month long negotiations involving the Jewish Agency, JDC, HIAS, Rav Tov, IRC, and the governments of Israel and Austria it was decided to close the refugee hostel (*maon*). Evidently only émigrés with first-degree relatives went to the "enclosed" hostel. All others went directly to the city and came under the care of other agencies including HIAS. The Jewish Agency believed that many émigrés did not reveal having first degree relatives in order to avoid being sent to the hostel (Memo, Akiva Kohane to Ralph Goldman, April 30, 1982, JDC files).[24] Thereafter, the Austrian police would meet the émigrés and send all those wanting to go to the West to a hotel where Jewish Agency emissaries would try to persuade them to go to Israel. For those not wanting to go to Israel, the Jewish Agency would transfer them to JDC, in writing, all émigrés with relatives in the West; all others were free to go to other agencies. JDC would then interview those it received and turn over all non-Jews to other agencies (Notes, Meeting in Jewish Agency in Jerusalem, June 24 1982 [JDC files] and Working draft/ notes, Meeting of JDC Transmigrant Program Staff in Rome, October 7–8, 1986, JDC files).[25]

In late 1980 JDC made its Vienna office consisting of a single secretary, "non operational." By the summer of 1982 it closed its Ladispoli office, shut downs its medical services, computer section and Jewish education program in Rome and cut its Rome staff from 64 to 8 (Transcript/notes of phone conversation between Akiva Kohane and Ralph Goldman, June 2, 1982 and Report of Dr. Akiva Kohane at August 23, 1982 Meeting, JDC files). In contrast HIAS remained more active in Vienna and Rome. Since April 13, 1982, HIAS had resumed its "historic role of offering HIAS services to any Jew in the world who is in need" (Memos, Ted Feder to Ralph Goldman, April 29, 1982 and Akiva Kohane to Ralph Goldman, April 30, 1982, JDC files). It accepted Jewish émigrés in Vienna who did not have close family ties in the United States. Since JDC refused to care for these people, HIAS provided them with care and maintenance as well as helping them get visas to the United States and elsewhere. This increased HIAS's financial burdens in Europe despite partial reimbursement by the United States government (Letter, Edwin Shapiro to HIAS Board Members, October 1, 1982, HIAS files).[26]

Nevertheless, the drop in Soviet emigration adversely affected HIAS. Its overall caseload which determined its governmental subsidies (on a per capita basis) declined. This was compounded by a sharp drop in its Indochinese refugee case load. For example, it had assisted 12,589 individuals in 1981; 8,137 of these were from the Soviet Union and 3,909 from Indochina. It estimated its overall caseload in 1983 at fewer than 3,000 persons including 1,100 Soviet Jews, 700 "other" Jews and about 1,200 refugees from South East Asia. It expected a slight increase in 1984 (CJF LCBC Highlights, Plenary Session #2, November 15–16, 1983, CJF files, box 593). Consequently, it reduced its staff in the United States and overseas from 352 persons in 1979 to 187 at the end of 1981. It planned to reduce the number to 140 by June 30, 1982.

Second, its overall budget dropped from about $16m in 1980 to $10m in 1981 and then to around $6m in 1982 (Memo, Henry J. Goodman, to Joseph B. Manello, chair, LCBC, March 15, 1982, CJF files) and Minutes, Annual HIAS Board of Directors, March 10, 1982 (HIAS files).[27] By 1984 it would be under $5m ("Report of LCBC Subcommittee on HIAS" March 31, 1982, CJF files, box 696 and CJF LCBC Conference Highlights, Plenary Session #2, November 15–16, 1983, CJF files, box 593). At the height of Soviet Jewish immigration in 1979, the United States government provided 76 percent of HIAS income. By 1982 and 1983 federal funding covered 26 and 28 percent respectively. HIAS shifted its funding efforts to the CJF's LCBC which had set up a subcommittee on HIAS in November 1981. The latter proposed that HIAS appeal to federations for supplemental allocations to avoid borrowing from banks. Ironically, many federations assumed that with the drop in the flow of Soviet refugees HIAS's needs also declined. There were very few supplemental allocations (Minutes, HIAS Board of Directors, June 2, 1983, HIAS files).[28]

During this time the Jewish Agency in Israel also faced a serious budget crisis which had been exacerbated by its role in absorption of Soviet Jewish immigrants. It had amassed a deficit of $630m (Minutes, CJF Executive Committee Meeting, April 22, 1982, Shoreham Hotel, D.C., CJF files box 659).[29] In response the Americans on the Board of Governors began to rethink its purposes and functions.[30] They demanded reforms and changes in many areas including immigrant absorption. Later, in 1983, Jerold Hoffberger, succeeding Max Fisher as Chairman of the Board of Governors, tried to have the

Jewish Agency removed from immigrant absorption by transferring its absorption functions and facilities to the government of Israel. The Jewish Agency bureaucracy in Jerusalem fought these efforts (Interview, Howard Weisband, December 25, 1995; Katz 1987, Lazin 1991 and Goldberg 1996:353)[31] The massive waive of Soviet Jewish immigrants as well as Ethiopians in late 1988 would delay implementation of an agreement for the Jewish Agency to leave the field of absorption (Lazin 2001, 2001b).

UNITED STATES REFUGEE POLICY

In the early 1980s, United States policy toward Jewish refugees from the Soviet Union remained on a low burner. The reduced number of émigrés and a freeze in U.S.-USSR relations reduced the likelihood of significant policy changes and possible American intervention on the subject. Nevertheless, there were some efforts to rethink American policy toward refugees in general and Soviet Jewish refugees from the Soviet Union in particular. Moreover, the Liaison Bureau and some of its American Jewish supporters worked to alter American policy toward Soviet Jewish refugees.[32] Opposing them were the CJF, HIAS, and other groups.

The 1980 Refugee Act established the principle of a "well founded fear of persecution" which conformed with United Nations Protocol and Convention Relating to Status of Refugees (Salitan 1992:130; Goldberg 1996:184). The 1980 Act defined eligibility as "Any person who is outside any country of his nationality or in the case of a person having no nationality, is outside any country in which he last habitually resided, and who is unable or unwilling to return to, and is unable or unwilling to avail himself of the protection of that country because of persecution, or a well founded fear of persecution, on account of race, religion, nationality, membership of a particular social group, or political opinion" (Reimers 1985:191). The act provided funding for care, maintenance and resettlement.[33] The new law required that refugees be sponsored by a selected group of non-profit organizations which took responsibility for their initial (first 90 days) resettlement. While setting a limit of 50,000 refugees a year, it also stipulated that the actual number of refugees permitted each year be set in consultation between the President and/or his representative and the Judiciary Committees of Congress. The intent was for the executive branch to propose, the legislative branch to comment and then for the President to decide.[34]

Until 1982 (and thereafter) the United States had accepted almost all Soviet Jewish émigrés as refugees. Official United States policy had been committed to the principle of freedom of choice ("HIAS Quits Plan for Settling Soviet Jews," *NYT*, May 2 or 6, 1982). Accordingly, the United States government supported the HIAS decision to abandon its temporary support of Dulzin's policy and return to its policy of aiding all Soviet Jews upon request.

By 1982, some American officials discussed curtailing refugee entry into the United States. In March 1982, Howard Eugene Douglas, U.S. Ambassador at Large and Coordinator for Refugee Affairs in the State Department met with leadership in various federations including Los Angeles, Chicago and Cleveland and with leaders and officials in HIAS and CJF.[35] He discussed with them proposed changes in government regulations which would curtail refugee immigration into the United States. He made specific references to Soviet Jews as well as to other groups of refugees.

The Israelis may have influenced his thinking on Soviet Jewry. He met with Raphael Kotlowitz, the head of the Immigration and Absorption Department of the Jewish Agency. He also discussed "dropouts" with Yehuda Lapidot who replaced Levanon as head of the Liaison Bureau. Rather than request a change in United States policy (which Prime Minister Begin opposed), Lapidot explained to Ambassador Douglas the Israeli policy of invitations, which involved a commitment to absorb emigrés and to give them citizenship (Interview, Yehuda Lapidot, June 26, 2002).[36] He also explained that the same policy existed for Romanian Jews who also arrived as immigrants to Israel. He asked Douglas why the United States did not consider them refugees too. Why was American policy different vis-à-vis Jews from the Soviet Union? Realization that Soviet Jews had the alternative of immigrating to Israel in the context of an overburdened American refugee load may have led Ambassador Douglas to reconsider the American policy of granting all Soviet Jewish emigrés refugee status (Interview with Lapidot, June 2002).[37]

Ambassador Douglas told Carmi Schwartz of CJF in May 1982 that there was a need for an across the board curb on refugees entering the United States. He referred to Cambodians, Vietnamese, Haitians, Cubans and Soviet Jews. More specifically he wanted to limit entry to Soviet Jews with first degree relatives "in keeping with the government of Israel's policies vis-à-vis Soviet Jewish immigrants" (Memo, Carmi Schwartz to Martin Citron "Proposed U.S. Administration New Regulations" [2 drafts], May 20, 1982, CJF files, box 660). He had favored Soviet Jewish emigrés leaving on Israeli visas to be resettled in Israel. In his view Israel needed and wanted their valuable human resources and their going to Israel satisfied the higher echelons of the KGB and the Communist Party of the Soviet Union. It would also reduce the refugee burden of the United States. He favored both the American government and American Jewish community helping to fund the resettlement in Israel (Interview, H. Eugene Douglas, June 29, 2004).[38]

One Los Angeles Federation official wrote that Ambassador Douglas had bought the Israeli line that "the principle reason for closing of the gates with regard to Soviet Jews is the fact that they are using exit visas to go to places other than Israel" (Letter, Ted Kenner to Ralph Goldman, Leonard Seidenman, Karl

Zukerman, April 21, 1982, JDC files). Carmi Schwartz told Ambassador Douglas that most American Jewish organizations would oppose such proposals as they had been in the forefront of urging the United States government to liberalize its posture and regulations on refugees. Second and more importantly, the argument that the new policy was in accord with Israeli policy "would be totally unacceptable to the Jewish community and its organizations and institutions." Schwartz urged that he not link the proposed policy changes to the needs of Israel or what might be deemed the supposed wishes of the American Jewish leadership. "These new regulations should not be overtly or covertly construed as a Jewish issue or in response to Israeli or Jewish policies or wishes. Any attempt to connect this new policy to the Jewish community would . . . be terribly deleterious to the interests of the United States and to the interests of the Jewish community." It was imperative, argued Schwartz, "that if . . . new policy must be enacted, it be related exclusively to United States' interests alone." He urged that the total generic rationale for curtailing all refugee numbers be linked to the state of the economy, high rate of unemployment and the sense of Congress and the Administration (Memo, Carmi Schwartz to Martin Citron, May 20, 1982, CJF files, box 660).[39]

HIAS officials believed this apparent desire to shift refugee policy reflected a general concern by the Administration with difficulties in settling some non-Soviet refugee groups with high public assistance dependency rates. This brought considerable pressure on Congress to curtail funded benefits and services and to reduce the number of refugees admitted. A reduction in entry could be accomplished either by Congress setting lower admissions numbers or by stricter interpretations of existing regulations. While Soviet Jewish refugees and other Jewish refugees in general "were recognized as not presenting a resettlement problem, [HIAS feared that] these tendencies in government would affect them also" (Memo, Bruce Leimsidor to Cooperating Agencies, "Minutes, Committee of Families Agencies Meeting" [June 1982] Minneapolis, July 3, 1982, CJF files).[40]

Evidently, some of the changes proposed by Ambassador Douglas would mean that many more Soviet Jews would have to come in as immigrants and not as refugees (Memo, Leimsidor, July 3, 1982, CJF files). Proposed INS regulations would require "that the parent, child or spouse of a United States citizen enter the United States as 'immigrants' rather than as 'refugees'" (Memo, "Policy Issues and Concerns," November 16, 1982, CJF files, box 660). In the past, the memo explained, those with first degree relatives could enter either as refugees or as immigrants. Almost all preferred to enter as refugees. Thus, a relative or agency would have to file an affidavit of support pledging to keep his incoming relative free of public dependency for three years. This disqualified the immigrant from most government benefits e.g. Medicaid, Social Security insurance and public assistance unless stateside relatives' income was low enough to warrant qualification for such benefits. The numbers of potential immigrants would be small but would increase as more and more Soviet Jews became American citizens. The number of Soviet Jews eligible for citizenship doubled from 1983 to 1984 (Ibid.).[41]

The new arrangement would create problems for relatives and agencies like HIAS. American citizen relatives of potential immigrants would be responsible for resettling them in the United States.[42] HIAS was aware that many new "Soviet" U.S. citizens refused to assume responsibility for first-degree relatives wanting to come to the United States.[43] "Thus, local Jewish communities may be asked to provide financial support and increased services to newly arrived immigrants" (Working draft of notes of meeting of JDC Transmigrant program staff in Rome, October 7–8, 1986, JDC files).[44]

Representative Hamilton Fish (Republican New York), ranking minority member of the Subcommittee on Immigration, Refugees and International Law of the House Judiciary Committee wrote Ambassador Douglas that he opposed a change in policy that would result in limiting Soviet Jewish refugee admissions to family reunification cases because Soviet Jews presumably would not qualify under higher priority categories. In explaining his position he argued that the Holocaust justified "special consideration of the plight of Jewish refugees" (Letter, Hamilton Fish to Eugene Douglas, July 23, 1982, CJF files, box 659).[45] Representative Fish suggested that a dramatic change in U.S. admissions policy toward the admission of Soviet Jews "would exacerbate the fears of a number of members of Jewish communities that only Israel stands ready to provide refuge for the Jewish people." He went on to emphasize that the United States has been encouraging the Soviet Union to allow the Jewish population to leave. To now call for limiting entry would make us seem hypocritical. Moreover, our setting a high ceiling on Soviet Jewish refugees would be sending a signal to the Soviet Union that America was committed to the principle of freedom for Soviet Jews; to change this policy would send the wrong signal now.

Congressman Fish dismissed the Israeli/Liaison argument that dropouts influenced the Soviets to close their gates to Soviet Jewish emigrants. He noted that it was unlikely that the Soviets preferred them to go to Israel because of Arab pressures. He also noted that he never "heard American government officials place credence in the argument that the Soviet Union would be more inclined to allow its Jews to leave if the United States refuses to prove a haven to persons who do not meet family reunification criteria." He closed: "My hope is that the United States will adhere to its practice of admitting Soviet Jews regardless of whether they have relatives currently living in this country. The unsettled conditions in the Middle East provide an additional reason for allowing Soviet Jewish refugees the option of living outside of Israel." CJF and other American Jewish groups probably had contacted Fish and "advised him" on writing the letter.

A month later Ambassador Douglas wrote Congressman Fish that it "would be unthinkable that we would precipitate any action which might impede the ability of Jews to leave the Soviet Union." He explained that they were weighing withdrawal of the sixth priority, region by region and then worldwide (Letter, Eugene Douglas to Hamilton Fish, August 23, 1982, CJF files, box 710).[46] He emphasized that a public discussion of withdrawal of sixth priority for Soviet Jews "could well weaken the Jewish emigration program from the Soviet Union; none of us would wish to do that."

He went on to restate many of the Liaison Bureau arguments. He also supplied a document, possibly generated by the Liaison Bureau's, quoting various Soviet diplomats and officials saying that dropouts angered Soviet authorities and adversely affected Soviet emigration policy. He emphasized that "It is absolutely incongruous that we are competing with Israel for Soviet Jewish refugees when basically Israel is the *country of first resettlement*.[47] He talked about long-range deleterious consequences for Jewish emigration due to the large number of dropouts. This would reduce the first-degree relative pool in Israel! He did add: "Of course this is just an excuse for their cutting down emigration, but it is one we have been giving them." Competition with Israel he suggested contradicted our policy of encouraging other countries to be prime resettlement sites for ethnics that related to them. (Letter, Douglas to Fish, August 23, 1982).

He closed: "Our doors are open to Soviet Jews and will continue to be open to them as long as I am coordinator and the philosophies of this country and the Reagan administration stand." Douglas reassured Fish that he had no intention of going ahead with the proposed changes. Rather he would consult and review the ideas with various departments and with Congress and might set up a working team to analyze the scope and implications of proposed policy changes.

Later, Ambassador Douglas claimed that he had been overruled by Congress. He believed that the "Jewish lobby" (CJF, HIAS and other organizations) had "gotten to Congress." He thought that the organized American Jewish community, especially HIAS, feared loosing Soviet Jews to Israel. He argued that HIAS's continuing existence in the 1980s required the Soviet Jews to go to the United States. He also suggested that the Israeli government and Liaison Bureau refused to help him in dealing with American Jewish opposition to his proposed changes which would have brought more Soviet Jews to Israel (Interviews, H. Eugene Douglas, February 3, 2004 [telephone] and June 29, 2004).

At this time Congress debated the issue of a ceiling on refugees. A Senate bill by Alan K. Simpson (R WYO) proposed a ceiling for legal immigration of 425,000 persons per year, mostly for family reunification and not including refugees. A second bill by Senator Walter D. Huddleston (D KY) also set a 425,000 limit but included refugees.[48] A coalition of CJF, AJC, HIAS and many federations and officials from the Reagan administration supported Simpson's bill and opposed Huddleston's. They argued that the President and administration wanted flexibility to be able to respond to a crisis; that the United States must maintain leadership as the nation that cares about human rights; that a single numerical ceiling would be divisive domestically putting various refugee aid groups at odds with one another; and to limit flow to the United States would reduce U.S. leverage to influence other nations to accept more (CJF Washington Action Office Bulletin on Immigration Bill, September 1982, CJF files, box 696). In effect they feared that Soviet Jews might loose their special status of automatically being considered refugees.[49]

At the same time Jewish organizations worried about proposed revisions in the Simpson Mazzoli bill with respect to the processing of asylum applications. The bill would reduce the role of the State Department and leave the matter with the INS which it feared "May also remove some political considerations in defining the concept of well founded fear of persecution as applied to asylum seekers from various parts of the world, . . . definition of persecution may become somewhat more uniform and restrictive, so that the applicants for asylum from . . . Iran, USSR, . . . may face the same test as applicants of El Salvador or Haiti." It may not bode well for asylum seekers from the Soviet Union (Memo, Leonard Seidenman to Coordinating Agencies re: Simpson-Mazzoli Bill, September 1982, CJF HIAS files).[50]

In February 1983 HIAS remained cautious about the standing of Soviet Jews as refugees in the United States. An official reported that the United States Government continued to support us. They "accorded exceptional treatment to Soviet refugee program, as being in the national interest; this special treatment takes the form of financial support of HIAS in both processing and resettlement as well as in representations to the Soviet authorities to facilitate the exit of Soviet Jews." The source urged caution. There are "foreboding winds signaling a deterioration of eventual cutbacks in financial support in context of the government deficit and the current unfavorable political climate for refugee assistance" (Minutes, HIAS Board of Directors Meeting, February 28, 1983, HIAS files). By the summer of 1983 HIAS was less than satisfied by legislative developments in Washington (Letter, Leonard Seidenman, to Cooperation Agencies RE: Current U.S. Government Developments, July 6, 1983, CJF files, box 659).[51] CJF also remained cautious. It informed Ambassador Douglas that although it did not like the administration's removal of priority (clause) six on refugees it understood it as a measure of expediency and as part of a global strategy ("Introductory Remarks for Martin E. Citrin at Presidential Advisory Group," March 13, 1983, CJF files, box 695).[52] CJF saw many problems that could adversely effect the immigration of Soviet Jews to the United States. It emphasized that the Jewish community always opposed cap and preferred to leave the current system with its provision for "unlimited family reunification" (CJF memo, "Issues in Immigration Reform," January 26, 1984). Most of these fears proved unfounded as United States policy would continue to grant almost all Soviet Jewish émigrés refugee status and entry into the United States until early 1988. By the end of the decade, however, the CJF would reverse its position on this issue!

In contrast to the position of the CJF the Liaison Bureau and its supporters including NCSJ continued to urge that Soviet Jews go to Israel. At the 1984 General Assembly Morris Abram, President of the NCSJ, speaking on "Soviet Jewry in Crisis" focused on repatriation to Israel citing "the right of Jews to repatriate to Israel is the right of any member of a national minority to settle freely in his national state." He did note, however, that some prefer "certain countries of the West." He emphasized that the priority of Soviet Jewry is tied to the "prosperity and vibrancy of the State of Israel" (Abrams 1984). Nevertheless, NCSJ refrained from supporting Ambassador Douglas's proposals for refugee reform which might have limited the entry of some Soviet Jewish émigrés as refugees. NCSJ did not challenge the CJF on this issue (Interview, H. Eugene Douglas, June 29, 2004).

THE POLICIES OF MENACHEM BEGIN TOWARD SOVIET JEWISH ÉMIGRÉS AND ADVOCACY

Menachem Begin as Prime Minister exerted important influence on Israel's Soviet Jewry emigration policy. His humanitarian concerns on the issue of Soviet Jewry and dropouts surprised many. He gave important consideration to the issue of family reunification even if it resulted in émigrés resettling in countries other than Israel. While Begin had rejected a proposal from the head of the Liaison Bureau to request that the President of the United States deny refugee status to Soviet émigrés (see above), he favored a policy of maximizing Soviet Jewish immigration to Israel ("Dodging the Issue," *JP*, April 8, 1983). He asked American Jews to stop aiding Soviet Jewish émigrés in Vienna who exited on Israeli visas. As noted in chapter 4, he failed to win concessions from American Jewish leaders who favored freedom of choice. They rejected his efforts to compromise at the CJF General Assembly in Detroit.

Noteworthy was Begin's decision to change leadership in the Liaison Bureau which may well have weakened Israeli influence on American Jews in the Soviet Jewry advocacy movement. Almost all of the senior personnel in the Liaison Bureau had strong ties and ideological commitments to the Labor Party. Begins election in 1977 constituted a revolution in Israeli politics. For the first time in 27 years the Labor Party did not form the government (Peretz and Doron 1998:81–83). Initially, Menachem Begin decided to keep Nehemia Levanon as head of the Liason Bureau (Interview, Aryeh Naor, Secretary to the Cabinet [Begin Government], December 30, 2002).[53] When Levanon retired in November or December 1980 Prime Minister Begin appointed Yehuda Lapidot to replace him. Lapidot was a Professor of Chemistry and member of the Likud Party and a Begin loyalist. He had no special knowledge, expertise or experience with Soviet Jewry or the Soviet Union. American Jewish leaders soon became aware of the "shortcomings" of the inexperienced head of the Liaison Bureau. The 1967 break in diplomatic relations with the Soviet Union diminished significantly direct contact between the Israelis (and Liaison Bureau) and Jews in the Soviet Union. In contrast direct contacts and visits by American Jews expanded. Many activists in the Union of Councils as well as the NCSJ came to believe that they knew as much or more than the Israelis as to what was happening in the Soviet Union. In 1985, Mr. David Bar Tov, fluent in Russian with prior personal experience in the Soviet Union, replaced Lapidot as head of the Liaison Bureau.

Most significantly, Prime Minister Begin increased the public presence of Israel in the Soviet Jewry advocacy movement. In deciding to hold the Third Brussels Conference in Jerusalem he brought Israel "out of the closet" on the issue of Soviet Jewry. The Brussels International Conferences of 1971 and 1976 were important events for the Soviet Jewry movement. Initiated and organized by the Liaison Bureau working through the Jewish Agency and other groups, they helped to coordinate and mobilize a world wide Soviet Jewry advocacy movement. The Conferences brought together Jewish and non-Jewish activists, intellectuals, government leaders, politicians and former Soviet Jewish Prisoners of Zion in a major public relations event which captured the interest of the world press and media. Between conferences, the World Conference of Soviet Jewry, controlled by the Liaison Bureau, coordinated the efforts of national and local Soviet Jewry groups around the globe. The Brussels III conference would be of crucial importance to focus world attention on the fact that the Soviet Union had closed its gates to Jews wanting to reunite with family abroad and in their homeland.

The Conference was scheduled for October 1982 in Paris. In a June 1982 meeting Menachem Begin hinted that the Soviets had pressured to postpone the meeting (Hand notes of Ralph Goldman at meeting with Prime Minister on *Noshrim*, June 17, 1982, JDC files).[54] According to Yehuda Lapidot an activist in Europe who had been instrumental in organizing previous meetings in Brussels refused to cooperate with Prime Minister Menachem Begin (Interview, Jerusalem, June 2002).[55] Lapidot arranged for the renting of a hall at Versailles with a local French Jew picking up the tab. A problem arose when French President François Mitterrand let it be known that he would not receive Prime Minister Begin as a guest of the French Government. He agreed, however, to allow Menachem Begin to enter France and participate in the conference as a private citizen. In ensuing negotiations the French government agreed to provide Menachem Begin with "state lodgings" at Versailles but still as a private citizen. This was unacceptable to Begin.

At the time Begin met with a group of French Jewish leaders including Lord Rothschild who were attending the funeral of Nahum Goldmann in Jerusalem. They advised him not to go to Versailles. The Prime Minister then asked the head of the Liaison Bureau to find another European site. This proved a very difficult task. Begin then suggested holding the conference in Jerusalem between March 15–17, 1983.

Many, however, felt that it would be a mistake for Israel to be identified so openly and closely with the Brussels Conference and the Soviet Jewry movement. Opposing the Jerusalem venue were Aryeh Dulzin of the Jewish Agency, Edgar Bronfman of the WJC, and leaders of B'nai B'rith. Other Americans in the Soviet Jewry movement who did not see Israel as the central focus of their cause also opposed the Israeli venue. Some leaders felt that holding it in Paris would give the impression of wider support and many more world leaders would come (Freedman 1989b:80).[56] In a short period of time the location was no longer an issue. B'nai B'rith, WJC and the Jewish Agency cosponsored the conference. Over 1,500 delegates from thirty countries participated. The NCSJ, assisted by NJCRAC, Philadelphia CRC and Greater New York Conference of Soviet Jewry brought an American delegation of 430 persons.[57] Ambassador Jeanne Kirkpatrick made the opening presentation on behalf of President Ronald Reagan. The conference called for ending the barriers to emigration and focused on anti-Semitism in the Soviet Union (Highlights of Plenary Session of LCBC CJF meeting, April 15, 1983, CJF files box 593).[58]

In 1984 Menachem Begin retired and new elections brought a government of national unity. Shimon Peres of Labor and Yitzhak Shamir alternated as Prime Minister and Foreign Minister respectively. Some in the Liaison Bureau thought that Peres was indifferent to the issue of Soviet Jews.[59] He wanted to reestablish diplomatic relations with the Soviet Union which he hoped would improve Israel's ability to negotiate with them about Soviet Jews. He opposed exerting public pressure on the Soviet Union.

Yitzhak Shamir, while not enthusiastic about Soviet Jewry advocacy in the early 1980s would become more interested as time passed. Importantly, he broke ranks with Menachem Begin on the issue of dropouts. In January 1984 Shamir's view was the "negation of the status of refugees for any Russian Jew who has an Israeli visa" (Memo, Akiva Kohane to Ralph Goldman, January 20, 1984, JDC files). He wanted all to be brought to Israel. He believed that once in Israel those wanting to leave to join relatives abroad could emigrate. Mr. Yehuda Lapidot, head of the Liaison Bureau, supported Shamir's policy shift. He believed that Begin's policy of compromise with American Jewish leaders had not worked ("Summary of Discussions with Yehuda Lapidot" March 7, 1984, JDC files). He urged Prime Minister Shamir to meet with American Jewish leaders.[60] Via the head of the Liaison Bureau, Shamir made his views known to Mr. Morris Abram of the NCSJ and the AJC and to Ambassador Douglas in the State Department.[61] Ambassador Douglas told the head of the Liaison Bureau that "there would be no problem in effecting this change in the status of Soviet Jews with Israeli visas if there are no objections from the American Jewish organizations" (Memo, Akiva Kohane to Ralph Goldman, January 20, 1984, JDC files).

In June 1984 in Jerusalem JDC, HIAS, and Jewish Agency renewed the dialogue on dropouts (Michael Schneider, "Meeting in Jerusalem's Binyanei Huma," June 27, 1984, JDC files).[62] They established a working committee consisting of Karl Zukerman of HIAS, Ralph Goldman of JDC and Howard Weisband of the Jewish Agency. Their charge was to develop "a unified Jewish (Israeli) position on how to maximize the flow of Soviet Jews to Israel" (Letter, Robert Israeloff [HIAS] to Chuck Hoffberger, November 19, 1984).

In a December 1984 draft the working committee raised the idea of "direct flights," a proposal which had been discussed often by Israelis. Because passage to Israel via a free country (Austria) resulted in a high dropout rate, direct flights via Romania would probably increase the number going to Israel. However, this might result in fewer Jews leaving the Soviet Union and discontent among those with families in the United States. It is interesting that Ralph Goldman argued that the committee should not deal with direct flights since it was a matter between sovereign states—Israel, the Soviet Union, and a third government (Letter, Ralph Goldman to Karl Zukerman, January 3, 1985, JDC files). Later in the decade, several American Jewish leaders including Shoshana Cardin of CJF, would argue that the issue of freedom of choice did not apply to direct flights because they involved the sovereign state of Israel and other countries and not American Jewish organizations.

The committee also discussed criteria for determining country of settlement in terms of family and relatives. It considered not having HIAS and JDC provide assistance for those deemed to be "more appropriate[ly]" resettled in Israel. Those in this category not wanting to go to Israel would be kept for 3–6 months in Europe where HIAS, JDC and the Jewish Agency would try to convince them to go to Israel. One participant noted that if HIAS did not aid these people other groups would (Karl Zukerman to Ralph Goldman, Irving Kessler, Howard Weisband, December 20, 1984, CJF files).[63]

In April 1985 Howard Weisband issued a revised report in the form of a policy statement which called for maximizing the flow of émigrés, family reunification and the resettlement of Jews in Israel (as the principal goal). It presented several options for future consideration. One option would fly, at the expense of world Jewry, all émigrés without exception to Israel for 3 to 6 months (direct flights or via third country). In Israel, authorities would allow stateless persons the option of obtaining citizenship within six months. It also proposed that Western countries (United States, Canada) allow Soviet Jews who had been in Israel for up to six months without obtaining citizenship to apply as refugees. Those leaving Israel after six months could do so on their own but could be assisted by HIAS to settle in other countries. They would be given material aid to the extent that it was not provided by their relatives in other countries. According to Howard Weisband and Aryeh Dulzin the Jewish Agency and Israel would not accept the idea of having Jews being brought to Israel with the option to leave within six months.

The second option had the Jewish Agency receiving all émigrés holding Israeli visas in Vienna. It would transfer those wanting to join first-degree relatives (defined as spouse, parents, children and siblings) in the West to HIAS and JDC. It assumed that Jewish federations would not provide resettlement services to those without first-degree relatives. Assistance from HIAS and JDC would be to the extent that relatives in the West could not provide. It proposed to adopt this option for one year or for 10,000 persons on a trial basis. A third option dealt with Soviet Jews who had close relatives abroad and who would apply for visas to the West in Moscow (Howard Weisband, "Soviet Jewish Migration proposed policy statement for HIAS, JDC, and UIA leadership, April 22, 1985, JDC files).[64]

In September 1985 Karl Zukerman revised further the proposed new policies after consulting with HIAS and Jewish Agency personnel. He proposed that the Jewish Agency would refer to HIAS/JDC for processing and assistance all émigrés on Israeli visas with first degree relatives in the West. The Jewish Agency would take all other Soviet Jews with Israeli visas to Israel. HIAS, JDC and other American voluntary agencies would not assist them to go elsewhere. The Jewish Agency would undertake an intensive one-year absorption effort to convince Soviet Jews to remain in Israel. If after one-year the émigrés desired to leave, HIAS would be available to assist. If they wanted to go to the United States (provided that the American government agreed) they would come either as refugees or as immigrants. Zuckerman understood that the HIAS board, the Jewish Agency and the Israeli and American governments would have to approve these proposals (Memo, Karl Zukerman to Saul Cohen, Irving Kessler, Howard Weisband and Carmi Schwartz, re: "Maximizing Flow of Soviet Jews to Israel" September 24, 1985).

In *Haaretz* of November 15, 1984 Dan Margolit reported that senior ministers had backed an appeal to the U.S. government to no "longer grant refugee status to Soviet Jews who exit the Soviet Union on the false pretence that they are destined for Israel when . . . their paths are chartered for the '*Goldene Medina*' (United States)." The ministers hoped this would result in more coming to Israel. The paper noted that Foreign Minister Shimon Peres had not raised the issue when visiting the United States. Margolit argued that Peres realized that the American Jewish community would not accept the idea; that it now more than ever favored freedom of choice. Peres believed that if the American Jewish community rejected Israeli policy in the 1970s when Israel was more central to American Jews then all the more so now in the 1980s when Israel's luster had been tarnished in the eyes of many American Jews. Margolit also emphasized that the sad state of the Israeli economy, with so many young people leaving, undercut any demand by Israelis to request of American Jews to pressure Soviet Jews to come to Israel (Dan Margolit, "The *Noshrim* who Cost Us Dearly" *Haaretz*, November 15, 1984).[65]

Minister of Absorption Yakov Tsur, however, told the press that Israel was a free country and would not compel anybody to go anywhere. He implied that "no application would be made to the United States to deny refugee status to the dropouts" (Letter, Robert Israeloff to Chuck Hoffberger, November 19, 1984 and *JP*, November 12, 1984). He reiterated this position a month later when he blamed HIAS and the United States government for the dropouts because the latter gave them refugee status. He conceded, however, that "it would be difficult to convince HIAS and the United States. to withhold assistance to the émigrés." He believed, nonetheless, that Soviet Jews were better off leaving the Soviet Union than staying regardless of destination (*JTAB*, December 10, 1984).[66]

Several Liaison Bureau emissaries and American Jewish leaders including Ralph Goldman believed that Israeli leaders gave up the struggle over Soviet Jewish dropouts by not confronting American Jews (Interview, Ralph Goldman, December 2, 1996). Goldman continuously argued that the Israelis were not tough enough in challenging American Jewish supporters of freedom of choice (Interview, Ralph Goldman, December 6, 1996). Baruch Gur and Yoram Dinstein argued that Prime Minister Yitzhak Rabin in the 1970s did not want a confrontation with American Jewry over the dropout issue (Phone interview, Baruch Gur, January 1, 2003).[67] Goldman claimed that Begin refrained from raising the dropout issue and often backed down when it was raised and challenged. Yoram Dinstein similarly argues that Prime Minister Menachem Begin did not challenge American Jews on this issue and in particular Rabbi Alexander Schindler of the Conference of Presidents' for fear of causing an open break over Israeli settlement policies in the territories. Yehuda Lapidot believes that Menachem Begin did not challenge American Jews and in particular HIAS because he was ambivalent about fighting against the entry of Jewish refugees into the United States (Interview, Yehuda Lapidot, June 26, 2002). Dinstein (Interview, May 3, 2003) also faults Levanon for not pressuring Begin to be more forceful on dropouts with American Jews. He believes that Levanon, was never 100 percent sure on the issue so he was not stubborn.

Most ironic was the position on dropouts of JDC and its Executive Director Ralph Goldman on the issue of dropouts. Ralph Goldman was a staunch and committed advocate of having Soviet émigrés go only to Israel if they wanted the aid and support of the Jewish people. Also, the lay Executive Committee and Board of JDC generally supported the Jewish Agency and the Israeli government in their conflicts with HIAS over dropouts. Nevertheless, the JDC funded and supported most Soviet Jewish dropouts in Europe who applied for visas to the United States. Officials at HIAS and UIA believed that JDC was concerned about turf in Europe as well as the resources it received from the federal government and UJA for providing care and maintenance for Soviet Jewish émigrés. Had it refused to do so, then the CJF or American government would have turned to HIAS or other voluntary agencies to provide care and maintenance (Interviews, Karl Zukerman, November 8, 1996; Irving Kessler, August 16, 2001 and Yehuda Lapidot, June 26, 2002). It may be that the Liaison Bureau and the Israeli government viewed JDC as a partner and ally in the struggle for Soviet Jewry regardless of its support for dropouts. As noted in chapter 4, JDC funded many of the Liaison Bureau clandestine operations and later would fund its operations in the Soviet Union during the Gorbachev era.

Arthur Opolion, in an almost prophetic letter to the *JP* ("Hard Questions on Soviet Emigration," May 15, 1985), argued that "The [dropout] issue defies resolution because American Jewish leaders have no interest in changing the situation. They are pleased to have Soviet Jews come to the United States and to bask in the sunshine of their splendid achievements" Guilt ridden by the Holocaust they now sought to save their brethren not for altruistic reasons but to revitalize many American Jewish organizations. He thought that Israeli leaders had to decide what they wanted more "Soviet Aliyah {immigration} or the continued support of American Jewish leaders, whose interest do not coincide with Israel on this issue?" He thought the Israelis had leverage since American Jewish leaders "derive much of their power and influence from their relationships with Israeli leaders, and would go a long way to avoid rupturing such relations." He predicted that should the Soviet Union open its gates that immigration to Israel would not occur. Israel, he argued, must challenge American Jewish leaders and insist on their acceptance of its position. "Israel can be confident that if American Jewish leaders could keep Ethiopian Jews out of the United States they can do the same with respect to Soviet Jews."

Importantly, Opolion suggests that the American Jewish organizations and community viewed Soviet Jewry as a source of revitalization. The historian Henry Feingold (1981) made the same point at the General Assembly of CJF in 1981 when he argued that Jewish communities in the United States "who have accepted modernity with its acculturation and diminishing birth rate require outside supplementation to assure their survival. . . . Viewed through the prism of demography, one can conclude that Israel and American Jewry, since before the establishment of the State, have been vying for the same scarce pool of Jewish humanity which they both need."

ISRAELI EFFORTS TO COERCE MORE
SOVIET JEWISH ÉMIGRÉS TO RESETTLE IN ISRAEL

Before 1985 it became clear to the Liaison Bureau and Israeli political leaders that if the gates of the Soviet Union would open then most émigrés would choose the United States over Israel. At the same time, the Israelis, as late at 1984, may have thought that gates would not open in the foreseeable future. Speaking at the CJF General Assembly Yoram Dinstein (1984) told the delegates that two or three million Jews would remain in the Soviet Union at least for the next "twenty or thirty or forty years." Nevertheless, in addition to direct flights, Israeli leaders suggested various proposals to limit a potential mass exodus of Soviet Jews from going to the United States.

One proposal involved the bestowing of Israeli citizenship on Soviet Jews before their arrival in Israel.[68] This might make Soviet Jewish émigrés ineligible for American refugee status. An in-depth analysis prepared for HIAS, however, argued that granting citizenship would not preclude eligibility of entry into the United States as refugees provided the applicant establishes that he/she has not been firmly resettled in Israel and that the Israeli citizenship was acquired involuntarily as the only means of escaping the Soviet Union. The memo noted that United States law recognizing that an individual fleeing persecution who resorts to misrepresentations or obtaining fraudulent documents were excludable offenses under section 212 (a) (19) of the Immigration and Nationality Act. It also noted that the United States government consistently subscribed to the position that "no state is free to extend the application of its law or nationality in such a way as to reach out and claim the allegiance of whomever it pleases." Granting of citizenship also required that an individual perform an overt act indicating acceptance e.g. military service.[69] HIAS argued that Soviet Jews could still refuse to accept Israeli citizenship. Should Israel then refuse them a visa, Irving Haber argued, then the Soviet Union would appear to be more liberal on emigration than Israel (Mr. Irving Haber, "Soviet Jewish Program," September 11, 1984, HIAS files). Ralph Goldman opposed the idea of granting Israeli citizenship arguing that it would divide Israel and the Diaspora. He urged no unilateral action on this matter while recognizing that "any such action is the unilateral prerogative of the sovereign State of Israel (Memo, Ralph Goldman to Chaim Aharon, Chairman of Aliyah Department, Jewish Agency, JDC files).

Another proposal was to influence the United States not to allow entry of Soviet Jewish émigrés. This often involved the argument that Soviet Jews leaving on Israeli visas did not qualify as refugees. By early 1986 it became clear to CJF officials that Israel and its friends were urging some American Jewish organizations including the Conference of Presidents and the NCSJ to secure greater restrictions on the movement of Soviet Jews into the United States. This became a highly volatile and divisive issue in the American Jewish community (Hand letter of Carmi Schwartz to Jerold Hoffberger, March 16, 1986, CJF files, box 697).[70]

Later in February 1987 Mr. Yitzhak Shamir, Prime Minister of Israel publicly suggested that the United States not consider Soviet Jewish émigrés as political refugees. He called on the American Jewish leadership and organizations to support the Israeli position and called upon the American government to "institute more restrictive measures with regard to immigration and refugee status for Soviet Jews wishing to be resettled in the United States" (Freedman 1987b:86–90).[71] He and his chief of staff met with State Department officials on the subject (Interview, Richard Schifter, Washington, D.C., August 2, 1995). According to HIAS, Secretary of State George Shultz told Prime Minister Yitzhak Shamir that he would not act on the request "unless it receives a clear signal from the American Jews that this is what they want" (Letter, Robert Israeloff to HIAS Board, March 24, 1987, JDC files).[72]

The CJF responded that there was a clear consensus among American Jewish leaders and organizations "that indicates that American Jews will not undertake such an assignment—quite to the contrary, American Jewish leaders and organizations would continue to be committed to more liberal United States immigration and refugees policies and would seek to have such policies implemented on all United States government levels ("Notes for re: Soviet Jewish immigration, refugee status and direct flight issues" April 8, 1987, CJF files, box 667).[73] Shoshana Cardin, CJF President, stated that we were "disturbed that Prime Minister came over with proposal without consulting with American Jewry" and we are opposed to any change in the current emigration laws and regulations (Meeting of Large City Presidents and Executive Meeting and Notes [CJF], April 27, 1987, CJF files, box 696 and David Harris "The Controversy over Refugee Status of Soviet Jewish Émigrés," AJC publication, May 25, 1987, CJF files). There is a national understanding among HIAS, JDC, UIA, United Jewish Appeal and CJF "that there is no resettlement from Israel and Jews are resettled once as the responsibility of the federated movement." She explained that CJF authorized her to "lead a small delegation of national leadership to meet with Prime Minister Shamir to express what we believe are the feelings and concerns of federated Jewry." She also claimed that the United States government was looking to us before it would act. She explained that the last CJF Executive Committee concluded with little division that nothing CJF did should in any way "discourage free flow of Soviet Jewish emigration." Yet, CJF agreed with the Prime Minister that Israel should be the place that the émigrés should go. They should be encouraged to go to Israel. They also favored attempts to change the refugee status in this country to help the flow from Israel, if they went to Israel first. "No question there should be no change in our total commitment to freedom of choice of the Soviet Jewish emigrant. We must not in any way in spite of Israel's feeling impose the demand they must go to Israel." Finally it had decided to resettle Soviet Jews in the USA who had first gone to Israel (on direct flights) regardless of what the U.S. government decide on their refugee status (Meeting . . . April 27, 1987).[74]

Malcolm Hoenlein, Executive Vice President of the President's Conference, urged the CJF to avoid a crisis with Prime Minister Shamir and the Israelis (Notes of Meeting on Soviet Jewish Advocacy Issues, March 2, 1987, CJF files, box 667).[75] UJA President Stanley B. Horowitz wrote that the American Jewish community will oppose Israeli's interference in American policies and view it ironic "the specter of a Jewish State attempting to convince another nation to be less liberal towards the self determined desires of Jews" (Letter, Stanley B. Horowitz to J. Hoffberger, March 17, 1987, CJF files, box 697). He felt it contrary to what we had been fighting for years namely freedom of Jews to migrate anyplace they wanted. He suggested instead that the Israelis improve absorption.[76]

With Mikhail Gorbachev in power in March 1985 the necessary conditions for Détente came into place. This in turn would facilitate important political changes in the Soviet Union for Soviet Jews. Important developments would take place in terms of both emigration and cultural and religious freedom for Soviet Jewry. It was evident to both the Liaison Bureau and American Jewish leaders that most Soviet Jews, if given freedom to leave, would prefer to come to the United States. Until this time American Jewish leaders had resisted most Israeli efforts to limit "freedom of choice" for Soviet Jews whether it be in the form of reducing aid for dropouts or entry into the United States as refugees. The changes brought about by Gorbachev would also cause American Jewish leaders including those in the CJF to rethink their position on freedom of choice. The policies of Mikhail Gorbachev toward Soviet Jews and Jewish emigration and his summits with President Ronald Reagan are the subject of the next chapter.

NOTES

1. It also brought to a halt the emigration of Germans and Armenians.

Emigration from the USSR, 1980–1986

	1980	1981	1982	1983	1984	1985	1986
Germans	6,954	3,773	2,071	1,447	913	460	753
Armenians	6,109	1,905	339	194	88	110	246
Jews	21,471	9,448	2,692	1,314	895	1,140	914

Sources: Salitan 1992:59 and Fax from Israel (Probably Liaison Bureau) to JDC (New York City), August 10, 1995 "Annual FSU/Soviet Aliya" (JDC files).

2. Yoram Dinstein (interview, May 3, 2003) and Sara Frankel (1989) supported this position. The Minutes of HIAS Board of Directors of December 14, 1982 report that Prime Minister Begin told a private group that Soviet Foreign Minister Gromyko said that Soviet Jewish emigration depended on USA-USSR relations.

3. Also many in the Soviet Union saw the continued exodus of Jews, Germans and Armenians as hurting the Soviet economy and potentially causing a labor shortage

(Salitan 1992:97,98; Korey 1999:112 and Friedgut 1989:6,7). The United States boycotted the 1980 Olympic Games in Moscow. While the Liaison Bureau and establishment American Jewish groups wanted to participate in the Moscow Olympics the Union of Councils called for a boycott. The American decision to boycott resulted in Israel also boycotting (Applembaum 1986:630).

4. Salitan (1992:59-633) argues that there was a general clamp down on Western influence in the Soviet Union in the early 1980s. Soviet authorities jammed Voice of America (VOA) and British Broadcasting System (BBC) in August 1980. Hebrew teachers were harassed and many Jewish activists were arrested. By 1985, 26 Jews were in prison or labor camps for practicing Judaism. By 1986 there would be over 11,000 Refuseniks, Jews who had been denied permission to leave the Soviet Union.

5. In response to the War in Lebanon the Soviet Union increased its anti-Israel and anti-Zionist campaign at home and abroad. Friedgut (1989:6) suggested that at the Twenty-sixth Party Congress in 1981 Leonid Brezhnev offered to end quotas on Jews and anti-Semitism if Soviet Jews would cut ties to West. While some evidence suggested initial ending of some job discrimination, little changed for Soviet Jews. HIAS officials thought (Minutes, HIAS Board of Directors, December 14, 1982, HIAS files) that Andropov might let more Jews out and improve relations with Israel in order to improve relations with the West. Leonid Brezhnev died on November 20, 1982. Yuri Andropov who succeeded him died on February 9, 1984. He was succeeded by Konstantine Chernenko as First Secretary and then also as Head of State (Shapiro 1986:287). Within a year he died and was succeeded by Mikhail Sergeyevich Gorbachev on March 11, 1985 (Shultz 1993:124,471,526).

6. On October 11, 1982, *Pravda* printed a cartoon showing Hitler directing an Israeli soldier to kill Arabs (Shapiro 1983:218). The leaders of the Anti Zionist Committee were Jews including retired general David Dragunski, chair, Professor Samuil Zivs, first vice chair, Mark Krupskii, Igor Beliaev and Jurii Kolensnikov Vice chairs (Salitan 1992:62–63; Shapiro 1984:246). It functioned between 1983 and 1985 and ceased to exist by 1987.

7. At the General Assembly of the CJF in 1984, Professor Yoram Dinstein (1984), a former Liaison Bureau emissary, noted the sluggishness of the movement in the United States. While it had the staying power of many, many years, the decades since 1959 had tired out the activists.

8. Friedgut (1989:5) notes that at this time the Israeli government which had urged, inspired and coordinated "much of the international effort now found that it had no control and a diminishing measure of influence over this effort."

9. See comments by Arthur Herzberg (chapter 4) concerning his first meeting with Nehemia Levanon who *instructed him* how the American Jewish Congress should act on behalf of Soviet Jewry.

10. Via the AJC it reached out to UNESCO. Its newest constituent agency the Jewish National Fund planted a forest for Soviet Jews in Israel and twinned American Bar and Bat Mitzvah children with Jewish counterparts in the Soviet Union. It also sponsored American tours and meetings with former Soviet Jews now living in Israel.

11. According to Shachtman 2001:109,110) JDC funded many visits by both Americans and Israelis.

12. It had a staff of 12 persons; 4 professionals and 5 clericals in New York and 2 professionals and 1 clerical in Washington, D.C. Budgetary problems led to a shortage of handbooks for Congressmen.

13. Regular activities in Washington, D.C., included briefing the incoming House and Senate members, briefing delegations visiting the Soviet Union and circulating various petitions for Prisoners of Zion.

14. Naftalin of the Union of Councils (1999:233) represented the United State government as a public member of the American delegation to the Warsaw Review and Pamela Cohen also of the Councils played a similar role in the 1991 Geneva Conference.

15. While the LCBC validated $250,000 to NCSJ in 1983 and 1984, the NCSJ only received $193,000 of this. By 1985 CJF's contribution to NCSJ covered 47 percent of its budget (not including the Soviet Jewry Research Bureau). The CJF contribution in the 1986 projected budget dropped to 37 percent based on expected large contributions. NCSJ, "1985–1986" submitted to LCBC, November 13, 1985 (CJF files, box 667).

16. At the September 12, 1982, Quarterly in New York City, Lebanon became the major issue; no mention was made of Soviet Jewry in the initial agenda (Letter, Martin Citrin, CJF to Senators Moynihan and Cranston, August 11, 1982, box 659). There is no mention of Soviet Jewry in the Highlights of CJF Board meeting on March 4, 1984 (Martin Citrin to Board of Directors, CJF, January 27, 1984, CJF files, box 659) and none with announcement for a Board Meeting for April 20, 21, 1985 (Shoshana Cardin to CJF Board of Directors, March 15, 1985, CJF files, box 659) and agenda for April 20, 21 and September 5–8, 1985 Board of Directors of CJF (Cardin to Board Members, Federation Presidents and Executive Committee Members announcing meeting of September 5–8, 1985, CJF files).

17. JDC President Don Robinson talked about the dual responsibility for North American Jewry to help Soviet Jews emigrate and to provide assistance for those that would remain.

18. Talisman helped Congressman Tom Foley get 372 Congressmen to sign a petition protesting the treatment of Anotoly Sharansky. Foley hand delivered it to Yuri Andropov. Talisman had played a major role in developing the Jackson-Vanik amendment, block grants for resettlement of Russian refugees and the Refugee Act of 1980. He later participated in the Max Fisher–State Department meetings in 1989 concerning the entry of Soviet Jewish refugees.

19. President Reagan and his supporters in Congress sought American Jewish support for their domestic and foreign policies. During the 1970s when liberals called for defense cutbacks some pro-Israel groups and lobbyists supported the more conservative and Republican position (Ginsberg 1993:185–205). After 1980 a coalition of cold war warriors, defense establishment officials and pro-Israeli forces wanted more military spending and supported Reagan's military policies. Among them was Richard Perle. Ginsberg (1993:205) claims that the Reagan administration used the Israeli lobby for a Cold War arms buildup. For example Steve Solarz, a Democrat, supported Reagan on arms and foreign aid bill opposed by the (D NY) leadership. American Israel Political Action Committee and neoconservatives also pushed the idea of Israel as a bulwark against the Communist threat (208). In turn the Israeli government worked with the Reagan Administration on military and intelligence tasks in the Middle East and elsewhere (208–215). Goldman argues that Jewish groups including Anti-Defamation League helped Reagan undermine the Sandinistas. This Jewish-Republican alliance would decline with the collapse of the Soviet Union.

20. On June 15, 1983, together with the President's Conference, NCSJ brought together presidents of national Jewish organizations and major Jewish communities to

meet with Shultz. He reconfirmed his and President Reagan's commitment to Soviet Jewry.

21. Morris Abram (1984:2,3), President of the NCSJ, told the CJF General Assembly in November 1984 that the United States "has taken the plight of Soviet Jews very seriously indeed. As a matter of fact, on October 21, 1984 Secretary of Schultz, when he appeared before the National Conference on Soviet Jewry's Leadership Assembly, made it so clear that no one could doubt his determination and the determination of the American government to make this an item in the next negotiations when they occur with the Soviet Union—not a throw-away item, but an item of first-rank importance."

22. To mark the opening of Madrid meetings 139 Jews in Moscow and 6 other cities held a three day hunger strike (Shapiro 1981:237). From prison Anatoly Sharansky wrote the Madrid Conference about human rights and conditions in the Perm prison.

23. Half of those exiting were above the age of fifty.

24. He suggested that the Jewish Agency wanted to sever ties with HIAS and to deal with it in the same manner as it did with Rav Tov.

25. Before 1967 the JDC rarely questioned the Jewish identity of its clients. In the 1967–1968 post Gomulka era of Polish Jewish émigrés at least one member of a nuclear family had to be fully Jewish (both parents) in order to be processed by JDC and HIAS. They would not accept families with baptized minor children.

26. The estimated lifetime upkeep of five hard core cases (out of 275,000 since 1969) in Rome not wanting to go to Israel and rejected by the United States (physical disabilities) would be $500,000 per person ("Policy issues and concerns," November 16, 1982, CJF files, box 660).

27. It had a cumulative deficit for 1980 and 1981 of $565,000. UJA committed to fund $400,000 of the 1981 deficit leaving a net deficit of $198,791. HIAS established a capital reserve fund of $500,000.

28. In 1979 the federations and Federation-UJA of New York provided 22 percent of HIAS's budget. This increased to 40 percent in 1982. Edwin Shapiro reported that the U.S. Government would cover 21 percent of the 1983 HIAS budget (Minutes, Meeting of HIAS Board of Directors, December 14, 1982, HIAS files), Table IV. With reduced federal funding HIAS turned over to local communities a larger share of the federal per capita subsidy.

29. In 1979 the Jewish Agency set its debt ceiling at $650m. It sold off assets and cut its budget ("Draft resolution at CJF meetings on Jewish Agency debt" September 9, 1982, CJF files box 659). In 1984 it balanced its budget for the first time since 1974 (Minutes, CJF Board of Directors, April 16–17, 1983, CJF file, box 659).

30. Many of the leaders in the establishment Soviet Jewry advocacy movement in the United States also played major roles on the Jewish Agency Board of Governors. In the late 1960s Louis Pincus, Chair of the Jewish Agency Executive expanded the role of the Americans in the governance of the Jewish Agency. He found an ally in Max Fisher who became Chairman of the Board of Governors of a reconstituted Jewish Agency in 1971 (Golden 1992:217ff). The overseas non–Zionists received control of the Board of Governors and the WZO, representing Israeli political parties, retained control of the Jewish Agency Executive. While the Executive appointed heads of operating departments the Board of Governors retained a veto over their appointments (Silberman 1985:217).

In June 1983 the newly elected Board of Governors headed by Jerold Hoffberger refused to approve the reappointment of Rafael Kotlowitz as head of the Absorption Department *(Baltimore Jewish Times,* July 15, 1983 and Memo, Jerold Hoffberger to M. Droblas, January 27, 1984). He was a political appointee from Begin's Herut faction of the Likud (Stenographic notes of comments by Chuck Hoffberger at JDC Executive Committee Meeting, July 14, 1983, JDC files) and Jerold Hoffberger (Interview, December 3, 1996). Israelis in the Jewish Agency supported him so as not to embarrass the Prime Minister (Letter, Yehuda Domonitz to Ralph Goldman, December 23, 1982, JDC files and Memo, Carmi Schwartz to Martin Citrin, re: Visit to Israel, December 27, 1982, CJF files, box 660). The Secretary of the Begin government doubted that Begin cared that much about this matter (Interview with Aryeh Naor, December 30, 2002). Ralph Goldman hand notes on Hoffberger's comments, July 27, 1983 (JDC files) and Golden (1992:227).

31. The UJA's annual contribution of $300m is the budgetary core "of the Jewish Agency For Israel, the Jewish state's largest private social-service provider." Overall the Jewish Agency's half billion dollar budget is the largest single Jewish institution in the world excluding the government of Israel.

32. Richard Krieger of the staff of the Office of Refugee Affairs in the State Department (telephone interview, December 11, 2003) remembered being approached by Israelis in the early 1980s wanting to have most Soviet Jewish émigrés go to Israel.

33. Reimers (1985) notes that the support for financial assistance originated with the two California Senators who were concerned about the large number of Vietnamese refugees. Carmi Schwartz (Interview, September 6, 2001) argues that the 1980 Act made it easier for Soviet Jews to enter as refugees. He recalls at the time that he had reservations as to whether they were really refugees but was overruled by CJF lay leaders.

34. The consultation took place in early fall in order to set the number of refugees to be admitted in the coming Fiscal Year beginning on October 1, (Goldberg 1986:184 and Interview, Arnold H. Liebowitz, July 1995). The 1980 Refugee Act refers only to consultation between the Executive Branch and the Judiciary Committees of Congress. Nongovernmental organizations had access to Congress on this matter. For several years Mark Talisman of CJF represented the nongovernmental refugee aid groups before Congress (E-mail, Princeton Lyman to Fred Lazin, June 23, 2004).

35. The position was established by the Refugee Act of 1980 (PL96-212, March 17, 1980, Ninety-sixth Congress 94 Stat.102). The President with the Advise and Consent of the Senate appointed the Coordinator who held the rank of an Ambassador at Large. He was responsible to the President for developing and coordinating overall refugee admission and resettlement policy, liaison to voluntary organizations, governors and mayors and contacts with other countries.

36. He recalled that before meeting the President of the United States Menachem Begin asked for ideas to raise about Soviet Jewish dropouts. Lapidot told him that if you can convince the President to stop giving aid and considering them refugees then the problem would be solved. Begin answered "Never will I request from a non Jew not to allow Jews to enter his country." Lapidot felt that Yitzhak Shamir was willing to do anything; "a terrorist with no principles or values."

37. Richard Krieger (Telephone interview, December 11, 2004) of Douglas's staff suggests that the Ambassador's "first inkling was that the Russian Jews should go to

Israel." Krieger, a former Jewish federation professional who favored freedom of choice argues, that he convinced Ambassador Douglas that Soviet Jews should have the right to make their own decision as to where to live. The author's interview with Douglas (June 29, 2004) indicates that when in charge of refugee policy he did not favor freedom of choice. He believed it in the interest of both Israel and the United States for most Soviet Jewish émigrés to resettle in Israel.

38. By this time the United States had encouraged other nations to share the burden of refugee resettlement.

39. At the time Richard Krieger of Ambassador Douglas's staff told Schwartz that Douglas was angry that he had not been informed that the American Jewish community requested a $5m increase in aid for resettling Soviet Jews in Israel. Ambassador Douglas would support the increase but use it as an additional rationale to restrict entry of Soviet Jews to those with first-degree relatives. Again Schwartz argued against linking Soviet Jewish entry to the United States and Israeli and Jewish interests.

40. In testimony before the Senate Judicial Committee on September 23, 1982 (JDC files) Ambassador Howard Eugene Douglas expressed concern about "apparent misuse or over-utilization of our refugee public assistance programs," which remained the largest cost of domestic refugee resettlement programs.

41.

Soviet Jewish Emigres Eligible for American Citizenship

Year of Eligibility	Jewish Émigrés Eligible	Year of Arrival in USA
1982	6,838	1977
1983	12,259	1978
1984	28,878	1979
1985	15,630	1980
total	63,605	

42. Soviet émigrés with citizen relatives in the United States were kept in Vienna pending the signing of an affidavit of support by the U.S. relative. If not signed within three months the relative was removed from the care and maintenance caseload. The Austrians feared these persons might become public charges. The United States Refugee Program funded their transfer to Rome where JDC continued to provide care and maintenance (reimbursed by United States Refugee Program) and HIAS processed them.

43. Karl Zukerman of HIAS raised the issue whether HIAS should seek an agreement with the relatives in the U.S. If relatives did not agree, he queried, should the federation assume responsibility or should it seek to bring the individual as a refugee and thus eligible for block grant reimbursement?

44. The care and maintenance provided immigrants is not eligible for reimbursement under the block grant.

45. Fish sent a follow up memo on August 17, 1982. The six priorities for refugee admissions were: 1. compelling concern/interest; 2. former U.S. government employees; 3. family reunification (refugees who are spouses, sons, daughters, parents, or grandchildren of a person in U.S. who must be a U.S. citizen, lawful permanent resident

refugee or alien; 4. other ties to the USA (e.g. employed by U.S. foundation; 5. additional family renunciations (married siblings); 6. "Otherwise of National Interest: Other refugees in specified regional groups whose admission is in the national interest" (Letter, Richard Krieger to Carmi Schwartz, August 24, 1982, CJF files, box 710).

46. It had been already eliminated in Southeast Asia and South America to date. Richard Krieger (Letter, to Carmi Schwartz, August 24, 1982, CJF files, box 710) asked rhetorically what the efficacy of our programs would be if we don't include Soviet émigrés in our phase out of sixth priority? Douglas expressed this dilemma in meeting American Jewish leaders on the proposed changes. All favored more leaving the Soviet Union and a larger percentage going to Israel but did not agree on how to achieve these goals.

47. According to Princeton Lyman (e-mail message to Lazin, June 24, 2004) "it is standard refugee practice that refugees be processed in the first place of asylum. . . . This is to avoid 'asylum shopping' i.e. that refugees shop around for the most attractive places to resettle. . . . In the case of Soviet Jewish refugees it was recognized that the reason they all had (at that time) visas for Israel was that this was the only exit visa the Soviets allowed Jews."

48. Huddleston's Bill would eliminate the fifth preference for brothers and sisters of adult U.S. citizens; an unlimited number of visas for first degree relatives of United States citizens would be available but the number of visas issued for this purpose in a given year would be subtracted from the 350,000 available for family reunification in the next year.

49. According to the 1980 Refugee Act applicants had to "demonstrate on a case-by-case basis a well-founded fear of persecution" but Soviet Jews had virtual presumptive refugee status after a perfunctory interview in Rome. (Beyer 1991:141)

50. The Simpson-Mazzoli bill also provided voluntary agencies a role in the legalization program for aliens seeking amnesty.

51. Senator Simpson believes that extended family reunion was not in the best interests of the USA. He favored independent investors and professional admissions. Proposed changes could hurt Soviet Jews. Also applicants from Eastern Europe and minorities who were not actively persecuted might not fare well under definitions that would evolve. Finally, if violate status, they can't adjust in the USA. This would hurt HIAS caseload. HIAS thought the level of per capita funding low and that the law would limit HIAS's traditional advocacy role on behalf of its clients.

52. Clause 6 was removed for Haitian, Cuban, Latin American, Cambodian, Laotian and Vietnamese cases on January 1982. It was to be implemented for Eastern European refugees as of January 1, 1983 and to be removed for refugees from Africa on January 1, 1984.

53. Naor argues that Begin's policy in general was to keep people and not switch personnel.

54. The 1982 War in Lebanon probably influenced the Israelis to delay the Paris meeting.

55. He suggested that the activist opposed many of Begin's policies.

56. Aryeh Dulzin had Prime Minister Begin send the head of the Liaison Bureau to the United States to cool things off before the Jewish High Holidays of 1982 (Interview with Zissy Schnur, August 2002).

57. The NCSJ coordinated the American delegation. It recruited speakers and raised funds. It brought Ambassador Jeanne Kirkpatrick, Bayard Rustin, Newman Flannagan (President of National District Attorneys Association), Governor Thomas Kean of New Jersey and Christian leadership. (NCSJ report to LCBC, November 15, 1983, CJF files box 593). The estimated cost for Brussels III was $520,000. World Zionist Organization would put up $85,000, World Jewish Congress and B'nai B'rith $62,500 each, CJF federations $170,000, and the Jewish communities of Great Britain $11,500, France $20,000, Canada $20,000 (corrected to $15,000), Greece $250 and Panama $500 (Letter from Theodore R. Mann to Marvin Citron, July 1, 1982, CJF files Box 660). CJF endorsed a special one time grant to help defray the costs of the conference (Minutes of Board of Directors of CJF, January 17, 1983).

58. Chernin in a report to the CJF Board of Directors (Summary of Minutes, April 16–17, 1983, CJF files, box 659) emphasized "unprecedented role of United States government, the presence of representation of other Western democracies [and the] . . . level of participation of Christians."

59. In the 1970s Peres had reservations against forcing Soviet Jews to come to Israel. If they did not want to come here, they were better of in the United States where they could be Jewish then if they were to remain in the Soviet Union.

60. The JDC favored such a meeting at the end of June when most American Jewish leaders would be in Jerusalem for the Jewish Agency meetings. Telex, Ralph Goldman to Yehudah Lapidot, June 14, 1984 (JDC files). *Maariv* (July 17, 1984) reported that the Liaison Bureau stopped sending affidavits to Soviet Jews in order to reduce the dropout rate. It had not informed U.S. Jews of this policy change.

61. Lapidot claimed that he had persuaded Morris Abram to accept Shzmir's position.

62. Participants included Chuck Hoffberger, Henry Taub, Bob Israeloff, Ralph Goldman, Karl Zukerman and Michael Schneider.

63. Ralph Goldman asked Karl Zukerman (letter, January 3, 1985, JDC files) why we should compromise principles because of a fear of these groups?

64. Another paragraph dealt with those without relatives who would apply in Moscow for visas to the West.

65. Margolit presented a disclaimer on the Holocaust analogy, arguing that while the British kept Palestine closed as a potential place of refuge, a free and independent Israel now existed.

66. Israeloff wrote Chuck Hoffberger (November 19, 1984) that the Israeli Cabinet did not pass the resolution requested by Dulzin.

67. Dinstein (May 3, 2003) suggested that Rabin neglected American Jewry.

68. In the early 1970s the Knesset passed a law that allowed Soviet Jews to get citizenship by proxy in the Netherlands Embassy in Moscow. The Dutch never acted on this (Buwalda 1997:76)

69. An unsigned analysis in HIAS files argued that according to U.S. regulations that one would be ineligible if he/she has offer of nationality voluntarily and only if they entered that country. The memo noted that even accepting Israeli end visas meets a requirement of being firmly resettled in another county but since most dropouts did not continue to Israel, they were not considered firmly resettled. "Summary of Staff Analysis of Effects of Conferring Israeli Nationality on Soviet Jewish Émigrés," September 12, 1984 (HIAS files) and Memo Michael Gendel to Karl Zukerman, September 14, 1984 (HIAS files-*Noshrim*).

70. Schwartz voiced support for Minister Tsur's request that we not make it easy for Israelis in Europe to gain access to the USA. HIAS favored their quick entry into the USA outside of the quota.

71. He argues that the Soviets used emigration policy to advance their interests in the Middle East peace talks. Shamir told Gur-Gurevitz (1996:18) that he raised the issue twice with Bush and discussed it with Under Secretary of State Richard Schifter as well. Gur-Gurevitch claims that Shamir did not publicly ask for the United States to deny Soviet Jews entry as refugees.

72. He referred to the "bitter experiences 50 years ago when many European Jews fleeing Nazis were denied entry into this country."

73. In an editorial "Let Soviet Jews Decide" (March 8, 1987) the *NYT* favored allowing Soviet Jews to determine their place of refuge. Windmueller (1999:168) argues that some American Jews also entertained Shamir's idea of closing America to Soviet Jews. Morris Abram recalled that he had met Shamir on his arrival at the airport and begged him not to request a denial of refugee status. He thought Shamir made a mistake because the policy would not be changed (Dorot 30ff.).

74. In other words they would not be considered "Israelis." Steve Nasatir of Chicago argued that those without first-degree relatives would not be admitted to the USA.

75. CJF probably sponsored this meeting. Participants included Al Chernin of NJCRAC, Malcolm Hoenlein of Presidents' Conference, Karl Zukerman of HIAS, Jerry Goodman of NCSJ, Carmi Schwartz and Ted Comet and Elaine Morris of CJF. Hoenlein suggested that Shamir meant it as a trial balloon. He also reported that Shamir would allow all Soviet Jews to come to Israel for a six month trial period.

76. Interestingly, Carmi Schwartz of CJF supported the idea of direct flights to Israel as a means of insuring that Russian Jews would go to Israel.

6

The Reagan-Gorbachev Summits:
Moving toward a Resolution of
the Soviet Jewry Issue

This chapter looks at efforts of the Soviet Jewry advocacy movement and the NCSJ in particular to pressure the Reagan Administration to place the issue of Soviet Jewry on the agenda of the summit meetings between the President and Secretary Gorbachev. These bilateral talks led to an opening of the gates for Soviet Jewry by the end of the decade as well as cultural, religious and organizational freedom for those who remained. The latter development led many American Jewish organizations, the Liaison Bureau and the Jewish Agency to expand their cultural and educational activities in the Soviet Union (Schnur 1990:60–61).[1] Malcolm Hoenlein (1989:28) suggested that instead of the American Jewish communities adopting Soviet cities to foster emigration and resettlement that they should send over rabbis and teachers to help them be better Jews.

Importantly, during this time the Liaison Bureau continued to exert considerable pressure on the American Soviet Jewry advocacy movement to deny Soviet Jewish émigrés entry into the United States. While often resisting these efforts the CJF and NCSJ and most other establishment groups supported the Israeli plan for "direct flights" via Bucharest which would deny most Soviet Jewish émigrés the right to determine their own destination.

Mikhail Gorbachev became General Secretary of the Communist Party on March 11, 1985 succeeding Konstantin Chernenko (Gitelman 1987:263). Initially, little changed for Soviet Jews despite Gorbachev's policies of *glasnost* (openness) and *perestroika* (restructuring).[2] During his first year "conditions of Soviet Jewry worsened" (Freedman 1988). Emigration remained low in the first two years, there were more Prisoners of Zion and his regime conducted a crackdown on Jewish culture (Freedman 1989: xv and Schifter 199:137).[3] Gorbachev opposed unrestricted emigration by Soviet citizens including

Soviet Jews ("NCSJ 1985–1986" submitted to LCBC, November 13, 1985, CJF files, box 667; and Friedgut 1989:13). He feared the loss of human capital.[4] He also considered Soviet emigration a domestic (internal) matter. His stand and policies would be altered, however, when he sought to achieve détente with the United States. He was more willing than those before him to "pay the ide-ological and political costs of strengthening Soviet ties with the United States and to go along with the United States on human rights issue, inter alia, with regard to easing restrictions on Jewish emigration and on the promotion of Jewish cultural life" (Goldman 1995:349).

The President of the United States and his Secretary of State favored dé-tente with the Soviet Union which they hoped would end the Cold War, re-duce nuclear arms and expand U.S.-USSR trade. Early on they made it clear to their Soviet counterparts that détente required freedom of emigration for Soviet Jews (and other specific groups) who wished to emigrate.[5] At times the United States suggested freedom of emigration for all Soviet citizens wanting to leave. In Schifter's view (1999:137) Jewish emigration remained an essential part of the fabric of Soviet American relations without becoming a key issue. While supporting human rights in general and emigration of So-viet Jews in particular, the Reagan Administration did not favor their linkage to arms control (Buwalda 1997:150–152).[6]

Importantly, the Reagan Administration and Secretary of State George Shultz placed the issue of human rights and in particular the right of Soviet Jews to emigrate on the agenda in almost every official American-Soviet meeting.[7] In his first meetings with Soviet Foreign Minister Andrei Gromyko in the fall of 1982 Shultz (1993:119–124) raised "problems of Jews, dissidents, and families divided by Soviet refusal to allow emigration" and persecution of those monitoring Helsinki.[8] He (1993:277) told the Senate Foreign Rela-tions Committee on June 15, 1983: "We have made clear that human rights cannot be relegated to the margins of international politics."

The Secretary of State took a personal interest in the plight of Soviet Jews. For him it was an issue "of deep moral principle."[9] In his memoirs he notes that one of his most moving experiences as Secretary of State was in late 1987 when he received a call from Ida Nudel, a leading "Prisoner of Zion" and "Refusenik," informing him of her release from the Soviet Union and ar-rival in Israel (1993:990). On official visits to the Soviet Union, he met with Soviet Jewish Refuseniks. In April 1987, for example, he attended a freedom Seder in Moscow with Ida Nudel, Vladimir Slepak and 40 other Refuseniks at Spaso House, the Moscow residence of the American Ambassador. He told them: "You are on our minds; you are in our hearts. We never give up. We never stop trying and in the end some good things do happen. But never give up, never give up" (Shultz 1993:86).[10]

Most importantly, Shultz had the support of President Reagan on this is-sue.[11] Clearly the "liberation" of Soviet Jews should be recorded as an accomplishment of President Ronald Reagan. He took up the subject of human rights "at each of his meetings with Secretary Gorbachev and with most visitors from the Soviet Union in the Oval Office" (Shultz 1993:1094 and "President Links Rights in Soviet to Summit Success" *NYT*, October 8, 1986). For example, in a meeting with Soviet Ambassador to the United States Anatoly Dobrynin in February 1983 President Reagan spoke about human rights, divided families, Soviet Jewry and Refuseniks and Pentecostals.[12]

Spearheading the human rights issues for the State Department was Richard Schifter, Assistant Secretary of State for Human Rights and Humanitarian Affairs and himself a Jewish refugee from Hitler's Germany.[13] Ironically, some Israelis saw his being a Holocaust survivor as "hurting" the interests of Israel. One Liaison Bureau official argued that he could not distinguish between Vienna 1938 and Moscow 1988 and refused to hinder the entry of Soviet Jewish refugees into the United States (Interview, Jerry Shiran, February 28, 2003). Over the years he worked hard to get the maximum number of Jews out of the Soviet Union. At times he seemed surprised at the willingness of the Soviets to accommodate his requests.

In the past much of the success of the NCSJ, the Union of Councils and the Soviet Jewry advocacy movement in general had been with Congress and local and state elected officials. It had always been harder to reach the President directly.[14] Advocacy groups often used friends in Congress to influence the White House. In trying to influence United States policy on the Soviet Union in the mid-1980s the NCSJ and its chairman Morris Abram focused on the President and his dealings with Secretary Gorbachev. They hoped to make the issue of freedom of emigration for Soviet Jews a condition of détente.[15] Nehemia Levanon (1989:74) praised the American Jewish leadership for winning over the President to support the issue. Importantly, in planning overall strategy as well as specific actions, Morris Abram, the NCSJ and CJF consulted with the Liaison Bureau and with Nehemiah Levanon (Interview, Jerry Goodman, January 10, 2001).[16] In contrast, the Union of Councils acted more independently of the Israelis (Memo, Eli Boyer to LCBC, July 8, 1982 (CJF files). It did, however, consult with the Liaison Bureau.

FIRST REAGAN-GORBACHEV SUMMIT

In preparation for the first summit between President Ronald Reagan and Secretary Mikhail Gorbachev scheduled for November 19 and 20, 1985, in Geneva, the NCSJ rallied Soviet Jewry activists throughout the United States. It declared November 19, 1985 a special day for Soviet Jewry ("NCSJ 1985–1986" submitted to LCBC, November 13, 1985, CJF files, Box 667).[17] On September 9, 1985, a NCSJ delegation met with the President and Secretary of State (NCSJ statement of Morris Abram on Reykjavik, October 10, 1986, CJF files, box 667).

Leaders of the NCSJ including Morris Abram (1989:10) realized that the over-riding American interest in détente with the Soviet Union concerned arms control and reductions. Several years later he recalled that in 1985 he was reluctant to link arms reductions with freedom of emigration for Soviet Jewry (Abram 1989). He did not think it propitious to raise the issue of freedom of emigration as a condition for negotiations in arms reductions. Instead, Abram focused his appeal to the President on the issue of "trust." He would argue that since the Soviets did not abide by the 1975 Helsinki Accords that they "cannot be trusted to comply with any agreement—especially one effecting its vital interests such as armaments. Therefore, President Reagan is morally right to insist on change in Soviet Policy in these areas; he is stating a political reality that new agreements are implicitly linked by trust as tested by experience with existing agreements" ("NCSJ Wrap Up Leadership Report: Soviet Jews: The case of Emigration" n.d., CJF files, box 593).

At the meeting in the White House on September 9, 1985, Morris Abram told President Reagan: "At the outset of the talks, the Soviet Union should be informed that it is very unlikely that the American people will trust the Soviets on new agreements affecting the vital security of both countries while they persist in violation of the humane provisions of the Helsinki accords. Under these circumstances United States negotiators could not, if they wished, lay to rest American distrust of the Soviet (Union). . . . The responsibility for this state of affairs and opportunity to reverse it rests with the USSR. . . . Mr. President, we ask you to raise the issue of Soviet Jewry with General Secretary Gorbachev in context of the justified suspicion of sincerity of the Soviet word felt by the American government and people and indignation that the Soviets treat the human rights agreements as if they never happened" (Abram 1989:11).

To Abrams's surprise President Reagan agreed. In doing so, Reagan placed the issue of freedom of emigration for Soviet Jews on the negotiating table.[18] Importantly, in meetings in Moscow before the summit Secretary of State Shultz met with Gorbachev who agreed to a four part agenda for Geneva including human rights (Shultz 1993:586–594).

Morris Abrams later reported that President Reagan told Gorbachev at Geneva: "I am telling you, Mr. Gorbachev, that the American people have a deep suspicion which will be rectified and satisfied and quelled only if it is demonstrated that you live up to your promises in the field of human rights. Your credibility is on the line and I, the President, as a leader of a free people cannot guarantee anything beyond what the Senate . . . and the people of the United States find it reasonable in their hearts to accept" (Comments by Morris Abram at NJCRAC, "Soviet Jewry after . . . ," February 14–17, 1988, CJF files, box 667).

Lawrence Grossman (1988:196) reported that the summit "had produced optimism, bordering on euphoria that Soviet leaders were prepared to liberalize emigration policy."[19] Gitelman (1987:267) reported that a "senior Reagan administration official" said that if the Soviet Union "would allow a "significant movement" of Jews and others from the USSR, the United States would move to ease trade restrictions." Many observers, however, noted mixed Soviet signals on the Jewish issue (Gitelman 265).[20] More arrests and harassment were reported (NCSJ flyer "Washington Mobilization" "Gorbachev is Coming to Washington" c. January 1986).[21] While 1,140 Jews had emigrated in 1985 only 914 would be allowed to leave in 1986. An estimated 400,000 had applied for invitations from relatives (Gitelman 1988:344).

Prior to and following the summit, the Soviets let some notable persons, including Anatoly (Natan) Sharansky leave (in February 1986) without significant changes in Soviet policies of limited emigration, harassment and repressing Jewish culture (Dershowitz 1991:250).[22] The releases generated positive publicity for the Soviet Union at relatively little cost (David Harris "After Sharansky? What's next for Soviet Jews," *Washington Post*, February 13, 1986 and "Opinion" *Washington Jewish Week*, February 13, 1986). Ironically, in releasing Sharansky they provided the Soviet Jewry advocacy movement with an imaginative, dynamic, charismatic, clever and indefatigable activist and leader. He would play a major role in mobilizing Western support for the movement. He opposed quiet diplomacy and favored activism. He both cooperated and operated independently of the Liaison Bureau and mainstream American Jewish organizations including the NCSJ. Grossman (1988:197) argues that he was closer to the Union of Councils and SSSJ.[23] However, he actively cooperated with the NCSJ to organize the mass protest in Washington, D.C., in December 1987.[24]

By January 1986 disappointment on Soviet emigration policy led Morris Abram to call on "the American government to link any future arms control agreement with the Soviets to human rights" (Grossman 1988:196).[25]

A SUMMIT IN WASHINGTON, D.C.?

President Reagan and Secretary Gorbachev agreed to hold the next summit in Washington, D.C., in 1986 and a third in the Soviet Union in 1987. In early 1986, the NCSJ launched a campaign for Summit II designed to mobilize American Jewry to participate in a mass protest at the forthcoming Washington, D.C., summit ("The Campaign to summit II," July 15, 1986, CJF files, box 555 and Letter, Shoshana Cardin to Morris Abram, March 1986, CJF files, box 555).[26] The initial co-chairs were Robert E. Loup, Chairman of the Board of Trustees of the UJA and Shoshana Cardin, President of CJF. The writer, Holocaust survivor and 1986 Nobel Peace Prize Laureate Eli Wiesel agreed to serve as Honorary Chair. NCSJ appointed a summit II task force composed of lay leaders and professionals from most major Jewish organizations including the Union of Councils. The task force focused on communications, synagogue mobilization, interreligious and interethnic affairs, international parliamentarians, state and local officials, satellite Seder groups and a mobilization group that would develop the program for the event and bring tens of thousands of demonstrators to Washington, D.C., ("The Campaign to Summit II," NCSJ document, c. March 20, CJF files, box 555, and September 8, 1986, CJF files, box 684).[27] NCSJ staff would coordinate and provide background resources.[28]

The expected budget exceeded one million dollars with national organizations funding (or providing in kind services) for $800,000 (Memo, Shoshana Cardin and Carmi Schwartz to Federation Executives and Presidents on Summit II, c. March 20, 1986, CJF files, box 555).[29] The NCSJ budget for summit II was $309, 250 most of which would be funded by Jewish federations. CJF told each federation what its "fair share" contribution would be. These funds were to be over and above regular federation allocation to NCSJ (Memo, Shoshana Cardin and Carmi Schwartz to Federation . . . , c. March 20, 1986, CJF files, box 555).

Organizers saw the proposed event as an opportunity to publicize in the United States the plight of Soviet Jews which the current Soviet regime tried to thwart through the release of certain well known prisoners and the use of other public relations gimmicks. They hoped to set a solid foundation of American opinion on human rights before public attention could shift to other matters, demonstrate to the Soviets that the issue of Soviet Jewry must be favorably addressed before relations between the superpowers would be normal, show full support for United States human rights initiatives as set forth by the President, continue directing the focus of Congressional activities on behalf of Soviet Jews and to ensure the largest Soviet Jewry rally ever held in Washington, D.C.

The Summit II task force worked to activate Jewish communities to participate in local and national events. It proposed that every community event in federations and synagogues throughout the United States held prior to the summit, either adapt or change the program to focus on Soviet Jewry and Summit II events ("To Summit II" NCSJ and "Campaign to Summit II," n.d. c. February 1986 Jewish Community Council of Greater Washington, CJF files).[30] They also wanted every city council and state legislature to pass resolutions on Soviet Jewry to demonstrate to President Reagan and Secretary Gorbachev that human rights were of the utmost important to the American people (NCSJ, "The Campaign To Summit II," c. March 1986, CJF files, box 555). In the words of CJF President Shoshana Cardin: Summit II, was an extraordinary time to place "the plight and cause of Soviet Jewry on the agenda of all Americans. We wish to inform General Secretary Gorbachev that the

American people stand behind Soviet Jews and their desire to leave the Soviet Union" (Memo, Shoshana Cardin and Carmi Schwartz to Federation . . . , c. March 20, 1986, CJF files, box 555).

Activities continued into the spring. Mass mailings went out via constituency organizations. For example the UJA produced 150,000 copies of "Matzoth of Hope" featuring Natan Sharansky and Summit II and prepared an 11-minute film on "Sharansky, The Struggle Continues" (Memo, Myrna Sheinbaum to Jerry Goodman, re: National Agency Projects for "The Campaign to Summit II," May 2, 1986, CJF files). Cardin informed federations to establish a task force in their communities to mobilize action under the direction of NJCRAC (Memo, Shoshana Cardin and Carmi Schwartz to federation presidents, May 21, 1986, CJF files, box 555).

In July 1986 an ongoing conflict over turf in the Soviet Jewry advocacy movement between NCSJ and NJCRAC resulted in reorganization within the Campaign to Summit II. Jacqueline Levine, representing NJCRAC became chairperson of the "Washington Mobilization" (Memo, Barbara Gaffin to Jerry Goodman, re: "Washington Mobilization, The Campaign to Summit II," July 9, 1986, CJF files, box 555).[31] She and her committee expected that the forthcoming visit of Secretary Gorbachev would begin on a Sunday in the fall at 12 noon at the Capitol and end at the Lincoln Memorial. In early September 1986 Levine reported that 56 communities in 24 states had formed local task forces for Summit II; they expected to come to Washington in impressive numbers. In planning a program she and her committee considered inviting Mary Travers, Charlton Heston and Yolanda King, persons from all sides of the political spectrum not including extremists, prominent members of labor business, human rights and academia. They also discussed involvement of high school bands, a Refusenik orchestra, and agreed to hold multiple events in Washington, D.C. sponsored by different groups, during the weekend of the summit (Memo of Jacqueline K. Levine, Washington Mobilization to NJCRAC and CJF Member Agencies," September 5, 1986, CJF files, box 684).[32]

Earlier, in late spring 1986 Shoshana Cardin had informed the CJF executive that should the Soviet Union open its gates we should cooperate to ensure that a maximum number could leave and that all should be encouraged to resettle in Israel, especially those without first degree family relationships in Western countries. She emphasized that we should consider all émigrés to Israel as having been resettled. She noted that the UJA, Jewish Agency, UIA, JDC, HIAS, NCSJ and CJF subscribed to this policy ("Executive Committee Meeting of CJF," April 18, 1986, CJF files, box 695).

By September 1986, however, the NCSJ also emphasized the possibility of some Jews preferring to remain in the Soviet Union. This is clearly evident in a position paper on Soviet Jewry given to Secretary of State George Shultz. While the "primary goal remains repatriation to Israel and reunification with kin" the document argued that many Jews in the Soviet Union wanted to be able to pursue Jewish learning and tradition (NCSJ "Rescuing Soviet Jewry", A Position Paper Submitted to Secretary of State George P. Shultz, September 17, 1986, CJF files, box 667). It proposed a set of priorities of permitting exit and emigration (e.g. limit security restrictions to five years and an annual emigration quota of 50,000).[33] It called on the Administration and Congress to continue to demonstrate that this issue was a fundamental stumbling block on the path to improved bilateral relations. It proposed holding firm on Jackson-Vanik ("Rescuing Soviet Jewry," September 17, 1986).[34] It stated that the issue at hand was not a Jewish issue but "a fundamental matter of human rights recognized in the Universal Declaration of Human Rights, the International Covenant on Civil and Political Rights and the Helsinki Final Act."

The document also lambasted Secretary Gorbachev for not fulfilling the expectation of change and liberalization of emigration and cultural freedom within the Soviet Union. It cited the figure of 370,000 Soviet Jews that had received letters of invitation from relatives and more than 11,000 Refuseniks. It noted that a joint Reagan-Gorbachev statement at Geneva pledged "resolution of humanitarian cases in the spirit of cooperation" ("Rescuing Soviet Jewry").[35] Despite his pledges to liberalize emigration Gorbachev had changed little.[36] It charged harassment of Refuseniks in violation of Helsinki and a new suppression of cultural and intellectual Jewish life including severing of ties between Soviet and overseas Jews by not delivering mail and cutting phone lines.[37]

SUMMIT IN REYKJAVIK

By September 25, 1986, NCSJ staff talked about a Summit II Washington, D.C. protest on December 7, 1986 (Minutes of Summit II Task Force Meeting, September 25, 1986, CJF files, box 555). The United States and the Soviet Union, however, announced that a special summit between President Reagan and Secretary Gorbachev would be held in Reykjavik, Iceland, in early October 1986.

Prior to Reykjavik, President Reagan met in the White House with freed Soviet dissident Yuri F. Orlov.[38] At a press conference with Orlov, President Reagan stated that "a substantive improvement in Soviet human rights was crucial for a summit meeting with Mikhail. S. Gorbachev in the United States." This was the first time that he linked Soviet human rights policies with summit meetings ("President Links Rights in Soviet to Summit Success" *NYT*, October 8, 1986).[39] The White House announced that President Reagan would raise the issue of Jewish emigration at the summit. He would follow the approach of President Nixon believing that you can "accomplish more in private than you can making public statements." The President then took Orlov to a meeting in the White House with representatives of religious and human rights groups involved in U.S.-USSR relations.[40] There he stated, "I will make it amply clear to Mr. Gorbachev that unless there is real Soviet movement on human rights, we will not have any kind of political atmosphere necessary to make lasting program on other issues. . . . true peace requires respect of human rights and freedom as well as arms control. Our agenda at the Reykjavik meeting will deal not only with arms reductions, but Soviet human rights violations" ("President Links Rights in Soviet Union to Summit success," *NYT*, October 8, 1986).[41]

That same day Secretary of State George Shultz spoke before 300 to 400 Jewish leaders in the Department of State and told them "our message to the Soviets is simple. Token gestures for short term lowering of barriers will not suffice. What the American people want to see is a genuine and lasting improvement in the situation of Soviet Jews as part of a broader commitment on the part of Soviet authorities to allow their citizens to exercise basic human rights, including freedom of movement" (Statement of Morris Abram on Reykjavik, October 10, 1986, CJF file, box 667).[42] Shultz quoted article 13, paragraph 3 of the Universal Declaration of Human Rights which states that "everyone has the right to leave a country, including his own" Then Shultz turned dramatically to the back of the document and said: "I see here the signature of Mr. Brezhnev. I believe that we have a right and a duty to monitor adherence to these provisions and insist that they be complied with" (Statement of Morris Abram at Reykjavik, October 10, 1986, CJF file, box 667).

The NCSJ had supplied Shultz as per his request with several documents prior to his departure for the summit. One was a brief memo about the emigration situation. It cited Article 13 of the Universal Declaration of Human Rights and Article 12 of the International Covenant on Civil and Political Rights and Principle 7 of Basket I and Basket II of the Helsinki Final Act. It noted that 330,000 Soviet Jews presently in the Soviet Union had received invitations from Israeli citizens and were registered in the Israeli Foreign Office. They also presented Shultz with a list of the names of 11,000 Refuseniks, many of whom had waited at least 5 years or more to leave. Some had been sentenced to labor camps during Secretary Gorbachev's tenure. The NCSJ received this information from the Liaison Bureau and updated and edited it with information from travelers, and helpful journalists (Letter, Jerry Goodman to Fred Lazin, December 29, 2003).[43] The memo offered an olive branch in suggesting that should the Soviets open the gates then Congress would probably respond reciprocally, hinting at waving the Jackson-Vanik Amendment. The memo demanded that all Soviet Jews be allowed to leave (NCSJ, "Soviet Jews: A Case for Emigration," October 8, 1986, CJF files, box 667).

Morris Abram led a small group of leaders of the American Soviet Jewry advocacy movement to Reykjavik. The group included Jerry Goodman, Executive Director of NCSJ; Theodore Mann, President of the American Jewish Congress and immediate past president of NJCRAC; Seymour Reich, President of B'nai B'rith International (and President of the Conference of Presidents);

Michael Pelavin, Chair of NJCRAC; Albert D. Chernin, Executive Vice Chair of NJCRAC; Alvin Pesky, Chair of Coalition to Free Soviet Jews (formerly GNYCSJ) and Ruth Popkin, President of Hadassah. They came to support their President and to lobby for the right of all Soviet Jews to emigrate. They argued that millions of Americans "are determined that the Jewish people, one-third of whom were annihilated in the Hitler Holocaust, will not stand alone in their determination that one-fifth of world Jewry (who live in the USSR) will not now be lost in the memory hole of history" (Statement of Morris Abram at Reykjavik, October 10, 1986).

    Many had high expectations that the Reykjavik talks would be significant for human rights and emigration of Jews in the Soviet Union (Bernard Weintraub, "Soviet Jewish Emigration Gains in Agenda" *NYT,* October 11, 1986; Grossman 1988:197–198; and George P. Shultz, "Agreement to . . . " *NYT,* October 19, 1986).[44] Afterwards Secretary of State Shultz claimed that human rights as promised "were front and center in Iceland." In his memoirs (1993:775) Shultz describes Reykjavik negotiations as a "stupendous success." Bernard Weintraub reported that the issue of rights "emerged as secondary to arms control" (Bernard Weintraub "Arms Issues Overshadowed Question of Rights in Soviet," *NYT,* October 13, 1986). The failure of the two heads of state to agree on arms control, however seemed to be a setback for human rights and Soviet Jewish emigration.[45] Yet, in Abrams view the summit in Reykjavik marked a real breakthrough ("Statement of Morris Abram on Reykjavik," October 10, 1986, CJF files, box 667).[46] He argued that the Soviet Union accepted the Reagan Administration's proposal "to discuss the easing of certain emigration restrictions . . . [specifically it] agreed to create a [joint] working group at Reykjavik to deal with humanitarian issues" including Jewish emigration (Letter, Morris Abram and Jerry Goodman to *NYT,* October 18, 1986 and Comments by Morris Abram at NJCRAC "Soviet Jewry after . . . ," February 14–17, 1988, CJF files, box 667). In Shultz's view (1993:776): "Reagan and Gorbachev agreed that human rights would become a regular and recognized part of our agenda." This was to be announced in a joint communiqué but none was issued.

    The General Assembly of the CJF met in Chicago in November 1986 shortly after Reykjavik. The resolutions reflect an uncertainty about the Soviet Jewry issue. They exhibit pessimism at the continuation of closed gates and cultural suppression. One resolution emphasized that the situation of Soviet Jewry had worsened, despite the thaw in U.S.-USSR relations, the revival of cultural exchanges and claims by Soviet authorities that the situation of Jews had improved. It cited 20,000 Refuseniks denied emigration, 400,000 Soviet Jews holding invitations for resettlement in Israel and the arrest of Hebrew teachers. In contrast, other resolutions indicated a reserved optimism at the presence of the issues of human rights and free emigration in the summit negotiations between President Reagan and Secretary Gorbachev.

One resolution put a most positive spin on Reykjavik noting that Soviet Jewry was no longer considered an internal Soviet issue, which represented "a significant departure from long–standing Soviet positions" (Resolutions at 55th General Assembly in Chicago, November 1986, CJF files, box 659). The CJF's General Assembly called on all federations to mobilize constituents for the next summit to be held in the United States.

CJF President Shoshana Cardin and Executive Vice-President Carmi Schwartz suggested canceling the scheduled December 1986 mobilization in Washington, D.C. should a meeting between Secretary Gorbachev and President Reagan not materialize. They had doubts about the financial and participatory support of the federations and other groups (Letter, Carmi Schwartz to Jerry Goodman, December 5, 1986, CJF files, Box 555).[47] The mobilization was cancelled.

SOVIET EMIGRATION POLICY AND DIRECT FLIGHTS

On January 1, 1987, the Soviets introduced new exit regulations which permitted any person with first degree relatives abroad (including the United States) to apply to be reunited provided that they were not in possession of security information and would not leave behind dependent relatives that needed support.[48] Some saw this as codifying previous restrictive practices. They expected a reduction in emigration since it would limit *vysovs* (letters of invitation) to those with close relatives abroad and exclude those with state secrets and/or who supported others (Gitelman 1988:344 and 1989:357).[49] Others saw progress and change in the publication of the regulations, allowing visits by Soviet citizens to relatives abroad and by the promise of allowing *vysovs* from relatives in the West. The official American response was "subdued and qualified" reflecting American policy of welcoming change but reminding the Soviets of existing shortcomings in emigration policy (Schifter 1999: 138, 139). In practice the Soviets only required first degree relative invitations for new applicants. Previous applicants were required to submit a new *vysov* and new invitation from abroad without having to prove closeness to the inviting relative. Soviet authorities also allowed some long term Refuseniks to leave even if they did not have a first degree relative abroad. In February 1987, 146 persons left the USSR, the largest number in any month during the past four years. It soon rose to a rate of 400 and then 700 per month (Schifter 1999:139). On March 20, 1987 the *NYT* reported that 10,000 Jews were expected to emigrate in 1987. This would be 10 times the number allowed to leave in the previous year.[50]

On March 31, 1987 the *NYT* reported that the Soviet Union planned to allow a major increase in Soviet Jewish emigration (David Shipler, "Two Say Soviet Plans to Let Jews Leave," *NYT*, March 31, 1987 and Memo, Al Chernin to NJCRAC and CJF Member Agencies, "Report by Morris Abram on Trip to Moscow, April 1, 1987," CJF file, box 667). Shipler focused on the 3 day Moscow visit in March 1987 of Edgar Bronfman of the World Jewish Congress and Morris Abram of the NCSJ and President of the Conference of Presidents.[51] In meetings with top Soviet officials, they received promises of expanded emigration, direct flights via Romania and a liberalization of restrictions on Jewish cultural and religious life in the Soviet Union (NCSJ, news release statement by M. Abram, April 1, 1987, CJF files, box 667 and Freedman [1989b:90]).[52] Both Bronfman and Abram hinted that such changes could result in a relaxation of the Jackson Vanik and Stevenson resolutions (Gitelman 1989:358ff.).[53]

In a public statement Abrams qualified the Shipler article. He emphasized, however, that although *glasnost* (openness in public life) and "new thinking" in foreign affairs (Buwalda 1997:147,148) provided a window of opportunity, that on issues of emigration and freedom the test remained actual Soviet performances. As to Jackson-Vanik he suggested only considering waivers for the time being that would be based on "a very substantial and sustained emigration" (Abram, Press Release, April 1, 1987).

By October 1987 Richard Schifter and others in the State Department believed that the Soviets had changed their emigration policies toward the Jews. They had waived the first degree relative requirement for nationality groups for which the doors of emigration had opened (Jews, Armenians and Germans but not for others). On the second barrier—the consent of relatives—they removed the siblings but kept parents of spouse. In practice there were few objections. As for security clearance, it proved hard to enforce. In Schifter's view the Soviet Foreign Ministry was turning from an adversary to an ally (Schifter 1999:144, 145) This was later confirmed during the Reagan-Gorbachev summit in Washington, D.C. (1999:147).

Yet some remained skeptical. In fall 1987 Shultz (1993:994) noted greater progress with the emigration of Germans than with Jews in the Soviet Union. He sarcastically informed Soviet Foreign Minister Shevardnadze that the Jews too had a homeland and reminded him that he (Shevardnadze) had been quoted in Uruguay as saying that any Jew could leave.[54] Anthony Lewis (*NYT*, September 18, 1987) emphasized that for the time being the Soviets denied most Jews the right to leave while giving freedom to celebrity cases in hopes of reducing American pressures. A *NYT* editorial of October 19, 1987 "In Moscow, Rights by the Drop," expanded on this theme. While noting that emigration was up and that most Refuseniks would be allowed to leave, it called on Gorbachev "to change the rules for all, Jews and non-Jews, and not just bend them for a few."[55] Even Morris Abram admitted that emigration in 1987 was one seventh of what it had been under Brezhnev (Grossman 1989:227ff).

With prospects of increased Jewish emigration becoming a reality, the issue of dropouts and a potential conflict between proponents of freedom of choice and resettlement in Israel loomed large. Israeli political leaders and the Liaison Bureau realized that if the gates would open the overwhelming majority of Soviet Jews who wanted to leave would prefer the United States to Israel. To partially prevent this from happening the Liaison Bureau proposed "direct flights" from Eastern European cities to Israel which they hoped to begin by mid-1987 (David Harris "The controversy over Refugee Status of Soviet Jewish Émigrés," AJC publication, May 25, 1987, CJF files). This would involve Soviet Jews leaving the Soviet Union for Bucharest, Budapest or Warsaw and then flying to Israel. Chances for dropping out were minimal in these Communist dictatorships. Consequently, Soviet Jews not obtaining visas for the West would either stay in the Soviet Union or immigrate to Israel.

Bill Keller ("Soviet Said to Plan Emigration Shift Favored by Israel," *NYT*, March 30, 1987) reported that the Soviet Union had agreed that future émigrés to Israel would be sent by way of Romania.[56] Rabbi Arthur Schneier, President of the Appeal for Conscience Foundation, claimed that he had negotiated the deal with the Soviets in Romania and in Moscow (Interview, Conscience, August 2002).[57] He claimed to have the assurances from Alexander N. Yakovlev, Anatoly Dobrynin and President Nicolae Ceausescu (Keller, "Soviet Said . . . ," March 30, 1987).[58] According to Schneier the Soviets agreed because they thought without an option to drop out that fewer would emigrate. Gur-Gurevitz (1996:77,78) claims that Prime Minister Shamir got President Ceausescu's approval in May 1987 but that the Dutch refused to cooperate in Moscow as they favored freedom of choice.[59]

Unlike the late 1970s and early 1980s the leadership of the American Jewish establishment including the CJF exhibited a greater understanding of the Israeli position. Most leaders chose not to challenge Israeli efforts to insure a greater number of Soviet Jews going to Israel via "direct flights." In sharp contrast, they would oppose Prime Minister Shamir's efforts to have the American government deny Soviet Jewish émigrés entry into the United States as refugees. In supporting "direct flights," the CJF and most other major American Jewish organizations qualified their support for "freedom of choice." Officially, they continued to support it; in practice they abandoned it (John Goshko "Jewish Leaders Say Soviet May Let Thousands emigrate," *Washington Post*, March 31, 1987).

According to David Harris (AJC, May 25, 1987), "American Jewish organizations have, virtually without exception, voiced support for direct flights, recognizing that there would be few serious grounds on which to object." He added that if the Soviets would allow other Soviet Jews to join their families in the West then the problem would be solved. At the time, however, Soviet policy restricted the obtaining of visas to the West.[60]

The position of the CJF was almost ingenuous. It believed that "direct flights will solve many more problems than it will create and that direct flights is in fact the optimal approach for the rescue of Soviet Jews and their survival and continuity as Jews" (Minutes of Soviet Jewry Advocacy Study Committee, April 9, 1987, CJF files, box 667). The CJF viewed direct flights as intergovernmental arrangements which only involved the governments of Israel, Romania, and the Soviet Union. This is contrasted to the past situation in Vienna which involved non-governmental groups including the Jewish Agency, HIAS and JDC (Notes re: "Soviet Jewish Immigration, Refugee Status and Direct Flight Issues," April 8, 1987, CJF files, box 667). CJF admitted that while they may have some serious concerns about movement of Soviet Jews through Eastern Europe and boarding direct flights to Israel "all this will take place under governmental auspices . . . if there is some disruption in this process because of Soviet Jews demonstrate and the like it becomes the responsibility of government to act" (Ibid.).[61]

In the spring of 1987 the Union of Councils opposed direct flights (Gur-Gurevitz [1996:7] and Minutes of Soviet Jewry Advocacy Study Committee, April 9, 1987, CJF files, box 667). According to Naftalin (1999:236,237) while the Councils understood the needs of Israel they favored freedom of choice because that was the position of the Refusenik leadership.[62] They preferred a dual track system of allowing Soviet Jews to apply in Moscow to immigrate to either the United States or Israel.

At the CJF Quarterly in the end of April 1987 CJF President Shoshana Cardin met with American Jewish leaders and Jewish Agency officials in hope of reaching a consensus on advocacy for Soviet Jewry ("Notes for Shoshana Cardin on Soviet Jewish Emigration" April 27, 1987, CJF files, box 710).[63] She outlined three scenarios that were to be followed simultaneously as if the other two were not taking place. First she argued that Jewish Agency and Israeli Government officials "would welcome a program whereby Soviet Jews in the United States should aggressively pursue letters of invitation to their relatives in the Soviet Union for direct migration of these relatives to the United States under the framework of family reunification." She admitted that although *CJF had thought of this in previous years it had never been implemented vigorously "for fear may dilute the invitation program from Israel."* She argued that for this to succeed the Department of State had to transmit documents to the Soviet authorities and to get their consent for exit to the United States for family reunification.

Second, CJF et al. would meet with the leadership in Congress and the Administration "to facilitate a more realistic view of numbers of Soviet Jews who may arrive in the United States in this Fiscal Year (FY) and increase the numbers related to block grant to accurately reflect the number of Jews emigrating."[64]

Third, she reiterated that we agreed for some period of time "that direct flights would be the optimal way of bringing Soviet Jews to Israel and helping to maintain and enhance their Jewish profile and their Jewish future."

She repeated the Liaison Bureau line that this would also protect the "effectiveness and dignity of the Israeli visa" a concern for Israeli government and Jewish leadership. She argued that direct flights need not create serious problems and complexities: "All agree that all Soviet Jews arriving in Israel should be resettled in Israel as has been the case with each and every Jewish emigration from whatever land to Israel." Should they want to leave after they arrive free to do so on their own: "world Jewry and Israel . . . acquits itself of resettling Jews only once." For those arriving with relatives only in the West, she argued, the consensus was that they should be given the opportunity to reunite with their families under the auspices of the refugee status program.[65]

SUMMIT III—WASHINGTON, D.C.

The high point of the Soviet Jewry Movement in general and the NCSJ in particular was the Washington Demonstration on December 6, 1987, prior to Summit III involving President Reagan and Secretary Gorbachev.[66] In October 1987, President Reagan and Secretary Gorbachev issued a call to the summit in Washington, D.C., to discuss missile reductions, human rights, humanitarian issues and regional issues (Comments by Morris Abram at NJCRAC, "Soviet Jewry after . . . ," February 14-17, 1988, CJF files, box 667).

The NCSJ convened a coalition for mobilization for the demonstration. The CJF via its federations provided much of the funding and called on American Jewry to mobilize for Summit III (Minutes, CJF Board of Directors, November 18, 1987, CJF files, box 659 and Minutes of CJF Executive Committee Meeting, September 14, 1987, CJF files, box 695).[67] CJF expected that the mobilization in Washington, D.C. would be preceded by a campaign of rallies and other events throughout the United States and Canada in support of the American policy "that the Soviet Union must permit the emigration of Soviet Jews." The event "will provide the American Jewish community with an opportunity to demonstrate that the plight of Soviet Jewry is a burning national concern" (Meeting, CJF Board of Directors, September 15, 1987, CJF files, box 659).

The NCSJ in cooperation with eight other Soviet Jewry/umbrella organizations organized the demonstration. Over 50 national Jewish organizations and 300 local federations and community relations councils participated (Bulletin III Campaign to the Summit, October 21, 1987, CJF files, box 667) and (Grossman 1989:227ff.).[68] The Union of Councils participated fully. As with the Summit II campaign NJCRAC played a central role both in Washington, D.C. and throughout the United States.[69] Jacqueline Levine, its past President co-chaired and Eli Wiesel served as honorary chair (Memo, Jacqueline Levine to NJCRAC and CJF member Agencies, "Materials on Washington

Mobilization, Bulletin #3, October 23, 1987, CJF files, box 667).[70] Natan Sharansky traveled from city to city to recruit support and participants. His call for 400,000 or more demonstrators frightened some Jewish leaders who had doubts about mobilizing large number of American Jews for a rally in Washington, D.C. (Bayer 1989). When some had reservations about the rally he threatened to hold it himself. Some Israelis and American Jewish professionals believe that he challenged American Jews in a very positive way (Foxman 1989 and Frankel 1989).

CJF and others pressured NCSJ to appoint David Harris, the AJC's Washington, D.C. representative and a former NCSJ staff member as the national coordinator of the event in Washington, D.C., (Memo, Morris Abram to NCSJ Executive Committee, February 8, 1988, CJF files).[71] He headed a committee of several staff on loan from other Jewish organizations including Ted Comet of CJF. Behind the scenes the CJF pressured for broad and comprehensive cooperation among Jewish organizations (Memos, Dan Shapiro to CJF Advisory Study Committee, October 22, 1987 and November 3, 1987, CJF files, box 667).[72]

Harris realized that he had a difficult task. After the summit was announced; he had only 37 days to make final preparations for the rally on December 6, 1987. The largest Soviet Jewish rally in D.C. had never attracted more than 12,000 persons.

Harris and his steering committee put together a 90-minute program, which lasted for 2 hours and 15 minutes.[73] Harris did not want criticism of President Reagan or his policies that opposed linkage between Jewish emigration and disarmament.[74] Harris's committee excluded anti-communist elements. Speakers included Vice President George Bush, Speaker of the House, Richard Schifter, representatives of civil rights groups, labor, Ed Koch represented the National Conference of Mayors, Bishop William Keller of the National Conference of Catholic Bishops, Dr. Arie Brower of the National Council of Churches, Jane Fonda, Mary Travis and Pearl Bailey, presidential candidates, and members of Congress from both parties.[75] There was a minimum of Jewish speakers. Morris Abram as head of the Conference of Presidents spoke as did Elie Wiesel and several Soviet Jewish activists (Harris 1989:32). At the end Morris Abram, Elie Wiesel, Yuri Edelstein, Natan Sharansky, Yosef Mendelowitz and Ida Nudel locked arms and sang the Israeli national anthem *Hatikvah*. An estimated 250,000 persons had participated (Comments by Morris Abram at NJCRAC, "Soviet Jewry after . . . " February 14–17, 1988, CJF files, box 667).[76]

Many of the Jewish leaders at the rally thought of the Holocaust and the helplessness of the American Jewish community at that time to assist European Jewry. It may have been best articulated by Rabbi James Rudin (1990) who recalled: "But the guilt was there, and there was a sense of 'God damn it, we're going to do in '87 for the Soviet Jews what we could have done and should have done or might have done earlier.'" Harris (1989:21) later commented that in light of the helplessness in the 1930s, the Washington, D.C. rally was like an "empowerment of American Jewry, a realization of its own growth and maturation and size and power to things in the street when necessary."

The demonstration helped the American government convince the Soviets that the issue of "freedom of emigration" for Jews was important to the American people and their elected leaders. A person at the summit told Richard Schifter that after greeting Gorbachev at the White House, the President asked him: "Have you heard about the rally on the Mall last Sunday?" Gorbachev responded yes and that he wanted to get on with the business of the meeting, "But Reagan did not let him. He started to talk about the size of the turnout, how much the Soviet emigration issue meant to many Americans, and how important it was that the Soviet Union respond positively" (Schifter 1999:145–147).[77] David Harris (1988:19) claims that President Reagan said to Secretary Gorbachev: "You have seen on December the 6th the breadth and depth of American support—not American Jewish—American support for the issue. It won't go away."

In a meeting with Secretary of State George Shultz on January 6, 1988, Morris Abram found the Secretary cautiously optimistic. He said that the President told him that he expected substantial progress on the issue of Soviet Jewish emigration. Schultz believed that the Soviet leadership understood how important this issue was to us. Schifter believed that Schultz made this crystal clear to Shevadnadze.

Schifter concluded that by the time that Gorbachev left Washington, D.C., we were "reasonably optimistic that the human rights situation in the Soviet Union . . . would improve and so would Soviet emigration policy." (1999:147). In a short period of time he realized however that the breakthrough might be short lived. Evidently, some parts of the Soviet bureaucracy had different interpretations of Soviet policy (Schifter 1999:148). Some KGB officials on local levels refused to cooperate. In early 1988 there were problems again with matters of first degree relatives, support for relatives and security.

While about 8,000 Soviet Jews left the Soviet Union in 1988, nine times the number that emigrated in 1986, both NCSJ and Union of Councils expressed dismay that more had not been allowed to emigrate ("Soviet Jewry Emigration in 'Glasnost' Year: 8000" *Jewish Week*, January 15, 1988. The Union of Councils and SSSJ wanted to stand firm against the Soviet Union. They opposed a liberalization of American trade policy and concessions toward the Soviet Union until the gates opened. The SSSJ urged a boycott of American firms dealing with the Soviet Union. The NCSJ remained more cautious (Grossman 1989).

David Shipler, writing in the *NYT* in early January 1988 indicated that some high administration officials had reservations as to whether the Soviet Union

would allow free emigration of Jews (David Shipler, "Law on Emigration in
Effect in Soviet; U.S. Sees Tightened Rules—Earlier Preference for Jews now
Apparently at End," *NYT*, January 2, 1988). He wrote that the new Soviet law
would allow 30,000 to 40,000 citizens to emigrate yearly. Those eligible
would be close family members (limited now to parent, child, sibling and/or
spouse). The new law banned discrimination on the basis of racial, ethnic,
religious and other grounds, which "has been interpreted abroad as ending
the preference given to Jews in the past." Many Latvian, Lithuanian, German
and Ukrainians in the Soviet Union would now be able to emigrate. The Soviets had told Schifter that they did not intend to return to the mass emigration figures of the earlier Brezhnev period.

In effect, the Soviets might be willing to liberalize emigration across the
board for some while denying mass emigration for the Jews. This placed
American Jews in the Soviet Jewry advocacy movement in a dilemma. At
stake now was the general liberalization versus the interest of the Jewish minority in the Soviet Union. For the American Jewish leadership the latter took
precedence over the former (Hand notes, Soviet Jewry International Council, November 30, December 1, 1988, Jewish Agency archives).

This position is evident in the response of American Jewry to the 1987 Mc-
Clure Amendment denying the Most Favored Nation (MFN) status to the Soviet Union until it complied with all Helsinki clauses which meant freedom
of emigration for all Soviet citizens and not just for Jews. Morris Abram and
others from the NCSJ spoke with Senator Phil Gramm and told him that the
Jackson-Vanik Amendment was a Jewish amendment "and if you tie it to
general human rights, there can never be any incentive for the Soviet Union
to behave toward the Jews in anticipation of the relief in trade." Gramm influenced his fellow Senator to withdraw the amendment (Abram 1989:24).

By early February 1988, Morris Abram expressed guarded pessimism. He
noted that most of the Jews allowed to emigrate by Secretary Mikhail Gorbachev had been Refuseniks that had waited a long time to leave.[78] He and
others referred to tougher regulations for those wanting to leave. Also Gorbachev had spoken again about a "brain drain" problem when in Washington, D.C., in December 1987. Abram urged the Soviet Jewry advocacy movement to hold fast on Jackson-Vanik and to continue to pressure the United
States government and even American businesses that wanted to enter the
Soviet market (Comments by Dr. Arnold Horelick, Director Rand/UCLA Center for the Study of Soviet International Behavior and by Morris Abram at
NJCRAC, " Soviet Jewry after . . . ," February 14–17, 1988, CJF files, box 667).
He urged that American Jews push the issue in the forthcoming elections.[79]
Nevertheless, the Coalition to Free Soviet Jewry cancelled the March 1988
Solidarity Day demonstration which in the past had attracted over 100,000
persons annually in New York City (Grossman 1990:265).[80] The cancellation
indicates that many of the major activists in the Soviet Jewry advocacy move-

ment including those with very close ties to the Liaison Bureau, believed that significant change in Soviet Policy toward Jewish emigration and cultural and religious freedom had occurred.

Mixed signals continued to appear. Wolf Blitzer reported that the Soviets told Secretary of State George Shultz in February that they would not enforce the first-degree relative requirement for this year (Blitzer, 1988).[81] In the *Jewish Week* of March 11, 1988, an article quoted the American envoy to the UN Human Rights Commission in Geneva saying that his country believed that the changes in the USSR had been more superficial and cosmetic than fundamental" ("US Envoy Calls Glasnost Cosmetic," *Jewish Week*, March 11, 1988).[82]

THE FINAL REAGAN-GORBACHEV SUMMIT

President Ronald Reagan and Secretary Mikhail Gorbachev held a final summit in Moscow in late Spring 1988. Beforehand, Morris Abram, head of NCSJ and the Conference of Presidents gave Secretary of State George Shultz a memo "In preparation for the Moscow Summit: Emigration" which incorporated nine points approved by NCSJ at their March 10, 1988 meeting. It demanded free emigration for all Jews that wanted to leave, provisions for direct flights and full cultural, religious and educational rights for those that would remain (Letter of Morris B. Abram to George Shultz, April 13, 1988, CJF files, box 667).[83] It emphasized: "that in regard to Jewish emigration . . . the next procedure must be sustained, systematic and substantial." It demanded more opportunities to study at universities. It also called for a cessation of jamming of the Voice of Israel (Kol Israel) to the Soviet Union.

Abram and other Jewish leaders met with Secretary Shultz on May 3, 1988 (Minutes, CJF Board of Directors, April 19, 1988, CJF files, box 659). Also present was a CJF delegation headed by Richard Maass, former President of the NCSJ. CJF had brought a large delegation of Jewish leaders to Washington, D.C. for a summit action day for Soviet Jewry. They were briefed at the State Department and visited with members of Congress and with officials of non-governmental organizations and various envoys of Helsinki Accord signatory nations.

Several American Jewish leaders followed President Reagan to Helsinki where he stopped off on his way to Moscow from May 25–29, 1988.[84] They would also participate in activities in Moscow. Ted Comet recalls that Finnish authorities banned protests against Gorbachev in Helsinki. They did permit, however, a pro Reagan demonstration. In a speech in Helsinki President Reagan stated: "There is no true international security without respect for human rights. The greatest creative and moral force in this new world, the greatest hope for survival and success, for peace and happiness, is human freedom" He went on to ask bluntly "Why Soviet citizens who wish to exercise their right to emigrate should be subject to artificial quotas and arbitrary rulings. And what are we to think of the continued suppression of those who wish to practice their religious beliefs" (Shultz 1993:1101,1102).

At Helsinki Morris Abram invited Secretary Shultz to attend Friday night religious services at the Jewish Community Center in Helsinki. He agreed to go if it would help the cause. Before an audience of over a thousand people Shultz at a dinner after the services stated: "We're here because we know of the plight of Soviet Jewry and we want to make a statement about that on the eve of an important meeting." He added with indignation: "We really can't see for the life of us why people should not be allowed to live their lives as they want to live them, to worship as they want to worship" ("Shultz Makes a Pledge To support Soviet Jews" *NYT*, May 28, 1988).

In Moscow President Reagan hosted the Zieman family, Refuseniks who had applied to leave in 1977 and another 98 Refuseniks at Spaso House, during the first day of his talks in Moscow (Richter 1989:55).[85]

The Summit of May–June 1988 in Moscow led to an increase in exit visas and a liberalization in the cultural and religious life of Soviet Jews.[86] Officially CJF called on federations to remain active in the fight for the freedom of Soviet Jews to emigrate and for rights for those that chose to remain. Despite Gorbachev, the summits and *Glasnost* over 400,000 potential émigrés remained "trapped" in the Soviet Union" (CJF memo "Recommendations to Strengthen Soviet Jewry Advocacy," June 17, 1988, CJF files, box 667 and Arkin 1988). For years conservative elements who opposed emigration prevented the Soviet leadership from passing legislation to make emigration a civil right and enact procedures to convince Jews and others that an application to leave would not invite harassment and would succeed (Ro'I: 62). Nevertheless the stage was set for a massive exodus as well as the foundations for a revival of Jewish cultural and religious life in the Soviet Union.

CONCLUSION

During the Gorbachev period the Israelis reached an agreement in principal with the Soviets which allowed direct flights via Bucharest, Budapest and Warsaw. This was a means of preventing dropping out in Vienna. The American Jewish establishment supported the Israeli position. They had retreated from their previous commitment to freedom of choice. If the Israelis could achieve an agreement with the Soviets on direct flights then they would stand behind the agreement and not challenge it.

The Union of Councils in opposing direct flights argued in favor of a dual process of emigration with freedom for Soviet Jews in the Soviet Union to choose to emigrate either to the West or to Israel. This had been proposed earlier by the Liaison Bureau and adopted by the Committee of Eight. The Soviets, however, had not agreed to allow Jews in large numbers to apply in Moscow for visas for family reunification in the West.

Ironically, in late spring and early summer of 1988 the Soviets balked on the apparent agreement on direct flights via Eastern Europe. At the same time, Soviet authorities indicated that more Jews would be allowed to emigrate. The only way out for most Soviet Jews was on a visa for Israel. Increased emigration, therefore meant many more dropouts and Jewish refugees coming to the United States which angered the Israelis. American authorities and American Jewish leaders expected a dramatic increase in the number of Jewish refugees entering the United States. This in turn revived the issue of freedom of choice. As noted here, by 1988 the CJF clearly wanted most Soviet Jews to go to Israel. *In supporting the proposed direct flights the CJF had deserted the principle of freedom of choice. Would American Jewry desert it again in the face of its own government's reservations about accepting the expected large number of Soviet Jews who wanted to come to the United States rather than to Israel?*

NOTES

1. In writing speeches for Congressmen at the December 1987 D.C. rally David Geller emphasized emigration and cultural and religious rights for those that remained. By 1989 the Conference of Presidents of Major American Jewish Organizations called for expansion of Jewish life in the Soviet Union. In February 1988 (*Jewish Week*, February 19, 1988) the board of B'nai B'rith voted to open an office in Moscow. They believed that two million Jews would remain in the USSR.

2. Ambassador Douglas, Coordinator for Refugee Affairs, told a Congressional Subcommittee in April 1985 that "All of us sense that there may be some improvements coming in the Soviet Jewish exits from the Soviet Union . . . . We may not know by the summer whether this is going to be true."

3. Gorbachev would end the life of the Soviet Public anti-Zionist Committee which had been set up on April 21, 1983. It functioned actively until late 1985. By the fall of 1987 it was clear that the Soviet government had decided to abandon the Committee which proved anomalous to the détente (Korey 1989; Spier, 1989). Ironically the new freedom in the Soviet Union allowed the anti-Semitic organization Pamyat to surface and become active (Dershowitz 1991:267).

4. Morris Abram (1989:9) claimed that Secretary Gorbachev told President Reagan during the last summit "no reason why this brain drain should be allowed to continue." In 1987 Gorbachev told Tom Brokaw that the campaign for Jewish emigration was an attempt to "organize a 'brain drain'" and that the Soviet Union would "never accept a condition when people are being exhorted from the outside to leave their country" (Gitelman 1989:357). Ro'i (1996: 62) argues that even when the gates would be open that Gorbachev wanted to create incentives to have Jews stay because he wanted their talents and skills for the success of perestroika.

5. Vice President George Bush in a meeting in Moscow after Gorbachev took office told the new Soviet leader that he must "understand that this issue (human rights) is extremely important to the President and the American people" (Shultz 1993:531). Bush mentioned the denial of Jewish emigration, the persecution of Hebrew teachers, the treatment of dissidents and the violations of the spirit of the Helsinki accords (Buwalda 1997:148).

6. Shultz (1993:488) favored addressing every "issue on its merits: we would press on what was right for Soviet Jews whether things were going well or poorly on other issues of concerns." While Shultz (1993:265,266) also preferred quiet diplomacy and avoiding embarrassing the Soviet Union, he often acted otherwise.

7. Shultz served as Secretary from June 1982 (following Haig's resignation) until January 21, 1989 (Shultz 1993:xi,3).

8. Prior to the meeting, Shultz (1993:121) met with American Jewish leaders and with Avital Sharansky, wife of imprisoned Anatoly (Natan) Sharansky. He told her: "The President and I will never give up on pressing the cause of human rights and the case for your husband's release."

9. Schifter (1999:156,157) argues that within the government Shultz is the "person deserving special thanks and special credit." Some Jewish leaders had reservations about Shultz's appointment due to his association with the Bechtel Corporation. They considered him an "Arabist" and anti-Israel. Max Fisher did not agree. He had easy access to Shultz (Golden 1992:434). Nehemia Levanon considered Senator Jackson and Secretary Shultz to be the two Americans who helped most on Soviet Jewry. According to Morris Abram (1989:18–20): "Shultz's attitude was, and is, I shall leave a deposition so strong, so firm, that it never can be erased." While appreciative of the efforts on behalf of Soviet Jewry by President George Bush and Secretary of State James Baker, Abram felt that they lacked Schulz's passion. Baker discontinued Shultz's practice of meeting American Jewish leaders before each summit.

10. The Seder was broadcast to the United States and the rest of the world. Later that night he met with Gorbachev who protested his participation in the Seder (Shultz (1993:886 and Gitelman 1989b:358).

11. In 1984 Reagan received almost 35 percent of the Jewish vote. Thereafter, Max Fisher and others established the National Jewish Coalition in Washington, D.C. to sensitize Republican decision makers to concerns of Jews and to encourage Jewish participation in Republican Party politics (Golden 1992:447 and Charlotte Jacobson 1990).

12. Several Pentecostal Christians took refuge in the American Embassy in Moscow in 1978. Secretary Shultz used Max Kampleman, the chief negotiator in Madrid who had close ties with a KGB General in the Soviet delegation, to negotiate their release and emigration (Shultz 1993:165–171,281).

13. Some referred to him as the Zionist in the State Department (Interview, August 2, 1995). Schifter (1999:136) thought often of his failure to rescue his parents from Hitler in 1941when 45 years later "it fell to me to help initiate the third major Jewish exodus from the Soviet Union."

14. According to Yoram Dinstein (1989:23) the Soviet Jewry advocacy movement had little influence in the White House until the Leningrad trial.

15. In May 1985 the NCSJ intensified efforts with the corporate world, Congress and the White House ("NCSJ 1985–1986" November 13, 1985 submitted to LCBC (CJF files, box 667 and Note: Morris Abram to Robert H. Naftaly, October 20, 1986 (CJF

files, box 667). "It hoped to establish "Policy Advisory Committee" to involve academicians, former government officials, corporate executives and other influential people. "On April 7, 1987 the Congressional Coalition for Soviet Jews, a NCSJ affiliate with 86 Senators and 235 Congressmen, Congressional Wives for Soviet Jewry and NCSJ's National Advisory Council sponsored a national freedom Seder for Soviet Jews in Washington, D.C. House and Senate leaders from both parties served as honorary chairpersons (*Jewish Week*, April 17, 1987; "NCSJ Congressional Update" 2 #2, March 13, 1987, CJF files, box 593).

16. After leaving his position as head of the Liaison Bureau, Levanon remained in contact with many leaders and activists in the Soviet Jewry Movement. Goodman and others suggest that Morris Abram paid deference to Levanon; others see Levanon as Abram's guru. In 1987, Morris Abram checked with Levanon before accepting an invitation from Edgar Bronfman of WJC to visit the Soviet Union (Levanon 1989). Also see Comments by Morris Abram at NJCRAC, "Soviet Jewry after . . . ," February 14–17, 1988 (CJF files, box 667).

17. In September 1985 it hosted the International Council of the World Conference of Soviet Jewry in Washington, D.C. and placed an ad in the *NYT*.

18. According to David Harris (1989:60–68) the genius of American diplomacy of the 1980s was to seek to weave the issue of Soviet Jewry into the broader fabric of Soviet American relations. This prevented the Soviets from separating security and trade issues from human rights. Gur-Gurevitz (1996:13) notes that Prime Minister Margaret Thatcher supported President Reagan's linking of human rights and Soviet Jews with disarmament.

19. In Schifter's (1999:137) view the American delegation returned from Geneva with optimism. A few weeks before the summit rumors circulated about a Soviet offer to release 15,000 Soviet Jews (Freedman (1989b:83) says 20,000) who would be flown directly to Israel prior to the summit. Nothing ever came of this (Sheldon Engel Mayer, "Mass Airlift Seen near for Soviet Jews," *Jewish Week*, November 1, 1985). Gitelman (1987:265) suggests that Shimon Peres indicated that the French government would be willing to fly Soviet Jews to Israel should the Soviets change their policy in exchange for their inclusion in Middle East peace negotiations. According to Freedman (1989b:91ff) Shamir opposed their inclusion. He reported on a meeting in France between the Soviet and Israeli Ambassadors in July of 1985. They discussed renewal of diplomatic ties, emigration and Soviet involvement in Middle East Peace talks. Israel wanted a resumption of diplomatic relations and free emigration and the Soviets wanted a partial withdrawal from Golan, that émigrés go to Israel and that Israel cease its anti-Soviet activities in the United States. Freedman argues that Soviet Middle East politics and not Soviet Jewry influenced Soviet Israeli relations at this time. Freedman (1988) notes that shortly after Gorbachev came to power *Izvestia* published Israeli President Herzog's remarks on the fiftieth anniversary of the victory of the Allies over Hitler. Before resumption of diplomatic relations the Soviets approved of a renewal of Israeli diplomatic ties with Poland and Hungary.

20. Yaakov Ro'I (1997:60,61) has suggested that during this period that Soviet officials deliberately issued conflicting signals to deter would be émigrés. "There seemed to be a conscious obfuscation of the issue of security clearance, no one knowing exactly what professions or jobs might be excluded on these grounds, while the operation of OVIR seemed no less deliberately founded on unfathomable secret

circulars and obstructions in order to disseminate an "atmosphere of insecurity and unpredictability."

21. In August 1986 Soviet Foreign Ministry personnel met with Israeli consular officials in Helsinki for 90 minutes. The Soviets proposed to visit Israel but refused an Israeli request for a reciprocal visit (Buwalda 1997:149). A month later Israeli Foreign Minister Shimon Peres met with his Soviet counterpart Eduard Shevardnadze in New York (Freedman 1988).

22. Sharansky was released in Germany as part of a prisoner exchange between the United States and the Soviet Union. He had been arrested on March 15, 1977.

23. Alan Dershowitz (1991:251) defended Sharansky before Soviet courts. He reports that the Liaison Bureau urged that he "drop the Shcharansky case." Ruby argues that Liaison Bureau discouraged NCSJ and NJCRAC from highlighting Sharansky or involving themselves closely with Avital's campaign in the United States. They viewed Sharansky as a human rights activist and not as a Prisoner of Zion. They were afraid that he might subvert the Jewish cause (interview, Jerry Goodman, January 10, 2001). The *NYT* (December 7, 1977) reported that American Jewish organizations advised leading New York civil rights lawyer not to aid Andrei Sakharov because his efforts would taint the Soviet Jewish movement by threatening Soviet authorities. NCSJ supported this position at the time while the Union of Councils supported ties to the dissident movement and to Sharansky (Ruby 1999:208,209). Eventually the Liaison Bureau and Israeli political leaders declared him a Prisoner of Zion. There was always tension between Avital Sharansky and the NCSJ. In her trips to the United States, often financed by the Liaison Bureau, Avital Sharansky was always accompanied by *Gush Emunim* (True Believers) activists who were the ideological vanguard of the West Bank settlers movement. The Union of Councils handled her in Washington, D.C. Leaders of the SSSJ often traveled with her. Rabbi Zvi Tau in the Rav Kook Yeshiva was the head of an international committee to free Sharansky. Rabbi Avi Weiss (1989) was very much involved with her activities in the United States. Dershowitz suggested an understanding between the Israelis and Soviet governments by which the Israelis would be concerned only with Refuseniks and Prisoners of Zion.

24. Grossman correctly states that Sharansky took a "hard-line anti-Soviet position." He would oppose the resumption of Israel-Soviet consular ties. He criticized the cooperation between the American Bar Association and the Association of Soviet lawyers in the absence of any change in emigration policy. The Liaison Bureau and NCJS had favored such agreements as being useful influencing Soviet opinion and practices. Also see Dershowitz 1991:264.

25. In December 1985 Edgar Bronfman, President of the WJC, went to Moscow for private negotiations. His meager results led to Abram's statement. In December the Soviets released Eliahu (Ilya) Essas the head of the movement of newly observant Jews.

26. In early 1986 the NCSJ, together with Congressmen Jack Kemp and W. Fowler and the Congressional Coalition for Soviet Jewry arranged for a Special Order on Soviet Jewry for Congress on February 20 which coincided with the February 25 meeting of the Communist Party Congress in Moscow. The NCSJ urged local groups to use the "District Work Period, scheduled from March 27 to April 7 to present 'certificates of appreciation' to Senators and Congressman for their help on the Soviet Jewry issue." While noting Sharansky's release it urged publicity for the other 18 persons in jail, 27 former prisoners not allowed to emigrate and the 15,000 Refuseniks and hun-

dreds of thousands of others not allowed to leave (Memo, NCSJ to Board of Governors "Maintaining . . . " February 17, 1986).

27. The Anti Defamation League handled communications and newspaper ads; the AJC worked on inter-religious and inter-ethnic contacts; B'nai B'rith International coordinated the Parliamentarians; NJCRAC prepared a "Manual for local organizations" and coordinated certificates of appreciation to member of Congressional Coalition of Soviet Jews and Congressional Wives for Soviet Jews; and the Central Conference of American Rabbis, Rabbinical Council of America, Synagogue Council of America, and Union of American Hebrew Congregations agreed to organize their constituent members (Shinbaum 1999:180).

28. NCSJ staffers, Myra Sheinbaum in New York City and Billy Keyserling in Washington, D.C. worked full time on the event.

29. An undated memo in CJF files "NCSJ Special Funding" refers to allocations of $392,000 from 137 federations.

30. The following are some of the activities held in preparation for Summit II: March 24 mail out to Rabbis new Matzoth of Hope; March 27–April 19 tour of Eliyahu Essas; March 31 Midwest regional conference (Summit II); April 13 Detroit Rally for Summit II and Los Angeles Rally for Exodus 86; April 21 New England regional Conference Summit II; April 23–30 special Passover programs including a vigil at Soviet Embassy in Washington, D.C. and May 11 NY Solidarity Sunday. They also planned a " special event in D.C. for Christian groups on Capital Hill."

31. She met regularly with leaders of the UJA, CJF, NJCRAC and NCSJ.

32. Participating at a July 9 planning meeting were single representatives of the Union of Councils for Soviet Jewry, American Israel Political Action Committee, AJC, American Jewish Congress, Anti-Defamation League, B'nai B'rith Women, CJF, Jewish War Veterans, Naamat, National Council of Jewish Women, UAHC, UJA, Community Relations Councils (Baltimore and Richmond) NCSJ (8 persons) and NJCRAC (3 persons).

33. In early 1989 Golub (1989:7) argued that the Soviets had denied about 2,000 Soviet Jews the right to leave for security reasons (possession of state secrets). In December 1988 at the UN Secretary Gorbachev indicated that the Soviet Union would limit the security clause.

34. It also called for more Voice of America broadcasts, an expanded cultural exchanges with the Soviet Union, free delivery of mail and an end to forced assimilation

35. Shultz (1993:602) believed that this was an important precedent. The document noted that in 5 or 10 years Gorbachev said having state secrets clause would not apply. Gorbachev told François Mitterrand at dinner in Moscow that the Soviet Union was prepared for "international cooperation on humanitarian problems."

36. At the Bern Conference on Helsinki Basket 3 (April 15 to May 27, 1986) Soviet government tried to close the book on Soviet emigration by saying that they could not send to war zone in Middle East. They unsuccessfully try to limit visas for visits and family reunification to "participating states," that is, 35 signatories of Helsinki.

37. The document charged that all the above violates Basket 3 of Helsinki Final Agreements (reunion of families, emigration and cultural and religious rights). It hoped these issues would be raised in the forthcoming Vienna Review Conference in November.

38. Orlov, a physicist, founded the Moscow Chapter of Amnesty International in 1973 and the Moscow Helsinki Watch Group (which he chaired) in 1976. He was arrested in February 1977 and released and exiled to the United States in 1986 (Eddie Oshins "The Case of Yuri Orlov," *New York Review of Books* 30 (#1), February 3, 1983; "Committee of Concerned Scientists: Yuri Orlov biography, www.libertynet .org/ccs/orlov.htm (June 25, 2004 and Gitelman 1988:341).

39. The *AJYB, 1988* reported that prior to the summit President Reagan said that human rights and arms control would receive equal priority. Due to disagreements on arms control, human rights became a secondary issue (Gitelman 1988:343).

40. Morris Abram attended this briefing with 15 other persons.

41. President Reagan made reference to Jehovah's Witnesses in the Soviet Union.

42. Abram also met that same day with Admiral Poindexter.

43. Pratt (1989:23–25) claimed that Reagan had passed the list on to Soviet authorities (who agreed to receive it) at Reykjavik. George Shultz (1993:989) refers to a NCSJ position paper on emigration given to him that he gave to Soviet Foreign Minister Eduard Shevardnadze in September 1987 which provided figures on the number of Jews wanting to emigrate. Schifter (1999:157) praises Eduard Shevardnadze "who had shaken off the Bolshevik shell and (who) . . . responded to our appeals" and thus set a new tone for the Soviet Foreign Ministry. Buwalda (1997:148) confirms this. In an Op Ed piece in the *NYT* "Agreement To Expand Contacts," October 19, 1986, Secretary of State Shultz wrote: "In Reykjavik, the President drew heavily on materials provided by the NCSJ and other organizations. It made for a strong and convincing presentation. We believe the Soviets will consider it carefully. We hope it will have an impact in the months ahead." Friedgut (1989:13) says the Shultz prior to Reykjavik agreed that freedom of emigration would be the litmus test of any human rights agreement.

44. The issue of the status of Soviet Jews emerged in advance as a topic of meetings. Weintraub argued that Reagan and Shultz promised that it would be central.

45. Some thought that Reagan's stand on Star Wars insured the summit's failure. In his memoirs (1993:746–772) Shultz describes much of the discussion at Reykjavik on arms and not human rights.

46. Buwalda (1997:151) supports Abram, arguing that Shultz's first human rights victory was at Reykjavik when the Soviets agreed to his demand that human rights issues be open and on the agenda. (Shultz 1993:1095). After the summit Gorbachev ordered Alexander Yakovlev, Secretary of the Central Committee of Communist Party of the Soviet Union to set up a section on humanitarian issues and human rights in the Party's Department of International Information.

47. In 1986 and 1987 CJF failed to raise from the federations the amount it budgeted for NCSJ for the Campaign to Summit II. By December 31, 1986, CJF owed NCSJ $84,536. On April 16, 1987, Mark Heutlinger of NCSJ (Memo to Shoshana Cardin and Robert Loup "Financial Summary of Summit II, CJF files, box 555) argued that NCSJ could not pay its bills due to a $64,000 shortfall from CJF. In August 1987 CJF told NCSJ to request $42,219 from UJA to cover funds not delivered by CJF from the federations (Memo Carmi Schwartz to Morris Abram, August 6, 1987, CJF files, box 555).

48. The Soviets announced the new policy earlier in August (Gitelman 1988:344) and in November 1986 (Schifter 1999:138 and David Harris "The Controversy over Refugee Status of Soviet Jewish Émigrés," May 25, 1987, CJF files). In a visit to Wash-

ington, D.C., in the summer of 1986 Yuri Kashlev, head of the Soviet Foreign Ministry Humanitarian Affairs Administration told Richard Schifter that they were reconsidering emigration but would not give Jews special treatment (Schifter 1999:138) In July 1987 head of all Union OVIR (Ministry of Interior) Rudolf Kuznetsov said all former Soviets, now citizens of other countries, could send *vyzovs* to their relatives for the purpose of visits or emigration. They also allowed some visas for emigration directly to Australia (Friedgut 1989:18,19). In 1987 Secretary Gorbachev also set up a Commission to supervise and speed up the granting of visas by OVIR. In April 1987 Eduard Shevardnadze, at George Shultz's suggestion, appointed a Soviet counterpart for human rights (Schifter 1999:140). While exit visas had increased 10 fold over 1983–1986 Schifter wanted more and an end to restrictions. In his view the Soviet Foreign Ministry was way out front on the issue of human rights issues, more so than other Soviet bureaucracies (1999:142). In the fall of 1987 he found Soviet officials much more flexible, having been instructed "to initiate a genuine dialogue" (1999:143).

49. Herbert Teitelbaum, head of the NCSJ legal committee (and son-in-law of Abram) had the "white shoe" law firm, White and Case review the Soviet practice of restricting emigration on grounds of knowledge of state secrets in comparison with standards on international law and politics. Their "pro-bono" report concluded that the policy was against "all civilized standards." They gave the report to Secretary of State George Shultz (NCSJ 87-88 Summary for LCBC," November 17, 1987, CJF files, box 593 and e-mail, Herbert Teitelbaum to Fred Lazin, June 28, 2004.

50. This was the first time a high Soviet official (Sergei Ivanko, member of board of state running the features syndicate *Novosti*) had mentioned a figure. The previous day in the *NYT* (March 19 1987) Morris Abrams wrote in a letter to the editor that rumors of liberalization in emigration had proved barren.

51. Morris Abram used the occasion to bring in (on Bronfman's private jet) 5,000 prayer books and other religious items which were shipped out by taxi at the airport (1989:16).

52. Abram indicated that all Refuseniks and families would be allowed to emigrate (via Romania) to Israel within one year except for national security cases; first degree relatives could emigrate for family reunification purposes within an established time frame (could be flexibility on current narrow interpretation of "first degree relative"; Soviets to review cases of those Refuseniks in category of "never allowed to emigrate"; all Jewish religious books may be imported; synagogues will be opened where there is a demonstrated need; Soviet Jews to be allowed greater access to Rabbinical training including United States; teaching of Hebrew in school or synagogue settings will be considered; to open kosher restaurant in Moscow and to make liberal provisions for ritual slaughter).

53. Avi Weiss of SSSJ and Center for Soviet Jewry opposed relaxing Jackson-Vanik. He did not trust the Soviets. Ruby (1999:218–222) writes that many American activists and grassroots groups and Refuseniks criticized the Abram-Bronfman meetings. They saw the WJC as appeasing Soviet leaders. Natan Sharansky and Josef Mendelevich publicly criticized both men at the 1986 Solidarity Sunday March in New York City.

54. Secretary of State Shultz reported that his discussions with Shevardnadze no longer focused on individual cases but the broader issues of changes in laws, misuse of psychological institutions, religious freedom and the right to emigrate.

55. It also noted the increased cultural and religious freedom for Jews and other minorities.

56. Grossman (1989) reports on an agreement in principle by the end of 1987 between Israel, the United States and the Soviet Union and other parties "to route flights from USSR through Romania to Israel." Details had to be worked out.

57. The Foundation, a New York based coalition of business and religious figures deals with issues of religious freedom. As early as 1966 it sponsored a mission to the Soviet Union which may have been coordinated with the Liaison Bureau (Irving Spiegel, "Interfaith Mission Finds Fear Prevalent Among Jews in Soviet," *NYT*, February 11, 1966).

58. Naftalin (1999:237) claims that Morris Abram had worked on a similar deal with the Soviets in 1986 offering an end to Jackson-Vanik in exchange for direct flights. Representatives of the Liaison Bureau belittle the role played by Rabbi Schneier.

59. As Prime Minister Shamir as Prime Minister had met with President Ceausescu. The American government which opposed direct flights may have pressured the Dutch not to cooperate. One source claims they feared direct flights would result in Soviet Jews lining up at the American Embassy in Moscow for visas to America. Buwalda (1997:169–172) says that the Israeli Ambassador in Holland proposed that the Dutch raise a Bucharest route with the Soviets and that they put a stamp on exit permits that were valid only for Bucharest. According to Buwalda (1997:154–157) Gorbachev approved direct Moscow Israel flights in 1987 but the KGB objected.

60. Until 1973 several thousands of Soviet Jews, primarily from Moldavia, flew to Israel via Bucharest. Israel paid Romania a per head charge (Sanders 1988:594–597). According to Gur- Gurevitz (1996:79–84) the Soviet Foreign Ministry vetoed an agreement between the Liaison Bureau and Aeroflot for direct flights from Moscow. Thereafter, the Liaison Bureau and Jewish Agency competed on negotiating on direct flights. With Prime Minister Shamir's support, the Liaison Bureau negotiated a high cost deal with the Soviets. On January 1, 1990 an El Al plane returned to Israel with 125 immigrants directly. The Soviets then cancelled the agreement because of Arab pressure.

61. CJF Executive Vice President Carmi Schwartz stated that the federation position is that direct flights are best, recognizing that there are many problems (Minutes, of Soviet Jewry Advocacy Study Committee, April 9, 1987, CJF files, box 667).

62. Pam Cohen and Micah Naftalin of the Union of Councils attacked the idea of direct flights via Romania in an Op Ed piece in the *NYT* of June 18, 1987. They indicated that the Soviets may have been promised trade concessions and a role in the Middle East Peace process. Morris Abram indicated that if direct flights from Romania continued then he might try to permit reentry of Soviet Jews from Israel to the United States ("Report by M. Abram on Trip to Moscow, April 1, 1987, CJF file, box 667). On possibly changing American laws to allow refugee status for Soviet Jews who first went to Israel and became citizens, they noted that Secretary of State George Shultz, a proponent of freedom of choice "is aware of the difficulty of changing the definition of refugees in order to accommodate Soviet Jews without similar accommodation for refugees from other regions." Richard Schifter of the State Department may have considered changing United States laws (*JP*, July 8, 1988). Technically, even if granted citizenship by Israel Soviet Jews would be eligible to apply for refugee status to the United States. See chapter 5.

63. On the advice of Israeli officials she cancelled a public meeting on Soviet Jewish issues at the Quarterly. They feared it might jeopardize negotiations between the Israeli and Romanian governments on flights. Attending were leaders of the UIA, UJA, JDC, HIAS, Jewish Agency, Conference of Presidents and NCSJ.

64. She noted that in current FY October 1, 1986 through September 30, 1987 the block grant approval is for 1,000 Soviet Jews. The trend of the last 8 or 10 weeks indicates at least 3,500–4,000 Soviet Jews before September 30, 1987. At this rate there would also be insufficient visa slots in 1987. Notes for re: Soviet Jewish Immigration, Refugee Status and Direct Flight Issues, April 8, 1987, CJF files, box 667).

65. Cardin argued that all Jewish leadership including Prime Ministers Meir, Begin and Shamir, have subscribed to reunification of Soviet Jews with first-degree relatives in the West. Earlier in the month (Minutes of Soviet Jewry Advocacy Study Committee, April 9, 1987) CJF considered altering U.S. refugee laws to enable Soviet Jews to enter the USA after spending a year in Israel. They realized, however, that this "is a far fetched idea and in order for it to work would require very detailed negotiation, both with government circles in Israel as well as in the United States." In meetings with Israelis American Jewish leaders urged drastic improvement of absorption.

66. Some would see the event as rejuvenating the Soviet Jewry advocacy efforts in the United States while others believed that it turned the protest into a movement (Rudin 1990; Document of CJF Soviet Jewry advisory Study Committee, February 4, 1988, CJF files, box 667 and Abram 1989).

67. CJF urged federations to subsidize the participation of constituents so as to "demonstrate to America, the world at large, and the leadership of the Soviet Union our commitment to Soviet Jewry and their freedom." CJF approved NCSJ request of $240,000 for the mobilization. It assessed its constituent federations fair share amounts to pay. Other organizations provided in kind services and staff. By November (Memo of Carmi Schwartz to Federation Executives, November 6, 1987, CJF files box 667) CJF admitted that it had underestimated expenses. The revised budget stood at $430,000 and final expenditures were $405,000. The NCSJ estimated budget for 1987 was $838,000 and the projected budget for 1988 $997,000 (NCSJ 87-88 Summary for LCBC" November 17, 1987, CJF files, box 593).

68. Community Relations Councils had a major role. Anti Defamation League handled ads; AJC the involvement of Christian organizations; Jewish Community Council of Washington, D.C., local logistics; NCSJ's Washington, D.C., office and other Washington, D.C., representatives of national organizations worked with Congress; NCSJ Washington, D.C., representative Barbara Gaffin served as liaison to operations committee; New York Coalition to be involved in planned program and promotion of event; and Morton Yarmon of the AJC handled Public Relations subcommittee. Rabbi Alexander Schindler (UAHC) mobilized congregations while leaders of Hadassah, B'nai B'rith and other organizations recruited members to come to Washington (Harris 1988:38).

69. Abe Bayer (1989) argues that NJCRAC and its Executive Director Al Chernin played a major role. Its mobilization committee had been in place for over two years.

70. She wrote her "summit" memos on NJCRAC paper. Al Chernin, Executive Director of NJCRAC, wrote Community Relations Councils and NJCRAC about Summit III as though it was a NJCRAC operation. Many Summit III materials used pictures and quotes of Natan Sharansky.

71. CJF had established a committee headed by Dan Shapiro to resolve the turf issues between NCSJ and NJCRAC. Abram believed that it may be fair "to say that the appointment of David Harris was generated by these discussions." Shapiro claims the CJF made financial support conditional on Harris being in charge (Interview with Dan Shapiro, July 2002).

72. Cardin argued that CJF helped NCSJ design a most effective professional task force headed by David Harris. She served as a member of the leadership group of the volunteer task force.

73. He wondered at times whether Gorbachev might ask to speak as Shevardnadze had done at a protest rally in Uruguay. He also feared possible violence and disruptions from the followers of Meir Kahane.

Harris was aware that the situation in the Soviet Union had become "nuanced." Things were improving and more Jews were leaving. He believed then that Mikhail Gorbachev clearly wanted change and reform.

74. Weiss (1989) writes that the rally allowed the establishment to pat itself on the back. Grossman 1989:227ff argues that when the *NYT* quoted Abram as saying that the "demonstration will be in support of American policy" that the coalition almost broke up. Glen Richter of SSSJ accused Abram of signaling a position of weakness. Rabbi Avi Weiss was not allowed to speak. From his seat on dais he raised a sign in protest. Josef Mendelevitz shouted linkage from the stage.

75. Before the rally B'nai B'rith held a special meeting for Congressmen who did not speak with Refuseniks (Richter 1989 and Weiss 1989:39). The SSSJ wanted a week's protest rather than one day. They began their activities on Friday night with a demonstration at Aeroflot offices and held a demonstration after the march.

76. Abram claims that two weeks prior to the summit, President Reagan told representatives of the Soviet Jewry movement that "I wish I could be there" and after the summit he wrote "Congratulations on your extraordinarily successful demonstration." The Voice of America broadcast much of it to the Soviet Union.

77. Another source quoted a letter from Reagan saying that he "declared the cause of Soviet Jewry as a concern for all Americans." A *Jewish Week*, February 19, 1988 article "B'nai B'rith to test Soviet by opening Moscow office," quoted a Reagan letter to Morris Abram in which the President pledged "to continue to press the human rights question" (which for him) "will always be a front-burner issue."

78. Slater ("Transmigrants Report," March 16, 1988, JDC files) reported that 20 percent of the increased number of Soviet emigrés in past year were 60 years of age or older and that many have chronic diseases which double JDC medical bills.

79. David Shipler ("Law on Emigration in Effect in Soviet: U.S. Sees Tightened Rules–Earlier Preference for Jews Now Apparently At end," *New York Times*, January 2, 1988) quoted Professor Stephen F. Cohen that "when it comes to the emigration of Jews, no other human rights question has such a well-organized American constituency." Cohen referred to the NCSJ and Union of Councils.

80. This had been an ongoing major event since the early 1970s. Some felt it reflected a changed environment in the USSR; others felt that glasnost made the "strategy of mass rallies obsolete" (Grossman, Ibid.). Jerry Goodman believes that the Washington Rally had such an impact on the White House and Congress that the New York City effort and event had become less important (letter, Jerry Goodman to Fred

Lazin, December 29, 2003). Lynn Singer of the Union of Councils supported the decision while SSSJ considered the cancellation an outrage.

81. While Soviets were seen as dragging their feet on some immigration issues, they were also willing to be flexible in interest of U.S.-USSR relations realizing in Shultz's words that human rights are "integral part of the relationship." Also see Susan Birnbaum, "Soviet Jewish Emigration Up Slightly," *Jewish Week*, March 11 1988.

82. An Israeli source, possibly from Liaison Bureau told *Jewish Week* ("Soviet Softening Stance on Emigration, Mideast," May 20, 1988) that the Soviets were enforcing first degree for those going to Israel even though they said they would not.

83. Memo cited White and Case study showing that "secrets" criteria outside "the common core on which civilized nations agree." Jerry Goodman (Memo to Morris Abram, re: Summit Strategy, April 13, 1988, CFJ files, box 667) argued in favor of shifting from reliance on Basket 2 of Helsinki Final act to a bilateral framework. He proposed offering restraint in certain areas and even concessions for example, if progress act to end Stevenson Amendment. He proposed contacting all candidates at all levels during the next 4 weeks and to do the same with corporate executives who were going to Moscow and a nationwide campaign of letters to the President.

84. Abram led a NCSJ delegation of 50 persons (including Mayor David Dinkins of New York City) to Helsinki. The NCSJ conducted a silent vigil while the SSSJ and Union of Councils held more activist protests (Grossman 1990:264ff.)

85. In an op ed piece, "Glasnost May be Glasnost, but Prison is Prison" (*NYT*, May 28, 1988), Sharansky called for linkage with human rights. He argued that although many had been allowed to emigrate, "But for the broad mass of Soviet Jews who want to leave or want to live as Jews, little was changed. In some ways, they are worse off." In the opinion of Richard Schifter (1999:155 it would take the Soviet Union until 1990 to allow free emigration of Soviet Jewry.

86. A new Rabbinic academy would be opened in Moscow and there was less harassment of Hebrew teachers ("Moscow's Climate of Change . . . and the Danger Clouds" June 11, 1988 JP? and "U.S. Expects increase in Soviet Jewish Emigration," *JP*, June 11, 1988). Shifter in Israel told the Prime Minister that Soviet Union would let more leave and those remaining would be allowed to practice their religion and cultural life more freely. At the summit Shultz gave the Soviets 400 names of Refuseniks. During the 3 days of summit talks 20 percent of the list got exit visas.

7

The Conflict over Turf
in the American Soviet
Jewry Advocacy Movement:
The Dominance of the CJF

With success almost at hand in the American Soviet Jewry advocacy movement a controversy over turf and functions developed between the National Conference on Soviet Jewry (NCSJ) and the National Jewish Community Relations Advisory Council (NJCRAC) (Yitzhak Rabi, "NCSJ to Coordinate Soviet Jewry Policy Under CJF Restructuring Plan," *JTA*, June 15, 1988).[1] Each wanted to be responsible for control of Soviet Jewish advocacy in the American Jewish Community. Tension between these two organizations dated back to the establishment of the NCSJ and its predecessor, the American Jewish Conference for Soviet Jewry.

Whereas in the 1960s and 1970s the Israeli Liaison Bureau exerted significant if not dominant influence in the politics of Soviet Jewry advocacy within the American Jewish establishment, in 1988 it wielded far less. Now the CJF had almost sole control of the decision making process which determined the outcome of this conflict among major American Jewish organizations. This suggests that by 1988 the CJF had become the most powerful organization in American Jewish politics.

In his book on American Jewish politics J. J. Goldberg (1996:52) argues, "The CJF theoretically is the most powerful body in the American Jewish community. But its power is largely illusory, for the council consists of 190 local federations—each a private corporation answerable to its own directors and jealous of its independence. If the CJF can ever win the right to govern its members, it indeed will be the most powerful body in American Jewish life; meanwhile it is a sleeping giant."[2] Goldberg may have missed something. By the 1980s the CJF dominated American Jewish organizational politics; it exerted growing influence and power within the American Soviet Jewry advocacy movement. It had become the dominant force in an issue/

policy area of extreme importance to the American Jewish community. In a crucial power struggle over turf within the American Soviet Jewry advocacy movement in the late 1980s, both parties, NCSJ and NJCRAC formally accepted the adjudication of CJF.

BACKGROUND TO THE CONFLICT

The American Jewish Conference on Soviet Jewry, Conference of Presidents of Major American Jewish Organizations and many of their constituent organizations including NJCRAC established the NCSJ in 1971 to set overall policy for Soviet Jewry advocacy in the United States.[3] They also gave NJCRAC a specific role in Soviet Jewry advocacy. While the NCSJ set policy, NJCRAC was responsible for implementation at the community level and for supervision of local Soviet Jewry action committees (Memo, Jerry Goodman to CJF Subcommittee Review Taskforce, March 5, 1985, CJF files, box 667).[4] This made the NCSJ dependent on NJCRAC in dealings with federations and local Soviet Jewry committees. The unclear boundary between policy making and implementation contributed to ongoing friction between these organizations. As early as 1976, a CJF subcommittee of the LCBC investigated conflicts between the NCSJ and NJCRAC and organizational shortcomings of the NCSJ (Memo, Phil Bernstein to Dan Shapiro, Shoshana Cardin and Carmi Schwartz, August 21, 1987 and Memo of Mrs. Marvin Shapiro to Community Delegates, re: Funding Soviet Jewry Community Relations Community" (November 20, 1976, CJF files, box 667).

"Israeli influence" may have also contributed to the tension between NJCRAC and NCSJ. The Israelis continued to have tremendous influence over the NCSJ. Its leaders and staff either followed the direction of the Liaison Bureau or sought its advice on most major decisions. Liaison Bureau members participated in staff, executive and board meetings of NCSJ in both New York City and in Washington, D.C. NJCRAC, in contrast, was more an American directed Jewish organization. Its dominant professional director through 1975, Isaiah Minkoff, was a one time Bundist whom the Liaison Bureau did not trust. It took more independent positions even though some of its officers and senior staff (Abraham Bayer in particular) wanted to follow the Israeli lead on the issue of Soviet Jewry. Minkoff's successor, Albert Chernin, cooperated with the Liaison Bureau.

NJCRAC professionals had always wanted to lead the American Soviet Jewry movement. They believed that NJCRAC could add Soviet Jewry to one of its many concerns in the area of community relations. It had staffed the American Jewish Conference on Soviet Jewry until the establishment of the NCSJ. By the mid-1980s, if not before, NJCRAC leaders, staff and supporters were highly critical of NCSJ. They demanded a greater policy making role for

NJCRAC in the Soviet Jewry advocacy movement. A CJF subcommittee on the Soviet Jewry movement brought together the operating officers from the two organizations in 1984 in hopes of increasing cooperation and understanding (Memo, Phil Bernstein to Don Shapiro et al., August 21, 1987 and Memo, Al Chernin to Jerry Goodman, March 18, 1985, CJF files, box 667).[5] Basically, NCJRAC argued that in setting up NCSJ its organizers "formally recognized the role of NJCRAC as the coordinator and catalyst of community activity on behalf of Soviet Jewry" (NJCRAC, "Preliminary Report of Review Committee, February 17, 1986," CJF files, box 684). In 1986, NJCRAC made known its interest in opening an office in Washington, D.C., which had become a center of NCSJ operations. While possibly infringing on the NCSJ, the idea of a Washington, D.C. office also angered the defense agencies—AJC, American Jewish Congress and Anti-Defamation League who also operated in Washington, D.C. (Summary, Minutes of CJF NJCRAC Liaison Committee, April 16, 1986, CJF files, box 684).[6]

In response to the friction between these two organizations and other Soviet Jewry advocacy groups including the New York City based Coalition for Soviet Jewry (formerly the GNYCSJ) and the Union of Councils, the CJF and the UJA–Federation of New York each established committees to examine the Soviet Jewry advocacy movement.[7] Both committees investigated the Soviet Jewry movement in general and the functioning of both organizations and their ties to each other.

Judah Gribetz, headed the UJA–Federation of New York task force established in early 1986, "to determine whether funds are being used effectively to carry out the mandates of the agencies involved with Soviet Jewry and to make recommendations . . . regarding future funding of the organization" ("Soviet Jewry Task Force [UJA–Federation of New York]," July 24, 1986; Memo, Task Force of Soviet Jewry, March 4, 1986 and "Soviet Jewry Task Force, May 12, 1986, CJF files, box 667).[8] Officially the committee focused its efforts on NCSJ, NJCRAC, Coalition for Soviet Jewry and planned later to look at the Long Island Committee for Soviet Jewry and the SSSJ. In practice, however, it concentrated on the NCSJ and the Coalition for Soviet Jewry.

Considerable tension and apparent competition existed between these two organizations. Both had been established at the same time: one to focus on national policy and the other to be concerned about activities in metropolitan New York. Over the years some of the New York organization's activities had a national impact on the Soviet Jewry movement. For example, its annual solidarity marches became one of the major events of the Soviet Jewry Movement in the United States. National politicians vied to participate. Changing its name to the Coalition for Soviet Jewry, with no mention of New York, led some to think that it wanted to become a national agency. A former director denies this intent (Interview, Zeesy Schnur, August 12, 2002). A conflict over the 1986 Solidarity Sunday March of the Coalition exacerbated relations with the NCSJ. According to Ms. Schnur the NCSJ wanted to co-sponsor the 1986 March because of Natan Sharansky's involvement. Both organizations had sponsored the first marches but then NCSJ left the event to the New York Conference to organize.

In appearances before the Gribetz committee, lay and staff of the Coalition charged NCSJ with making policy on its own without consulting with its constituent members. It claimed NCSJ had usurped program functions of NJCRAC, the Coalition and other local Soviet Jewry committees while failing to "service" these local groups. It also accused the NCSJ of incompetence in Washington including the hosting of Natan Sharansky (Memo, Task Force of Soviet Jewry, March 4, 1986, CJF files, box 667). Finally, it suggested that the Coalition was now making its own policy.[9]

In his appearance before the Gribetz task force, Jerry Goodman of the NCSJ attacked the Coalition for overemphasizing the national sphere, competing with NCSJ and NJCRAC and neglecting the local sector. He cited a drop off in attendance at the Solidarity Sunday marches ("Soviet Jewry Task Force," July 24, 1986, CJF files, box 667). In his testimony Morris Abram emphasized that the relationship between NCSJ and NJCRAC had never been clearly defined; NCSJ was to make policy and provide activity guidelines to be implemented by CJF and NJCRAC through local community relations councils and federations. "Where policy development left off and program development began was not clarified." He explained that NCSJ had also developed its own relationships with local groups.

The Gribetz Committee did not meet from June 1986 until April 9, 1987 ("Soviet Jewry Task Force," April 9, 1987, CJF files, box 667). In the meantime in early 1987, CJF established a committee on Soviet Jewry advocacy to study the current functions, structures, effectiveness, responsibilities and relationships of NCSJ, NJCRAC and other organizations (Letter, Dan Shapiro to Morris Abram and others, February 18, 1987 and Hand notes [probably Carmi Schwartz], February 9, 1987, CJF files, box 667).[10] CJF invited NCSJ and NJCRAC to participate but not the Union of Councils and SSSJ. All four organizations would be invited to testify. The cooperation given CJF by the lay leadership and professional staff of both NCSJ and NJCRAC indicates the apparent power of the CJF to decide on their future roles and functions within the Soviet Jewry advocacy movement. CJF funded both organizations.[11] Dan Shapiro would chair the committee ("Soviet Jewry meeting," February 10, 1987, CJF files, box 667).[12]

The CJF Committee would only concern itself with advocacy on behalf of Soviet Jewry and not with emigration and resettlement issues. Nevertheless, participants at a March 2, 1987 meeting noted that advocacy for emigration has always included encouragement for resettlement in Israel. "Let my people go . . . to Israel has been the assumption." It urged those involved in debate on resettlement (Israel versus "freedom of choice") to avoid discussions with the press and if necessary to speak and then emphasize "maximizing emigration from USSR" (Meeting, notes on Soviet Jewish Advocacy issues of March 2, 1987, March 4, 1987, CJF files, box 667). All present agreed on the need to find ways to increase the number going to Israel without rescinding refugee status to the United States.

Executive directors of NCSJ and NJCRAC complied with the Shapiro Committee's request to submit position papers on the reorganizations of the Soviet Jewry advocacy movement. In his memo of April 1987, Jerry Goodman lists the following three purposes of the NCSJ: to enable Jews to leave the USSR, to "help those Jews who choose to remain in the Soviet Union live as Jews with the same rights accorded every other nationality and religious minority," and to assure that the plight of Soviet Jewry is kept in the forefront of deliberations of our government as well as in the public and private sectors (Memos, Jerry Goodman to Carmi Schwarz, April 7, 1987 and Carmi Schwartz to Dan Shapiro, July 9, 1987, CJF files, box 667).[13] He explained that budget shortages had reduced community involvement of the NCSJ. He also noted that there were few if any community (federation) leaders on the NCSJ Executive Board.[14]

In his memo for the Shapiro Committee, ("Issues and Propositions for Examination by CJF Subcommittee" April 9, 1987, CJF files, box 684) Albert D. Chernin of NJCRAC, chastised NCSJ. He charged that it did not consult on policy issues with constituent members, supply adequate information about happenings in the Soviet Union, fulfill its spokesperson role in Washington, D.C., and provide innovative new programs and coordinate efforts of member organizations. Rather than act as a catalyst for other agencies in the field, NCSJ "operates . . . as a restraining agent."[15] He also accused NCSJ of failure to assign tasks to member organizations and debrief adequately those persons and groups that it sent to the Soviet Union. He suggested that the NCSJ had often been sluggish in reacting to important events. For example, he argued that it was NJCRAC that had prodded NCSJ action on the Reykjavik Summit. Other than citing a 1978 memo proposing that NCSJ and NJCRAC occupy the same quarters and be under one supervisor, Chernin had no specific proposals for organizational changes.

The Shapiro Committee met on April 9, 1987, to discuss the memos from Goodman and Chernin. Before Abram's arrival, those present expressed dissatisfaction with both NCSJ and NJCRAC. Several persons criticized the performance of NCSJ's Executive Director (Minutes of Soviet Jewry Advocacy Study Committee, April 9, 1987, CJF files, box 667).[16] Shapiro proposed several organizational options including the establishment of a joint task force involving both NCSJ and NJCRAC. Morris Abram opposed the idea of a new task force. In the present emergency situation, he argued, NCSJ could not afford to restructure even if it was necessary (Memo, Carmi Schwartz to Dan Shapiro, July 9, 1987).[17]

At its next meeting on May 8, 1997, the Shapiro Committee proposed that NCSJ, in partnership with NJCRC, set up an ad hoc (six month time limit) consultative process on issues related to Soviet Jewry advocacy. Committee members wanted to involve NCSJ, NJCRAC, New York Coalition, Union of Councils, SSSJ (where appropriate), Conference of Presidents, AJC, American Jewish Congress and Anti-Defamation League (maybe) B'nai B'rith, National Council of Jewish Women, and at least six federations (Los Angeles, San Francisco, Chicago, Philadelphia, Miami and a leading intermediate and small size federation). This group would develop a modified approach according to the principles of partnership between NCSJ and NJCRAC with the participation of other key national and local players as part of the deliberation and networking process (Memo, Carmi Schwartz to Al Chernin and Jerry Goodman, May 8, 1987, CJF files, box 667). During the six-month period the Shapiro Task Force would continue to examine the relationships and structures of advocacy for Soviet Jewry.

NCSJ responded positively to the CJF's Strategic Task Force's charge. Jerry Goodman reported on NCSJ decisions to expand the Executive Committee and the creation of a Strategic Assessment Task Force headed by Edward Robin to guide the Jewish community and NCSJ constituencies on the subject of Soviet Jewry advocacy. He also reported on plans to strengthen NCSJ's Board of Governors (with the involvement of NJCRAC and CJF) and development of a Council of Associates (Letter, Jerry Goodman to Carmi Schwartz, May 11, 1987, CJF files, box 667).[18]

NJCRAC also accepted the idea of a joint task force to operate for six months along the lines suggested by Shapiro (Letter, Michael Pelavin to Dan Shapiro, May 22, 1987, CJF files). It proposed that NJCRAC appoint one of the co-chairs of the task force. It wanted it jointly staffed by Jerry Goodman (NCSJ) and Al Chernin (NJCRAC). It also proposed renewing an earlier practice that the head of NJCRAC be a vice chair of NCSJ. In addition, it wanted NCSJ and NJCRAC to set up two joint committees—one on travel to the Soviet Union and a second on regional consultations.

In a short period of time the proposed joint task force became a reality as a NCSJ operation with NJCRAC appointing a co-chair. Carmi Schwartz, Executive Director of CJF, continued to meet with Jerry Goodman and Al Chernin to discuss issues of consultations and cooperation between the two organizations. He wanted them to develop a joint document, which proposed revised roles for each organization in the Soviet Jewry advocacy movement. He recommended joint operation of an enhanced travel program, regional and local seminars on Soviet Jewry advocacy and program implementation and agenda development and direction of NCSJ Strategic Planning Task Force (Memo, Carmi Schwartz to Al Chernin and Jerry Goodman, May 27, 1987, CJF files, box 667). On a higher level, Dan Shapiro continued to meet with Morris Abram and Michael Pelavin, presidents of NCSJ and NJCRAC respectively.

Goodman and Chernin agreed to have NCSJ invite NJCRAC to choose a co-chair for the new NCSJ Strategic Planning Task Force, work together on planning and developing an enhanced travel program (with a role for Israelis) and a "conscious exchange and engagement of top leadership in each other's governance ranks where appropriate" (Memo, Schwartz to Chernin and Goodman, May 27, 1987, CJF files, box 667). Almost nothing, however, had been put in writing. In a follow up memo to Al Chernin and Jerry Goodman, Carmi Schwartz suggested that they jointly prepare the agenda for the next Shapiro Committee meeting on July 30, 1987 to convey the "nature of our inner-agency communication and coordinating efforts" (Memo, June 12, 1987, CJF files).[19]

In a meeting on June 19, 1987, Dan Shapiro, Morris Abram and Michael Pelavin agreed that Arden Shenker of NJCRAC would co-chair with Edward Robin the NCSJ Strategic Reassessment Task Force. Abram also agreed to have Michael Pelavin elected a vice chair of NCSJ but did not view this position as being reserved for the NJCRAC President. He also objected vehemently to Dan Shapiro's intent to invite Pam Cohen of the Union of Councils to the next task force meeting which would be held in Chicago (Letter, Dan Shapiro to Morris Abram and Michael Pelavin, June 25, 1987, CJF files, box 667).[20]

In early July Jerry Goodman submitted a joint proposal on behalf of himself and Chernin and Chernin submitted guidelines on the proposed role of NJCRAC (Memo, Carmi Schwartz to Dan Shapiro, July 9, 1987, CJF files, box 667). Goodman proposed joint regional seminars for professionals with NCSJ preparing materials and providing speakers and NJCRAC working with local community relations councils to arrange the meetings. He suggested leaving responsibility for travel to the USSR under the auspices of NCSJ with NJCRAC helping to coordinate briefings. In effect, Goodman wanted NCSJ to continue to define goals and needs and NJCRAC to work with local community relations councils and federations. Later Chernin submitted a very different proposal concerning regional meetings and travel to the USSR (Notes and Minutes, Meeting of "Soviet Jewish Advisory Study Committee," July 30, 1987, CJF files).

At the July 30, 1987, meeting of the Soviet Jewry Advisory Study Group Morris Abram again admitted that the exiting structure was not "most desirable, but that it had to be lived with."[21] He argued for increased funding to enable NCSJ to meet its responsibilities and to achieve greater visibility. While the NCSJ is well known to American officials, he argued, "it is not well known in the Soviet Union as the Union of Councils, nor is its work sufficiently known in the communities due to the bifurcated structure with NJCRAC. Because of the need for greater NCSJ visibility," he rejected a notion of parity with NJCRAC on travel and regional meetings presented in Chernin's proposal.[22] Pelavin urged greater cooperation as NJCRAC spent one third of its budget and assigned two full time staff on Soviet Jewry advocacy.

Rather than leave deliberation and negotiations with the professionals of the Soviet Jewry advocacy groups Carmi Schwartz proposed bringing in former CJF Executive Director Phil Bernstein to monitor the discussion and determine the consensus concerning the restructuring of the Soviet Jewry advocacy movement. All present accepted the idea.

Phil Bernstein initially met with Morris Abram, Shoshana Cardin, Carmi Schwartz and Dan Shapiro. He then interviewed the chairs and executives of the national advocacy organizations including the Union of Councils and some local and community groups as well (Memos, Dan Shapiro to members of Soviet Jewry Advisory Study Committee, October 22 and November 3, 1987, CJF files, box 667). The activities for Summit III (December 6, 1987), however, put off actions by both Bernstein and the Shapiro Task Force. Following its meeting on July 30, 1987, the Task Force did not officially meet again until January 19, 1988. Shapiro emphasized that the cooperative approach to Summit III reflected the good work of his committee.

At the January 19, 1988, meeting, Phil Bernstein reported that Morris Abram had rejected the idea of a joint NCSJ-NJCRAC committee to coordinate Soviet Jewry advocacy. Abram also opposed a proposal to relocate NCSJ headquarters to Washington, D.C. (Hand notes by Elaine Morris of Soviet Jewry Advocacy Study Task Force, January 19, 1988, CJF files, box 667).[23] Emphasizing that *glasnost* required fresh thinking, changes in policy and more sophisticated operations, Phil Bernstein presented several restructuring options for discussion. One option had NCSJ taking over the NJCRAC functions in Soviet Jewry advocacy to unify policy making and implementation in one organization. This would mean "full concentration on Soviet Jewry in one body, the National Conference" ("Options draft" Soviet Jewry Advisory Committee," February 1988, CJF files, box 667). This option also called for more funding from federations and UJA and for a cessation of outside funding for the Research Bureau (a quasi Liaison Bureau operation). Bernstein and others may have been concerned about the clandestine funding arrangements for the Research Bureau. Prior to the NCSJ it had been operated by Moshe Decter for the Liaison Bureau in a building on the grounds of the American Jewish Congress in New York City. After Decter left in 1975, Jerry Goodman integrated its activities (of supplying data on Soviet Jews to the media, Congress, State Department) into the NCSJ. Funding came from many sources including the Jewish Agency (Decter 1990:34 and Jerry Goodman, telephone interview, July 1, 2004). The other options dealt with minor modifications. Significantly, none of Bernstein's original recommendations called for NJCRAC to take over the functions of NCSJ.

Bernstein's options were quickly revised and updated. The following are from a revised version of the February 1988 (Soviet Jewry Advisory Committee, "Options Draft" (CJF files, box 667). Option 1 would continue the present structure with minor modifications. NCSJ would upgrade its Washington,

D.C. office and it would counsel communities directly with visits and phone calls. Option 2 would continue present structures but with some transfer of responsibility between NCSJ and NJCRAC. Option 3 would have NCSJ and NJCRAC employ joint staff but keep their autonomous structures. Option 4 had NCSSJ taking over NJCRAC functions to unify policy making and implementation in one organization. Options 5 through 8 dealt with other Soviet Jewry advocacy organizations and their functions; Option 7 proposed giving the Union of Councils a formal role and or representation in the NCSJ and including it in Washington, D.C. delegations to the Department of State and White House. Option 9 urged the closest ongoing relationships with Israel and the Liaison Bureau, in coordination with NCSJ.[24] Option 11 urged more financing; it noted that limited support until now "severely restricted actions" of Soviet Jewry advocacy. It suggested that increased involvement of communities in national organizations might help fundraising. The various options were to be tested by 15 criteria. For example: What will achieve the most effective advocacy for Soviet Jews? What will assure the strongest influence in Washington, D.C., in the media, and so on?

Michael Pelavin of NJCRAC favored restructuring with NJCRAC absorbing NCSJ but allowing NCSJ to retain its name and board. He believed that disbanding the NCSJ would give the wrong message to Soviet authorities. Abram opposed this idea; NCSJ would be lost if absorbed within NJCRAC even if allowed to keep its name and board. He favored instead a separate Soviet Jewry advocacy organization with its own identity.

Shapiro's committee soon reduced the options to four ("CJF Soviet Advisory Study Committee Document," February 4, 1988, CJF files, box 667).[25] Option one would continue the roles of both organizations with more community (federation) representatives on NCSJ committees, greater lay oversight of NCSJ administration, an upgrading of staff in NCSJ's Washington, D.C. office and a greater overlap of board members. NCSJ would transfer to NJCRAC responsibility for coordinating national bodies. There would be a joint committee for travel to the USSR and special staff linkages. Option two would give NCSJ and NJCRAC joint staffs or alternatively to have both employ the same executive vice president. Option three would have the NCSJ take over all NJCRAC Soviet Jewry functions. Option four would give NJCRAC full authority over Soviet Jewry advocacy with NCSJ retaining its name, identity, and distinct organizational and lay structure. NCSJ would continue to direct relations with the government and the media. Again the criteria for choosing an option would be the most effective advocacy, strongest influence in Washington, D.C., most inclusive national umbrella, and soundest policies.

In February 1988 Morris Abram informed the NCSJ Executive Committee about the proposals presented by the Shapiro Committee. While he emphasized NCSJ's financial dependence on CJF he suggested that the Shapiro Committee could make recommendations but that it lacked the power to effectuate change. He believed, however, that the NCSJ would emerge more unified, better funded and a stronger national organization (Memo, Morris Abram to Executive Committee of NCSJ, February 8, 1988, CJF files).[26]

By the time a subcommittee of the Shapiro Committee met on March 9th, it became clear that CJF was leaning in favor of NCSJ becoming the sole lead agency for Soviet Jewish advocacy in the United States (Memo, Dan Shapiro to subcommittee members with Memo, "CJF Soviet Jewry Advocacy Options Revised February 1988," February 26, 1988, CJF files, box 667). Phil Bernstein had reported that in January 1988 the Large City Executives of CJF endorsed a freestanding, full service National Conference of Soviet Jewry without a role for NJCRAC. They were prepared to provide necessary funding but wanted the main office to be in Washington, D.C. He also noted that 12 of 13 intermediate city executives and 7 of 8 lay leaders favored "centralization in one organization" (Memo, Phil Bernstein to Dan Shapiro and Carmi Schwartz, March 3, 1988, CJF files, box 667, Hand notes [probably Carmi Schwartz] January 31, 1988, CJF files, box 695).

Despite the contents of his memo, Phil Bernstein was less certain as to whether NCSJ or NJCRAC should be the organization to take charge. He feared that local community relations councils loyal to NJCRAC might influence local federations to oppose the proposed changes. In addition, the CJF demanded more federation and local input into NCSJ and preferred the main office to be in Washington, D.C., which Morris Abram opposed (Soviet Jewry Advocacy Notes, March 9, 1988, CJF files, box 667).[27]

The full committee would meet at the upcoming CJF quarterly in Philadelphia on April 17–19. In preparation CJF sent out a revised proposal to federation executives and presidents and members of the CFJ Board listing two options ("CJF Reports: Proposals for Discussion; Soviet Jewry advocacy—Future National Organization and Service," April 7, 1988, CJF files, box 660).[28] CJF urged adoption of the option that would be most effective for Soviet Jewry, provide the greatest support for Refuseniks, have the strongest influence in Washington, D.C. and in media, be the best national local link and attract the highest level lay leadership and staff ("CJF Reports for Discussion; Soviet Jewry Advocacy, Future National Organization," April 7, 1988, CJF files, box 660).

Option one would centralize all Soviet Jewry advocacy in NCSJ. It would continue to determine policy, be the central spokesperson in Washington DC and to media, conduct strategic planning, coordinate national organizations and do research. It would contact communities directly and provide information, guidance and assistance. Because of the NJCRAC tie to local Soviet Jewry committees via community relations councils, the NCSJ would retain a link to NJCRAC. If possible the New York office of NCSJ would adjoin NJCRAC offices or be in the same building ("Relations Between NCSSJ and NJCRAC, Final Version" March 22, 1988, CJF files, box 667). NJCRAC staff specialists on Soviet Jewry and community service would be transferred or be loaned to NCSJ and NJCRAC's Associate Executive VP "might" serve as a consultant to NCSJ for one year. There would be joint staff meetings and NCSJ would clear requests for community action with NJCRAC. NJCRAC chair or another officer would be vice chair of NCSJ and there would be an overlap of lay leadership. A NJCRAC leader would co-chair a NCSJ committee on oversight of community services. The chairperson of NJCRAC would continue to be part of delegations at national and international events including the World Council of Soviet Jewry and its executive.

Reasons for this option were the need for a single full time organization involved only in Soviet Jewry advocacy. Moreover, the NCSJ had a high profile in Washington, D.C., and in the media and it could act quickly on behalf of the Jewish community. In contrast NJCRAC has many other concerns including Israel and Ethiopian Jewry. Moreover, as a coordinating umbrella organization it would first need to achieve consensus among its autonomous constituent organizations in order to act.

Option two proposed unifying central responsibility for Soviet Jewry advocacy within NJCRAC. In order not to harm the standing of the advocacy movement in the eyes of Soviet authorities NCSJ would retain its name, lay leaders, full time staff, budget, comprehensive membership of national organizations, and serve as a spokesperson in direct relations with government and media. It would become, however, a distinct substructure of NJCRAC. NJCRAC would administer its operations and its New York and Washington, D.C., staff would be transferred to NJCRAC. The NJCRAC staff in New York City would focus on national and community coordination, program assistance and travel to the Soviet Union. The staff in Washington, D.C., would handle liaison with government, the Congress and mass media and conduct research and analysis ("CJF reports . . . ," April 7, 1988).

The proposal justified option two by citing NJCRAC's experience in networking and advocacy on behalf of Soviet Jewry and its critical role in national strategic planning process including the December 6 demonstration and the Reykjavik summit. It also expounded on NJCRAC's extensive experience with community relations councils and federations, the press and travel to the Soviet Union. It portrayed NJCRAC as a multi issue agency with the priority of Soviet Jewry being second only to its concern for Israel. It argued: "Effective advocacy for Soviet Jewry focuses on target groups who join Jewish agencies in responding to other issues on the Jewish agenda and the issue of Soviet Jewry gains strength from those relationships. The role of NJCRAC and its member agencies is to nurture these relationships." Finally, it noted that most Soviet Jewry committees of communities are units of Community Relations Councils that are served by NJCRAC.

Regardless of the option adopted the document emphasized the need for reorganization with greater involvement of community (federation) leaders

of local Soviet Jewry committees in the governance of the national organization. All of the largest community Soviet Jewry committees would have representative on the governing board with a rotation of representatives from
intermediate and small communities. This would provide the restructured
national advocacy agency with a constituency now lacking in the NCSJ.[29]
The new agency would report more often, more fully and more promptly to
national organizations and communities and provide periodic assessments
and reports. There would be one address for travel to the Soviet Union, better utilization of national organizations, and a specified, continuing structural
and procedural relationship with the Union of Councils, SSSJ, Appeal of Conscience Foundation and the UJA. It would also coordinate policy with Liaison Bureau and Israeli government. The Coalition for Soviet Jewry would be
involved in planning and governance with the new agency. The document
expressed uncertainty as to whether the new organization would have its
headquarters in New York City or Washington, D.C. Regardless of option the
Soviet Jewry Advocacy movement required much greater funding in the future ("CJF reports . . . " April 7, 1988).[30]

The CJF Quarterly in April discussed the proposal without reaching a de-
cision. It was decided to poll the federations and to hold a special CJF Board
Meeting in June or July to resolve the issue (Minutes, CJF Board of Directors,
April 19, 1988, CJF files, Box 659 and Letter, Mendel Berman to CJF Board of
Directors, Federation Executives and Federation Presidents, April 25, 1988,
CJF files). In May CJF set the meeting for June 9 in Chicago. It would be held
over CJF's satellite network thus maximizing participation throughout the
United States (Letter, Mendel Berman to CJF Board of Directors, Federation
Executives and Federation Presidents, May 20, 1988, CJF files, box 667).[31]

By the time of the June 9 Board Meeting consensus had been reached by
CJF to go with option number one (Minutes, Special CJF Board Meeting, June
9, 1988, CJF files, box 667). At the meeting Dan Shapiro noted that a "vast majority of federations were interested in Option 1 for an independent National
Conference and wished to eliminate totally the bifurcation of this vital responsibility." On the other hand all were concerned that "NJCRAC's expertise
in community service and Soviet travel still be utilized for the benefit of Soviet Jewry." Therefore the CJF would centralize "the authority, responsibility
and accountability for Soviet Jewry advocacy in the National Conference but
with specific recommendations for maintaining its "special relationship" with
NJCRAC modified by experience and future needs."[32] He emphasized that the
NCSJ would receive a budget increase from CJF of $223, 000 over the LCBC
validated budget ("Minutes . . . June 9, 1988).[33] Dan Shapiro explained that
Morris Abram, Albert Chernin, Jerry Goodman and Michael Pelavin had indicated that they "could work within the proposed plan."

In his comments to the CJF board Morris Abram "commented upon the retirement of Jerry Goodman as Executive Vice President of NCSJ." Although

Goodman had announced his planned retirement six months before and stayed on during the negotiations with CJF, his removal may have been a condition of CJF.[34] Chernin voiced support for the proposal and stated: "NJCRAC is looking forward to working with the National Conference and enhancing its effectiveness." The vote was 67 in favor, 2 against and 2 abstain. In a statement to the meeting Michael Pelavin indicated that "We entered these discussions in good faith; we enter this renewed relationship in good faith, and we look forward to working in harmony with the reconstituted National Conference within the framework of the special relationship set forth in the proposal and in the supplementary memorandum from Bill Berman and Dan Shapiro to Morris Abram and Michael Pelavin" (Memo with proposals of June 9 Meeting of CJF, CJF files, box 667).

At a news conference after the meeting. Morris Abram stated that the National Conference is now "the final ultimate authority" in the movement on behalf of Soviet Jewry in America (Rabi "NCSJ to coordinate . . . ," June 15, 1988). Dan Shapiro seemed to confirm Abram's assessment. He told the CJF Executive Committee that the federations on June 9, 1988 voted to give the NCSJ the principal role in Soviet Jewry advocacy with special relations to be developed with NJCRAC (Minutes of CJF Executive Committee, September 8, 1988, CJF files, box 695). Clearly Abram had managed to keep his organization intact, central and relatively independent. It would still have financial difficulties.[35] He succeeded in keeping the NJCRAC at a distance especially in matters concerning national policy and Washington, D.C. Their special relationship on the local level would remain unchanged.

Yet the real victory belonged to the CJF. Its leaders and staff had orchestrated the entire process of redefining roles. The ascendancy of CJF was evident. What clearly changed in the formal reorganization of the Soviet Jewry advocacy movement in the United States was the increased representation of CJF federations on the governing boards of the NCSJ. It may also be significant that Shoshana Cardin, former President of CJF, succeeded Morris Abram as head of NCSJ in 1988 (Larry Cohler, "The Soviet Jewry Movement Gets Ready for a Shakeup," *Jewish World*, April 15 [15–21], 1988).[36] As Mandell Berman would note in September 1988, "the National Conference now becomes the responsible authority and totally accountable agency to American Jewry on behalf of advocacy for Soviet Jewry" ("Notes for Mandell L. Berman," September 7 [or 8], 1988, CJF files, box 696). To be accountable to American Jewry was to be accountable to CJF.

As we will see in the next chapter when the gates of the Soviet Union opened for Soviet Jewry and the potential refugee flow to the United States created serious concerns for the American and Israeli governments it was the CJF and not the NCSJ which represented the American Jewish community and the Soviet Jewry advocacy movement in dealings with the American government.[37]

NOTES

1. Both were umbrella institutions with most constituents being establishment organizations. NJCRAC also had 114 local community relations councils.

2. Sachar (1992:924) argues the local CJF leaders triumphed over the Israeli oriented UJA leadership.

3. At the start of the Soviet Jewry advocacy movement in the 1960s Liaison Bureau representatives tried to limit the role of NJCRAC due to their suspicions of its Executive Director Isaiah Minkoff (see chapter 2). NJCRAC provided office space and staff for the American Conference on Soviet Jewry. When the American Conference proved inadequate because of the events in the Soviet Union in 1970 and 1971, rather than expand its activities the Israelis pressured for a separate, single purpose Soviet Jewry organization with its own staff and budget.

4. Many local community relations councils served as the local Soviet Jewry action committee. Both were affiliated with local federations and NJCRAC.

5. Members in March 1985 were Nat Kameny, (Chair), Philip Bernstein, Albert D. Chernin (NJCRAC) and Jerry Goodman (NCSJ).

6. At the Soviet Jewry Task Force meeting of April 9, 1987 Jacqueline Levine of NJCRAC proposed setting up a national task force on Soviet Jewry to operate out of a proposed national NJCRAC office in Washington, D.C.

7. In New York City the Jewish Federation and the local UJA were a single unified agency. It provided 70 percent of the funding for the GNYCSJ and considerable funds to NCSJ and NJCRAC.

8. Other members included Froma Benerofe, David Gottesman, Judith Peck, Steve Shalom, Joan Cohen, Stanley Lowell, Peggy Tishman and Leonard Kersten. Staff were Gloria Blumenthal and Rabbi David Cohen.

9. According to Rabbi Avi Weiss (1989:35) Natan Sharansky wanted to meet with the President alone but Morris Abram wanted to accompany him. Sharansky suggested that Maury Shapiro of the Union of Councils and Rabbi Avi Weiss of SSSJ also join them. Morris Abram opposed this and then agreed that Sharansky meet the President alone.

10. Participants at a planning meeting on February 9, 1987 were Michael Pelavin (NJCRAC), Dan Shapiro (CJF), Morris Abram (NCSJ) and Elaine Morris (CJF). In a letter to Dan Shapiro and Carmi Schwartz, February 9, 1987, (box 667) Abram recommended the appointment of Sandra Weiner of Houston, Bob Loup of Denver and possibly Charlotte Jacobson to represent the Zionists. When the Gribetz Task Force resumed its meetings, it confined its scope to activities in the greater New York region. "Soviet Jewry Task force of UJA–Federation of New York," May 21, 1987. Dan Shapiro and Judah Gribetz were appointed to each other's committees.

11. The 1987 NJCRAC budget was $1.3m (70 percent from CJF Federation Fair Share; 12 percent national agency dues; 2 percent New York UJA–Federation of New York; and $10 Community relations councils service fees. It spent 23 percent of its budget on Soviet Jewry issues.

12. CJF Executive Vice President Carmi Schwartz and Elaine Morris provided staff support. Initial candidates were to be Michael Pelavin, Morris Abram Dan Shapiro Judah Gribetz (hold), Richard Wexler, Esther Ritz, Robert Loup, Alan Pesky, Charlotte Jacobson (Zionists) (cross off), and Sandra Wiener of Houston. Shoshana Cardin (ex

officio), Robert Naftaly of Detroit and chair of LCBC as resource person. On February 18 invitations to join went out to Abram, Pesky, Loup, Pelavin, Ritz and Wexler and a different letter to Naftaly (Message from Steve Solender, March 12, 1987, CJF file, box 667). At the meeting Michael Pelavin complained the NCSJ had not allowed NJCRAC to attend its executive meetings. Morris Abram admitted to NCSJ's weak board. Dan Shapiro and Michael Pelavin both criticized NCSJ staff especially Jerry Goodman. On March 23 Dan Shapiro invited Betsy Gidwitz, Earl Raab and Judah Gribetz to a meeting of the Soviet Jewry Advocacy Study Committee (Letter from Dan Shapiro, March 23, 1987, CJF files, box 667).

13. This suggests that NCSJ and the Israeli Liaison Bureau expected that many Jews would remain in the Soviet Union. Goodman commented that if we are concerned about their being Jewish then we should send more Rabbis, Cantors and teachers to visit the Soviet Union.

14. The present board consisted of one delegate from each constituent organization plus 25 delegates from welfare funds (CJF) and Community Relations Councils designated jointly by NJCRAC and CJF. He talked of expanding a National Advisory Council to include 300 to 400 influential persons.

15. He praised David Harris who headed the NCSJ Washington, D.C. office from 1981–1984 (interview, David Harris, August 8, 2002).

16. Attending were Morris Abram, Shoshana Cardin, Betsy Gidwith, Robert Loup, Michael Pelavin, Alan Pesky, Earl Raab, Esther Leah Ritz, Richard Wexler and CJF staff Carmi Schwartz and Elaine I. Morris.

17. Someone proposed restructuring NCSJ, moving the office to Washington, D.C., and appointing Billy Kaiserling director. Jerry Goodman would become vice-chair and policy coordinator on Capitol Hill. Following the meeting Earl Raab wrote Carmi Schwartz (April 16, 1987, CJF files, box 667) supporting the idea of a joint task force involving NCSJ, NJCRAC and CJF. He also recommended that the NY Coalition, Union of Councils, HIAS, the Conference of Presidents and several federations participate.

18. The Strategic Task Force's recommendations would be submitted to the NCSJ Executive Committee or to its Board of Governors for approval and implementation. Morris Abram had appointed Robin (Letter, Edward Robin to Ted Comet, May 20, 1987, CJF files box 667).

19. At this time, Richard Wexler of Chicago complained that the Shapiro Committee had stopped meeting (Memo, Richard Wexler to Dan Shapiro, June 8, 1987, CJF box 667). In a memo to Al Chernin and Jerry Goodman (June 12, 1987) Carmi Schwartz mentioned that the last meeting of the Shapiro Committee had been two months ago.

20. Pelavin agreed to provide NCSJ with a list of chairs of all local Soviet Jewry Committees.

21. Attending were Dan Shapiro; Morris Abram and Jerry Goodman from NCSJ; Betsy Gidwitz from Boston; Alan Pesky of NY Coalition; Bernice Tannenbaum of WZO, Richard Wexler of Chicago Federation and Carmi Schwartz and Ted Comet from CJF.

22. He expressed frustration at NJCRAC for not providing names of heads of local Soviet Jewry Committees.

23. Participating were Morris Abram, Betsy Gidwitz, Judah Gribetz, Alan Molod (LCBC), Michael Pelavin, Esther Leah Ritz (Milwaukee), Connie Smuckler (Philadelphia

and NCSJ), Richard Wexler (Chicago); and Carmi Schwartz, Phil Bernstein and Elaine I. Morris (CJF). The minutes report that Jerry Goodman had resigned as Executive Director of NCSJ. He would stay on until June. He complained that NJCRAC had yet to supply names of local chairs. Richard Wexler (letter to Daniel Shapiro, January 20, 1988, CJF 667) took exception with Abram's implied assertion that the status and clout of NCSJ depended on him being President. Wexler felt the clout of the organizations reflected the clout of American Jewry. He said that Abram wanted to replace Goodman.

24. It noted that the Liaison Bureau "staffs the International Council for Soviet Jewry."

25. In a covering letter Shapiro emphasized that the federations wanted to strengthen advocacy for Soviet Jews to secure emigration of all who want to leave and to obtain the rights of those who remain in Soviet Union to live as Jews and practice Judaism, free from persecution and discrimination.

26. He credited the committee for the cooperation in the Washington, D.C. demonstration and the appointment of David Harris to coordinate the event.

27. Michael Pelavin argued that the community relations councils favored NJCRAC taking over advocacy but he remained in the minority. Present at the meeting were Morris Abram, Michael Pelavin, Carmi Schwartz, Elaine Morris and Phil Bernstein. Some suggested that the NY Coalition cease being concerned with policy issues.

28. In a letter to Dan Shapiro on April 8, 1988 (CJF files, box 667), Earl Raab argued that neither option would work. He preferred the status quo with a transfer of some functions from NCSJ to NJCRAC. He proposed establishing a task force of NCSJ, NJCRAC, Union of Councils, Coalition and others to serve as a policy-making clearinghouse.

29. The intent was not to structurally affiliate the local Community Relations Councils and Soviet Jewry Committees with the new national body.

30. Steve Nasiter of the Chicago Federation favored the NCSJ as the sole agency. He wanted it "owned" by UJA and CJF and controlled by federations who fund it. Moe Stein of Dallas wanted a separate NCSJ with its own executive but supported by NJCRAC. Jeff Solomon of UJA–Federation of New York favored NCSJ and pulling NJCRAC entirely out of Soviet Jewry activities.

31. The letter noted that the new framework calls for federations to increase by 33 percent their financial allocations for national Soviet Jewry advocacy and a 43 percent increase in national constituent agency dues to NCSJ.

32. While wanting to accommodate Chernin's objections to option 1, Philip Bernstein refused to alter the provision allowing NCSJ direct contact with local Soviet Jewry committees (Memo, Philip Bernstein to Dan Shapiro, June 2, 1988, CJF files, box 667). In a revised proposal of June 7, 1988 and in a letter of commitment the next day, CJF stated that if option one is adopted that it would work to bring NCSSJ and NJCRAC into negotiations to define future elements in their "special relationship." "CJF will recommend to the NCSJ that . . . it should utilize NJCRAC for coordination of local implementation of national policies" (Memo, of Intent, Mendel Berman and Dan Shapiro to Morris Abram and Michael Pelavin, June 8, 1988, (CJF files, box 667). CJF would also recommend that both form a committee of oversight of community services. Finally, CJF would monitor the fiscal relationship of CJF member federations to a new dimension of Soviet Jewry advocacy until member federations' allocations were commensurate with the necessary increase

in financial requirements outlined in proposed budget of May 13, 1988. "Soviet Jewry Advocacy," June 7, 1988 (CJF files, box 667).

33. Chernin attended the meeting but Pelavin was in the hospital.

34. Interview with Jerry Goodman, May 2003. Goodman admits he was pressured to leave at the time.

35. In August 1988 LCBC promised to try to collect $60,000 from delinquent federations who had not paid their fair share of a $400,000 pledge to NCSJ (CJF Board of Directors, April 19, 1988, CJF files, Box 659). NCSJ required a one-time transition amount from CJF for the period of September 1, 1988 through August 31, 1989 of $325,000 to $400,000 depending on whether or not the Soviet Jewry Research Bureau allocation is cut by $75,000. The LCBC advised NCSJ to submit a budget of $1,432,000 which is $232,000 higher than at the time of satellite meeting. Dan Shapiro had recommended that NCSJ become a LCBC fair share agency. Molod hoped to get the approval for this at CJF and LCBC meetings in September and then formal approval at the CJF General Assembly ("NCSJ 1988–1989 Transition Budget" September 6, 1988, CJF files, box 696).

36. Cohler wrote that the CJF involvement in the Soviet Jewry movement was a milestone "in the federations' advance as powerful players on matters of policy." The emergence of "Federation Judaism." Leaders in 19 large city and 21 intermediate cities played a major role in decision-making policy.

37. See "Recommendations to Strengthen Soviet Jewry Advocacy," June 17, 1988, box 667 sent with letter of June 20, 1988, of Mandell Berman.

8

The Final Struggle over Soviet Jewish Emigration: A Quota That Ended the Freedom of Choice Debate

With the opening of the gates of the Soviet Union to Jewish emigration in the late 1980s many American and Israeli sources expected several hundred thousand or more Jews would emigrate during the next few years (Gur-Gurevitz 1996:18 and *Refugee Reports* IX, no. 7, July 28, 1989).[1] With a probable drop-out rate of almost 90 percent the expected number of Soviet Jews coming to the United States far outnumbered the available refugee slots.[2] This possible scenario created a series of dilemmas for Soviet Jews, the American government, American Jewish leaders and the Israeli government and Liaison Bureau. Many Soviet Jews strongly favored resettling in the United States and other Western countries; most did not want to immigrate to Israel regardless of incentives and Israeli absorption policies. The American government did not want to accept all those wanting to come. Officially it had a relatively small numbers of places for millions of refugees from around the world and limited funding to resettle them. The American Jewish establishment wanted to help their brethren in the Soviet Union but was concerned about their government's policies, the interests of other American refugee support groups who objected to preferences for Soviet Jews, the high economic costs of resettlement in the United States and Israeli pressure for all Soviet Jews to be resettled there. Finally the situation shocked and angered the Israeli government and Liaison Bureau who feared that free emigration might result in Israel loosing immigrants from the Soviet Union ("Notes of JDC Transmigrants Program Staff, Rome, October 7–8, 1986, (JDC files).[3] They deemed Soviet Jews to be essential for Israel's well being and survival. They contrasted the skills and education of Soviet Jews to the poorly educated immigrants from Arab lands who settled in Israel in the 1950s and 1960s.[4]

At the same time changes instituted by Mikhail Gorbachev's regime radically improved the possibilities of renewed Jewish cultural and religious life in the Soviet Union. Many Jewish leaders in the Soviet Union, the United States, Western Europe and Israel believed that viable Jewish life was now possible in the Soviet Union (Salitan 1992:65–69 and Blank 1995:64).[5] By 1988 *glasnost* had resulted in a renewal of Jewish cultural life with expanded activities including freedom to practice religion without harassment, opening and expansion of Jewish schools and organizations, teaching of Hebrew, grassroots Jewish cultural groups and international ties with Jewish organizations (Gitelman 1990:380–386 and 1991:343–345 and Grossman 1990:264ff).[6] While Soviet Jews initiated some of these activities, the Jewish Agency and Liaison Bureau separately and sometimes with the support of the WJC, JDC, and B'nai B'rith initiated, supported and/or provided educational and cultural activities in the Soviet Union.[7] The changed situation would also influence the response of the United States government and American Jewry to demands from Soviet Jews to resettle in the United States.

This chapter focuses on the response of the American Jewish establishment to the Soviet policy of allowing free emigration of Jews, a change in American policy which limited the refugee status for most Soviet Jews, and Israeli pressure to have more Soviet Jewish émigrés resettle there. While initially fighting for 'freedom of choice' for all Soviet Jewish émigrés, the American Jewish establishment, led by CJF, eventually supported an American government quota on Soviet Jewish refugees and an Israeli policy of direct flights which denied Soviet Jewish émigrés the option of dropping out. Ironically, several members of Congress who opposed an American government policy of restricting the entry of Soviet Jews as refugees in 1989 found that they had lost the support of many in the American Jewish establishment. Finally, when the American gates closed to most Soviet Jews, hundreds of thousands preferred to go to Israel rather than remain in the Soviet Union.

DIRECT FLIGHTS

The Israelis proposed "direct flights" as a solution to the potential dropout phenomena. Uri Gordon, head of the Jewish Agency Absorption Department stated, "If we find a way to make a straight flight from the Soviet Union, not stop in Vienna, then the Jews would come." Asked if they would come "only because they had no choice?" he replied, "That's right!" (Joel Brinkley "Israel Feels Growing Anguish as Immigration Flow Falters" *NYT*, June 17, 1988). On June 19, 1988 the Israeli cabinet voted 16–2 with 3 abstentions to compel Soviet Jews to fly directly to Israel via Bucharest upon receipt of a permit to leave the Soviet Union. The Dutch embassy in Moscow, however, refused to cooperate.[8] The Dutch obstacle might be overcome when the Soviets allowed Israel to reopen its consular section and Embassy (Andrew Silow Carroll "Israeli policy change on visas may not impede freedom of choice," *JTA*, June 21, 1988; Gitelman 1990:381; Elaine Sciolino, "Meeting of Shamir and Shevardnadze Set for This Week," *NYT*, June 7, 1988 and "Israel Chief Meets Soviet Aide to UN," *NYT*, June 10, 1988).[9] Nevertheless, through mid-1989, Israel never denied a Soviet Jew a visa regardless of the likelihood of their final settlement in Israel (Buwalda 1997:172ff).

Mendel Kaplan and Simcha Dinitz, joint heads of the Jewish Agency, endorsed the cabinet decision (*JP*, June 20, 1988 and *Refugee Reports*, IX (6), June 24, 1988).[10] Initially some overseas members of the Jewish Agency Board of Governors objected but later that month the Jewish Agency Assembly passed a resolution welcoming the decision by the government of Israel to secure "direct flights from the USSR to Israel for Soviet Jews" (Memo, Howard Weisband to Jewish Agency Representatives of the Coordinating Committee, January 26, 1988).[11] Several American Jewish leaders expressed concern for violations of freedom of choice. For example, Rita Hauser, Vice President of the AJC, deemed the policy unsound as it might discourage some Jews from leaving the Soviet Union (Michael R. Gordon "Israeli Decision on Émigré Curb Splits U.S. Aides," *NYT*, July 4, 1988 and Grossman 1990:267).[12] In the words of the Union of Councils: "if Jews in the Soviet Union believe Israel is the only way out—after 40 years of anti-Israel propaganda and little knowledge of Israel except the terrible things they've heard—they may be discouraged from exercising the right to emigrate" (Grossman 1990:267).

Most American Jewish leaders, however, supported the decision (Michael R. Gordon, "Exit for Soviet Jews, Conflict for Americans," *NYT*, August 14, 1988). For example, Morris Abram, now President of the Conference of Presidents, welcomed it as a "positive response to recent changes in Soviet emigration policy." In a letter to the editor of the *NYT* (July 14, 1988) he explained that Soviet Jews would have freedom of choice within the Soviet Union where they could apply for visas to the West. He noted that this year three times the number of permits to emigrate to the West had been granted. Earlier on May 9, CJF reconfirmed its support for direct flights. It also called for balancing direct flights with "invitations to Western countries for Soviet Jews not wishing to settle in Israel (CJF "Soviet Jewry Direct Flight Statement" May 9, 1988 and "Notes for Mandell L. Berman," September 8, 1988, CJF files, box 659)."[13] In June 1988, Morris Abram told Secretary of State George Shultz that American Jewry "feels that majority of Jews leaving the Soviet Union should go to Israel, because there they will be redeemed as Jews having been stripped of their traditions for 70 years," (David Friedman, "New Visa Policy Won't Limit Freedom of Choice, Shultz Told," *JTA*, June 23, 1988.).[14] Freedom of choice, he argued, should be preserved in Moscow. The Union of Councils also supported the proposed two track system. In doing so it understood that the Israelis would fly Soviet Jews directly to Israel (*Refugee Reports* IX (7), July 15, 1988).[15] It joined 10 other American Jewish groups that endorsed the cabinet move on the "condition that Soviet authorities also loosen emigration procedures so that Jews could more easily come directly to the United States and Canada" (Gordon, "Exit for Soviet Jews . . . " and Golub, 1989:45).[16]

In a meeting with Shultz on September 16, 1988 American Jewish leaders endorsed direct flights (Memo, Myrna Sheinbaum to Executive Committee of NCSJ, Member Agencies, Federations and CRCs, re: "Meeting with Shultz," September 19, 1988, CJF files, box 667).[17] Abram emphasized that the American Jewish community supported a two-track system and opposed a change in the legal definition of a refugee. Shultz replied that he had no argument with the Israelis but "Soviet Jews are at risk. . . . Let's get them out first and . . . then worry about where they want to go. . . . If I could tell them (Soviet Jews) where to go, I would tell them Israel. . . . However, they shouldn't be forced to go where they don't want to go."[18] Shultz assured Abram and the others that he would press the Soviets to respect American visas given to Soviet Jews. He expressed the view that Soviet regulations denying free emigration are violations of international agreements. He also promised to speak out publicly on these issues ("Israel Seeks to Control Émigrés Destination," *NYT*, June 20 1988).[19]

At the time HIAS organized a national effort to get American Jews to invite relatives from the Soviet Union to immigrate to the United States. It expanded its letter of invitation staff, advised cooperating agencies and instituted a tracking system. It remained uncertain, however, as to whether the Soviets would accept letters of invitation from the West in the same manner that they accepted those from Israel (Memo, Karl Zukerman (HIAS) to HIAS Board of Directors and Cooperating Agencies, re: "Change in Content of Israeli Letters of Invitation," April 20, 1988, JDC files).

In mid August 1988, in a change of policy, the Soviet authorities facilitated direct processing of Soviet émigrés by the American Embassy ("Statement of Gerald Coyle," INS, *Processing of Soviet Refugees: Joint Hearing Before the Subcommittee on Europe and the Middle East of the Committee on Foreign Affairs and the Subcommittee on Immigration, Refugees, and International Law of the Committee on the Judiciary House of Representatives, 101st Cong. 22 (1989)* hereinafter "*Processing.*"[20] Most of those applying were Armenians. Previously, Soviet Armenians left via Accelerated Third Country Processing for refugees; eligible persons first applied at the American Embassy in Moscow, then traveled with permission of Soviet authorities to Rome where they received a refugee visa for the United States at the American embassy.[21] Soviet authorities continued to deny Evangelical Christians the right to exit to the United States. They allowed them, however, to leave on visas for Israel. Most dropped out in Vienna and received refugee visas to the United States in Rome. About 10 percent of those in the

Vienna-Rome pipeline in FY88 were non-Jews. In July 1989 non-Jews would constitute 21 percent of the dropouts ("Prepared Statement of Nancy Kingsbury," (GAO), "Processing . . . " 95ff).[22]

The possibility that the Soviets might not allow large numbers of Soviet Jews to apply for American visas in Moscow led certain State Department officials and American Jewish leaders to discuss allowing Soviet Jews to apply for American refugee status from Israel (Wolf Blitzer, "Split in US over Soviet Jews," *JP*, July 5, 1988 and A.M. Rosenthal, "Justice at State" *NYT*, July 12, 1988).[23] Israeli leaders and their American Jewish supporters opposed this idea (Letter, Paul Berger to Elie Likhovski, January 5, 1989, JDC files).[24] The idea that Soviet Jews in Israel would be considered refugees incensed most Israeli leaders (Gordon, "Israeli Decision . . . " *NYT*, July 4, 1988). The State Department did not confirm the proposed change and INS called the reports erroneous. While Secretary of State George Shultz was committed to freedom of choice he was aware "of the difficulty of changing the definition of refugees in order to accommodate Soviet Jews without similar accommodations for refugees from other regions" (Cohen and Naftalin, "Give Soviet Jews a Choice," *NYT*, June 18, 1987).

A CRISIS IN UNITED STATES VISAS

Officially the United States government and American Jewish organizations favored a dual track system which would allow Soviet Jews to apply in Moscow to emigrate to either Israel or the United States and other Western countries (*JTA*, June 21, 1988 and *Refugee Reports* IX (6), June 24, 1988).[25] While Soviet consent and cooperation remained uncertain in early 1988, an unexpected problem arose in the United States which threatened to derail the dual track solution. On July 4, 1988 the United States Embassy in Moscow stopped processing visa applications for all Soviet citizens until October 1, 1988 (*Refugee Reports* IX (7) July 15, 1988 and IX (8) August 12, 1988).[26]

Officially, reception and placement money had run out. According to Golub (1989:46, 47), the estimated shortfall needed to resume processing until October 1, is $8 million. CJF, JDC, HIAS, and NCSJ urged their government to reopen the visa process in Moscow in order to signal to the Soviets that the two track system would work ("Meeting of CJF and others at HIAS on U.S. Embassy Problem in Moscow" July 8, 1988, CJF files, box 667).[27] In a letter of protest to Secretary of State George Shultz, Jewish leaders called the "temporary measure" cruel. They emphasized the irony that as the Soviets were opening their gates were closing ours (Letter, Ben Zion Leuchter, Mandell Berman and Morris Abram to George Shultz, July 11, 1988, CJF files, box 695 and Memo, Carmi Schwartz to CJF Presidents and Executives "Temporary Suspension of US Visas by US Embassy in Moscow," July 14, 1988, CJF files, box 695).[28]

The apparent change in American policy toward Soviet refugees focused on the Armenians. In May, State Department lawyers ruled that many Armenians had been accepted as refugees "without any finding that they have been persecuted in the Soviet Union" (Philip Taubman, "U.S. Embassy holding up Visas for Soviet Émigrés," *NYT*, July 8, 1988 and *Refugee Reports* IX (6) June 24, 1988). Importantly, Armenian American organizations did not support their status as refugees. They, as did most Soviet Armenians, viewed emigration from the Armenian homeland in the Soviet Union as a form of betrayal. Ros Vartian, chair of the Armenian Refugee Coordinating Committee in the United States stated: We accept the fact that many, if not most, of the Soviet Armenians currently emigrating to the United States may not qualify as refugees as mandated by the Refugee Act of 1980" (*Refugee Reports* IX [11], November 11, 1988). An op-ed piece in the *LAT* (June 8, 1988) argued: that "They are leaving in search of freedom and a better life. This is not the province of refugee policy" (Also see *NYT* May 29 and June 6, 1988).

What the *LAT* said about the Armenians could be said about many Soviet Jews. The temporary closing of visa processing may well have been intended by Washington to signal to Soviet Jews and their American sponsors and advocates that the United States government was unwilling to accept all Soviet Jews who wanted to enter as refugees. Until this time there had been a presumption of refugee status for all Soviet Jews. This changed shortly after the Moscow closing of visa processing. Attorney General Edward Meese following consultation with the State Department and INS wrote Colin Powell, Assistant to the President for National Security Affairs on August 4, 1988 that "current practices in processing Soviet émigrés appear not to conform with the requirements established by the Immigration and Nationality Act of 1980." Therefore, "procedures followed by the Embassy in Moscow must be brought into sync with INS procedures" (Rosenberg 2003:428). Meese urged officials to "be as generous as possible in their application of the refugee definition and attentive to facts brought to their attention by the Department of State and other reliable sources" (Letter, Meese to Powell . . . , "Soviet Refugees," Hearing before the Subcommittee on Immigration, Refugees, and International Law of the Committee on the Judiciary, House of Representatives, 181, first session on H.R. 1605 and H.Con. Res. 73 Emergency Refugee Act of 1989, 101st Cong., 128–130 [1989] hereinafter "Soviet Refugee").[29] For the first time Soviet Jews applying for refugee status in both in Moscow and Rome would have to prove in interviews with consular authorities "a well founded fear of persecution (Golden 1992:469; Beyer 1991:145). The Attorney General stipulated, however, that all Soviet Jews not granted refugee status would be "considered for entry in the United States under my parole authority" (Beyer 1991:146).

Meese did not want to continue to provide parole to large numbers "unless the Administration is also simultaneously supporting a longer term legislative solution" (Letter, Meese to Powell, August 4, 1998). In December 1988 Attorney General Thornburgh announced expanded parole authority—up to 2,000 per month—to cover persons rejected in Moscow and all persons rejected as refugees from Rome (*Refugee Reports* IX [12] December 16, 1988). Officially, for the time being, no Soviet Jews would be denied entry into the United States.

Parole, however, required sponsorship by friends and relatives (or federations) that had to guarantee in an affidavit that the parolee would not become a public charge (Testimony of Alan Nelson, INS "Soviet Refugees," 106). Parolees were ineligible for medical benefits, government transportation to the United States, and resettlement funding [or reimbursement to sponsors] [Rosenberg 2003:428]). Moreover they were ineligible for permanent resident status which made it more difficult to eventually obtain citizenship (*Refugee Reports*, November 11, 1988). It is not surprising, therefore, that many offers of parole were not accepted. In the period from October 1, 1988 through March 1989 American authorities offered parole to 4, 889 persons (2,073 in Rome and 2, 816 in Moscow) but only 482 persons (22 in Rome and 460 in Moscow) accepted and departed for the United States (Letter, J. Moore to Congressman Bruce Morrison, April 10, 1989 ["Soviet Refugees"]).[30]

This change in policy clearly reflected a refugee quagmire in Washington, D.C. There was a huge increase in requests for refugee status from Armenians, Pentecostal Christians and Jews in the Soviet Union but a limited number of refugee slots and insufficient funding for processing and resettlement. Also, some members of Congress pressured for a uniform application of the law; they felt that a stricter standard had been applied to people from Indochina than to would be Soviet refugees (Robert Pear "U.S. Bars Some Soviet Jews and Armenians as Refugees," *NYT*, December 3, 1988 and Kathleen Teltsch "Groups Are Bracing to Help More Refugees on Slim Funds" *NYT*, January 11, 1988).[31]

The seriousness of the situation was evident in the announcement of FY1989 refugee ceilings in September 1988. For the estimated 15 million refugees in the world, the United States provided for a total of 94,000 slots, 10,000 of which were not funded (http://www.refugee.org/world/statistics/WRS97_table2.htm [last visited July 22, 2004].[32] For the Soviet Union there would be 16,000 funded and 2, 000 unfunded refugee slots (*Refugee Reports* X (1) January 27, 1989). In making the announcement Secretary of State George Shultz emphasized budgetary and legal problems; there were insufficient resources to meet the growing number of refugees in the world including the Soviet Union and it was unclear as to whether many of the applicants were really refugees (*Refugee Reports* X (10) October 14, 1988). The backlog in Moscow included 9,500 persons who had been granted exit visas but were waiting for an interview at the United States Embassy.[33] In November 1988

Secretary of State Shultz instructed the new Attorney General to apply the uniform standard of refugee determination namely "a well founded fear of persecution" in Rome and Moscow (*Refugee Reports* IX (12) December 16, 1988 and X (1) January 27, 1989).[34]

Thereafter, the consular section in the American Embassy in Rome rejected an increasing number of visa applications from Soviet Jews. For example, it rejected 11 percent in January, 19 percent in February and 36 percent in March 1989 (*Refugee Reports* X (4) April 28, 1989).[35] Visa rejections were higher in Moscow where most of the applicants were Armenian. From October 1, 1988 through March 31, 1989 4, 919 applications out of 18, 487 were rejected (*Refugee Reports* X (4) April 28, 1989). It was the first time that the United States had denied a "significant number of Soviet Jews" refugee status (Golub 1989:1, 2 and Harris 1989: 70–72,103).[36]

The rejections in Rome increased dramatically the size of the Jewish émigré community under the care of JDC in Ladispoli near Rome. The numbers grew from 5,000 in January 1989 to at least 16,000 in July 1989 including 4,400 who had been rejected (Prepared Statement of Nancy Kingsbury, GAO, "Processing," 103, 104; Windmueller 1989:169 and Jay Bushinsky "Soviet Jewish Emigrants Find Selves in Italian Limbo," *Chicago Sun Times*, January 30, 1989 and "Israel Seeks to Stem Flow of Soviet Refugees," *Chicago Sun Times*, February 9, 1989). This increased the costs for the American Jewish organizations as well as the American government who reimbursed many of the maintenance expenses.[37] The mood among the émigrés deteriorated as many had their applications for refugee status rejected. Congressman Barney Frank called the situation in Ladispoli "appalling" and GAO described it as chaos ("Soviet Refugees," 16).[38] As INS processing time decreased in Rome the processing time of the voluntary agencies expanded; the increased numbers made it more difficult for HIAS and other organizations to get sponsorship assurances in the United States. This resulted in a shortfall of 6,500 refugees in FY89 (Testimony of Nancy Kingsbury, INS, September 14, 1989).[39] Eventually, the desire to effectively deal with the plight of Soviet Jews in Ladispoli would lead American Jewish leaders to seek a compromise with their government over Soviet Jewish refugees.

Leaders of the American Jewish community protested their government's rejection of Soviet Jews as refugees. Many expressed anger and alarm. They charged consular officials with discrimination against Soviet Jews. Some noted that many INS personnel had no familiarity with the Soviet Union and with Soviet Jews. Others charged INS with "institutional bias against special treatment for particular group of refugees" which reminded some of the anti-Jewish policies of American consular officials in Germany in the 1930s (Lazin 1979, Morse 1968 and Feingold 1970).[40] A delegation from HIAS, CJF, AJC and others met with Attorney General Dick Thornburgh and presented him with a brief against the new refugee policy toward Soviet Jews. The brief argued that in light of history and experience Jews in the Soviet Union had well founded fears of persecution (Beyer 1991:147). They received no formal response to the brief. The Attorney General denied the charges and made it clear that the government had neither the slots nor the funds (Leuchter 1993:105; Zukerman [1993:142] and Liebowitz [Interview, July 1995]).

A few voices raised publicly the issue of refugee status of Soviet Jews. In September 1988 a State Department document asked whether in the era of *glasnost*, "conditions are such for Soviet Jews that all emigrants from the USSR automatically merit refugee status." Nevertheless it admitted that in spite of the thaw "Jews in particular suffer from both religious and ethnic discrimination and have only limited access to higher education and senior government employment" (Golub 1989:2).[41] Susan Jacoby (*Newsday*, January 27, 1989) questioned whether the Soviet Jews should be classified as refugees at all. She argued that most of those wanting to come to the USA were not politically or religiously motivated. She believed that anti-Semitism and quotas in the Soviet Union did not add up to persecution. Mark Talisman ("Processing," 144) commented: "I think there is a feeling . . . on the part of some individuals in the government that Soviet Jews are not refugees period. . . . I think that there are some Sovietologists in this country who have made a strong case that under *glasnost* and *perestroika*, things have so improved for the Russians they are no longer refugees." Finally, Senator Alan Simpson (R WYO) noted before a Senate hearing in September 1989 that some Soviet Jews had said that they would rather stay in the Soviet Union than go to Israel. "If they would rather remain than go to Israel, that says something about the level of persecution . . . no other group of refugees on earth gets a choice of country of first asylum" (*Refugee Reports* IX (9), September 22, 1989).

Privately, several prominent American Jewish leaders shared the view that Soviet Jews were not political refugees as defined in American law. They expressed these views at closed meetings, off the record or kept them to themselves. In March 1989, Morris Abram (1989:30) commented, "They are not refugees, in my judgment. If you come out of a country and have access and automatic citizenship to a free country, you're not a refugee. They came here because they are 'refugees' and get the benefits of being refugees, payments of cash, money and medical services and other things."[42]

Phil Baum, longtime American Jewish Congress Executive Vice President felt that deep in their hearts American Jews did not believe that Soviet Jews were refugees in the classical sense of the word for they were not suffering in the Soviet Union in a way that was associated with refugees, especially not today. He resented "devoting my energies and efforts . . . to persuading Congress to make funds available so that they can be more comfortable when they come here" (Baum 1989:50). He added that the more we emphasized persecution the more understanding we got from the various administrations. David Harris (1989:73) called them "privileged refugees" having a choice. Another slant on the matter was expressed by then CJF Executive Vice President Martin Kraar (1993:340): "The implication for the Federation field is that if they're refugees, we still continue to get federal funding. If they're immigrants, then the federal funding dries up and the Federation system has many more financial obligations." His predecessor Carmi Schwartz (Interview, September 6, 2001) claimed that he had reservations in the 1980s as to whether Soviet Jews were refugees but that the CJF leadership overruled him.

By early November 1988 there was a visa/interview backlog of almost 10,000 persons at the U.S. Embassy in Moscow. It grew to 19,000 by the end of February 1989 and reached 40,000 by October 1989 (Ambassador Moore at "Processing," 80 and Gerald Coyle, INS "Soviet Refugees," 22).[43] Eighty percent of the applicants were Armenians and the remainder Jews and Pentecostal Christians. HIAS wanted refugee numbers increased via emergency consultation between the Administration and Congress. It also strongly opposed the American government policy to shift resettlement costs onto the Jewish community by encouraging refugees and sponsors to pay transportation and other admission expenses. It felt that the administration ignored past expenses incurred by the Jewish community of at least $14m in FY88 and $66m in FY89. It argued that refugee admission policy is an expression of American foreign policy goals and humanitarian commitments and should not be sold to the highest bidder (*Refugee Reports* IX (11) November 11, 1988).[44]

CLOSING THE GATES OF THE UNITED STATES

At a dinner in November 1988 honoring Morris Abram on his retirement as head of NCSJ, Under Secretary of State Richard Schifter predicted a major change in American policy toward Soviet Jewish émigrés. He suggested that the "United States may one day limit entry of Jews from the Soviet Union" (*JTA*, November 2, 1988). He emphasized that this was due to the large number of those being let out and "particularly when there is another country of refuge—Israel." He reported that the present emigration rate was twenty times the rate of January 1987. He also noted that much of the financial burden for resettling Soviet Jews would rest with American Jewry (Grossman 1990:267, 268).[45] Whereas Ambassador Douglas had suggested a similar policy in the early 1980s and met insurmountable opposition from American Jewish organizations, in 1989 the American Jewish establishment would support the new American restrictions on refugee status for all Soviet Jews. It would abandon freedom of choice.

In the meantime American Jewry protested policy changes in the Administration. The American Jewish establishment and Jewish grassroots Soviet Jewry advocacy organizations focused their efforts on Congress. On December 13, 1988, the 160 member Congressional Human Rights Caucus protested to President Reagan recent actions by the American government in Rome and Moscow affecting Soviet Jews. They charged these actions had handed "the Soviets an undeserved public relations victory by permitting them to claim that they are releasing more Soviet Jews than the United States is willing to receive." On January 30 a similar letter of protest was sent by 51 Senators to Secretary of State James Baker and Attorney General Dick Thornburgh. They called on the new administration to revert to its former policy of granting refugee status to all Soviet Jews citing the rise of anti-Semitism under the freedom of *glasnost* (Golub 1989).

In December 1988, the Reagan Administration reallocated 7,000 refugee admission slots from Southeast Asia and the Near East and transferred them to the Soviet Union to handle the backlog of Armenian and Jewish applications. This raised the refugee allocation for Soviet émigrés in FY 89 to 25,000. Interestingly, several American Jewish organizations joined Asian American refugee advocates in protesting the transfer (Golub 1989).[46]

In early December 1988 several Congressmen from both parties on the Subcommittee on Immigration, Refugees and International Law wrote Secretary of State George Shultz. The contents of the letter as well as it being in the files of JDC suggest that they had contact with several Jewish organizations (Letter, Charles Schumer, Hamilton Fish, Howard Berman, Bill McCollum and John Bryant to Secretary of State George Shultz, December 9, 1988, JDC files). They expressed concern about the situation in Rome where 173 Soviet Jews had been denied refugee status, which "constitutes a departure from longstanding U.S. policy." They also were surprised to learn that Soviet émigrés seeking U.S. visas in Moscow were told to expect delays "of a year or more in processing their visas." They argued that the increase in numbers should not "compromise the Administrations laudatory achievement of gaining increased emigration from the Soviet Union." It urged the following actions. First, in order to eliminate the tremendous backlog of refugee applications in Rome and Moscow they proposed front loading of all available Soviet refugee numbers for FY 89 to the second quarter for processing. They were willing to convene emergency consultations "to raise the refugee ceiling to accommodate the increases in the number of individuals expected to leave the Soviet Union." However, they did not want to dip into resources allocated for other refugee populations.

Second, they proposed that the administration borrow from the current balance of $30m in State Department Emergency Refugee and Migration Assistance Fund to meet emergency funding for refugee resettlement processing.[47] Third, they called for an increase in INS officers in Rome to speed up the interview and processing time; recent delays increased costs for the government and non-profit organizations. Finally, they encouraged the administration to "reverse its departure from longstanding policy of considering all

Soviet Jews as refugees. This policy is founded on a long history of discrimination, anti-Semitism and limited opportunities for Jews in the Soviet Union.
Despite reforms initiated by President Gorbachev, Soviet Jews still face persecution in their practice of their religion. Modifications that affect such sensitive issues as status classification should be brought to the immediate attention of Congress and not implemented through unilateral action."[48]

In his response, Assistant Secretary of State Edward Fox reiterated the State
Department's "open door policy" toward Soviet Jewry by noting that those denied refugee status are "still . . . offered the opportunity to come to the USA"
(Letter of J. Edward Fox, Assistant Secretary of State for Legislative Affairs to
Charles Schumer HR, c. January 5, 1989, JDC files). The Attorney General had
extended his parole authority which was not offered to other persons from any
other nation.[49] He argued that no Soviet emigrant was denied refugee status
because of budgetary limitations, which we had done in other parts of the
world. Moreover, he emphasized the United States was not "requiring Soviet
refugees to accept settlement elsewhere, as we normally do under our policy
of 'international burden sharing.'"[50] He reiterated that despite anti-Semitism in
the Soviet Union a refugee applicant had to qualify as a refugee under section
101 (a) (42) of the Immigration and Nationality Act. Regardless, Fox emphasized that the number of Soviet emigrants who qualified for refugee status was
greater than the "currently available refugee numbers."

To alleviate this, he wrote, the administration was trying to apply existing
authorities and resources to increase the admissions numbers and funds
available for Soviet refugees. He noted that they were working to make available for Soviet refugees additional 6,000 admission numbers for which the
private sector would pay for transportation and initial resettlement costs.

He suggested that the new administration might want to hold consultations with Congress to increase refugee admissions ceilings and funding for
the Soviet Union.[51] He indicated that after the holiday break INS would resume refugee and parole processing in Moscow. Nevertheless, he expected
the heavy load, limited numbers and a personnel ceiling in Moscow "will
cause backlogs to persist for some time to come." The challenge facing the
United States, he said, was to "solve in the fairest way possible . . . dilemma
of our human rights and foreign policy success in a way that does not distort
or compromise our other commitments to maintain an equitable worldwide
refugee admission and assistance program."

In testimony before a congressional panel in April 1989 Secretary of State
James Baker reiterated his support for the Justice Department policy to grant
refugee status on a selective basis to Soviet Jews wishing to enter the United
States. Several Jewish groups criticized him and the Bush Administration for
continuing the Reagan Administration policy of not giving refugee status automatically to all Soviet Jewish emigrants ("Baker Backs Policy on Denying
Refugee Status to Some Jews," *JTA*, April 4, 1989).

The exodus of Soviet Jews increased in 1989 with almost 90 percent wanting to resettle in the United States (Michael Parks, "Soviet Émigrés to United States in '89 to Hit 60,000," *LAT*, January 3, 1989).[52] Some estimated that as many as 50,000 to 60,000 would leave in 1989 (CJF, Washington Action Office, "Soviet . . . "). The United States government had been caught by surprise. It had expected 12,000 to 14,000 Soviet Jewish refugees and had budgeted for admission of 12,500 in FY89.

In March 1989 the Administration initiated emergency consultations on refugee ceilings for FY89 with Congress.[53] On June 19, 1989 President Bush signed the Presidential Determination (89-15) certifying a refugee emergency which increased the refugee ceiling for FY89 from 94,000 to 116,500 refugee slots. This added 22,500 additional slots for Eastern Europe and the Soviet Union whose ceiling now stood at 50,000. At the time Congress also passed a funding bill for the 22,500 slots including 6,000 that had been partially funded before. This left only 4,000 unfunded (*Refugee Reports* X (3) March 17, 1989 and X (6) June 16, 1989).[54]

Failing to win over the Administration on the status of all Soviet Jews as potential refugees, American Jewish leaders supported the Lautenberg Amendment. Enacted in November 1989, it lowered the burden of proof of persecution for Soviet Jews, Evangelical Christians and members of the Ukrainian Catholic and Ukrainian Autocephalous Orthodox Church to obtain entry as refugees to the United States (Beyer 1991:148ff. and Goldberg 1996:264).[55] These groups would have "strong likelihood of qualifying for admission to the United States as refugees because their groups have a history of persecution" (*Refugee Reports* X (7) July 28, 1989).[56] It required immigration officers to consider whether "historical circumstances" might give refugees a "credible basis for concern," rather than the "well-founded fear" they had been required to prove (Goldberg 1997:264–265; Statement by Senator Frank R. Lautenberg, Xerox n.d. c. 1993; Grossman 1999:188; Pear "U.S. Drafts . . ."; and Beyer 1991). Some believed the amendment made every Soviet Jewish émigré a potential refugee (Beyer 1991).

Regardless of support for the Lautenberg Amendment and previous efforts to obtain refugee status for all Soviet Jewish émigrés, the American Jewish establishment, excepting HIAS professionals and some federation personnel, abandoned the demand to resettle most Soviet Jewish émigrés in the United States. They decided to compromise on freedom of choice and to support their government's restrictive policy and encourage most Soviet Jews to go to Israel.

Several factors influenced this position. Perhaps most important was the realization that their government was unwilling to accept all potential Soviet Jewish emigrants as refugees (Pear "U.S. Drafts Plans . . ."). Recent events including the cessation of visas in Moscow in July 1988, the Meese letter to Powell and subsequent rejection of visa applications in Moscow and Rome made clear the position of the Administration not to accept most Soviet Jewish émigrés as refugees. The slots were not available and neither was the funding. American Jewish leaders were either not interested or unwilling to challenge their government on this issue.[57] They realized that in the worst-case scenario, the émigrés could go to Israel.

Second, the expected large number of Soviet Jewish refugees meant fewer slots for refugees from other countries (Orleck 1999:71). This created problems with other American resettlement organizations with whom HIAS and JDC and many federations had cooperated with for years. For example Caritas and the Catholic charities worked hard on behalf of Vietnamese refugees. To push for more Soviet Jewish slots risked confrontation and potentially embarrassing conflicts with these groups. David Harris (1989:104–108) commented: "There are feelings among some of the other professionals in other non-Jewish agencies that too much privilege, too much attention is paid to Soviet Jews." [58] These conflicts could raise the sensitive issue of the status of Soviet Jews as political refugees. It had become increasingly difficult to prove "that (Soviet) Jews are political or religious refugees" (Pear, "U.S. Drafts Plans . . . ").

Third, the cost factor was important. The American government indicated it would not have funding for all those it was willing to accept as refugees, which meant that the federations would have to cover more of the costs. They would also have to fund many of those coming in as non-refugees. Many federations as far back as 1979 had found it difficult to raise the funding and resources necessary to absorb Soviet émigrés in their communities. Moreover, the federations found it easier to raise money to settle Jews in Israel than in the United States (Hoenlein [1989:15] and Frankel [1989]).[59]

Related to costs and financial burden was the situation in Ladispoli with more than 15,000 Soviet Jewish émigrés and more coming daily. The situation became unacceptable for American Jewish leaders and federations. The émigrés were distraught and the expense overburdening for the American Jewish community. There was no solution in sight (Robert Pear "Why U.S. Closed the Door Halfway on Soviet Jews," *NYT*, September 24, 1989; Berman 1993:43; and Kraar 1993:342).[60]

The cost factor may clearly have been the major reason for deserting freedom of choice. Jacqueline Levine articulated well the changed position. She recalled that in 1979 there had been the issue of freedom of choice but in June 1989 it was not a matter of freedom of choice "as much as it was . . . a matter of finances . . . Finances will help to make the decision for us . . . In addition, in many federations and at many national meetings . . . I see and hear people not quite so willing to underwrite Soviet Jews in their communities . . . people seem to be more anxious and ready to pay and give the extra money if the Soviet Jews will go to Israel than they are to have Soviet Jews come into their community" (Levine 1989:2,24,25).[61] Stanley Horowitz

(1993:264) former Executive Vice President of UJA recalled that while the American Jewish community might have protested the upper limit on Soviet Jewry now there was an "inaudible sigh of relief from Federations, some of whom felt incapable of keeping up with the financial and service demands of unlimited resettlement in the communities."

Finally, in contrast to the 1970s, the American Jewish establishment in 1989 was more willing to support the Israeli demand that Soviet Jews be resettled in Israel. Many felt Israel needed them and that Israel provided a better opportunity for their remaining Jewish and part of the Jewish people. An important organization policy shift occurred in 1989 when ADL publicly favored restricting Jewish communal funding of travel and resettlement for Soviet Jews to those going to Israel. Its leaders held that American Jewry had an obligation to help free Soviet Jewry, but once free, American Jewry could condition their continued financial support on Soviet Jewry going to Israel. Rather than forcing Soviet Jews to go to Israel, ADL argued, it had decided where to send their aid (Foxman 1989:20 and Carp 1989).[62] American government policy to limit the entry of Soviet Jews together with pressure from other refugee support groups and the cost of resettlement made the Israeli option more attractive for most American Jewish leaders on both the local and the national levels.

In recalling this period many years later several Jewish lay leaders and professionals argue that they and the majority of American Jewry remained committed to freedom of choice; that Soviet Jews are entitled to choose where they want to live. We may have preferred that they go to Israel, they would argue, but we cannot decide for them and once in the USA we cannot allow them to become destitute (Golden 1992:470 and Kraar, "Freedom of Choice" 1993). To a great extent, however, by 1989, the CJF leadership and the American Jewish establishment had qualified and then abandoned their support for "freedom of choice."

NEGOTIATIONS TO SET A *QUOTA* ON SOVIET JEWISH REFUGEES

Passage of the Lautenberg Amendment might have led to a confrontation between Congress and American Jewry against the Administration over the status of Soviet Jews as refuges. The Administration, therefore, sought a compromise.[63] By expanding the number of Soviet Jewish refugees entering the United States, the Administration hoped that it could reach an understanding with American Jewish leaders and their supporters in Congress about the need to limit the number of Soviet Jews entering the United States.

Max Fisher negotiated on behalf of the American Jewish establishment (Interview, Max Fisher, February 1996; Gur-Gurevitz 1996:22; Kotler 1993:iv; and Letter, Ben Zion Leuchter to Max Fisher, August 11, 1988, HIAS files).[64]

He had the support or backing of the CJF, Conference of Presidents, and the NCSJ (Kraar 1993:343). He briefed and informed various Israeli officials about the negotiations.[65] He established a "no-name" committee to negotiate with the Administration for an increase in "the number of Soviet Jewish refugees to be admitted into the United States," to clean up and close down the refugee havens in Vienna and Ladispoli (Rome) and to insure that Soviet Jews would be able to leave the Soviet Union if they so desired (Kotler 1993: iv and Mark Talisman, interview, July 20, 1995). The members of the committee were Shoshana Cardin, the head of the NCSJ and past head of the CJF, Mandell (Bill) L. Berman, President of CJF, and Mark Talisman, the CJF Washington, D.C., lobbyist.[66]

Negotiations involved the State Department, INS, Justice, the White House and members of Congress.[67] The entire negotiation was part of the annual consultation between the President and the Legislative branch to determine refugee ceilings for FY90 (Interview, Princeton Lyman, February 12, 2004). Therefore, the "Soviet Jewish aspects" were only a component of the overall refugee ceiling and related procedures. The Soviet authorities became involved; they had to agree to facilitate the obtaining of American visas in Moscow and "direct" flights to Israel. Finally, the Israelis were consulted by the American government (as well as by Fisher who sought their approval). At a particular stage the Israeli government indicated to the State Department that it would accept the proposed arrangement (Interviews, Anita Botti, August 3, 1995 and Jerry Shiran, February 2003).[68] They would have preferred to either lower the 40,000 figure or to close the gates of the United States.

Once the parameters were set on the agreement Under-Secretary of State for Management Ivan Selin and two of his staff, Princeton Lyman (Director of Refugee Programs at the State Department) and Priscilla Clapp worked out the details with the various departments and Jewish groups (Interview, Ivan Selin, August 1995). Thereafter, other Jewish organizations had to be consulted. (See letter, Ben Zion Leuchter to Max Fisher, August 11, 1989.)

The Administration announced the new policy at Congressional hearings on September 14 and 15, 1989 (Beyer 1991:148). After October 1, 1989 refugee visas for Soviet citizens would be issued only in Moscow; processing of Soviet émigrés in Vienna, Rome and elsewhere in Europe would cease.[69] Beginning with FY89, the United States would allow up to 50,000 persons annually from the Soviet Union, most of them Jews, to enter as refugees.[70] Of the expected 40,000 Jewish refugees, the United States government would only fund 32,000 (Kotler 1993: iv). The American Jewish community had to fund, without government reimbursement, the placement of up to 8,000 Soviet Jewish refugees (Carp 1989:7 and Gur-Gurevitz 1996:23). Priority would be given to applicants with close relatives in the United States. Those without relatives or other ties to the United States would be ineligible or moved so far down the list that they would not be called for interviews.[71] Pamela Cohen of the Union of Councils called the scheme a "selection plan" because it bars "Soviet Jews without close relatives in the United States" (Pear, "U.S. Drafts . . . " and Gur-Gurevitz 1996:22). To facilitate the process of receiving American visas, INS would process the applications in Virginia and not Moscow.[72] This ostensibly reduced the need for HIAS to open an office in Moscow.[73] Interviews would be in Moscow and the paper work processed in the D.C. area. There would be a dual track system for Soviet Jews to leave the Soviet Union. They could either apply to go to Israel or apply for refugee status at the American Embassy in Moscow. Soviet authorities realized that the number of persons applying at the American Embassy would be limited. In contrast, an unlimited number of Soviet Jews could apply to leave for Israel.

Finally, first priority among qualified refugees would be given to the 30,000 persons in the Vienna-Rome pipeline and 41,600 persons in the backlog in Moscow (*Refugee Reports* X (9), September 22, 1989). These two groups would use up all the visas during the first year allocation and some of the second. Most émigrés in Ladispoli would be allowed to enter the United States as refugees.[74]

Soviet Jews exiting after November 6, 1989 would not be allowed to apply for visas as refugees at American Embassies in Europe (Letter, Ben Zion Leuchter to Simcha Dinitz, December 22, 1989, HIAS files). In addition aid for dropouts in Europe from HIAS and JDC would be curtailed.[75] This "ended" the dropout phenomenon. According to Rabbi Israel Miller (1990: 32), the dropout problem "was resolved by the United States Government by creating a quota."

Finally, the agreement curtailed the potential consequences of the Lautenberg Amendment which made most Soviet émigrés eligible for United States refugee status. The refugee ceilings set by the President in consultation with Congress and not the Lautenberg Amendment would determine the number of Soviet refugees allowed to enter the United States.

This arrangement of a two-track system in Moscow resulted in Israel becoming, "by default, the destination for the vast majority of Jews seeking refuge" (Naftalin 1999:237).[76] In the words of Mendel Kaplan, then chair of the Jewish Agency Executive, "in one decisive step, Max Fisher has changed the course of Jewish history" (Golden 1992:468). In effect the "change by the American government . . . produced the large waves of immigrants to Israel" (Zuckerman 1993:153). The U.S. quota filled quickly for the first two years. Consequently Soviet Jews who wanted to leave could either wait a few years for a possible visa to the United States or a third country or go immediately to Israel. For Soviet Jews without close relatives in the United States or other Western countries, Israel offered a free ticket out of the Soviet Union. The uncertainty about the future of the Soviet Union at the time led to an unprecedented exodus of Soviet Jews to Israel. The numbers might also suggest that in the 1970s if the American Jewish community had stopped aiding dropouts to resettle in the United States then many Soviet Jews may have preferred going to Israel rather than remain in the Soviet Union.

For the time being the Soviets did not allow direct flights to Israel. To make sure that Soviet Jewish émigrés did not drop out, Israel took the precaution of flying them via Eastern European countries. These countries did not allow emigrants to stay and agreed not to raise issues of freedom of choice. The Jewish Agency and Liaison Bureau set up transit sites in Bucharest, Warsaw and Budapest.[77] There was also a station in Finland which became a problem for the Israelis when the Finnish government insisted that Soviet Jews in transit be allowed to stay for up to five days and that each person sign a free-consent form before flying to Israel. The Israelis, therefore, limited the number of Soviet Jews they brought through Finland (Dominitz 1996; Gur-Gurevitz 1996).

During the negotiations between the State Department and Fisher's "no name" committee some expressed concern that if there were to be a regime change in the Soviet Union that Jews could find themselves prisoners once again (Testimony of Karl Zukerman, "Processing," 141).[78] The Selin team developed a fall back plan whose details are unavailable (Princeton Lyman, interview, February 12, 2004). It apparently involved other ways of getting Jews out of the Soviet Union and flying them to the United States from a third country. At the September 14, 1989 House hearing ("processing") on the plan Gerald Coyle of INS stated: "We would still reserve the capability and right to send people through Rome and Vienna if it was not going to be possible for them to get out of Moscow." It is significant that during the negotiations the Israeli government rebuffed an American request to provide visas for Israel as part of a fall back plan; the Israeli government informed the Americans that it would no longer permit Israeli visas to be used for Soviet émigrés not intending to settle in Israel (Interview, Princeton Lyman, February 12, 2004). Selin said (Interview, August 17, 1995) that Israeli Prime Minister Shamir and Israeli Ambassador Zalman Shuval were approached for letters of invitation and that Shuval refused to provide them.

The increase in Soviet Jewish émigrés coming to the United States created a tremendous burden for federations, CJF and UJA. During the 1970s, almost 80 percent of Soviet Jewish émigrés in the United States resettled in the federations of greater New York City, Los Angeles, Chicago, Philadelphia, and Boston and its North Shore (Berman 1993:50). The largest number came to the New York area where New York Association for New Americans (NYANA) settled them. During 1989 and 1990 the overwhelming majority came to these same communities. NYANA, for example, settled almost 40 percent of the refugees. In practice, funds raised by UJA and earmarked for Israel were being used for settling Soviet Jews in the United States. This angered the Israelis and the Jewish Agency.[79] Other federations who had to absorb large numbers of refugees were also stressed economically. In contrast some federations received few Soviet Jews.

This situation led CJF to set up a special Blue Ribbon Committee to deal with the domestic resettlement issue (Kotler 1993:v).[80] HIAS President Ben Zion Leuchter (1993:97) believed that the purpose of the committee was to find a solution for the 8,000 non-funded refugee slots. At a special CJF General Assembly in Miami, Florida on February 6, 1990 the participants voted overwhelmingly "to share the costs of providing services for domestic resettlement on an equitable and collective basis" (Kotler 1993:1). Each community was responsible for a proportional share of re-settlement costs under a formula based on 85 percent on its annual fundraising campaign and 15 percent on its Jewish population. There were three scenarios: First, the federation could resettle their fair share of refugees thus spending their fair share of costs; second, they could reset-tle fewer refugees than fair share and pay into a national pool $1,000 per refugee they did not resettle; and third, they could resettle more refugees than their share and receive $1,000 per additional refugee from the national pool.[81] The actions taken by the General Assembly in Miami can be understood as the CJF endorsing the decisions taken by Fisher's no-name committee in D.C. in early 1989.[82]

Also at the February 1990 General Assembly in Miami the CJF concep-tualized the idea for Passage to Freedom, a $75m fundraising campaign to "offset the cost of resettling Soviet Jews in the United States and Israel." Actually, the money was intended to cover the cost of funding the 8,000 unfunded refugee slots. CJF pressured the UJA to raise the money.[83] For the first time in its history the UJA agreed to raise money for domestic use with the allocation being set from the start (Lender 1993:240). Some would argue that the CJF piggybacked on Israel in that American Jews usually gave more when Israel was in trouble. The campaign proved unsuccess-ful (Lender 1993:236). Berman thinks that many federations dragged their feet and may have siphoned off UJA funds. He thought the decision had been taken in haste (Berman 1993:51). Dan Shapiro (1993:70) thought that it failed to raise the set goal "because there was ambivalence about hav-ing a campaign that was designed only to bring Jews here."[84] It was harder to raise funds for resettlement in the USA (Golden 1992:82,85). More suc-cessful was the Exodus Campaign set by UJA as a supplementary cam-paign to raise funds to resettle Jews in Israel. It was to raise $420m over three years but succeeded to raise over $500m in two. It was also ap-proved at the General Assembly in Miami in February 1990 (Golden 1992:473; Windmueller 1999:169).[85]

CONCLUSION

When the Administration's plan for Soviet Jewry was presented to the rel-evant House Committee Hearing in September 1989 several Congressmen

reacted critically. Howard Berman (D CA) suggested that the administration should "hang out a sign on the door in Moscow that says: 'For 1990,
Soviet refugees need not apply because there are no numbers for them.'"[86]
Barney Frank (D MA) spoke angrily to Princeton Lyman: "I am bothered by
the suggestion that family reunification is a high priority. I think the general refugee situation is a high priority too. You are beginning to down-
grade that. I worry some, and this has something to do with the disparity
between the refusal rates in Moscow and Rome; the more abstracted the
paperwork process becomes, the less there is a chance for human interaction and for people to be advised, dealing with people and the foreign language, the higher the refusal rate will be" ("Processing," 145). Hamilton
Fish (R NY) urged a return to the previous system of "presumed refugee
status." He commented: "I applaud the readiness that the State of Israel
shows in providing a home to Soviet Jews, but I believe the United States,
a compassionate, humane nation, must also offer a haven" (152).

In sharp contrast Mark Talisman of the CJF Washington office "seemed less
combative toward the government's initiative" (*Refugee Reports* IX (9) September 22, 1989). He responded at the hearings that "actual elements of the
plan are very solid." This reflected the CJF's commitment to the new arrangement which involved limiting the entry of Soviet Jews to the United States.

While the senior professional in HIAS Karl Zukerman criticized the plan,
HIAS President Ben Zion Leuchter gave it qualified support.[87] He supported
the two track system if "satisfactory arrangements for processing Soviet Jewish refugees can be worked out."[88] As for the "principle of freedom of
choice" he wrote in August 1989, "it seems likely that not every Soviet émigré who wishes to resettle in the United states will be able to do so—at least,
not with U.S. government financial assistance. Of course, the overriding difference between 1939 and 1989 is that today there is an Israel. Today there
is an alternative, so that any Jew who is denied admission to the United
States, for whatever reason, can still renew his or her life in a free land . . . in
a Jewish state" (Ben Zion Leuchter, "Article for CLAL Special on Soviet
Jewry," August 14, 1989 [Xerox], HIAS files).

Regardless of the support given by the American Jewish establishment, for
many American Jewish leaders the imposition of a quota remained a very sensitive issue. The Executive Director of the Jewish Federation of Chicago, Steven
Nasatir (1993:221) argued, "Well, we didn't agree to a cap. I think that is not the
right way to put it. I think that what happened was the United States government indicating what its cap would be and the American Jewish community by
and large not fighting about it, and there is a difference . . . American Jewish
people, who remember a time in our history when the doors of this country
were not open during the Hitler years, resulting in the death of many people,
and as a community, we could never, set a quota . . . we kind of acquiesced to
what the government thought was fair. . . . We can't ever go public in terms of

saying, we don't want these people." Actually they had agreed to a quota. Most may have come to accept the new situation. According to David Harris: "A growing number of American Jews are coming to believe that limits on refugee entry to the United States would not be so terrible if they result in greater voluntary migration to Israel" (Peach "U.S. Drafts . . . ").

According to Carmi Schwartz (1993:89) former Executive Vice President of CJF, "Freedom of choice is no longer an item on the American Jewish communal agenda, simply because to have freedom of choice would bring 200,000–300,000 Jews into this American environment. The American Jewish community couldn't handle this number economically, and the government of the United States doesn't want them to come in these numbers and would not participate, not only in its economics but in the necessary policies related to those kinds of numbers. So freedom of choice was dropped from our vocabulary and 'destination Israel' was re-inserted into the vocabulary. "Family reunification" became the new code-word for the arrival of Soviet Jews into this country as opposed to freedom of choice for all" (Schwartz 1993:8–9).

Marvin Lender, a UJA lay leader (1993:246) suggested that most American Jews favor freedom of choice but "Jews generally will demonstrate their true feeling with their pocketbooks . . . they are not necessarily willing to back up their philosophy of freedom of choice. So it is freedom of choice as a philosophy, but the reality is we would rather see Soviet Jews go to Israel."

NOTES

1. Some estimated that a million Soviet Jews would emigrate in the coming decade. There were an estimated 2.2 million Jews in the Soviet Union along with 600,000 Pentecostal Christians. The American embassy in Moscow estimated that 100,000 Soviets would register in 1989 to emigrate and 250,000 more in 1990. This did not include the 30,000 Soviet émigrés in the Vienna-Rome pipeline.

2. Buwalda (1997:160,173) reports a 97 percent drop out rate in October 1988. Salitan (1992:65) cites an 88.6 percent dropout rate in 1988. In March 1989, Richard Maass and Phil Baum estimated that about 90 percent of Soviet Jewish émigrés preferred to go to the West.

3. The Israeli government blamed the United States and American Jewish organizations for giving Soviet Jews refugee status and benefits, which provided a "viable and desirable alternative" to Israel.

4. Former Prime Minister Yitzhak Shamir (interview, July 17, 1996) noted the "primitive " character of Jews from Arab lands. He emphasized that the more intelligent Jews from North Africa, Iraq and Iran had settled in France, Great Britain and the United States respectively.

5. In meetings from November 30–December 1, 1988 members of the Soviet Jewry International Council associated with the Brussels Conference (Hand notes, Jewish

Agency files) endorsed immigration to Israel but also emphasized the need to foster Jewish culture and values within the Soviet Union.

6. By December 1988 B'nai B'rith established a lodge in the Soviet Union. The WJC and Jewish Agency helped establish the Solomon Mikhoels Cultural Center in Moscow. It closed after opening due to funding problems.

7. Edgar Bronfman (WJC) proposed a Jewish Peace Corps for the Soviet Union. Simcha Dinitz of the Jewish Agency wanted "tripling" between cities and towns in Israel, the United States and the Soviet Union (Hand notes . . . , November 30 . . .). While remaining committed to emigration the JDC, Jewish Agency and Liaison Bureau helped those staying to rebuild their community (Goldman 1995:16–18). By spring 1989 Soviet Jewish cultural organizations held a national conference with 185 representatives from 48 organizations. In December 1989 Soviet Jews established Vaad, a national coordinating body. In the early 1990s, the Liaison Bureau, with JDC support, competed with the Jewish Agency for control of activities "Jewish" in the former Soviet Union (Yitzhak Shamir, interview, July 17, 1996).

8. The *JP* ("The Bucharest Option," April 29, 1988) reported on an earlier agreement "by Israel with Romania, the Soviet Union and the Netherlands." On May 20 1988 Kol Israel (Voice of Israel) announced that Israel had not implemented the Romanian visa policy. See Philip Taubman "Jewish Emigration From Soviet Union Continues to Rise," *NYT* May 18, 1988. Buwalda (1997:172–177) argues that the Dutch continued to issue visas for Israel without regard to proposed destination. The Dutch balked, he argues, when it was clear that the U.S. Embassy in Moscow was not able to handle a two-track system.

9. Israeli Prime Minister Yitzhak Shamir discussed reestablishing diplomatic relations and repatriation of Soviet Jews with Soviet Foreign Minister Eduard Shevardnadze at the UN in June 1988. Shevardnadze told Shamir that there "are some restraints (military secrets), but no obstacles" to Jewish emigration. He also indicated that the USSR would recognize the right of Soviet Jews to immigrate to countries other than Israel. Later the Soviets allowed an Israeli Consular Section to operate within the Dutch Embassy after six Israeli diplomats arrived in Moscow in July 1988. With the reestablishment of diplomatic relations on January 3, 1991, the Israeli Embassy resumed the issuance of visas.

10. Shevarnadze had told Shamir that they did not want to force Soviet Jews to go to Israel.

11. Rabbi Moses Rosen of Romania viewed the decision as one that would shame Herzl and create new Prisoners of Zion (David Landau "Romanian Criticizes Visa Decision; Diaspora Leaders Balk, as Well," *JTA*, June 27, 1988). According to Buwalda (1977:173) the *JP* and *Haaretz* and many leading Russian Jewish activists in Israel opposed direct flights. Natan Sharansky argued that direct flights could lead to fewer l eaving and also hurt Israeli's image among Soviet Jews. Yuri Shtern of the Union of Council's–affiliated Soviet Jewry Education and Information Center charged that the Soviets were now saying more humanistic things than the Israelis; they claimed that they did not care where Soviet Jews went (Naftalin 1999:233). In contrast, the Soviet Prisoners of Zion organization in Israel and longtime Moscow Refusenik Yuli Kosharovsky supported the direct flights policy (Hillel Butman, "An Answer to Ida, Nathan and Yosef," *JP*, July 6, 1988). Writing in the *JP* ("The Cold War Against Israel," June 30, 1988) Mikhail Agursky argued that freedom of choice should take place in Moscow.

12. Charles Hoffman in the *JP* ("The New 'Prisoners of Zion,'" July 2, 1988) argued that the Soviets were accusing Israel now of denying freedom of choice.

13. Previously, in April 1987, the CJF had endorsed direct flights (Chapter 6).

14. By late July Shultz had not responded to the proposed Israeli policy of direct flights. He focused on getting the Soviet Union to let Soviet Jews join relatives in the United States (Michael R. Gordon "Shultz Holds Off on Soviet Émigrés," *NYT*, July 22, 1988).

15. Jerry Goodman (Interview, January 10, 2001) claimed that while supporting direct flights NCSJ did not push them in order not to jeopardize the objective of a maximum number of Jews leaving the Soviet Union. David Landau and Hugh Orgel ("Soviet says Israeli Cabinet Decision Restricts Peoples' Freedom To travel." *JTA*, June 22, 1988) reported that a Soviet Foreign Ministry official said that if Soviet Jews had invitations from the USA they could go there.

16. Buwalda (1997:173) argues that the Union of Councils strongly opposed direct flights.

17. Shultz held the meeting in preparation for his talks with Shevardnadze on September 22–23. Joining Morris Abram were Shoshana Cardin, CJF; Rabbi David Hill, Myrna Sheinbaum and Mark Levin of NCSJ; Malcolm Hoenlein, Conference of Presidents; Carmela Kalmanson, Hadassah; Morton Konreich, UJA; Ivan Novak, Zionist Organization of America; and Alan Pesky, Coalition to Free Soviet Jews.

18. He later joked, "The Israelis are not against freedom of choice, they just want to rig the system a little bit," *Refugee Reports* X (10), October 14, 1988.

19. The American Embassy in Tel Aviv argued that the direct flights would contradict an American policy that supports freedom of travel.

20. In FY 88 Soviets allow 300 Jews with letters from the United States to leave directly for the United States; this was triple the number allowed in 1987 and ten times the number allowed in 1986 (*Refugee Reports* IX (7), July 15, 1988). *Refugee Reports*, IX (10) October 14, 1988 noted that Soviet authorities announced intent to facilitate direct exit to the United States without the need of a letter of invitation from a close relative. In addition they planned to allow judicial review for children whose parents did not allow them to emigrate and place a time limit on state security reasons for denial of emigration requests. In 1986 only 1,854 people emigrated from the Soviet Union. The number increased to 25,747 in 1987 and during the first six months of 1988 over 29,000 ethnic Germans, Armenians and Jews left the Soviet Union.

21. Only 246 Armenians left in 1986 and 2,350 in 1987. Authorities expected that almost 12,000 would reach the United States in 1988 (*Refugee Reports* IX (3), March 18, 1988). The Israelis went along with the use of their visas by non-Jews. Prime Minister Shamir told the Dutch Ambassador in May 1989: "I am not against saving also non-Jews from the Soviet Union (with Israeli visas) if that is the only possibility."

22. Buwalda (1997:185) notes that Soviet authorities sometimes issued exit permit without a letter of invitation. Use of a visa for Israel required giving up citizenship.

23. Reportedly Assistant Secretary of State Schifter favored the idea while his colleague Richard Murphey of the Bureau of Near Eastern and Southeast Asian Affairs did not.

24. Shoshana Cardin (Interview, February 2003) opposed a suggestion by Richard Schifter to change the law. HIAS also indicated its opposition. A *JP* editorial ("Stateless Refugees, They're Not," June 24, 1988) supported a proposal to allow those coming to

Israel for six months or a year to then enter as refugees to the United States. Sharansky and Ida Nudel opposed as did *Haaretz* (Buwalda 1997:173,174). The Israeli Law of Return gave Soviet Jews citizenship upon arrival.

25. In June 1988, President Ronald Reagan added 15,000 refugee numbers for Eastern Europe and the Soviet Union for FY88. The additional slots, which were not initially funded, were for 12,000 Soviet Armenians, 2,000 Soviet Jews and 1,000 persons from Eastern Europe. At the same time government funding for resettling Armenian refugees in the United states was cut to $300 per person.

26. Less than two weeks later the Embassy allowed another 400 Armenians to depart for the United States. Another 3,000 applicants would have to wait for funding on October 1. Alternatively, private sources could fund them.

27. The group discussed ways to pressure Congress to intercede.

28. They asked him to either transfer funds or request of Congress "in the strongest possible terms that it enact supplemental appropriations to subsidize this humanitarian program through the end of the current fiscal year." NJCRAC (memo, Abraham Bayer to NJCRAC and CJF Agencies re: Suspension of visas," July 13, 1988, (CJF files box 667) urged federations and community relations councils to mail and phone President Reagan, Secretary Shultz and their Congressmen to fund and reinstate the process. Morris Abram met with National Security Council officials on July 13, 1988.

29. At hearings in April and September INS Commissioner Alan Nelson noted that the Armenian issue had triggered the Meese letter.

30. Some Soviet Jews rejected the offer of parole because it implied that "Soviet Jews are not persecuted as a group, but only in individual cases" (Besser, December 16, 1988 and Liebowitz, interview, July 1995). Beyer (1991:146) argues that HIAS urge them not to accept parole in order to bring pressure on the INS to reverse the decision.

31. Beyer (1991:142) notes that on September 13, 1988 Secretary of Shultz stated that people have an international right to emigrate and return to a country but not to immigrate into any country of one's choice. Authorities expected an exodus of 1,000 Armenians in 1988 but 1,000 were applying per month. Soviet Jewish immigration to the United States also increased from 641 in 1986 to 5,708 in 1987 and it reached 12, 794 through December 1988 (Pear "U.S. Bars Some . . . .").

32. The site reports on 14.4m refugees in 1988 and 15.1 m. 1999.

33. HIAS also claimed that there were 650 Jews stranded in the Soviet Union (*Refugee Reports* IX (11), November 11, 1988).

34. At his confirmation the new Secretary of State James Baker noted that we had more refuges at our gates than resources to accept them.

35. The first Soviet Jewish applicant was rejected in Rome on September 14, 1988. By the end of 1988, 7 percent of HIAS clients from the USSR had been rejected. Rejection rates at the American Embassy in Moscow were 46 percent (Letter, Ben Zion Leuchter to Max Fisher, September 5, 1989 [Leuchter family archive]). According to Pear ("U.S. Drafts Plans to Curb Admission of Soviet Jews," *NYT*, September 3, 1989) 19 percent of the 28,767 Jewish applicants had been denied refugee status since September 1988.

36. Clyde Haberman ("A Very Crowded Vestibule of the Western World," *NYT*, January 25, 1989) reported 20 percent rejection of applications since January 1, double the rate of December.

37. Ambassador Lyman estimated the cost to the government to be $34m a year ("Processing," 88).

38. During this time the Jewish Agency sent emissaries to work with Soviet Jews and to organize tours of Israel. Simcha Dinitz commented (Interview, July 31, 1996) that he was pleasantly surprised that HIAS gave the Jewish Agency access.

39. She also blamed the shortfall on the inadequate number of INS staff in Moscow.

40. Nancy Kingsbury, GAO ("Soviet Refugees," 141ff) found inconsistent adjudication by INS staff of refugee applications in Rome and Moscow, guidelines had changed, staff lacked knowledge of the Soviet Union, Jews and other groups. In response INS held staff seminars on the Soviet Union, Pentecostal Christians, Jews, etc. Mark Talisman's Statement ("Soviet Refugees") noted that INS ask HIAS to help with training seminars. Over half of INS rejections of Soviet Jews would be overturned by appeal (Rosenberg 2003:431).

41. Pear ("U.S. Drafts Plans . . .) notes that while many American officials believed that persecution of Jews had abated during the Gorbachev era, "many members of Congress and American Jewish groups say Mr. Gorbachev's policy of *glasnost*, or openness, has allowed freer expression of virulent anti-Semitic sentiments by grassroots organizations."

42. According to Naftalin (1999:238) at a London meeting of the World Conference of Soviet Jewry Morris Abram stated that the Soviet Jews have no right to immigrate to America as a persecuted minority. Their goal, he argued, is economic advantage. Naftalin added that Abram said the movement was an *Aliyah* movement and not a human rights movement. In a public press statement, however, he referred to it as a humanitarian movement.

43. The GAO claimed that at the end of August 1989 the Moscow backlog stood at 41,600. *Refugee Reports*, November 11, 1988.

44. Buwalda (1997:190) reports that HIAS suggested processing dropouts in Vienna rather than Rome. Also the American Embassy proposed processing refugee applications in Western Europe. Both ideas were rejected.

45. The problem of funding became acute. The budget for the first half of FY 1989 ran out two months into the year and processing was put on hold. This budget crunch would mean that Jewish groups would have to provide more funding for Soviet Jewish immigrants (James D. Besser, "So Close and Yet So Far," *Baltimore Jewish Times*, December 16, 1988). Secretary of State George Shultz opposed the idea of "frontloading budget" from the second half of the year because he did not want to burden the incoming administration.

46. At Congressional hearings in April 1989 HIAS President Ben Zion Leuchter stated ("Processing," 180): "HIAS opposed the transfer of these numbers, however needed, as bad refugee policy with unfortunate domestic consequences." Arnold Liebowitz (Interview, August 1995) said that the transfer angered the Vietnamese in the United States. Several American Chinese language newspapers attacked HIAS. This sensitized HIAS. Later, when HIAS would request additional refugee slots for Soviet Jews, they would emphasize that at least 20 percent be for non-Jews.

47. They committed to work to restore funds borrowed and to assure that funds would be available for other emergencies. They also indicated that Jewish communal organizations are "prepared to meet their total financial responsibilities with regard to increased immigrant flows, in continued partnership with the federal government."

48. A subsequent memo from the CJF Washington Action Office ("Update on Soviet Jewish Issues," January 3, 1989) repeated many of these arguments. It proposed to return to the policy of presumption of refugee status for all Soviet Jews, Pentecostals, Tartars and Ukrainian Catholics and an INS staff increase to process the backlog in Rome and Moscow. (*LAT* of January 3, 1989 estimated the wait for an interview in Moscow was more than a year and that in Rome 65 days).

49. Beyer (1991:142–145) noted incorrectly that parole was not "extended to any other group of refugee applicants seeking resettlement in the United States." Pricilla Clapp told a House Committee that the United States gave blanket parole to Vietnamese in Ho Chi Minh City ("Processing," 72 and Golub 1989:47). Fox hoped to alleviate the problem of Parole through legislation. The new Administration proposed a new category of immigrant for those whose admission was deemed "to be in the foreign policy interest of the United States." On April 5, 1989 the Administration submitted a bill to establish a new category of "special immigrant" to give the United States flexibility to "admit for permanent resettlement person of humanitarian and foreign policy concern who do not qualify under current immigrant or refugee provisions" (*Refugee Reports* X (4), April 28, 1989). The bill would allow entry of 30,000 immigrants per year for five years. These immigrants would be on a citizenship tract. In addition the bill would grant permanent residence status to parolees who entered between August 15, 1988 and September 30, 1989 (Rosenberg 2003:429).

50. Several persons in the administration noted the special treatment that Soviet Jews received with respect to refugee status. For example Alan C. Nelson, INS commissioner in April 1989 ("Soviet Refugees," 105) testified that only Soviet refugees had priority six (eligible but having no ties to the United States). With respect to Soviet Jews, he noted that they "have a clear freedom of choice when they have left the Soviet Union. Just about any other person leaving a country who has a firm offer of resettlement as the Soviet Jews do from Israel are barred against coming in as refugees to the United States." Finally he added that we "give 100 percent financial assistance to refugee applicants in the Vienna/Rome pipeline again for the Soviets and that is not done for other groups" (92).

51. Fox said that they had already frontloaded some numbers to the first and second quarter. He felt an additional increase would "present an unnecessarily critical situation too early in the tenure of the new Administration for it to be able to effectively react." Moreover it would be "inconsistent with a commitment made by the Secretary not to operate at a rate higher than for which funds are available." He objected to use of balance of Emergency Refugee and Migration Assistance (ERMA) fund to finance refugee admissions as funds needed for higher urgency life saving emergencies (Kurds, Southern Sudan Namibia). He noted that Congress had cut funding for admissions programs from $195m to $173m from FY 87 and FY 89 despite the increase in over 1m refugees worldwide.

52. In 1988 30,000 Soviet citizens entered the United States as refugees, parolees and immigrants. By 1989 Soviets allowed emigration without nominal invitation from relatives abroad. The Soviets also allow citizens to go to the U.S. Embassy before getting Soviet exit documents (Washington Action Office of CJF "Soviet Jewish Emigration: The current situation," March 1989, Jewish Agency archives).

53. In March 1989 Congressman Bruce Morrison (letter to Dick Thornburgh, March 23, 1989, JDC files) estimated that the disapproval ratio had reached fifty percent with-

out the administration offering "convincing evidence that the treatment of Jews in the Soviet Union has materially improved." CJF reported that since September 1988 over 1,000 Soviet Jews had been denied refugee status after an INS interview. In 1989 more than 15 percent of applicants were denied (CJF Washington Action Office 'Soviet . . . ." March 1989, Jewish Agency archives). A March 1989 CJF Washington Action Office memo ("Soviet Jewish Emigration: The Current Situation") claimed that 7,000 Soviet Jews were waiting in Rome and Vienna to enter USA and that new applicants in Moscow were told to expect a two year wait for an interview. Former Under-Secretary Richard Schifter disputed the figures on rejections (*Moment*, March 1989). He claimed that fewer than 10 percent of Soviet Jewish applicants had been rejected in 1989. He charged that the Administration's response had been "hasty, ill advised and inartfully executed." He believed that the current policy raised disturbing questions about the integrity of our refugee and asylum process. It also increased processing costs and created a serious hardship for refugees and refugee applicants. Soon thereafter Morrison asked the administration to double the number of Soviet refugees entering the United States ("Justice Department Urged to Speed Émigré Processing," *Washington Post*, March 24, 1989). In March 1989 Congressman Howard Berman introduced a bill to allow additional refugees in FY89 and to transfer funds from State Legalization Impact Assistance Grants (SLIAG) to cover costs. CJF "Summary of the Emergency Refugee Act of 1989" (HR1605). CJF estimate that $100m sufficient to cover needs of JDC, HIAS and CJF matching program (memo, CJF, Mark Talisman and Ellen Whitman to Federation Executives and Government Relations Network, re: "Legislation to assist Soviet Jewish Refugees," March 24, 1989, Jewish Agency files).

54. The expectation was that 14,000 additional visas would be made available in Rome and 10,000 in Moscow. The Backlog in March 1989 was 19,000 in Moscow and 7,000 in Rome.

55. The amendment was enacted for one year and subsequently extended throughout the 1990s. Also was adjusted parole status to permanent resident status if denied refugee status from August 15, 1988 to September 30, 1989. Bruce Morrison introduced a similar amendment in the House. INS regulations weakened the amendment but later accommodated demands of HIAS and other major American Jewish organizations (Zukerman 1993:142,143). Princeton Lyman (interview, February 12, 2004) suggests that Congressional pressure influenced INS to accept the Lautenberg Amendment.

56. The American Jewish position was expressed in a letter from the Combined Jewish Philanthropies of Greater Boston to Senator Edward Kennedy on April 5, 1989: "A thousand years of terror is sufficient reason for a well founded fear of persecution, even if they are followed by six months of liberalization" ("Soviet Refugees"). Similarly a lawyers group affiliated with the Union of Councils argued "in spite of recent reforms . . . , anti-Semitism remains a potent force in Soviet society" (Appendix 1 Ibid., Jonathan Baum et al. "Report to Subcommittee . . . " March 29, 1989).

57. Grossman (1991:189) agues that a key factor in inducing American Jewry to stress Israel as the appropriate destination for Soviet Jews "was the clear determination of the American government to clamp down drastically on the flow of refugees into the United States." Buwalda (1997:192) argues that changes by Gorbachev which ended persecution of Soviet Jews influenced both Congress and American Jews on the refugee issue; Congress would not legislate and fund significant refugee increases from the Soviet Union and American Jewry would not raise additional funds.

58. Harris argued that it is hard to defend that the Soviet Jews are the only national group with P6 eligibility (Gitelman 1991:342 and Orleck 1999:71). One federation professional Joel Carp (1989:7) wrote: "Given the reality of the limited annual number of refugee slots available, the financial problems of the United States government, and the clear morality which suggests that we Jews do not have the right to insist that only our refugees be permitted access to the United States., only a portion of the Soviet Jews interested in getting into the United States will be admitted." He believed that the denial of refugee status to Soviet Jews was about money and not law.

59. According to Grossman (1991:189,190) "organized American Jewry strained to absorb the cost of Soviet Jewish resettlement . . . American Jewish agencies felt overwhelmed by the financial burden of resettling immigrants in their communities gradually became more receptive to the Israeli argument that the Soviet Jews should be channeled to Israel." American Jewish leaders "declared frankly that in light of the financial burden of resettling the Soviet Jews in the US, they would not fight the new arrangements." At the time Malcolm Hoenlein feared collapse of social service networks for settlement and absorption if the federations did not receive $95m from the federal government.

60. Support for émigrés in Ladispoli cost JDC about $3.5m per month. Strapped for funds, JDC took out a $2.5m loan. Clyde Haberman ("A Very Crowded Vestibule of the Western World, *NYT*, February 2, 1989) reported on 5,500 Soviet Jews in Ladispoli in January 1989. By September the number reached 14,000 (Robert Pear "Why U.S.Closed . . . " *NYT*, September 24, 1989). "Proceedings" 103 report 16,000 Soviet refugees in Rome in July 1989 (prepared statement of Kingsbury," [GAO], "Processing,"103). Princeton Lyman (Interview, February 12, 2004) argues that the situation in Ladispoli united a divided American Jewish community to action; they wanted to help the refugees and empty the camps. Max Fisher (Interview, February 1996) recalled that the situation in Ladispoli had prompted his action. A United States Refugee Program policy of limiting reimbursement increased the financial burdens of the American Jewish community (Schneider 1992:190). The overwhelming majority did not want to go to Israel. For example, Jewish Agency emissaries convinced only 72 families (240 persons) to immigrate to Israel between July and October 1989 (Gur-Gurevitz 1996:23,24).

61. Schwartz (1993) concurred arguing that to bring Soviet Jews to the United States "became prohibitive in costs for the American Jewish community." According to Grossman (1991:190) American Jewish leaders "declared frankly that in light of the financial burden of resettling the Soviet Jews in the United States, they would not fight the new arrangement" to limit the entry of Soviet Jews.

62. Shoshana Cardin recalled going to an ADL meeting in 1989 and convincing them to endorse the idea that Jewish communal aid (UJA) should be used only to resettle Soviet Jews in Israel. Mendel Kaplan of the Jewish Agency argued that we in Israel do "not believe in Soviet Jews going to America—in moving them from one Diaspora to another." Jews should have the right to move where they want but not "use public Jewish funds to do it" (Golden 1992:471; Gur-Gurevitz (1996:22).

63. In April 1989, United States Coordinator of Refugees Jonathan Moore told Congress that the Department of State has convened "a comprehensive interagency policy review of the whole subject of Soviet emigration" ("Soviet Refugees"). Buwalda (1997: 190) refers to a new Policy Coordinating Committee on U.S, Policy on Soviet

Refugees under Secretary of State Baker. One of the early proposals called for stopping the processing of applicants "with other offers of resettlement . . . (e.g. Visas for Israel) [and to] encourage other countries, such as Israel . . . to accept them. This proposal would, . . . bring the processing of Soviet refugees in line with overall refugee policy."

64. Fisher had entrée with the Republican administration. He had been a major Republican fundraiser since the days of President Richard Nixon. He was friendly but not close with President Bush (Golden 1992:456).

65. Fisher claimed that Prime Minister Shamir asked him to help with Soviet Jews (Interview, February 1996).

66. Berman (1993:41) recalled: "it was really Max and Mark Talisman's venture." Max worked with the Administration and Mark with Congress. He suggests that the cause got a lot of support from "more religious Christian members of those (congressional) committees . . . " who saw this as a civil rights issue. Many of them were not pro-Israel.

67. According to Deborah Bodlander (interview August 14, 1989) of Representative Gilman's staff Larry Eagleburger of the State Department put them in touch with Ivan Selin and Priscilla Clapp with whom interested Congressmen met with several times.

68. Yitzhak Shamir (interview July 16, 1996) did not object to American visas for Soviet Jews in Moscow (Letter, Yossi Ben Aharon to Simcha Dinitz, May 17, 1989). According to Jewel LaFontant, Refugee Coordinator, Deputy Foreign Minister Benjamin Netanyahu told her that he "is all for the Soviet Jews who want to come to the United States. He doesn't feel his government or our government should tell them where to go" ("Processing," 71). Liaison Bureau personnel continued to pressure Congress and the Administration to restrict entry of Soviet Jews as refugees. It is beyond the scope of this research to further document this issue. Ellen Whitman (interview, August 16, 1995), who worked with Mark Talisman in the CJF Washington office, recalled that wherever she went to lobby for the "Fisher Position" she would see Jerry Shiran of the Liaison Bureau leaving. According to Peter Kovar (interview, August 1995) of Congressman Franks staff Shiran met with many Congressmen.

69. This would save the government $34m a year for care and maintenance of émigrés in Rome and allow potential refugees to know whether they would be admitted to the United States before leaving the Soviet Union (*Refugee Reports* X (9), September 22, 1989).

70. Liebowitz (interview July 1995) claimed they agreed to 80 percent for Jews and 20 percent for Pentecostals. No Armenians would be included. Persons could also enter as immigrants if children or spouse of citizens but this could involve a 6 to 8 year wait. Talisman (interview, October 3, 2002) claimed that an upper limit was not set (it would be determined by law each September). Shoshana Cardin (interview, September 3, 1995) claimed that the Administration had offered 25,000 slots and her group wanted 40,000 (Golden 1992:473).

71. The State Department explained that because of the overwhelming number of potential applicants there was a need to prioritize as to whom to invite for an interview: "Those with immediate family member (spouse, parents, children, brother, sister) who are citizen or legal resident of the United States" ("Processing," 187, Addendum #6 FACT Sheet State Department "Changes . . . " Pear "U.S. Drafts . . .). At the time about half the Soviet Jewish applicants were in 'priority 6' category (otherwise of national interest) and would be ineligible (Golub 1989).

72. Americans could also register in Virginia the names of relatives in the Soviet Union (Talisman, Interview, July 1995). According to Leuchter of HIAS (letter to Fisher, August 11, 1989) the negotiators first considered flying Soviet Jews into the United States and placing them in Fort Dix for processing (as was done with Hungarian refugees in 1956). HIAS opposed this and proposed opening an office, with CJF support, in Moscow to counsel applicants and coordinate the flow with communities in the United States (Gur-Gurevitz 1996:23). Liaison Bureau and Jewish Agency officials convinced CJF Executive Vice President Martin Kraar to oppose the idea. Karl Zukerman (Interview, November 8, 1996) stated that the State Department had proposed HIAS open an office in Moscow but the Jewish Agency convinced American Jewish leaders to veto the idea. Dan Shapiro (1993:73) had discussed the need for such an office but faced strenuous Israeli objections and dropped the idea. Kraar (1993:359) hints that the United States government may have favored HIAS opening an office in Moscow to advise applicants and coordinate resettlement (Letter, Ben Zion Leuchter to Max Fisher, September 5, 1989). In August 1989 an official at the State Department's Refugee Bureau suggested the possibility of an interdenominational American office in Moscow under a neutral name to help in the processing of Soviet Refugees for whom appointments had already been set by INS. He proposed 8 caseworkers for Jews and 4 for Pentecostals and Baptists. See comments of Clapp ("Processing," 65). Max Fisher (Interview, February 1996) thought that HIAS wanted a Moscow office to remain active with refugees.

73. The processing in the United States also got around Soviet limitations of American staff in Moscow (Interview with Ivan Selin, August 17, 1995). According to Pear "U.S. Drafts . . . " the FBI had concerns about sending more INS staff to Moscow since the Soviets would assert a reciprocal right to send staff to D.C. Princeton Lyman (interview, February 12, 2004) argues that the Soviets did not demand an equal number of additional staff in Washington D.C.

74. LaFontant ("Processing," 84) stated that they would clear out all, including those previously rejected. Berman (1993:44) recalls a meeting in New York City with two Deputy Assistant Attorney Generals "who with a straight face told us that they had re-examined the law and were reinterpreting it and obviously that would help solve the problem." Lautenberg bill facilitated clearing up of Ladispoli. According to *Refugee Reports* XI (1) January 31, 1990 the approval rate for refugee applications in Rome in January 1990 was 99 percent.

75. Carp (1989:11) reported that HIAS and JDC would only provide an additional 30 days of support after an émigré turned down the option to Israel or to the United States as a parolee.

76. With the opening of the gates in 1989 most Soviet Jewish émigrés chose to go to Israel. Almost 400,000 did so between 1989 and 1992. Far fewer went to the United States. Buwalda (1997:199) notes that many Soviet Jews waited in November and December 1989 to see what would happen; then in January 1990 thousands began to apply to leave for Israel.

77. Dominitz (1996:124) comments that they chose the way stations in Europe very carefully to avoid Vienna. Simcha Dinitz (Interview, July 8, 1996) claimed that when several Arab States pressured and threatened Eastern European countries against allowing transit sites that a senior State Department official ordered American ambassadors in those countries to guarantee American protection for the émigrés in transit.

78. Ellen Whitman of Talisman's staff (Interview, August 16, 1995) recalled sleepless nights worrying that the doors might close.

79. At the height of immigration to the United States NYANA received $25m out of several hundred million raised by UJA (Horowitz 1993:271). However, the year or two before the sum had been a mere one or two million dollars. Also see Hassenfeld 1993:170-172.

80. Charles Goodman of Chicago and Miriam Schneirov of Philadelphia chaired the committee to find better ways to facilitate domestic resettlement. See Shapiro (1993:75–78).

81. Kraar (1993:345–359) reported in 1992 on a 95 percent compliance with fair share.

82. According to Leuchter (1993:97–100), "HIAS asked to participate in the decision making as to whether we should accept the 40,000 ceiling influencing the 8000 unfunded." They were told not to attend the Miami meetings.

83. Berman (1993:48) recalls that he told UJA that unless they raised the money the federations would skim the funds from UJA contributions. Grossman (1991:187) describes a sharp conflict between Israelis, Jewish Agency and American federations. Dinitz objected to getting only 25 percent so shift NYANA funding from overseas to domestic (Grossman 1991:188).

84. By end of 1989 UJA announce $50.1m in pledges and $33m collected (Grossman 1991:189). According to David Harris (1989:77) American Jews seemed to like Soviet Jews from afar. Gur-Gurevitch (1996:21,22) claims that "American Jews responded apathetically" to "Passage to Freedom."

85. Lipoff (1993:290) claims that Exodus 1 raised $500m and Exodus 2 $400m. Lender (1993:248) said that by December 31, 1990 they had raised $420m in addition to the regular $750m UJA campaign. They then expand Exodus to $1b campaign. Goodman (1993:332) refer to $600m being raised in 3 years by the Exodus Campaign. Eventually part of Operation Exodus was used to help resettle Soviet Jews in New York (Rosenthal 2001:179).

86. Buwalda wrote (1997:192): "It was in many ways an embarrassing situation for those, both in the administration and in the Jewish community, who had struggled for so long to induce the Soviet Union to let its Jewish citizens go." They were well aware that the proposed changes would "turn away thousands of Soviet Jews who had hoped to begin a new life in the United States."

87. In his prepared statement before a Congressional committee ("Processing") Zukerman doubted that the American Embassy could conduct fair interviews for Soviet Jews due to past rejections, the absence of a HIAS office in Moscow (to counsel and advise applicants), fear by Soviet Jews to speak freely within the Soviet Union, and the poor communication link between Washington and Moscow.

88. In June of 1989 he voted for a resolution at the Jewish Agency Assembly which affirmed Israel as the "central address for all Jewish worldwide migration [and] "recognized that free choice of destination may be implemented by appropriate visa and direct transportation arrangements for those who choose to migrate to Diaspora countries."

9

American Jews, Soviet Jewry Advocacy, Israel, and American Politics: American Jewish Leaders Redefine Their Political Interests

COMPARISONS WITH THE 1930s

A study of the response of leaders of the American Jewish Committee to the crisis of German Jewry in the 1930s found sick and old men, lacking influence in the American political arena, insecure about being Jews and often more busy with business and family than with the plight of German Jewry (Lazin 1979). In sharp contrast this study of the Soviet Jewry advocacy movement in the United States during the 1970s and 1980s presents a very different picture of Jewish leaders and organizations. At least four major differences are worth noting.

First, a single organization, the American Jewish Committee, had an initial advantage on access and ties to the Roosevelt Administration in Washington. It was the major Jewish organization in American politics. There were other establishment organizations on the scene with considerably less influence, including the American Jewish Congress, B'nai B'rith (with its Anti-Defamation League) and the Jewish Labor Committee.

In the 1970s there were many Jewish organizations, establishment and grass roots, operating actively on local, regional and national levels in the struggle for Soviet Jewry. Many had influence and access in Washington, D.C. There was active competition between the grass roots and the establishment and within the establishment. For example NCSJ competed (and cooperated) on the national and local levels with CJF, NJCRAC, the Conference of Presidents of Major American Jewish Organizations and the Coalition for Soviet Jewry (formally the GNYCSJ) as well as with the Union of Councils, representing the grass roots. All of these organizations had varying degrees of access and influence with Congress and the Administration.[1]

A second significant difference is the quality of leadership. The top eche-
lon of the American Jewish Committee of the 1930s consisted of very wealthy
and professionally successful men. Many however were older, often sick and
over extended; other commitments both professional and personal limited
their time and involvement in concerns and activities of the Committee. For
example, it failed to find members to represent it "at home and abroad in
meeting and conferences on the German Jewish crisis. The wealth and position of its members sometimes facilitated contact with Europe and European
Jewry, but when business did not permit a trip or vacation, the Committee
was not represented" (Lazin 1979: 303).[2] Family concerns also interfered. "In
May, 1939, realizing that the situation of Jews in Germany was desperate, the
Committee wished to schedule additional meetings on Sunday. The plan
failed, however, because in the spring so many of the members went to the
country for weekends" (Lazin 1979:304).

Most of the organizations in the 1970s and 1980s had an overabundance
of qualified and dynamic lay leadership, both men and *women*, with
countless replacements waiting in the wings.[3] Persons active in Jewish organizational life, often persons of means, dominated the lay leadership of
the Soviet Jewry advocacy movement. Unlike their counterparts in the
1930s, however, most took leave from their other organizational, professional and business pursuits and committed themselves full time to the Soviet Jewry advocacy movement.[4] Importantly, for many their personal,
peer and communal status was earned via activism in a particular Jewish
organization.

Many of these organizations in the 1970s and 1980s had extensive and expanding professional staffs especially in existing and long established organizations like CJF, NJCRAC, AJC, JDC and HIAS. In sharp contrast the ad hoc and
newer organizations were hampered by staff shortages reflecting a lack of fiscal stability. The NCSJ, for example, suffered from a shortage of staff throughout which harmed its activities and effectiveness.[5]

Third, and most importantly, establishment Jewish leaders during the
1930s were insecure as American Jews. They often refrained from pressing
"Jewish issues and Jewish causes." They sought Christian allies to fight anti-
Semitism "without American Jews appearing in . . . [the struggle]" (Lazin
1979:291). The American Jewish Committee, for example, adopted "quiet
diplomacy" "believing it to be the most effective and preferable to more public approaches which lent themselves to anti-Semitism and general public
criticism of Jews and their cause" (Lazin 1979:285). At one point the President of the AJC feared that if his own government were to criticize Hitler that
it "might give substance to anti-Semitic charges that the American Jews controlled the government" (Lazin 1979:288).

In contrast most leaders and professionals in the 1970s Soviet Jewry advocacy movement felt comfortable with being both Jewish and American. They

took up the cause of Israel and Soviet Jewry without concern as to what non-Jewish Americans thought.[6] They did not see a conflict between Jewish and American concerns. They were comfortable in pressuring their government to act on behalf of Soviet Jews. They believed that the well being of Soviet Jews was a legitimate demand to make on their Congressmen and President. They justified their Jewish interests in terms of national interest and democratic and American values. To some extent, American Jews were no longer a minority but part of a majority in a psychological sense (Goldberg 1996:4ff). Representative is Mark Talisman, the CJF lobbyist in Washington, D.C. When asked about pressing for the entry of Soviet Jews as refugees, he claimed that he was not concerned about what non-Jews would think. He acted on behalf of the principle of family reunification.

The Cold War helped their case on behalf of Soviet Jewry since American Jews were seeking support and benefits for a population being persecuted by a Communist regime. This created a lot of general sympathy for the Soviet Jews in the United States. Many members of Congress were strongly anti-Communist and anti-Soviet. Senator Henry Jackson, for example, was a Cold War warrior fighting evil in the guise of the Soviet Union.[7] They saw the Soviet Union as evil. The issue of Soviet Jewry attracted them and their support required very little and had few political liabilities. Refugee resettlement became a key instrument in the fight against Communism (Russell 1995:47) and "Emigration from the former Soviet Union—or the lack of it—was a major concern of United States foreign policy during the cold war era" (81). Newland (1995:190) adds that during the Cold War refugee policy was a "handmaiden of foreign policy . . . meant to contribute to . . . damaging and ultimately defeating Communist countries."[8]

Ironically, Israeli policy on Soviet Jewry complicated the "*Cold War*" context of the Soviet Jewry advocacy struggle. Israel's Liaison Bureau consistently chose not to be anti-Soviet even in the face of persecution of Jews and refusal to allow emigration. It opposed contact between Jewish activists in the Soviet Union and Soviet dissidents who wanted to reform the Soviet regime. Led by NCSJ, the American Jewish establishment adopted this position. In sharp contrast the Union of Councils often favored the anti-Soviet line.

Another factor influencing the political behavior of American Jewish leaders in American politics in the latter period was the existence of Israel. In Ralph Goldman's words (1995:4,5): "The establishment and impact of the State of Israel psychologically changed the Jewish image from that of victim to victor. Jews around the world identified with Israel's struggles, its needs, its institutions, and its emissaries. Jewish political power and Jewish pride, whether real or perceived, escalated with the establishment of the State of Israel." Many of the leaders of the Soviet Jewry movement confirmed that Israel's existence and its 1967 victory had instilled in them a sense of pride and security.

Nevertheless, some leaders exhibited a certain restraint about emphasizing Jewish interests. Ralph Goldman of JDC, perhaps representative of an older generation who grew up in the 1930s, often urged caution. Citing this sensitivity does not, however, confirm assertions by Goldberg (1996:3–7) that many American Jews still see themselves as an "isolated, vulnerable minority." He emphasizes a growing awareness of rising anti-Semitism, insecurity and a lack of self confidence. He describes this as "the gap between the Jews' self-image of vulnerability and the reality of Jewish Power." Ginsberg (1993:7) raised a similar theme. Writing in the early 1990s he argued that in contemporary American life anti-Semitism "has begun to reemerge as a prominent political force, and in all likelihood will grow in importance in the coming years" (Ginsberg 1993:224).[9]

While these feelings may have surfaced in the 1990s, they were not central themes in the deliberations of the American Jewish establishment in the 1970s and 1980s. Possibly, the comfort and security felt by American Jewry in the 1970s and 1980s and described best by Silberman (1985) may have been a passing phenomenon. The situation of American Jews today may be significantly different from the 1980s and much closer to the descriptions of Goldberg and Ginsberg. For example, Frank Rich wrote recently in response to Mel Gibson's *The Passion*: "Speaking as someone who has never experienced serious bigotry, I must confess that . . . the fracas over *The Passion* has made me feel less secure as a Jew in America than ever before" (*NYT*, March 7, 2004).

A final difference between the two periods concerns the personalities of those holding public office. President Franklin D. Roosevelt did not "protest" Germany's persecution of its Jews until after the *Kristallnacht* pogroms in November 1938. His protest involved recalling the American Ambassador for consultations. Later, although he may have been less indifferent than other allied political leaders toward the plight of European Jews he did little or nothing to deter or prevent the German genocide against the Jews of Europe (Wyman 1984). In comparison several American Presidents in the 1970s and 1980s willingly spoke directly with Soviet leaders about Soviet Jews. President Ronald Reagan, for example, placed their right to emigrate and cultural and religious freedom on the agenda for summit meetings with his Soviet counterpart. He even met with refuseniks while on an official state visit to the Soviet Union.

The difference in Secretaries of State is even starker. In the 1930s American Jews could barely get an off the record comment about the persecution of Jews in Germany from Secretary of State Cordell Hull (1933–1944). He was aloof, cold, indifferent and formal on all matters relating to Jews and Germany. With respect to Soviet Jews, President Reagan's Secretary of State George Shultz (1982–1989) was the opposite. He was passionately involved in trying to pressure Soviet authorities to improve their well being and allow them to emigrate. He even chastised American Jews for deserting "freedom of choice" in the late 1980s, emphasizing that the goal should be to get Jews out of the Soviet Union regardless of where they wanted to resettle. His sympathy touched on philo-Semitism. He took a personal interest in the plight of many Soviet Jews. According to his memoirs (1993:990), the release of Ida Nudel was "one of the most moving moments of my years as Secretary of State." On missions to the Soviet Union he visited Soviet Jews denied exit visas, attended a Passover Seder with well known Refuseniks and encouraged Soviet Jews to persevere in their struggle for freedom. This would be the equivalent of Roosevelt's Secretary of State Cordell Hull visiting Germany after the passage of the Nuremberg Laws in 1935 and meeting there with German Jews and urging them to struggle on with reassurances of United States government support.

JEWS IN AMERICAN POLITICS TODAY

Many of the findings here are relevant for understanding American Jews today as an ethnic group and as individual actors in the American political system. The study confirms substantial Jewish influence and power in American politics. In contrast to the reserve, weakness and ineffectiveness of the American Jewish response to the plight of European Jews during the Holocaust, the American Jewish community of the 1970s and 1980s was very assertive, influential and effective in lobbying on behalf of Soviet Jews. The American Jewish establishment influenced Congress and then the Administration to pressure Soviet authorities to allow freer emigration for Soviet Jews and cultural and religious freedom for those that remained, accept most Soviet Jewish émigrés as refugees (until 1988), and fund their resettlement in Israel and the United States. These efforts along with their support of the Jackson-Vanik Amendment attest to Goldberg's (1996:16) assertion that "a powerful machine has arisen (in the United States) in the last quarter-century to advance Jewish interests."[10]

Goldberg (1996:xxi) explains Jewish power in terms of political influence. He describes Jewish votes as an electoral prize—while less than three percent of the voters they are a "key swing bloc. They are concentrated in a few populous states that control nearly half the Electoral College votes.[11] They are also energetic volunteers. Perhaps more important, they are prodigious givers, providing between one fourth and one half of all Democratic campaign funds" (xxiv–xxv). Several important members of the House and Senate have strong backing from activists in the American Jewish establishment.[12]

Also of importance was the growing presence of Jewish members of both Houses of Congress. Whereas in the 1960s and 1970s many American Jews may have been too timid to run for office (Isaacs 1975:198–238), by the 1980s

"Jewish members of Congress had become one of the most important bases of organized Jewish political power in the United States. Working frequently as a solid bloc, they formed the core of pro-Israel activity in Washington. They led the efforts to maintain and increase foreign aid . . . for Israel. . . . They won passage for legislative initiatives to extend American help to oppressed Jews in the Soviet Union and Ethiopia. They crafted and fought for laws to guarantee U.S. visas for Soviet Jewish refugees. They led the fight against school prayer, year after year" (Goldberg 1996:253–254).[13]

In addition Jewish men and women served as senior staff to members of Congress and on various Congressional Committees. Some of these staffers gave the Soviet Jewry issue a sensitive ear (Interviews, Deborah Bodlander and Peter Kovar, August 14, 1995). Stern (1979:22) credits Congressional staffers Richard Perle (of Senator Jackson's staff) and Morris Amitay (of Senator Ribicoff's staff) with shaping the Jackson-Vanik legislation to link Soviet Jewish emigration and trade. Another example is Mark Talisman. As a member of Congressman Vanik's staff he also played an important role in the Jackson-Vanik Amendment. Later, as a CJF lobbyist, he worked on the matching grant program for resettlement of Soviet Jews, the 1980 Refugee Act, briefed Congressional staff on Soviet Jewry and led orientations for freshman members of the House and Senate (Interview, Deborah Bodlander, August 14, 1995).

Yet at the height of its power, the American Jewish community exercised restraint. While pushing and pressuring for the maximum entry of Soviet Jews into the United States when the gates of the Soviet Union opened, American Jews accepted a quota on Soviet Jews allowed to enter the United States. They were not inclined to challenge the administration on this issue.

The agreement to accept a quota may have surprised and even shocked some observers due to the recent experience of the Holocaust when restrictive quotas limited the entry of European Jews trying to flee Nazi persecution. Revelations by Arthur Morse (1966), Henry Feingold (1970) and David Wyman (1984) contributed to a collective American Jewish awareness of American Jewish inaction and indifference of American officials toward the persecution and death of millions of European Jews. These realizations haunted many American Jewish leaders in the 1970s and 1980s. Countless activists and leaders in the Soviet Jewry advocacy movement recounted the tragic times when American Jews did almost nothing as six million Jews perished.[14]

This collective memory had made American Jewish leaders more concerned about Jewish survival and the situation of Jews in the Soviet Union and in Israel. "Never Again," a term used by Meir Kahane had been adopted by mainstream American Jewish leaders.[15] In fact the Liaison Bureau and the American Soviet Jewry movement used the memory of the Holocaust and Holocaust guilt to pressure American Jews to act on behalf of Soviet Jewry.

These sentiments helped to defeat Israeli generated proposals to cease aiding Soviet Jewish dropouts at the CJF General Assemblies in 1976 and in 1981. Despite wanting most Soviet Jews to go to Israel, many American Jews felt it wrong to support a policy which would deny Jews entry into the United States of America; after the Holocaust how could the American Jewish community ask its government to close the gates of the United States to Jews from the Soviet Union? The collective memory of the Holocaust, however, faded quickly.

What is often overlooked is the evidence presented here that as numbers of Soviet Jewish immigrants to the United States increased in the late 1970s, many major CJF affiliated Jewish federations began to retreat from their support of "freedom of choice." Several federations restricted resettlement in their community to persons with first-degree relatives. They preferred Soviet Jews to be resettled in Israel. If the Soviet emigration had not tapered off in 1981 and 1982 it is likely that more and more federations would have supported policies to restrict the entry of Soviet Jews into the United States. This controversy ended temporarily when the Soviet Union closed its exit gates in 1982.

By the late 1980s, however, when Mikhail Gorbachev proposed free emigration for Soviet Jews, the Jewish establishment initially retreated from support of freedom of choice behind the cover of "direct flights" via Bucharest. This denied Soviet Jews the option of dropping out en route to Israel. Shortly thereafter, they agreed to a quota on Soviet Jewish refugees allowed to enter the United States.

The reluctance of their government to accept more Soviet Jews, the limited federal funding and overall economic burden of resettlement, the desire not to alienate other groups sponsoring refugees and Israel's willingness to accept all Soviet Jewish émigrés explain their support of the quota of 40,000 Soviet Jewish refugees per year based on family reunification.[16] Nevertheless, the general lack of publicity that American Jewish organizations gave the negotiations between Max Fisher's "No-Name" committee and the State Department indicates the sensitive nature of American Jewry supporting a quota on Jewish refugees. As Steven Nasatir, the Executive Director of the Jewish Federation of Metropolitan Chicago, argued (1993:221), "American Jewish people, who remember a time in our history when the doors of this country were not open during the Hitler years, resulting in the death of many people, and as a community, we could never, set a quota . . . we kind of acquiesced to what the government thought was fair. . . . We can't ever go public in terms of saying, we don't want these people." Mark Talisman (interview, October 3, 2002) continued to deny that a quota had been adopted; technically the annual ceiling of Soviet refugees would be renegotiated each year between the White House and Congress.

The abandonment of "freedom of choice" casts doubt on the political significance of Novick's (1999:168) conclusion that the Holocaust had become

the primary concern among many individual American Jews and organized
local Jewish communities by the 1980s. The concern about "never again"
may not have been as profound or deep as evidenced by the willingness, if
reluctantly, to support a quota on Soviet Jewish refugees in 1989. American
Jewish leaders had learned to distinguish between the emotional awareness
and collective memory of the Holocaust and pragmatic political interests. In
dealing with Soviet Jewish advocacy and especially issues of resettlement after 1985, American Jews were more concerned about their own well being
and prosperity as a community and as individuals. This took precedence
over the desire of Soviet Jews to resettle in the United States. Importantly,
they had the option of going to Israel or remaining in the Soviet Union which
by the late 1980s was offering Jews greater cultural, religious and organizational freedom.

An interesting issue today would be the response of American Jewry to a
decision by the President of the United States to actively oppose a policy of
the government of Israel. How would the American Jewish establishment react? The experience of the Soviet Jewry advocacy movement suggests a preference by American Jewish leaders to pursue the self-interest of the American
Jewish community regardless of whether it is supportive of Israeli interests.

"SPONSORED POLITICS:" ISRAELI INVOLVEMENT IN AMERICAN POLITICS

The findings here about the Soviet Jewry advocacy movement in the United
States also provide important insights into understanding "sponsored politics" (Portes and Rumbaut 1996:109) in which the "old country" organizes
new immigrant groups in the United States to further its own interests. Newland (1995:203,204) argues: "The impact of refugee policy on broader U.S.
foreign policy objectives is often magnified—and in some cases virtually
created—by concerted political action on the part of refugee communities
resident in the United States. A number of Diaspora groups have developed
sophisticated political lobbyists with strong influence on politics and policies
in the countries where they or their forebears found refuge."

Even though most American Jews did not come from Israel, Israeli political leaders and most American Jewish establishment leaders assumed a special political relationship resembling that of "sponsored politics." Therefore,
the findings should be relevant for comparison with other immigrant groups
in the United States, especially those on the rise in the twenty-first century
who are mobilized and directed to act in the American political system by
their "native" countries.[17] This case may be all the more interesting for comparison because the powerful Jewish group of the 1970s was very marginal
and weak politically four decades earlier.

Rosenthal (2001:1) describes the strong identification among American Jews for Israel after the 1967 War. He writes that "by 1975, American Jews' identification with Israel and their loyalty to the Jewish state had become so strong that such emotions appeared unremarkable and routine. American Jews had embraced Israel as the culmination of Jewish history, as the highest expression of Jewish virtue, and as an indispensable component of modern Jewish identity. They saw their roles as providing automatic financial and political support for whatever goals or policies the Jewish state chose to pursue. Critics of Israel were simply read out of the organized American Jewish community."[18]

In the case studied here, Israel used American Jews to further its own interests (Soviet Jewry) within the American political system. They urged, cajoled and at times manipulated the American Jewish community to pressure its government to act on behalf of Soviet Jews with the ultimate goal being immigration to Israel. Personnel of the Liaison Bureau of the Prime Minister's Office in New York, Washington, D.C. and elsewhere catalyzed the Soviet Jewry movement in the United States. They placed the issue of Soviet Jewry on the agendas of American Jewry and the American public. Once the American Jewish establishment organized an umbrella organization for Soviet Jewry, Liaison Bureau personnel played active roles in its executive and policy making bodies. Leaders of the NCSJ consulted with Liaison Bureau personnel on important decisions.[19]

At a certain point, however, the sponsored became independent of the sponsoring country. This occurred in the mid-1970s when Soviet Jewish émigrés arriving in Vienna chose to resettle in the United States rather than immigrate to Israel. This caused a disagreement between American Jews and Israelis over the issue of whether Soviet Jews should exercise "freedom of choice" or be forced to go to Israel and whether the American Jewish community should assist and subsidize the resettlement of those not going to Israel. The Israeli government supported by Max Fisher and other American Jewish leaders and organizations proposed that HIAS and JDC cease aiding Soviet Jewish dropouts. Carl Glick, President of HIAS, opposed the Israeli position. Alone, Glick and HIAS lacked the resources and clout to defeat Israeli pressure on the American Jewish leadership. It was the local federation leadership, lay and professionals, motivated by memories of the Holocaust and an America closed to Jewish refugees who defeated the Israeli proposals at the CJF General Assemblies in Philadelphia (1976) and in Detroit (1981).[20] They favored freedom of choice.

After 1976 the CJF, representing federations throughout the United States, and not NCSJ, played a controlling role in the Soviet Jewry advocacy movement in the American Jewish establishment. Importantly, the Israelis had far less influence in this organization than they had in the NCSJ.

By the 1980s both Rosenthal and Goldberg explain a growing gap between Israel and the American Jewish community marked by greater American

Jewish independence vis-à-vis Israeli political leaders. Rosenthal points to the settlement policies, the War in Lebanon, demographic changes in Israel and greater assimilation in the United States to explain the chasm. Goldberg focuses on the debate over the issue "Who is a Jew" in 1988.[21]

Both authors present the American Jewish community as being reactive; it defined its relationship to Israel in response to Israeli politics and policies. The evidence here suggests a more proactive American Jewish community which defines its relationship to Israel in terms of its own interests and at times independently of what is happening in Israel. The evidence here supports a point made by Friedman (1999:8) that the Soviet Jewry movement led to a greater willingness for American Jewish leaders to challenge Israel (except on defense issues). While Israel used its exalted position in the minds of mainstream American Jewish leaders to bring the American Jewish community into the Soviet Jewry movement, involvement in the movement changed American Jewish attitudes toward Israel. It was a not a quick change but one that developed over the years.

American Jewish leaders in CJF, UJA, the federations, JDC, and HIAS were very pro-Israel in the late 1960s following the Six Day War. The entire community was involved in fund raising efforts and communal activities in which Israel stood at the center. Israel easily tapped this combination of good will, involvement and Holocaust guilt to foster the Soviet Jewry movement among the American Jewish community. Ironically the participation of American Jews in the Soviet Jewry movement helped direct them away from concern with Israel to focus on Jews elsewhere and eventually in their own communities.[22] By the 1970s while raising money to help Israel they were also funding resettlement services for Soviet Jews who had recently arrived in their own communities. They came to see their "Jewish interest" differing from that of the Israelis. Some even challenged Israel's claim of needing the Soviet Jews and put forth an American claim for a maximum number of Soviet Jewish émigrés (Jim Rice, Comments at Board of Trustees, UAHC, Los Angeles, December 4, 1976).[23] Many American Jewish leaders put "freedom of choice" before "Israel's national interest." This contributed to a new awareness and a new Jewish identity (more inward than Israeli oriented). To a great degree the centrality of Israel gave way to local and internal concerns.

Naftalin (1999:239,240) confirms this when he writes that new Jewish leaders "are further from the Holocaust; are more psychologically distanced from Israel; are less guided by a deep sense of Jewish responsibility; and seem more inclined to support secular institutions such as hospitals, universities, museums, symphonies and opera companies than the needs of their brethren abroad. . . . There is more than a suggestion that American Jews are turning inward, away from the needs of Israel, certainly away from the issues of Soviet Jews." They are most concerned today about being decimated "through assimilation."

Symbolically, the CJF had come to control the Soviet Jewry advocacy movement in the United States by the 1980s. It had also become the major "Jewish" organization in American politics. In the conflict over turf, function and leadership in Soviet Jewry advocacy in the United States between the National Conference of Soviet Jewry and the NJCRAC, the CJF arbitrated. When Max Fisher negotiated with the American government over a quota for Soviet Jewish refugees, he coordinated his efforts with the CJF. In contrast with the NCSJ which the Israelis had initiated and guided the CJF was an American organization whose leaders and professionals placed the interests and concerns of American Jews first. While many had sympathy for Israel and defined themselves as Zionists, they were more concerned about the needs of the American Jewish community. For some in fact, the more Soviet Jews that came to America, the more American Jewry and the Jewish people benefited.

Israel had begun the struggle for the liberation of Soviet Jewry and their immigration to Israel. Its leaders realized that success required the support of the American government. They achieved this through the mobilization of an American Jewish community whose leaders at the time were more than willing to follow the lead of Israel. Involvement in the Soviet Jewry advocacy movement shifted the interests of American Jewish leaders away from concern with Israel. Initially, American Jewish leaders defended freedom of choice against Israeli pressure to cease aiding Soviet Jewish dropouts to enter and resettle in the United States. When Gorbachev opened the gates of the Soviet Union to most Soviet Jews who wished to emigrate in 1989, the American Jewish leadership abandoned freedom of choice, supported a quota and favored Soviet Jews resettling in Israel. In doing so they were not bending to Israeli demands. Rather, they had succumbed to pressure from their own government and other sponsors of refugees and to the enormous economic expense of resettlement in the United States. It was cheaper to resettle them in Israel.

NOTES

1. The Union of Councils had considerable influence in Washington. Its influence and ties with Jews in the Soviet Union may have even surpassed that of the NCSJ.

2. During the 1930s the Committee decided to act on requests from European Jewish leaders to send a high-ranking "Committee member . . . to Europe for a year or two to serve as a liaison with European Jewry. . . . The Committee was unable to find an appropriate member . . . to fulfill this function."

3. Jewish women held leadership positions in several organizations including the American Jewish Congress, CJF, JDC, NJCRAC, NCSJ and Union of Councils.

4. Goldberg asserts (1996:76) Jewish leadership" has acquired the popular image of a self-appointed elite that controls the Jewish institutional world through its money."

5. Many senior leaders in the Soviet Jewry movement continuously criticized the staff at NCSJ. The poor performance of senior officials hurt HIAS in the 1980s.

6. Feingold (1995) argues that many politically active Jews in the 1930s were secular Jews without a sense of being Jewish.

7. According to Goldberg (1996:164), Henry Jackson a Lutheran of Norwegian ancestry had liberal views on domestic policy but was "one of the most unbending anti-Communists on Capitol Hill."

8. Ambassador Douglas (Interview, June 29, 2004) confirmed this. Also see Zolberg 1995:122.

9. Both Ginsberg (221) and Goldberg, focus on President George H.W. Bush's attack against the pro-Israel lobby over the issue of loan guarantees in the summer of 1991; "the Bush speech marked the first time in nearly forty years that an American president had questioned the legitimacy of pro-Israel lobbying efforts by American Jews" (Ginsberg 1993:223,224).

10. Goldberg (1996:4,5) cites Washington's $3b a year aid to Israel, rescue of Iranian and Ethiopian Jewries, and construction of the Holocaust Museum. Jewish power is also felt in civil rights and affirmative action, abortion rights, and church state separation issues. The Jackson-Vanik Amendment, he argues, gave "the Jewish community a veto over America's commercial links with Moscow." Newland (1995:208) writes: "Today the number and the political economic abilities of the Jewish-American population make it impossible to ignore their concerns."

11. They constitute 18.3 percent of the electorate in New York State and 5.8 percent in California (Goldberg 1996:xxx).

12. In a meeting of Jewish leaders at the White House on June 8, 1979 (Notes of Irving Kessler, JDC files) Richard Clark, Special Ambassador on Refugees thanked Jerold Hoffberger of Baltimore for getting Congressman Long to refinance an Emergency Fund for Refugees. Marvin Lender, a senior UJA lay leader, emphasized his close ties to Congressman Bruce Morrison who played a major role in matters of refugees and immigration during the 1980s (Interview, February 1997).

13. In 1991 there were 33 Jews in the House (7.5 percent) and 10 Jewish Senators. In the 109th Congress (2005) there are 11 Jewish Senators and 26 Jewish members of the House of Representatives (http://www.Jewishvirtuallibrary.org/sources/us-israel/Jewishcong108.html, July 4, 2004; M. Berger, "Congress says Goodbye to Two Jews, Hello to Two New Jewish Women," *Jewish News Weekly of Northern California*, November 5, 2004).

14. Some of the Soviet Jewry activists were children of Holocaust survivors. This cohort also became active in federations around the country.

15. Novick (1999:174) writes: "The responsive chord struck by Kahane's repeated invocation of the Holocaust gave rise to a fear among established Jewish organizations that he was establishing a kind of rhetorically ownership of it. In order to block this takeover bid by the usurper, they themselves began to talk more about the Holocaust."

16. Moreover, the resulting massive flow of Soviet Jews to Israel benefited the country which wanted and needed the human capital from the Soviet Union.

17. According to Newland (1995:211): "The political activism of Cuban-, Jewish-, and Armenian-Americans is seen as a model by other refugee communities such as the Vietnamese and Haitians."

18. Goldberg (1996:xix) notes that most major American Jewish organizations "share a long tradition of refusing to question Israeli government policy decisions." He cites (205–209) the case of the American Jewish organization *Breira* in the mid-1970s which challenged Israel on the Palestinian issue when "The right of Jews to dissent from Israeli policy" was a painful issue in the American Jewish community. Israel cracked down with its Ambassador Simcha Dinitz meeting with the Conference of Presidents and NJCRAC. They agreed on guidelines for behavior in the American Jewish community. Two of the tenets were that the Israelis were the only ones entitled to decide Israeli policy for they bore risks and that American Jews had to stand publicly united with Israel and air disagreements only in private.

19. In contrast the Union of Councils acted independently of the Liaison Bureau.

20. Some professionals were motivated by a desire to bring more Soviet Jews to the United States.

21. At the November 1988 CJF General Assembly, American Jewish leaders protested an agreement made by Prime Minister Shamir with the ultra-Orthodox over who is a Jew (Goldberg 1996:338–342).

22. Rosenthal 2001:33 notes that the low rate of immigration of American Jews to Israel after 1967 indicates that "despite their emotional support of Israel, American Jews' priorities remained overwhelmingly American."

23. Jim Rice rejected the Israeli claim to Soviet Jews based on its absorption of so many uneducated Jews from North Africa in the 1950s. Rice pushed a counter "American Jewish" claim for Soviet Jews since the community had not been replenished since Congress had closed the gates of America to massive immigration in 1924. He clearly articulated a point made by the historian Henry Feingold (1981), who suggested that the American Jewish community has competed with Israel for "Jews since the 1940s."

Appendix 1: Statistical Information

Table 1.   Immigrants to Israel from the Soviet Union, 1948–1966*

Year	Number of Immigrants
1948–53	18
1954	53
1955	105
1956	753
1957	149
1958	12
1959	7
1960	102
1961	128
1962	182
1963	388
1964	539
1965	1,444
1966	1,892
Total	5,772

*In addition, between 1957–1959, the Soviet Union repatriated 25,000 Jews to Poland; many of them immigrated to Israel.

Source: Fax, Israeli Source (probably Liaison Bureau) to JDC (NY), "Annual FSU/Soviet Aliyah," August 10, 1995 (JDC files).

Appendix 1

**Table 2. Arrivals of Soviet Jews to
Israel, 1966–1975**

Year	Number
1966	2,054
1967	1,403
1968	304
1969	3,019
1970	992
1971	12,839
1972	31,652
1973	33,477
1974	16,816
1975	8,531
Total	111,007

Source: Edelman 1976: 159.

Table 3. Soviet Jewish Emigration, 1954–1994

Year	Total Number Emigrating	
1954	53	
1955	105	
1956	454	
1957	149	
1958	12	
1959	3	776 (for decade above)
1960	60	
1961	202	
1962	184	
1963	305	
1964	537	
1965	891	
1966	2,047	
1967	1,406	
1968	229	
1969	2,979	8,840 (for decade above)
1970	1,027	
1971	13,022	
1972	31,681	
1973	34,733	
1974	29,628	
1975	13,221	
1976	14,261	
1977	16,736	
1978	28,865	
1979	51,320	225,494 (for decade above)
1980	21,471	
1981	9,447	
1982	2,688	
1983	1,315	
1984	896	
1985	1,139	
1986	914	
1987	8,155	
1988	18,919	
1989	71,196	181,802 (for decade above)
1990	181,802	
1991	178,566	
1992	108,292	
1993	102,134	
1994	34,437	605,231 (from Jan. 1990 to May 1994)

Overall total May 1954–May 1994 = 976,481

Source: Action for Post Soviet Jewry, suite 306, 24 Crescent Street, Waltham MA 02154 USA & Goldman 1995: 359.

Table 4.   Exit, Aliyah and Dropouts of Soviet/FSU Jews 1968–1992

Year	# Leaving USSR/FSU	# Invitations Sent to Families	# Immigrating to Israel	# Drop Outs	Percent Drop Outs
1967	1,162		1,162		0
1968	231	1,550	231	—	0
1969	3,033	10,267	3,033	—	0
1970	999	4,307	999	—	9
1971	12,897	22,933	12,839	58	.4
1972	31,903	40,546	31,652	251	.7
1973	34,733	40,576	33,277	1,456	3.6
1974	20,767	33,305	16,888	3,879	18.7
1975	13,363	28,041	8,435	4,928	36.9
1976	14,254	33,088	7,250	7,004	49.1
1977	16,833	44,209	8,350	8,483	50.4
1978	28,956	82,766	12,090	16,866	58.2
1979	51,331	99,825	17,278	34,053	66.3
1980	21,648	48,628	7,570	14,078	65.0
1981	9,448	23,143	1,762	7,687	81.4
1982	2,692	11,818	731	1,961	72.8
1983	1,314	8,743	861	453	34.5
1984	896	6,367	340	556	34.5
1985	1,140	7,574	348	792	69.5
1986	904	6,657	201	703	77.8
1987	8,155	20,068	2,072	6,083	74.6
1988	18,961	100,000	2,173	16,788	88.5
1989	71,005	300,000	12,117	58,888[f]	82.9
1990	228,400	1,000,000[a]	183,400[b]	45,000	19.7
1991	187,500	—	147,520[c]	39,980	21.3
1992	122,398[d]	600,000[e]	64,648	57,750	47.2
1993	101,887	65,953	66,145[g]	—	—
1994	100,830	69,974	68,079	—	—

[a]Number of family reunion invitations sent from Israel in hands of Soviet Jews
[b]Add to this number 868 tourists who settled in Israel
[c]According to Israeli Ministry of Immigrant Absorption
[d]This number includes 45,000 to the US and 10,000 to Germany
[e]Holding invitations according to the data of Israeli Ministry of Absorption
[f]Until 1989 numbers given include Jews who arrived in Vienna, dropped out and proceeded to countries in the West, and since 1990 include Jews who emigrated directly from the Former State Union (FSU) to the West.
[g]1993 and 1994 figures to Israel based on Israeli Ministry of Immigrant absorption statistics.

Sources: Jewish Agency for Israel Report. 1993: Report of the Jewish Agency's Immigration Department to the General Assembly, June 1995 & Fax, Israeli Source (probably Liaison Bureau) to JDC (NY), "Annual FSU/Soviet Aliyah," August 10, 1995 (JDC files).

Table 5.   Emigration from the Soviet Union

Year	Jewish	Armenian	German	Evangelical Protestant	Total
1971	13,022	886			13,908
1972	31,681	75	3,315		35,071
1973	34,733	185	4,436		39,354
1974	20,628	291	6,345		27,555
1975	13,221	455	5,752		19,428
1976	14,261	1,779	9,626		25,666
1977	16,736	1,390	9,119		27,245
1978	28,864	1,123	8,276		38,263
1979	51,320	3,581	6,947		61,848
1980	21,471	6,109	6,653		34,233
1981	9,447	1,905	3,595		16,852
1982	2,688	338	1,958		4,984
1983	1,315	193	1,447		2,955
1984	896	88	913		1,897
1985	1,140	109	406		1,655
1986	914	247	783		1,944
1987	8,155	3,248	14,488		2,5891
1988	19,292	10,981	47,572	2,000	79,845
1989*	27,200	2,834	49,154	6,062	8,5250

* January–July 1989
* Thus far in 1989 total emigration running at an annualized rate of 146,000 and Jewish emigration is running at an annualized rate of more than 46,000.
* Monthly rates of Jewish emigration 2,796 in January, 2,425 in February, 4,325 in March, 4,991 in April, 3,840 in May, 4,462 in June, and 4,628 in July.
* In late 1988 and early 1989 the emigration figures do not include growing backlog of Armenians (and to a lesser degree, Jews) who have exit permission or good prospects of getting it but have not been processed by the U.S. Embassy, or have been advised by the Embassy to hold off on obtaining exit permission. This backlog amounts to some 34,000 persons.

Source: Department of State, Office of Soviet Union Affairs, July 13, 1989 in "Processing of Soviet Refugees" 1989: 205.

Table 6. Designated Areas of HIAS Assisted Soviet Jewish Arrivals, 1966–1975

Year	Area USA	Canada	Australia	New Zealand	Latin America	Europe	Totals
1966	36	—	11	—	3	2	52
1967	72	—	4	—			
1968	92	—	—	—			
1969	156	2	9	—			
1970	124	—	3	—			
1971	214	24	12	—			
1972	453	11	17	—			
1973	1,449	196	46	—			
1974	3,490	398	119	—			
1975	5,250	847	305	47			
Grand Total	13,336	1,478	526	47			

Source: Edelman 1976: 159.

Table 7. Resettlement of HIAS Assisted Arrivals in the United States, in Selected Communities, 1971–1975

City	Jewish Pop	Number of HIAS Assisted Arrivals Resettled in					
		1971	1972	1973	1974	1975	Total
Baltimore	94,000	3	4	36	83	150	276
Boston	180,000	—	2	49	83	140	274
Chicago	253,000	7	16	73	146	260	502
Cleveland	80,000	2	27	60	113	145	347
Detroit	80,000	3	4	49	120	157	333
Los Angeles Metropolitan	463,000	16	23	90	229	428	786
New Jersey	95,000	—	5	25	62	67	159
Miami	225,000	1	5	16	94	124	240
NYC	1,998,000	138	276	731	1,572	2,247	4,964
Philadelphia	350,000	13	4	85	195	281	578
Pittsburgh	52,000	4	2	7	27	43	83
St Louis	60,000	—	—	11	37	77	125
San Francisco	75,000	5	1	6	40	69	121
Washington, D.C.	112,400	—	—	10	27	11	48
Others	1,614,900	22	84	201	662	1,051	2,020
Totals	5,732,900	214	453	1,449	3,490	5,350	10,856

Source: Edelman 1976: 168.

Table 8. Initial Resettlement of HIAS Assisted Arrivals in the United States, in Selected Communities, 1976–1979

City	Jewish Pop	Number of HIAS Assisted Arrivals Resettled in				
		1976	1977	1978	1979	Total
Baltimore	92,000	88	175	238	668	1,169
Boston	170,000	105	174	355	713	1,347
Chicago	253,000	266	499	1,031	2,099	3,895
Cleveland	75,000	174	170	377	814	1,535
Detroit	75,000	116	139	283	485	1,023
Los Angeles Metropolitan	455,000	397	383	819	1,832	3,431
New Jersey	95,000	123	84	219	525	951
Miami	225,000	111	101	271	528	1,011
NYC	1,998,000	2,363	2,974	5,134	12,213	22,684
Philadelphia	295,000	240	290	514	1,369	2,413
Pittsburgh	51,000	56	82	120	357	615
St Louis	60,000	60	94	162	396	712
San Francisco	75,000	87	145	235	765	1,232
Washington, D.C.	160,000	49	51	97	217	414
Others	1,781,900	1,277	1,481	2,410	5,813	10,981
Totals	5,860,900	5,512	6,842	12,265	28,794	53,413

Source: Edelman 1981: 59.

Table 9. HIAS Assisted Migrants by Area of Origin

Year	USSR	Other	Total
1954–1960	0	45,121	45,121
1961	0	7,156	7,156
1962	0	7,156	7,156
1963	0	5,194	5,194
1964	0	10,599	10,599
1965	0	12,142	12,142
1966	52	8,754	8,806
1967	76	6,166	6,242
1968	96	6,442	6,538
1969	182	6,178	6,360
1970	135	6,242	6,377
1971	265	2,909	3,174
1972	540	1,742	2,822
1973	1,773	4,713	6,486
1974	4,110	2,376	6,486
1975	6,676	4,629	11,305
1976	5,512	674	6,186
1977	7,985	741	8,726
1978	13,545	1,386	14,931
1979	31,931	5,082	37,013
Total	73,936	146,232	220,168

Source: www.hias.org/News/Statistics/origin.html (September 17, 2004).

Table 10.   HIAS Assisted Refugees Resettled in the United States, 1980–2002

Year	USSR FSU	Iranian Jews	Indo-China	Other	Total
			Country of Origin		
1980	15,461	419	5,157	3,959	23,996
1981	6,980	174	3,639	507	11,300
1982	1,327	148	1,503	253	3,231
1983	878	230	1,281	328	2,717
1984	480	375	1,294	258	2,407
1985	552	593	1,269	151	2,565
1986	577	789	715	152	2,233
1987	3,630	2,523	375	147	6,675
1988	10,330	1,610	244	82	12,266
1989	36,114	1,671	287	78	38,150
1990	31,645	1,076	476	121	33,318
1991	35,245	529	31	48	35,853
1992	45,871	336	156	16	46,379
1993	35,940	184	93	108	36,325
1994	32,912	278	35	114	33,339
1995	21,693	226	13	78	22,010
1996	19,501	347	16	224	20,088
1997	14,531	198	0	490	15,219
1998	7,371	261	4	418	8,054
1999	6,339	221	1	939	7,500
2000	5,881	248	35	738	6,902
2001	4,077	247	0	654	4,978
01/02–09/02	2,272	248	35	315	2,870
Total	339,607	13,060	16,624	9,083	378,374

Source: www.hias.org/News/Statistics/origin.html (July 30, 2004).

**Table 11.   Actual Refugee Admission to the U.S. and Ceilings on Refugee Admissions,
FY 75–89 (As of September 30, 1989)**

	Soviet Union		Total for U.S	
FY	Ceiling	Actual Admissions	Ceiling	Actual Admissions
FY 75–79		56,989		341,180
1980		28,444	231,200	207,116
1981	13,000	13,444	217,500	159,252
1982	20,000	2,756	140,000	97,355
1983	15,000	1,409	90,000	61,681
1984[a]	11,000	715	72,000	71,113
1985[a]	10,000	640	70,000	68,045
1986	9,500	787	67,000	62,440
1987[a]	12,300	3,654[c]	70,000	64,828
1988	30,000	20,421	87,500	76,487
1989[a]	50,000	39,553	116,500	107,230
Total FY 75–89		168,852		1,316,727
1990	58,300	50,716	125,000	122,326
1991[b]	46,500	38,661	131,000	112,811
1992[b]	61,400	61,298	142,000	132,173
1993[b]	49,775	48,627	132,000	119,482
1994	53,000	43,470	121,000	112,682
1995	48,000	35,716	112,000	99,490
1996	45,000	29,536	90,000	75,693
1997	48,000	27,072	78,000	70,085
1998	51,000	23,349	83,000	76,554
1999	23,000	16,922	91,000	85,006
2000	20,000		90,000	
total FY 90–00		377,438		

[a]Mid–year consultations in FY 84, FY 85, FY 87, FY 88 and FY 89 changed some regional ceilings but the overall ceilings changed only in FY 88 and FY 89.

[b]In FY 91, FY 92 and FY 93 Eastern Europe and the Soviet Union had separate ceilings. In all other years, the regions had a combined ceiling.

[c]According to www.refugees.org/world/statistics/WRSOO_table 6.pdf only 1,588 refugees from the USSR entered the United States.

Source for years 1980–1989: Refugee Reports X, no. 12 (December 29, 1989): 9.

Source for FYs 1990–2000: www.refugees.org/world/statistics/WRSOO_table6.pdf. (July 12, 2004).

Appendix 2: Glossary of Foreign Words and Acronyms

AJC	American Jewish Committee
AJCSJ	American Jewish Conference on Soviet Jewry
AJYB	American Jewish Year Book
Aliyah	Hebrew for immigration to Israel; literally, "ascent"
Aliyah Bet	Hebrew for illegal immigration, organization that moved Holocaust survivors from Europe to British Mandate of Palestine
BBC	British Broadcasting Corporation
Breira	Hebrew for choice; American Jewish organization
CJF	Council of Jewish Federations and Welfare Funds
CPSU	Communist Party of the Soviet Union
CSCE	Commission on Security and Cooperation in Europe
Evsektsya	Jewish Section of the Communist Part of the Soviet Union established in 1918
FSU	Former Soviet Union
FY	Fiscal Year (October 1–September 30)
GAO	Government Accounting Office
Geulah March	Redemption march
Glasnost	Russian for "openness"; the public affairs policy initiated by Mikhail Gorbachev
Goldene Medina	Yiddish for golden land (promised land); reference to the United States
Gush Emunim	Hebrew for true believers, West Bank settler's movement
Hatikvah	Hebrew for hope; the Israeli national anthem
HIAS	Hebrew Immigrant Aid Society

ICEM	(Intergovernmental) Committee for European Migration
INS	Immigration and Naturalization Service
JDC	American Joint Distribution Committee
JP	*Jerusalem Post*
JPS	Jewish Publication Society
JTA	Jewish Telegraphic Agency Bulletin
Judenraat	Jewish communal bodies set up by German authorities during the Third Reich
Kristallnacht	Pogroms in Germany and Austria, November 10, 11, 1938
LAT	*Los Angeles Times*
LCBC	Large City Budgeting Conference (CJF)
Lishkat Hakesher	Hebrew for Liaison Bureau
Maon	Hebrew for hostel
MFN	Most Favored Nation Status
NCRAC	National Community Relations Advisory Council
NCSJ	National Conference on Soviet Jewry
Neshira	Hebrew for "dropping out"
NGO	Nongovernmental Organizations
NJCRAC	National Jewish Community Relations Advisory Council
Noshrim	Hebrew for "dropout"; Soviet Jewish émigrés with Israeli visas who resettled elsewhere
NPPC	National Professional Planning Committee
NYANA	New York Association of New Americans
NYCSJ	Greater New York Conference on Soviet Jewry. In the 1980s it became the Coalition for Soviet Jewry
NYT	*New York Times*
Oleh (Olim)	Hebrew for immigrant (immigrants)
ORT	Organization for Rehabilitation and Training
OVIR	Office (Department) of Visas and Registration (USSR)
Pamyat	Anti-Semitic organization in the Soviet Union active in the 1980s
Perestroika	Russian for reconstruction; the reform policy of Mikhail Gorbachev
Piduyon Shvuim	Hebrew for rescue of prisoners.
Refuseniks	Russian Jews denied exit permits to leave the Soviet Union
Rosh Hashanah	Jewish New Year
SALT	Strategic Arms Limitation Talks
samizdat	Self-published literary works in USSR
SCA	Synagogue Council of America
Shaliach/ Schlichim	Hebrew for emissary/emissaries

Sovietische Heimland	*Soviet Homeland*, Yiddish journal in the Soviet Union
SSSJ	Student Struggle for Soviet Jewry
TCP	Third Country Processing
Tzedaka	Hebrew for Charity
UAHC	Union of American Hebrew Congregations
UIA	United Israel Appeal
UJA	United Jewish Appeal
UJC	United Jewish Communities, the new organization formed in the 1990s by the merger of CJF, UIA and UJA.
Ukase	Soviet administrative decree
USRP	United States Refugee Program
USSR	Union of Soviet Socialist Republics
Vysov	Russian for, literally, "summons"; the invitation to migrate to another country
VOA	Voice of America
WJC	World Jewish Congress
WZO	World Zionist Organization
Yeda	Hebrew for information; information agency of Liaison Bureau
Yevrei	Russian for Hebrew or Jew
Yordim	Hebrew for Jews who emigrate from Israel
Zapadniki	Russian for Jews who came from the Baltic republics and Moldavia that were annexed to the Soviet Union in 1939.

Bibliography

Abram, Morris. *Testimony*. New York: William E. Wiener Oral History Library of the American Jewish Committee, March 6, 1989.

———. "Soviet Jewry in Crisis." Address presented at the 53rd General Assembly of CJF, Toronto, November 14–18, 1984.

Adler, S. "Israel's Absorption Policy since the 1970s." In *Russian Jews on Three Continents: Migration and Resettlement*, edited by Noah Lewin-Epstein, Yaacov Ro'I, and Paul Ritterband,135–144. London: Frank Cass, 1996.

Alba, Richard, and Victor Nee. "Rethinking Assimilation Theory for a New Era of Immigration." *International Migration Review* 31, no. 4 (Winter 1997): 826–874.

Ami, Ben (Lova Eliav). *Between Hammer and the Sickle*. Philadelphia: Jewish Publication Society, 1967.

Appelbaum, Paul S. "The Soviet Jewish Movement in the United States." In *Jewish American Voluntary Organizations*, edited by Michael N. Dobkowski, 613–639. Westport, CT: Greenwood Press, 1986.

Arkin, Dan. "Israeli Army Broadcasts All the Time." *Maariv*, October 21, 1988 (Hebrew).

Baum, Phil. *Testimony*. New York: William E. Wiener Oral History Library of the AJC, May 24, 1989.

Bayer, Abraham. "American Response to Soviet Anti-Jewish Policies." In *American Jewish Year Book 1973* (74), edited by Morris Fine and Milton Himmelfarb, 210–225. Philadelphia: AJC and JPS, 1973.

———. *Testimony*. New York: William E. Wiener Oral History Library of the AJC, May 4, 1989.

Begin, Menachem. "Israel and the Jewish People." Address presented at the 49th General Assembly of CJF, Detroit, November 1980.

Berman, Mandell L. "Oral History." In *The Response of the North American Federations To the Emigration of Jews from the Former Soviet Union to the United States and Israel: The Growth of Collective Responsibility*, edited by Lawrence Kotler, 37–62. New York: CJF, 1993.

Bernstein, Philip. *To Dwell in Unity: The Jewish Federation Movement in America Since 1960*. Philadelphia: JPS, 1983.

Beyer, Gregg A. "The Evolving United States Response to Soviet Jewish Emigration." *Journal of Palestine Studies* 30, no. 1 (Autumn 1991): 139–156.

Biale, David. *Power and Powerlessness in Jewish History*. New York: Schocken Books, 1986.

Bialkin, Kenneth. "The Coming of Age of North American Jewry: A Political Affirmation." Address presented at 54th General Assembly of CJF, Washington, D.C., November 14, 1985.

Birman, Igor. "Jewish Emigration from the USSR: Some Observations." *Soviet Jewish Affairs* 9, no. 2 (1979): 46–63.

Blank, Naomi. "Redefining the Jewish Question from Lenin to Gorbachev: Terminology or Ideology?" In *Jews and Jewish Life in Russia and the Soviet Union*, edited by Yaacov Ro'I, 51–65. Ilford, Essex, England, and Portland, OR: Frank Cass, 1995.

Blitzer, Wolf. "Soviets Tell Shultz Old Emigration Rules Won't Be Applied." *Jewish Week*, March 4, 1988.

Bookbinder, Hyman. "The Jewish Role in the U.S. Political Process—Strategies for Effective Impact." Address presented at 54th General Assembly of CJF, Washington, D.C., November 14, 1985.

Briggs, Vernon M., Jr. *Mass Immigration and the National Interest: Policy Directions for the New Century*. 3rd ed. Armonk, New York: M.E. Sharpe, 2003.

Brubaker, William Rogers, ed. *Immigration and the Politics of Citizenship in Europe and North America*. Lanham, MD: University Press of America, 1989.

Buwalda, Petrus. *They Did Not Dwell Alone: Jewish Emigration from the Soviet Union 1967–1990*. Washington, D.C.: The Woodrow Wilson Center Press/Baltimore: The Johns Hopkins University Press, 1997.

Cardin, Shoshana. "Directions '85 . . . and Beyond." Keynote address presented at CJF Board Institute, Bal Harbour, FL, January 28, 1985.

Carp, Joel. "Absorbing Jews Jewishly; Professional Responsibility for Jewishly Absorbing New Immigrants in New Communities." Paper presented at Forum III of the World Conference of Jewish Communal Service, Jerusalem, Israel, July 4, 1989.

———. "The Jewish Social Welfare Lobby in the United States." In *Jewish Polity and American Civil Society*, edited by Allan Mittleman, Jonathan D. Sarna, and Robert Licht, 181–232. Lanham, MD: Rowman and Littlefield, 2002.

Chanes, Jerome A. "Jewish Advocacy and Jewish 'Interest.'" In *Jews in American Politics*, edited by L. Sandy Maisel and Ira N. Forman, 99–119. Lanham, MD: Rowman and Littlefield, 2001.

Chernin, Albert D. "Making Soviet Jews an Issue: A History." In *A Second Exodus: The American Movement to Free Soviet Jews*, edited by Murray Friedman, and Albert Chernin, 15–69. Hanover, NH: Brandeis University Press Published by University Press of New England, 1999.

Chiswick, Barry R. "Soviet Jews in the United States: Language and Labor Market Adjustment Revisited." In *Russian Jews on Three Continents: Migration and Resettlement*, edited by Noah Lewin-Epstein, Yaacov Ro'I, and Paul Ritterband, 223–260. London: Frank Cass, 1996.

Cohen, Richard. "With One Voice: A Day-by-Day Report on The Brussels Conference." *Congress Bi-Weekly* (March 19, 1971): 4–10.

———, ed. *Let My People Go*. New York: Popular Library, 1971.

Cohen, Roberta. "Israel's Problematic Absorption of Soviet Jews." In *Soviet Jewish Emigrants and Resettlement in the 1990s*, edited by Tanya Basok and Robert J. Brym, 67–98. Toronto: York Lanes Press, 1991.

Comet, Ted. *Testimony*. New York: William E. Wiener Oral History Library of the AJC, April 5, 1989.

Comptroller General of the United States. *U.S. Assistance Provided for Resettling Soviet Refugees: Departments of State and Justice*. Washington, D.C.: Comptroller General of the United States, June 20, 1977.

Cullen, Robert B. "Soviet Jewry." *Foreign Affairs* 65, no. 2 (Winter 1986): 252–266.

Dawidowicz, Lucy S. "A Century of Jewish History, 1881–1981: The View from America." In *AJYB 1982* (82), edited by Milton Himmelfarb and David Singer, 3–98. Philadelphia: AJC and JPS, 1981.

Decter, Moshe. *Testimony*. New York: William E. Wiener Oral History Library of the AJC, February 22, 1990.

De Jonge, Alex. *Stalin and the Shaping of the Soviet Union*. Glasgow: Collins, 1986.

Dershowitz, Alan M. *Chutzpah*. Boston: Little, Brown, 1991.

Dinstein, Yoram. *Testimony*. New York: William E. Wiener Oral History Library of the AJC, November 28, 1989.

———. "Soviet Jewry in Crisis." Address presented at 53rd General Assembly of CJF, Toronto, November 14–18, 1984.

Dominitz, Yehuda, "Israel's Immigration Policy and the Dropout Phenomenon." In *Russian Jews on Three Continents: Migration and Resettlement*, edited by Noah Lewin-Epstein, Yaacov Ro'I, and Paul Ritterband, 113–127. London: Frank Cass, 1996.

Edelman, Joseph. "Soviet Jews in the United States: A Profile." In *AJYB, 1977* (77), edited by Morris Fine and Milton Himmelfarb, 157–181. Philadelphia: AJC and JPS, 1976.

———. "Soviet Jews in the United States: An Update." In *AJYB, 1982* (82), edited by Milton Himmelfarb and David Singer, 155–164. Philadelphia: AJC and JPS, 1981.

———. "The Centenary of Jewish Immigration to the United States." *Judaism* 32, no. 3 (1983): 215–229.

Elazar, Daniel J. *Community and Polity: The Organizational Dynamic of American Jewry*. Philadelphia: JPS, 1976.

———. "The Noshrim and the Emerging Jewish Policy Process." Jerusalem Letter: Viewpoints, no. 20. Jerusalem: Institute for Federal Studies—Center for Jewish Community Studies, November 15, 1981.

———. "Introduction: The Jewish Political Tradition and the English-Speaking World." In *Jewish Polity and American Civil Society*, edited by Allan Mittleman, Jonathan D. Sarna, and Robert Licht, 1–9. Lanham, MD: Rowman and Littlefield, 2002.

Ettinger, Amos. *Blind Jump: The Story of Shaike Dan*. New York: Herzl Press, 1992.

Feingold, Henry. *The Politics of Rescue*. New Brunswick, NJ: Rutgers University Press, 1970.

———. *Bearing Witness: How America and Its Jews responded to the Holocaust*. Syracuse, NY: Syracuse University Press, 1995.

———. "The Jewish Immigrant Experience in North America: The Myth of Accommo-dation and the Myth of Survival." Address presented at 50th General Assembly of CJF, St. Louis, MO, November 10–15, 1981.

Fosdick, Dorothy. *Testimony.* New York: William E. Wiener Oral History Library of the AJC, February 22, 1990.

Foxman, Abraham. *Testimony.* New York: William E. Wiener Oral History Library of the AJC, November 9, 1989.

Frankel, Sara. *Testimony.* New York: William E. Wiener Oral History Library of the AJC, November 20, 1989.

Freedman, Robert O, ed. *Soviet Jewry in the 1980s: The Politics of Anti-Semitism and Emigration and the Dynamics of Resettlement.* Durham, NC: Duke University Press, 1989.

———. "Soviet Jewry as a Factor in Soviet Israeli Relations." In *Soviet Jewry in the 1980s: The Politics of Anti-Semitism and Emigration and the Dynamics of Reset-tlement,* edited by Robert O. Freedman, 61–96. Durham, NC: Duke University Press 1989b.

———. "Soviet Policy Toward Israel's National Unity Government in the Gorbachev Era." Jerusalem Letter/Viewpoint, no. 79. Jerusalem Center for Public Affairs, Oc-tober 2, 1988.

Freeman, G. P. "Modes of Immigration Politics in Liberal Democratic States." *Inter-national Migration Review* 29, no. 4 (Winter 1995): 881–902.

Friedgut, Theodore H. "Passing Eclipse: The Exodus Movement in the 1980s." In *So-viet Jewry in the 1980s: The Politics of Anti-Semitism and Emigration and the Dy-namics of Resettlement,* edited by Robert O. Freedman, 3–25. Durham, NC: Duke University Press 1989b.

Friedman, Murray. "Introduction: The Jewish Community Comes of Age." In *A Sec-ond Exodus: The American Movement to Free Soviet Jews,* edited by Murray Fried-man, and Albert Chernin, 1–12. Hanover, NH: Brandeis University Press published by University Press of New England, 1999.

Friedman, Murray, and Albert D. Chernin, eds. *A Second Exodus: The American Movement to Free Soviet Jews.* Hanover, NH: Brandeis University Press published by University Press of New England, 1999.

Geller, David. "Second World Conference on Soviet Jewry." In *AJYB 1977* (77), ed-ited by Morris Fine and Milton Himmelfarb, 153–156. Philadelphia: AJC and JPS, 1976.

———. *Testimony.* New York: William E. Wiener Oral History Library of the AJC, April 30, 1990.

Geller, Nate. *Testimony.* New York: William E. Wiener Oral History Library of the AJC, December 9, 1989.

Ginsberg, Benjamin. *The Fatal Embrace: Jews and the State.* Chicago: University of Chicago Press, 1993.

———. "Dilemma of Jewish Leadership in America." In *Jews in American Politics,* ed-ited by L. Sandy Maisel and Ira N. Forman, 3–27. Lanham, MD: Rowman and Lit-tlefield, 2001.

Gitelman, Zvi. "Soviet Immigrants in Israel." New York: Institute for Jewish Policy Planning and Research of the Synagogue Council of America, 1972.

————, and David Naveh. "Elite Accommodation and Organizational Effectiveness: The Case of Immigrant Absorption in Israel." *Journal of Politics* 38:963–986.

————. "Soviet Union." In *AJYB 1987* (87), edited by David Singer, 263–270. Philadelphia: AJC and JPS, 1987.

————. "Soviet Immigrant Resettlement in Israel and the United States." In *Soviet Jewry in the 1980s: The Politics of Anti-Semitism and Emigration and the Dynamics of Resettlement*, edited by Robert O. Freedman, 163–185. Durham, NC: Duke University Press, 1989b.

————. "Soviet Union." In *AJYB 1989* (89), edited by David Singer, 353–360. Philadelphia: AJC and JPS, 1989b.

————. "'From a Northern Country': Russian and Soviet Jewish Immigration to American and Israel in Historical Perspective." In *Russian Jews on Three Continents: Migration and Resettlement*, edited by Noah Lewin-Epstein, Yaacov Ro'I, and Paul Ritterband, 21–41. London: Frank Cass, 1996.

————. "Soviet Jews: Creating a Cause and a Movement." In *A Second Exodus: The American Movement to Free Soviet Jews*, edited by Murray Friedman and Albert Chernin, 84–93. Hanover, NH: Brandeis University Press published by University Press of New England, 1999.

Glick, Carl. *Oral History*. New York: UJA-Federation of Jewish Philanthropies of New York, August 30 and October 31, 1989.

Gold, Eugene. *Testimony*. New York: William E. Wiener Oral History Library of the AJC, January 10, 1990.

Gold, Stephen J. "Community Formation among Jews from the Former Soviet Union in the United States." In *Russian Jews on Three Continents: Migration and Resettlement*, edited by Noah Lewin-Epstein, Yaacov Ro'I, and Paul Ritterband, 261–280. London: Frank Cass, 1996.

————. "Post-Holocaust Jewish Migration: From Refugees to Transnationals." Unpublished manuscript (n.d.).

Goldberg, Arthur J. *Testimony*. New York: William E. Wiener Oral History Library of the AJC, January 17 and May 23, 1979.

Goldberg, J. J. *Jewish Power: Inside the American Jewish Establishment*. Reading, MA: Addison-Wesley, 1996.

Golden, Peter. *Quiet Diplomat: A Biography of Max M. Fisher*. New York: Cornwall Books, 1992.

Goldman, Marshall I. "Soviet-American Trade and Soviet Jewish Emigration: Should a Policy Change Be Made by the American Jewish Community?" In *Soviet Jewry in the 1980s: The Politics of Anti-Semitism and Emigration and the Dynamics of Resettlement*, edited by Robert O. Freedman, 141–159. Durham, NC: Duke University Press 1989b.

————. "Jackson-Vanik: A Dissent." In *A Second Exodus: The American Movement to Free Soviet Jews*, edited by Murray Friedman and Albert Chernin, 115–123. Hanover, NH: Brandeis University Press published by University Press of New England, 1999.

Goldman, Minton F. "United States Policy and Soviet Jewish Emigration from Nixon to Bush." In *Jews and Jewish Life in Russia and the Soviet Union*, edited by Yaacov Ro'I, 338–402. Ilford, Essex, England, and Portland, OR: Frank Cass, 1995.

Goldman, Ralph. "The Involvement and Policies of American Jewry in Revitalizing European Jewry, 1945–1995." Unpublished manuscript, 1995.

Golub, Judith. "The Dilemmas of Rescue: Current Policy Issue in Soviet Jewish Migration to the U.S." New York: American Jewish Committee—Institute of Human Relations, c. January 1989.

Goodman, Charles. "Oral History." In *The Response of the North American Federations to the Emigration of Jews from the Former Soviet Union to the United States and Israel: The Growth of Collective Responsibility*, edited by Lawrence Kotler, 317–336. New York: CJF, 1993.

Goodman, Jerry. "American Response to Soviet Anti-Jewish Policies." In *AJYB 1965* (66), edited by Morris Fine and Milton Himmelfarb, 312–319. Philadelphia: AJC and JPS, 1965.

———. "American Response to Soviet Anti-Semitism." In *AJYB 1969* (70), edited by Morris Fine and Milton Himmelfarb, 111–118. Philadelphia: AJC and JPS, 1969.

———. *Testimony*. New York: William E. Wiener Oral History Library of the AJC, September 18 and October 3, 1979.

Government Accounting Office (GAO). "Chapter 3: Resettlement of Soviet Refugees Outside Israel" (draft), October 15, 1976.

———. "U.S. Assistance Provided for Resettling Soviet Refugees" (ID 76–85), June 22, 1977.

Govrin, Yosef. "The Beginnings of the Struggle for Soviet Jewish Emigration and Its Impact on Israel-Soviet Relations." In *Jews and Jewish Life in Russia and the Soviet Union*, edited by Yaacov Ro'I, 327–337. Ilford, Essex, England, and Portland, OR: Frank Cass, 1995.

Greenberg, Anna, and Kenneth D. Wald. "The Contemporary Political Behavior of American Jewry." In *Jews in American Politics*, edited by L. Sandy Maisel and Ira N. Forman, 99–119. Lanham, MD: Rowman and Littlefield, 2001.

Grossman, Lawrence. "Jewish Communal Affairs." In *AJYB, 1988 (82)*, edited by David Singer. New York: AJC & JPS, 1988.

———. "Jewish Communal Affairs." In *AJYB, 1989* (89), edited by David Singer, 212–232. New York: AJC and JPS, 1989.

———. "Jewish Communal Affairs." In *AJYB, 1990* (90), edited by David Singer, 258–277. New York: AJC and JPS, 1990.

———. "Jewish Communal Affairs." In *AJYB, 1991* (91), edited by David Singer, 177–203. New York: AJC and JPS, 1991.

Gur-Gurevitz, Baruch. *Open Gates: The Inside Story of the Mass Aliyah from the Soviet Union and Its Successor States*. Jerusalem: Jewish Agency for Israel, 1996.

Halevi, Yossi Klein. "Jacob Birnbaum and the Struggle for Soviet Jewry." *Azure* 17 (Spring 2004): 1–21.

Harris, David. *Testimony*. New York: William E. Wiener Oral History Library of the AJC, March 7 and October 2, 1989.

Hassenfeld, Sylvia. "Oral History." In *The Response of the North American Federations to the Emigration of Jews from the Former Soviet Union to the United States and Israel: The Growth of Collective Responsibility*, edited by Lawrence Kotler, 159–193. New York: CJF, 1993.

Heckmann, Friedrich and Wolfgang Bosswick, eds. *Migration Policies: A Comparative Perspective*. Stuttgart: Ferdinand Enke Verlag, 1995.

Heitman, Sidney. "Jewish, German, and Armenian Emigration from the USSR: Parallels and Differences." In *Soviet Jewry in the 1980s: The Politics of Anti-Semitism and Emigration and the Dynamics of Resettlement*, edited by Robert O. Freedman, 115–138. Durham, NC: Duke University Press 1989b.

Hertzberg, Arthur. *A Jew in America: My Life, A People's Struggle for an Identity*. San Francisco: Harper, 2002.

Hoenlein, Malcolm. *Testimony*. New York: William E. Wiener Oral History Library of the AJC, June 14, 1989.

Isaacs, Stephen D. *Jews and American Politics*. Garden City, NY: Doubleday, 1974.

Jacobson, Charlotte. *Testimony*. New York: William E. Wiener Oral History Library of the AJC, January 16, 1990.

Johnston, Oswald. "Israel Seeking to Halt Soviet Emigrant Loss." *LAT*, November 9, 1976.

Katz, Israel, A. Globerson, Yakov Kop, Joe Neipris, and Jimmy Weinblatt. *The Jewish Agency Department of Immigration and Absorption: Options For Change*. Jerusalem: The Center for Social Policy Studies in Israel, 1987.

Kesler, Charles R. "The Promise of American Citizenship." In *Immigration and Citizenship in the Twenty-First Century*, edited by Noah M. J. Pickus, 3– 39. Lanham, MD: Roman and Littlefield, 1998.

Korey, William. "The Struggle Over Jackson-Vanik." In *AJYB, 1974– 75* (75), edited by Morris Fine and Milton Himmelfarb, 199–234. Philadelphia: AJC and JPS, 1974.

———. "The Struggle Over the Jackson Amendment." In *AJYB, 1976* (76), edited by Morris Fine and Milton Himmelfarb, 160–170. Philadelphia: AJC and JPS, 1975.

———. "The Soviet Public Anti-Zionist Committee: An Analysis." In *Soviet Jewry in the 1980s: The Politics of Anti-Semitism and Emigration and the Dynamics of Resettlement*, edited by Robert O. Freedman, 26–50. Durham, NC: Duke University Press 1989b.

———. "Jackson-Vanik: A 'Policy of Principle.'" In *A Second Exodus: The American Movement to Free Soviet Jews*, edited by Murray Friedman and Albert Chernin, 97–114. Hanover, NH: Brandeis University Press published by University Press of New England, 1999.

———. "From Helsinki: A Salute to Human Rights." In *A Second Exodus: The American Movement to Free Soviet Jews*, edited by Murray Friedman and Albert Chernin, 124–135. Hanover, NH: Brandeis University Press published by University Press of New England, 1999.

Kotler, Lawrence, ed. *The Response of the North American Federations to the Emigration of Jews from the Former Soviet Union to the United States and Israel: The Growth of Collective Responsibility*. New York: Council of Jewish Federations, 1993.

———. "Introductory Essay." In *The Response of the North American Federations to the Emigration of Jews from the Former Soviet Union to the United States and Israel: The Growth of Collective Responsibility*, edited by Lawrence Kotler, i–vii. New York: CJF, 1993.

Kraar, Martin. "Oral History." In *The Response of the North American Federations to the Emigration of Jews from the Former Soviet Union to the United States and Israel: The Growth of Collective Responsibility*, edited by Lawrence Kotler, 337–364. New York: CJF, 1993.

Lawrence, Gunther. *Three Million More*. Garden City, NY: Doubleday, 1970.

Lazin, Fred. "The Response of the American Jewish Committee to the Crisis of German Jewry, 1933–1939." *American Jewish History* 68, no. 3 (1979): 283–304.

——. "The Non-Centralized Model of American Jewish Organizations: A Possible Test Case." *Jewish Social Studies* 44, nos. 3–4 (1982): 299–314.

——. "The Third Sector and Immigrant Absorption: Lessons from the Israeli Experience." *Journal of Public Administration* 24, no. 11 (2001): 1211–1232.

——. "Israel's Efforts to Absorb Jewish Immigrants from the Soviet Union and Ethiopia, 1989–1993." *IMIS-Beitrage* 17 (2001b): 9–32.

Lender, Marvin. "Oral History." In *The Response of the North American Federations to the Emigration of Jews from the Former Soviet Union to the United States and Israel: The Growth of Collective Responsibility*, edited by Lawrence Kotler, 233–258. New York: CJF, 1993.

Leuchter, Ben Zion. "Oral History." In *The Response of the North American Federations to the Emigration of Jews from the Former Soviet Union to the United States and Israel: The Growth of Collective Responsibility*, edited by Lawrence Kotler, 87–124. New York: CJF, 1993.

Levanon, Nehemia. *Testimony*. New York: William E. Wiener Oral History Library of the AJC, December 3, 1989.

——. *"Nativ" Was the Code Name*. Tel Aviv: Am Oved, 1995 (Hebrew).

——. "Israel's Role in the Campaign." In *A Second Exodus: The American Movement to Free Soviet Jews*, edited by Murray Friedman and Albert Chernin, 70–83. Hanover, NH: Brandeis University Press published by University Press of New England, 1999.

Levine, Jacqueline K. *Testimony*. New York: William E. Wiener Oral History Library of the AJC, June 19, 1989.

Lewin-Epstein, Noah, Yaacov Ro'I, and Paul Ritterband, eds. *Russian Jews on Three Continents: Migration and Resettlement*. London: Frank Cass, 1996.

Lipoff, Norman. "Oral History." In *The Response of the North American Federations to the Emigration of Jews from the Former Soviet Union to the United States and Israel: The Growth of Collective Responsibility*, edited by Lawrence Kotler, 281–300. New York: CJF, 1993.

Liskofsky, Sidney. "United States Immigration Policy." In *AJYB, 1966* (67), edited by Morris Fine and Milton Himmelfarb, 164–175. New York: AJC and JPS, 1966.

Lookstein, Haskell. *Were We Our Brothers' Keepers? The Public Response of American Jews to the Holocaust*. New York: Random House, Vintage Books, 1988.

Lowell, Stanley H. *Testimony*. New York: William E. Wiener Oral History Library of the AJC, November 9, 1989.

Maass, Richard. *Testimony*. New York: William E. Wiener Oral History Library of the AJC, December 10, 1988 and March 17, 1989.

Maisel, L. Sandy and Ira N. Forman, eds. *Jews in American Politics*. Lanham, MD: Rowman and Littlefield, 2001.

Mandel, Morton. "CJF and Federations: New Goals for a New Decade." Address presented at 49th General Assembly of CJF, Detroit, November 1980.

Mann, Theodore R. "The Coming of Age of North American Jewry: A Political Affirmation." Address presented at 54th General Assembly of CJF, Washington, D.C., November 13–17, 1985.

Markowitz, Fran. "Israelis with a Russian Accent." *Jewish Journal of Sociology* 35, no. 2 (1993): 97–114.

———. "Emigration, Immigration and Cultural Change: Towards a Trans-national 'Russian' Jewish Community?" In *Jews and Jewish Life in Russia and the Soviet Union*, edited by Yaacov Ro'I, 403–413. Ilford, Essex, England, and Portland, OR: Frank Cass, 1995.

Markowitz, Herman. "Oral History." In *The Response of the North American Federations to the Emigration of Jews from the Former Soviet Union to the United States and Israel: The Growth of Collective Responsibility*, edited by Lawrence Kotler, 301–315. New York: CJF, 1993.

Mendelsohn, Ezra. *On Modern Jewish Politics*. New York: Oxford University Press, 1993.

Miller, Israel. *Testimony*. New York: William E. Wiener Oral History Library of the AJC, February 15, 1990.

Mittleman, Allan, Jonathan D. Sarna, and Robert Licht, eds. *Jewish Polity and American Civil Society: Communal Agencies and Religious Movements in the American Public Sphere*. Lanham, MD: Rowman and Littlefield, 2002.

Morse, Arthur D. *While Six Million Died*. New York: Random House, 1968.

Naftalin, Micah H. "The Activist Movement." In *A Second Exodus: The American Movement to Free Soviet Jews*, edited by Murray Friedman and Albert Chernin, 224–241. Hanover, NH: Brandeis University Press published by University Press of New England, 1999.

Nasatir, Stephen. "Oral History." In *The Response of the North American Federations to the Emigration of Jews from the Former Soviet Union to the United States and Israel: The Growth of Collective Responsibility*, edited by Lawrence Kotler, 207–232. New York: CJF, 1993.

Ne'eman Arad, Gulie. *America, Its Jews, and the Rise of Nazism*. Bloomington: University of Indiana Press, 2000.

Newland, Kathleen. "The Impact of U.S. Refugee Policies on U.S. Foreign Policy: A Case of the Tail Wagging the Dog?" In *Threatened Peoples, Threatened Borders*, edited by Michael Teitelbaum and Myron Weiner, 290–214. New York: W.W. Norton, 1995.

Novick, Peter. *The Holocaust in American Life*. Boston: Houghton Mifflin, 1999.

Orbach, William W. *The American Movement to Aid Soviet Jews*. Amherst: University of Massachusetts Press, 1979.

Orleck, Annelise. *The Soviet Jewish Americans*. Westport, CT: Greenwood Press, 1999.

Peretz, Dan, and Gideon Doron. *Government and Politics of Israel*. 3rd ed. Boulder, CO: Westview Press, 1997.

Peretz, Pauline. "Israel et le Mouvement de Mobilisation en faveur des Juifs Soviétiques 1964–1975." *Bulletin du Centre de recherche français de Jerusalem* 14 (Spring 2004): 50–67.

Pinkus, Benjamin. "Israel Activity on Behalf of Soviet Jewry." In *Organizing Rescue: Jewish National Solidarity in the Modern Period*, edited by Selwyn Ilan Troen and Benjamin Pinkus, 373–402. London: Frank Cass, 1992.

Portes, Alejandro, and Ruben Rumbaut. *Immigrant America: A Portrait*. 2nd ed. Berkeley: University of California Press, 1996.

Pratt, Yehoshua. *Testimony*. New York: William E. Wiener Oral History Library of the AJC, November 19 and December 4, 1989.

"Processing of Soviet Refugees." Joint Hearing Before the Subcommittee on Europe and the Middle East of the Committee on Foreign Affairs and the Subcommittee on Immigration, Refugees, and International Law of the Committee on the Judiciary House of Representatives, 101st Cong., 1st Sess. 54 (1989).

Raffel, Martin J. "History of Israel Advocacy." In *Jewish Polity and American Civil Society*, edited by Allan Mittleman, Jonathan D. Sarna, and Robert Licht, 103–179. Lanham, MD: Rowman and Littlefield, 2002.

Rager, Yitzhak. *Testimony*. New York: William E. Wiener Oral History Library of the AJC, June 8, 1990.

Refugee Act of 1980 PL 96–212, March 17, 1980, 96th Congress 94 Stat. 102.

"Refugee Assistance Act of 1985." Hearing before the Subcommittee on Immigration, Refugees and International Law of the Committee on the Judiciary. House of Representatives, 99th Congress first session on H.R. 1452 Refugee Assistance Extension Act of 1985 April 17, 1984 (Serial # 13). Washington, D.C.: GPO, 1985.

Reich, Seymour D. *Testimony*. New York: William E. Wiener Oral History Library of the AJC, February 2, 1990.

Reimers, David M. *Still the Golden Door: The Third World Comes to America*. New York: Columbia University Press, 1985.

———. "The Emergence of the Immigration Restrictions Lobby Since 1979." Paper delivered at the APSA Meetings, San Francisco, August 1996.

Rich, Frank. "Mel Gibson Forgives Us for His Sins." *New York Times*, March 7, 2004.

Richter, Glen. *Testimony*. New York: William E. Wiener Oral History Library of the AJC, April 17 and June 1, 1989.

Ritterband, Paul. "Jewish Identify among Russian Immigrants in the U.S." In *Russian Jews on Three Continents: Migration and Resettlement*, edited by Noah Lewin-Epstein, Yaacov Ro'I and Paul Ritterband, 325–342. London: Frank Cass, 1996.

Ro'I, Yaacov. "Soviet Policy Towards Jewish Emigration: An Overview." In *Russian Jews on Three Continents: Migration and Resettlement*, edited by Noah Lewin-Epstein, Yaacov Ro'I, and Paul Ritterband, 45–67. London: Frank Cass, 1996.

Rosenberg, Victor. "Refugee Status for Soviet Jewish Immigrants to the United States." *Touro Law Review* 19 (Winter/Spring, 2003): 419–450.

Rosenne, Meir. *Testimony*. New York: William E. Wiener Oral History Library of the AJC, November 10, 1989.

Rosenthal, Steven T. *Irreconcilable Differences: The Waning of the American Jewish Love Affair with Israel*. Hanover, NH: Brandeis University Press, published by the University Press of New England, 2001.

Rubin, Ronald I. "The Soviet Jewish Problem at the United Nations." In *AJYB, 1970* (71), edited by Morris Fine and Milton Himmelfarb, 141–159. New York: AJC and JPS, 1970.

Ruby, Walter. "The Role of Nonestablishment Groups." In *A Second Exodus: The American Movement to Free Soviet Jews*, edited by Murray Friedman and Albert Chernin, 200–223. Hanover, NH: Brandeis University Press published by University Press of New England, 1999.

Rudin, James. *Testimony*. New York: William E. Wiener Oral History Library of the AJC, April 12, 1990.

Rumbaut, Ruben G. "Assimilation and Its Discontents: Between Rhetoric and Reality." *International Migration Review* 31, no.4 (Winter 1997): 923–960.

Russell, Sharon Stanton. "Migration Patterns of U.S. Foreign Policy Interest." In *Threatened Peoples, Threatened Borders*, edited by Michael Teitelbaum and Myron Weiner, 39–87. New York: W.W. Norton, 1995.

Sachar, Howard M. *A History of Jews in America*, New York: Knopf, 1992.

———. *An Inquiry into the Contempory Jewish World*. New York: Harper and Row, 1985.

Salitan, Laurie P. *Politics and Nationality in Contemporary Soviet-Jewish Emigration, 1968–89*. New York: St. Martin's Press, 1992.

Sanders, Ronald. *Shores of Refuge: A Hundred Years of Jewish Emigration*. New York: Henry Holt, 1988.

Sarna, Jonathan D., and Jonathan J. Golden. "The Twentieth Century through American Jewish Eyes: A History of the American Jewish Year Book, 1899–1999." In *AJYB, 2000* (100), edited by David Singer and Lawrence Grossman, 3–102. New York: AJC, 2000.

Schachter, Herschel. *Testimony*. New York: William E. Wiener Oral History Library of the AJC, May 30, 1974.

Schifter, Richard. "American Diplomacy 1985–1989." In *A Second Exodus: The American Movement to Free Soviet Jews*, edited by Murray Friedman and Albert Chernin, 136–157. Hanover, NH: Brandeis University Press published by University Press of New England, 1999.

Schnall, David J. "Soviet Jewry: Malaise within the Movement." *Midstream* 16, no. 4 (April 1980): 8–13.

Schneider, Michael. "Oral History." In *The Response of the North American Federations to the Emigration of Jews from the Former Soviet Union to the United States and Israel: The Growth of Collective Responsibility*, edited by Lawrence Kotler, 185–206. New York: CJF, 1993.

Schnur, Zeesy. *Testimony*. New York: William E. Wiener Oral History Library of the AJC, April 25 and May 1, 1990.

Schroeter, Leonard. *The Last Exodus*. Jerusalem: Weidenfeld and Nicolson, 1974.

Schwartz, Carmi. "Oral History." In The *Response of the North American Federations to the Emigration of Jews from the Former Soviet Union to the United States and Israel: The Growth of Collective Responsibility*, edited by Lawrence Kotler, 1–35. New York: CJF, 1993.

Schwartz, Solomon. *The Jews in the Soviet Union*. Syracuse, NY: Syracuse University Press, 1951.

Sever, Rita. "Learning from the Experience? Israeli Schools and the Task of Immigrant Absorption." In *Russian Jews on Three Continents: Migration and Resettlement*, edited by Noah Lewin-Epstein, Yaacov Ro'I, and Paul Ritterband, 510–541. London: Frank Cass, 1996.

Shachtman, Tom. *I Seek My Brethren: Ralph Goldman and "The Joint."* New York: Newmarket Press, 2001.

Shapiro, Dan. "Oral History." In *The Response of the North American Federations to the Emigration of Jews from the Former Soviet Union to the United States and Israel: The Growth of Collective Responsibility,* edited by Lawrence Kotler, 63–85. New York: CJF, 1993.

Shapiro, Edward S. *A Time for Healing: American Jewry since World War II.* Baltimore: The Johns Hopkins University Press, 1992.

Shapiro, Edwin. *Testimony.* New York: William E. Wiener Oral History Library of the AJC, April 24, 1984.

Shapiro, Leon. "Eastern Europe." In *AJYB, 1965* (66), edited by Morris Fine and Milton Himmelfarb, 421–430. New York: AJC and JPS, 1965.

———. "Eastern Europe." In *AJYB, 1970* (71), edited by Morris Fine and Milton Himmelfarb, 460–468. New York: AJC and JPS, 1970.

———. "Soviet Jewry Since the Death of Stalin: A Twenty-five Year Perspective." In *AJYB, 1979* (79), edited by Morris Fine and Milton Himmelfarb, 77–103. New York: AJC and JPS, 1978.

———. "Soviet Union." In *AJYB, 1982* (82), edited by Milton Himmelfarb and David Singer, 229–239. New York: AJC and JPS, 1981.

———. "Soviet Union." In *AJYB, 1983* (83), edited by Milton Himmelfarb and David Singer, 213–222. New York: AJC and JPS, 1982.

———. "Soviet Union." In *AJYB, 1984* (84), edited by Milton Himmelfarb and David Singer, 212–223. New York: AJC and JPS, 1983.

———. "Soviet Union." In *AJYB, 1985* (85), edited by Milton Himmelfarb and David Singer, 242–250. New York: AJC and JPS, 1984.

———. "Soviet Union." In *AJYB, 1986* (86), edited by Milton Himmelfarb and David Singer, 287–293. New York: AJC and JPS, 1986.

Sharkansky, I. *Policy Making in Israel: Routines and Coping for Simple and Complex Problems.* Pittsburgh, PA: University of Pittsburgh Press, 1997.

Shinbaum, Myrna. "Mobilizing America: The National Conference on Soviet Jewry." In *A Second Exodus: The American Movement to Free Soviet Jews,* edited by Murray Friedman and Albert Chernin, 173–180. Hanover, NH: Brandeis University Press published by University Press of New England, 1999.

Shultz, George P. "Achieving a Just and Peaceful World Order." Address presented at the 52nd General Assembly of CJF, Atlanta, November 16–20, 1983.

———.*Turmoil and Triumph: My Years as Secretary of State.* New York: Charles Scribner and Sons, 1993.

Silberman, Charles E. *A Certain People: American Jews and Their Lives Today.* New York: Summit Books, 1985.

Simon, Rita. *In the Golden Land: A Century of Russian and Soviet Jewish Immigration in America.* Westport, CT: Praeger, 1997.

Sisco, Joseph. *Testimony.* New York: William E. Wiener Oral History Library of the AJC, March 2, 1972.

Smolar, Boris. *Testimony.* New York: William E. Wiener Oral History Library of the AJC, September, 1, 1983.

"Soviet Refugees." Hearing Before the Subcommittee on Immigration, Refugees, and International Law of the Committee on the Judiciary, House of Representatives,

181, first session on H.R. 1605 and H.Con. Res. 73 Emergency Refugee Act of 1989, April 6, 1989 Serial # 12. Washington, D.C., GPO, 1989.

Spiegel, Steven L. "American Jews and U.S. Foreign Policy." In *Jews in American Politics*, edited by L. Sandy Maisel and Ira N. Forman, 252–269. Lanham, MD: Rowman and Littlefield, 2001.

Spier, Howard. "Soviet Anti-Semitism Unchained: The Rise of the Historical and Patriotic Association, Pamyat." In *Soviet Jewry in the 1980s: The Politics of Anti-Semitism and Emigration and the Dynamics of Resettlement*, edited by Robert O. Freedman, 51–57. Durham, NC: Duke University Press 1989b.

———. "The West European Approach to the Soviet Jewry Problem." In *Soviet Jewry in the 1980s: The Politics of Anti-Semitism and Emigration and the Dynamics of Resettlement*, edited by Robert O. Freedman, 97–114. Durham, NC: Duke University Press, 1989b.

Spinner, Jeff. *The Boundaries of Citizenship: Race, Ethnicity and Nationality in the Liberal State*. Baltimore: The Johns Hopkins University Press, 1994.

Steinlight, Stephen. "The Jewish Stake in America's Changing Demography: Reconsidering a Misguided Immigration Policy." Washington, D.C.: Center for Immigration Studies, October 2001.

Stern, Paula. *Water's Edge: Domestic Politics and the Making of American Foreign Policy*. Westport, CT: Greenwood Press, 1979.

Stock, Ernest. *Partners and Purse Strings: A History of the United Israel Appeal*. Lanham, MD: University Press of America, 1987.

———. *Chosen Instrument: The Jewish Agency in the First Decade of the State of Israel*. New York: Herzl Press, 1988.

———. *Beyond Partnership: The Jewish Agency and the Diaspora 1959–1971*. New York: Herzl Press, 1992.

Szulc, Tad. 1991. *The Secret Alliance: The Extraordinary Story of the Rescue of Jews since World War II*. New York: Farrar, Straus and Giroux, 1991.

Taylor, Telford. *Courts of Terror: Soviet Criminal Justice and Jewish Emigration*. New York: Random House, 1976.

Teitelbaum, Michael S. and Myron Weiner, eds. *Threatened Peoples, Threatened Borders*. New York: W.W. Norton, 1995.

Troen, S. Ilan, and Klaus Bade, eds. *Home: Immigration and Absorption into Their Homelands of Germans and Jews from the Former Soviet Union*. Beer-Sheva, Israel: Hubert H. Humphrey Institute for Social Ecology, Ben Gurion University, 1994.

Weinstein, Lewis H. "Soviet Jewry and the American Jewish Community 1963– 1987." *American Jewish History* 4 (June 1988): 600–616.

Weisberger, Bernard. "A Nation of Immigrants." *American Heritage* (February–March, 1994): 75–91.

Weiss, Avi. *Testimony*. New York: William E. Wiener Oral History Library of the AJC, December 18, 1989.

Wiesel, Elie. *The Jews of Silence*. Philadelphia: JPS, 1967.

Windmueller, Steven. "'Defenders' National Jewish Community Relations Agencies." In *Jewish Polity and American Civil Society*, edited by Allan Mittleman, Jonathan D. Sarna, and Robert Licht, 13–66. Lanham, MD: Rowman and Littlefield, 2002.

———. "The 'Noshrim' War: Dropping Out." In *A Second Exodus: The American Movement to Free Soviet Jews*, edited by Murray Friedman and Albert Chernin,

161–172. Hanover, NH: Brandeis University Press published by University Press of New England, 1999.

Wyman, David S. *The Abandonment of the Jews: America and the Holocaust, 1941–1945*. New York: Pantheon Books, 1984.

Zolberg, Aristide. "From Invitation to Interdiction: U.S. Foreign Policy and Immigration since 1945." In *Threatened Peoples, Threatened Borders*, edited by Michael Teitelbaum and Myron Weiner, 117–158. New York: W.W. Norton, 1995.

———."Matters of State: Theorizing Immigration Policy." Draft manuscript, May 28, 1998.

Zukerman, Karl D. *Testimony*. New York: William E. Wiener Oral History Library of the AJC, April 5, 1990.

———. "Oral History." In *The Response of the North American Federations to the Emigration of Jews from the Former Soviet Union to the United States and Israel: The Growth of Collective Responsibility*, edited by Lawrence Kotler, 125–158. New York: CJF, 1993.

Interviews

The author conducted all the interviews. Most were held face to face with a few being done on the telephone. The author is most appreciative of those who were willing to discuss the subject of the research. Some have been quoted by name in the endnotes and some have not. Notes were taken by hand and they are stored in the personal archives of the author.

ISRAEL

Beer Sheva

Aryeh Naor, former Secretary to Israeli government cabinet, December 30, 2002.
Benjamin Pinkus, Historian, June 5, 2002.
Yitzhak Rager, former staff of Liaison Bureau, July 2, 1992.

Jerusalem

Steve Adler, staff, Ministry of Absorption, May 4, 1997.
Yehuda Avner, former adviser to Prime Ministers Yitzhak Rabin and Menachem Begin, July 3, 2001.
Zvi Barak, former director of Treasury Department, Jewish Agency, July 16, 1996.
Aryeh Barr, former director general, Ministry of Housing, August 4, 1996.
Yehoshua Barzel, former staff of Liaison Bureau, June 27, 2002.
Shoshana Cardin, former President of CJF and NCSJ, September 3, 1995.
Simcha Dinitz, former Chairman of the Jewish Agency Executive, July 8 and 31, 1996.

Yehuda Dominitz, former Director General, Jewish Agency Absorption Department, March 1, 1998 and July 3, 2001.

Leonard Fein, journalist, June 12, 2004 (telephone).

Sara Frankel, former staff, Liaison Bureau, June 26, 2002 and November 16, 2003 (telephone).

Baruch Gur (Gurevitz), former staff, Liaison Bureau, January 1, 2003 (telephone).

Harry Hurwitz, former advisor to Prime Minister Menachem Begin, December 25, 2001.

Mendel Kaplan, Chairman, Board of Governors, Jewish Agency for Israel, April 14, 1997.

Neale Katz, Director in Israel of UIA, November 30 and December 25, 1995.

Michael Kleiner, Member of Knesset, July 17, 1996.

Yossi Kutchik, former Director General, Ministry of Absorption, July 31, 1996.

Yehuda Lapidot, former head of Liaison Bureau, June 26, 2002.

Arnon Mantver, Director of JDC Israel, January 25, 1996.

Addisue Messele, Member of Knesset, July 13, 1998.

Moshe Nativ, Director General, Jewish Agency, July 8, 1996.

Daniel Pins, staff, Absorption Department, Jewish Agency, April 10, 1994.

Meir Roseane, former staff of Liaison Bureau, June 27, 2002.

Michael Ruikin, American Jewish activist, October 30, 1995.

Jonathan Sarna, historian, May 9, 2002.

Howard Weisband, former Secretary of Board of Governors of Jewish Agency, August 4 and December 25, 1996 and June 24, 2004 (telephone).

Tel Aviv

H. Eugene Douglas, former United States Coordinator for Refugees, February 3, 2004 (telephone) and June 29, 2004.

Uri Gordon, Head, Department of Absorption, Jewish Agency, March 28, 1996.

Marvin Lender, former Chairman, UJA, February 27, 1997.

Arnon Mantver, Director General, Absorption Department, Jewish Agency for Israel, April 29, 1994.

Yehoshua Pratt, former staff of Liaison Bureau, October 2002.

Yitzhak Shamir, former Israeli Prime Minister and Foreign Minister, July 17, 1996.

Jerry Shiran, former staff of Liaison Bureau, February 28, 2003.

UNITED STATES

Baltimore

Shoshana Cardin, former President of CJF & NCSJ, January 27, 2003.

Boston

Leon Jick, February 2004 (telephone).
Uri Rannan, Former staff of Liaison Bureau, February 2001 (telephone).

Chicago

Joel Carp, staff, Jewish Federation of Metropolitan Chicago, November 6, 1996.
Jim Rice, former Executive Vice President, Jewish Federation of Metropolitan Chicago, November 6, 1996.

Florida

Max Fisher, former President of CJF, UIA, UJA & Chair of Board of Governors of Jewish Agency, February 1996 and February 2001.
Richard Krieger, former staff, State Department employee, December 11, 2004 (telephone) and February 7, 2004.
Ben Zion Leuchter, former President of HIAS, January 23, 1997.

New Jersey

Henry Taub, former President JDC, May 29, 2003.

New York

Zelig Chinitz, former employee of Mr. Max Fisher, October 30, 1995.
Ted Comet, staff, JDC (former staff of CJF), March 4, 1999.
Yoram Dinstein, former staff of Liaison Bureau, May 3, 2003.
Ted Feder, former staff, JDC European Office, July 20, 1999.
Carl Glick, former President of HIAS, December 9, 1996, September 22, 1999 (telephone) and July 2001.
Ralph Goldman, former Executive Vice President, JDC, November 22 and December 6, 1996, January 21, 1998, July 12, 1999 and May 6, 2003.
Jerry Goodman, former Executive Director of NCSJ, January 20, 2001, May 1, 2003 and July 1, 2004 (telephone).
David Harris, Executive Vice President, American Jewish Committee, August 8, 2002.
Malcolm Hoenlein, Executive Vice President, Conference of Presidents, February 1, 2001.
Jerold Hoffberger, former President of CJF & United Israel Appeal & Jewish Agency Board of Governors, December 3, 1996.
Howard Israelov, former President of HIAS, January 13, 1997.

Charlotte Jacobson, past President of Hadassah & WZO (American Section), March 22, 2000.
Al Kastner, volunteer at IRC, July 2004 (telephone).
Martin Kraar, Executive Vice President, CJF, October 1, 1996.
Gunther Lawrence, former staff Union of American Hebrew Congregation (UAHC), July 3, 2003 (telephone).
Morton Mandel, former President CJF, August 6, 2001 (telephone).
Michael Schneider, Executive Vice President, JDC, November 22, 1996.
Rabbi Arthur Schneier, Founder and head of Appeal of Conscience Foundation & Rabbi of Park East Synagogue, August 9, 2002.
Zeesy Schnur, former Executive Director NYCSJ, August 12, 2002
Carmi Schwartz, former Executive Vice President, CJF, October 18, 1996 and September 6, 2001.
Edwin Shapiro, former President of HIAS, December 17, 1996.
Dan Shapiro, former CJF lay leader, July 31, 2002.
Steve Solender, former Executive Vice President of NY Federation-UJA, October 30, 1995, September 11, November 26 and December 1, 1996 and July 25, 2001.
Elie Wiesel, author and journalist, July 2001 (telephone).
Karl Zukerman, former Executive Vice President of HIAS, November 8, 1996.

Rhode Island

Irving Kessler, former Executive Vice President, UIA, June 26, 2001 (telephone) & August 16, 2001.

Washington, D.C.

Deborah E. Bodlander, staff of Representative Ben Gilman, August 14, 1995.
Anita Botti, staff, Department of State, August 3, 1994.
Larry Eagleburger, former Secretary of State, August 12, 2003 (telephone).
Peter Kovar, staff of Representative Barney Frank, August 14, 1995.
Mark Levin, NCSJ, July 14, 1995.
Arnold H. Liebowitz, HIAS counsel, July 26, 1995.
Princeton Lyman, former Director, Bureau for Refugee Programs (State Department), February 12, 2004.
Richard Schifter, former Assistant Secretary of State for Humanitarian Affairs, August 2, 1995.
Ivan Selin, former Under Secretary of State for Management, August 17, 1995.
Mark Talisman, former director of CJF Washington office, July 20, 1995 and October 3, 2002.
Martin A. Wenick, Executive Vice President of HIAS, July 14, 1995.
Ellen Whitman, former staff, CJF, Washington DC office, August 16, 1995.

Index

Abrahamov, Zalman, 65n96
Abram, Morris: and AJCSJ, 28; and anti-
  Semitism in Soviet Union, 27, 59n41;
  and direct flights, 222, 263–64; on
  Israel, 64n81, 192; and NCSJ, 67n107;
  and quotas, 269; and Reagan-
  Gorbachev summits, 213–15, 219–20,
  227–30; on refugees, 285n40;
  retirement of, 270; and Shamir, 194;
  and Shultz, 232n9; and turf conflict,
  246–47, 249–52, 254–55; and
  Washington Demonstration, 226
Abramov, Sh. A., 63n77
Abrams, Bobbie, 177n123
Abrams, Elliot, 68n121
academics, and freedom of choice, 104
Accelerated Third Country Processing,
  264
Ad Hoc Committee of Concern for
  Soviet Jewish Prisoners, 65n90
ADL. See Anti-Defamation League
Adler, Shmuel, 133
Afghanistan, 180
Agency of International Development
  (AID), 83, 112n14
Agursky, Mikhail, 119n58, 282n11
AIPAC. See American Israel Political
  Action Committee

AJC. See American Jewish Committee
AJCSJ. See American Jewish Conference
  on Soviet Jewry
AKSO. See Anti-Zionist Committee of
  the Soviet Public
Alexander II, tsar of Russia, 20
Aliyah, 2, 13n4, 95; 1968–1992, 310*t*
Aliyah Bet, 24
Allied Jewish Appeal, 15n20
Almogi, Yosef, 97, 99, 122n84
Alon, Yigal, 97
Althschuler, M., 57n27
Amalrik, Andrei, 76n186
American Council of Judaism,
  Philanthropic Fund, 111n10
American Israel Political Action
  Committee (AIPAC), 74n166, 203n19
Americanization, process of, 6
American Jewish Committee (AJC), 4, 9,
  293; and AJCSJ, 28; establishment of,
  16n23; Interreligious Affairs
  Committee, 66n106; and NCSJ, 37
American Jewish community, 3–8,
  293–305; and Begin, 152–53; and
  contemporary American politics,
  297–300; and direct flights, 223–24;
  and Dulzin, 155; and Israel, 3,
  133–38, 146, 197, 201; Liaison

Index